Bhutan

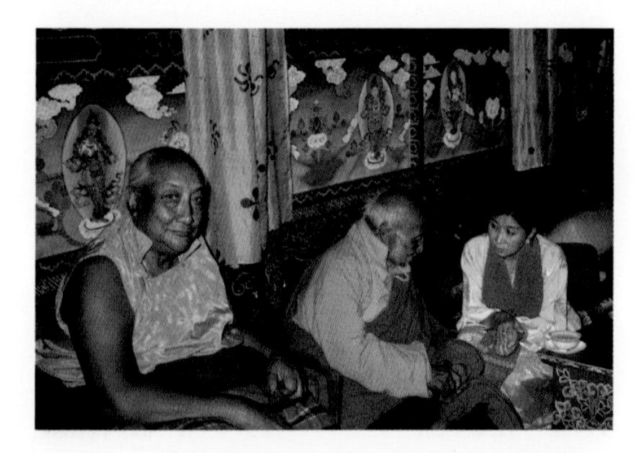

This book commemorates the 100th anniversary of the birth of Dilgo Khyentse Rinpoche and is dedicated to Her Majesty the Queen Mother of Bhutan, Ashe Kesang Choeden Wangchuck.

Bhutan

THE LAND OF SERENITY

Text and photographs by

MATTHIEU RICARD

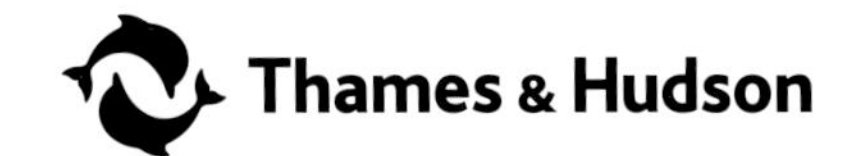

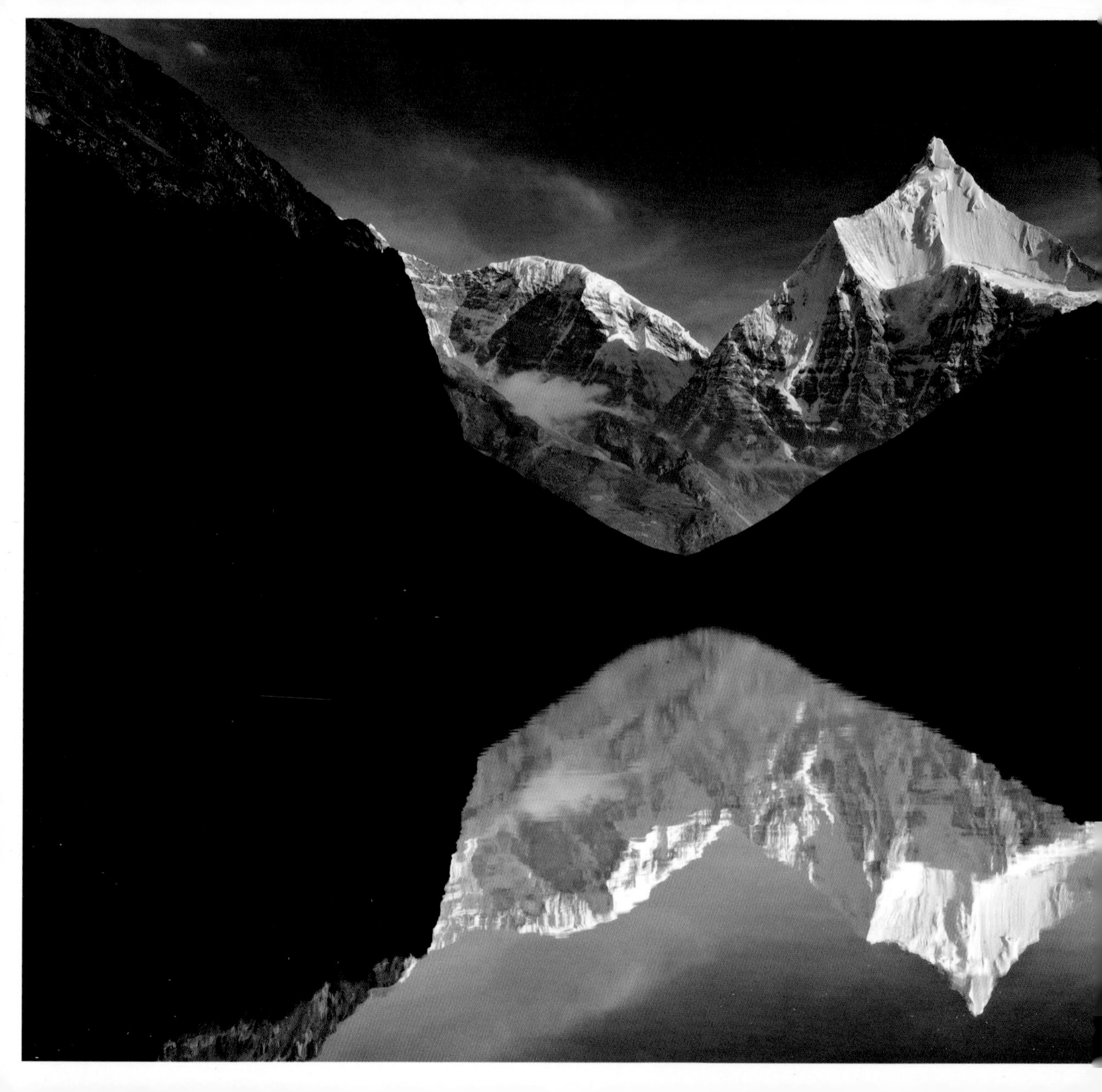

Contents

The summit of Jigchu Drake (6,989 metres), also known as Tsering Gang, reflected at dawn on the surface of Lake Tsophu (4,350 metres) in Bhutan, May 2007.

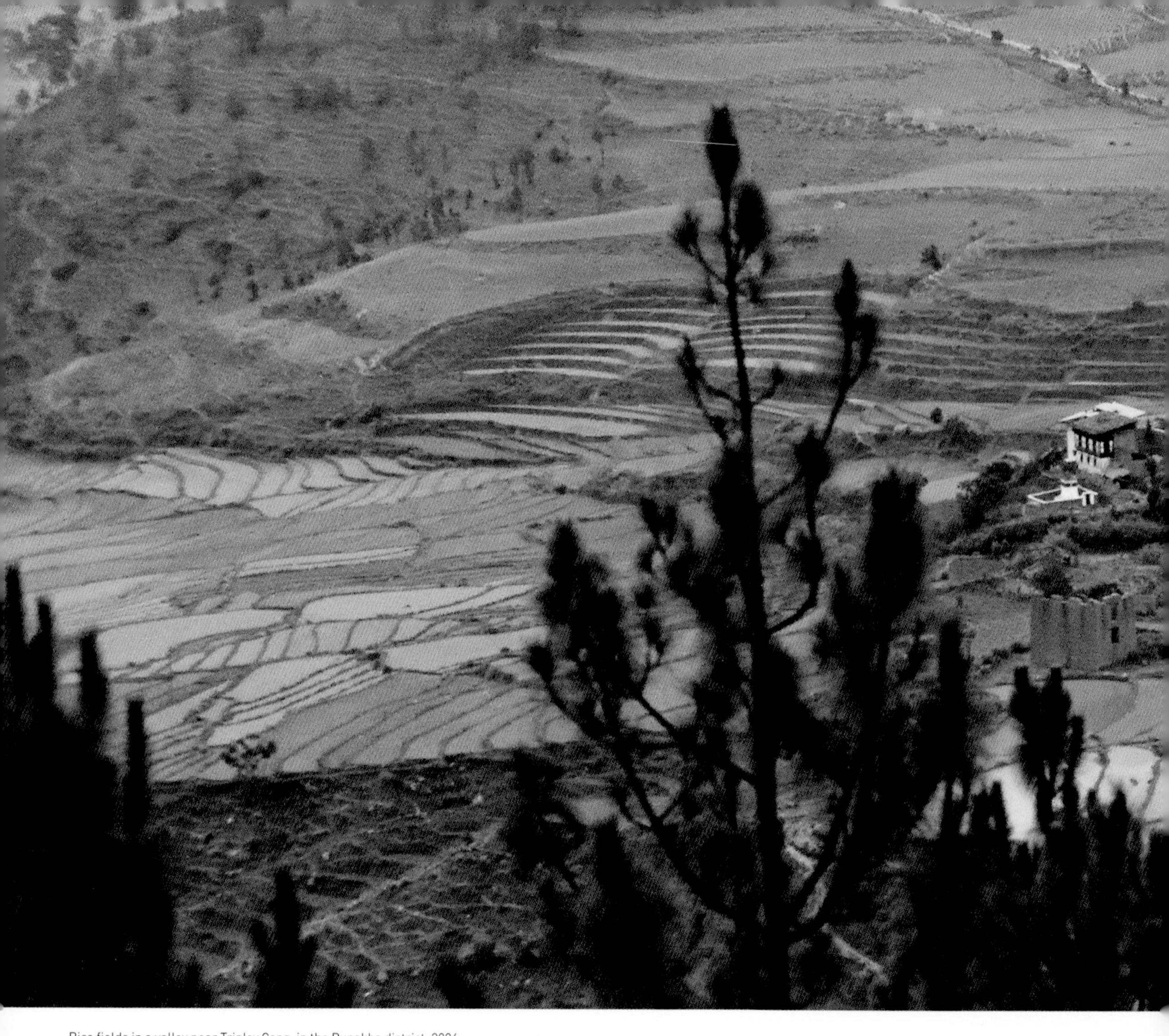

Rice fields in a valley near Trinley Gang, in the Punakha district, 2006.

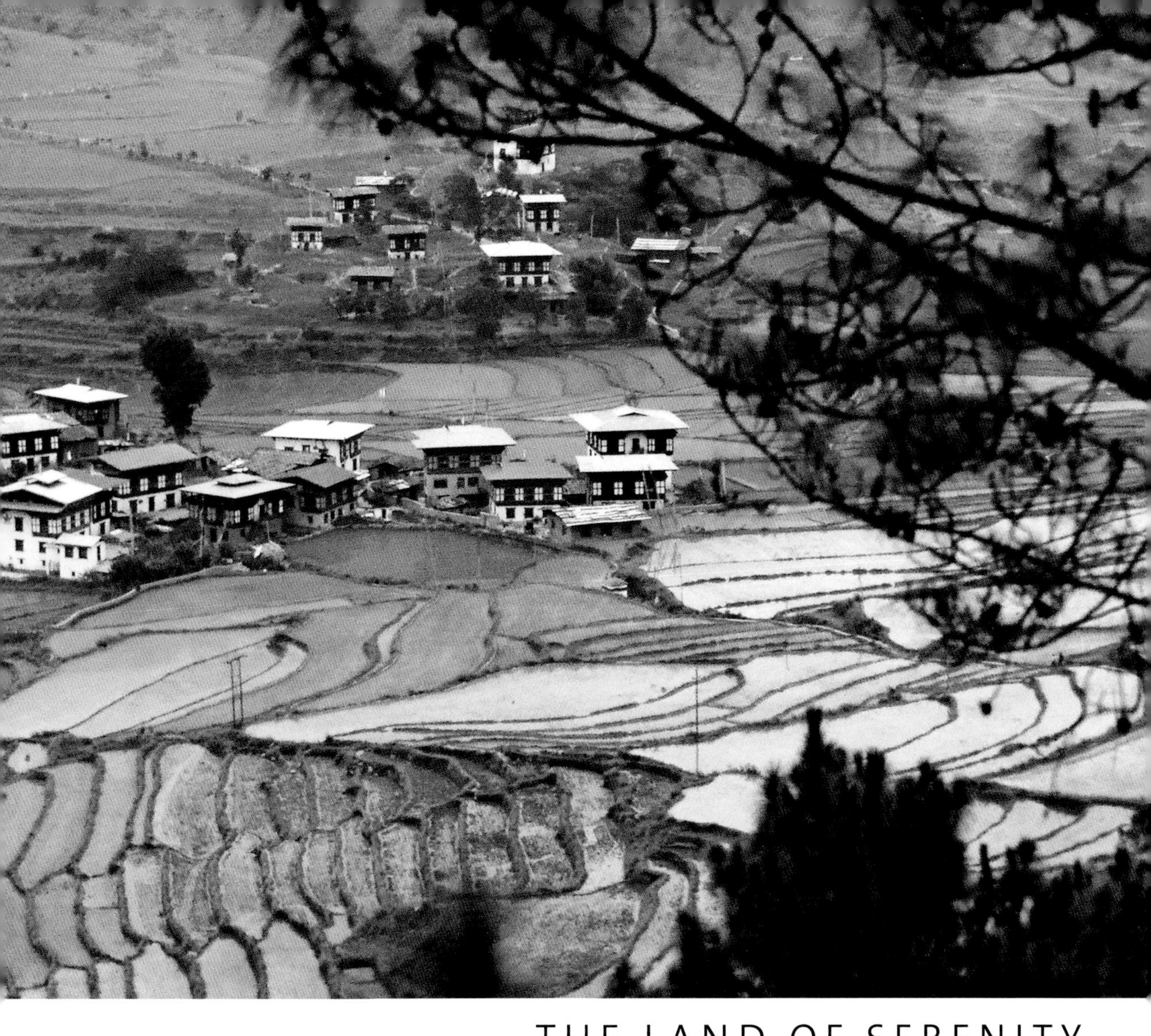

THE LAND OF SERENITY

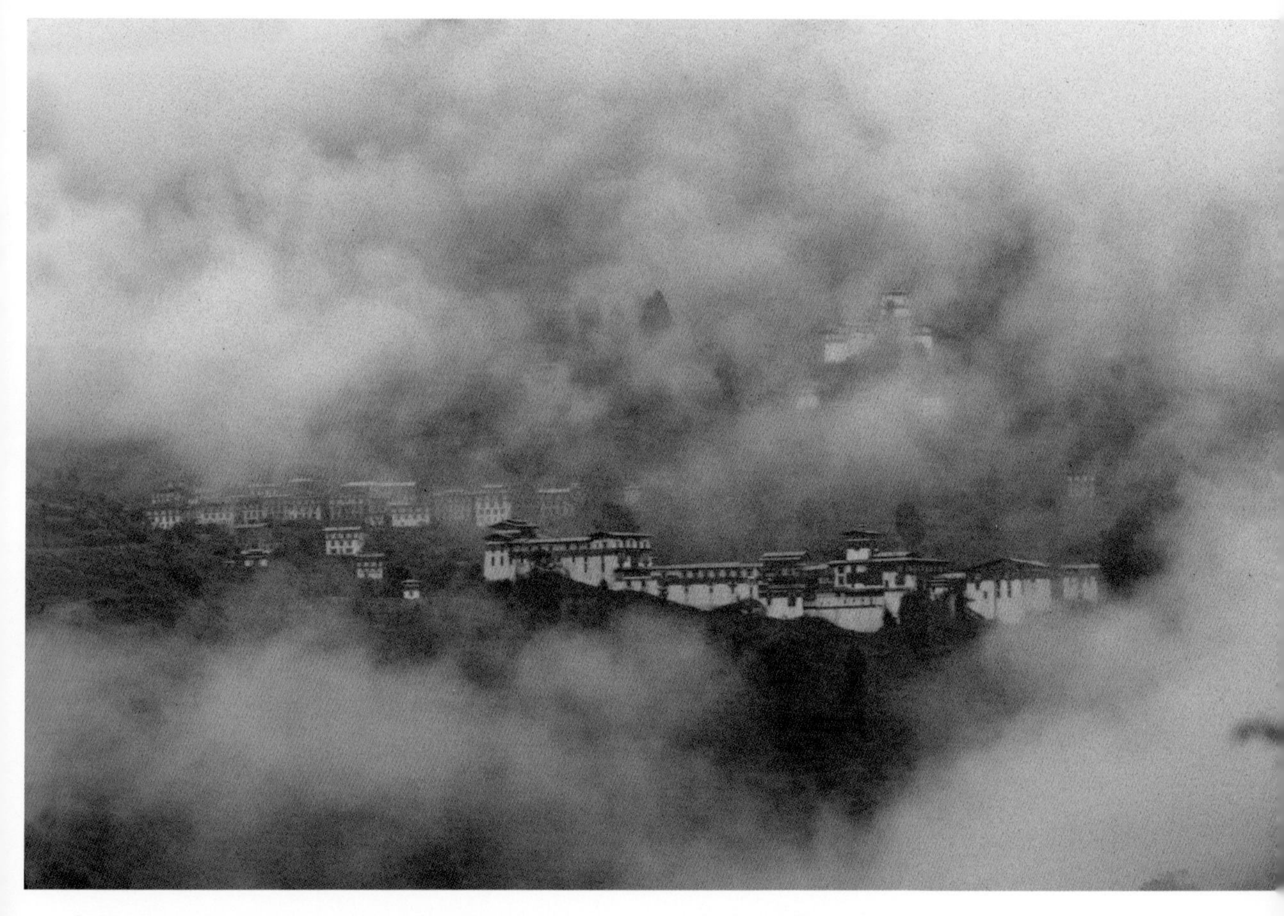

Trongsar monastery is home to several hundred monks. It was built in the 16th century on the side of a valley, at 2,000 metres, and is ringed with mountains.

The Land of Serenity

'Bhutan could become just like any other country in Asia, but no other country could be like Bhutan.' This remark was made by a Canadian high official who was instrumental in helping Bhutan join the United Nations and it underlines the uniqueness of this beautiful Himalayan kingdom. To this day, Bhutan has been remarkably successful in preserving its Buddhist culture while also drawing on the benefits of Western know-how, such as environmental conservation and improvements in public health and education.

Bhutan was influenced early on by Tibetan civilization, but over time it developed its own original culture. Today this culture is unique in its characteristics and achievements in ecology, spirituality, politics, architecture, textiles and other crafts, and still remains clearly distinct from other Himalayan regions. It continues to be a place of stability within a part of the world that is increasingly conflicted.

Bhutan – called Druk-Yul, 'Land of the Thunder Dragon', by its people – is pivotally positioned between those two Asian giants, India and China. To the north lies Tibet, along with the imposing barrier of the Himalayas, while extending to the east, south and west are the Indian states of Arunachal Pradesh, Assam, Bengal and Sikkim.

Much of the land is covered in lush and varied forests. Broad-leaf trees and conifers occupy three-quarters of its 46,500 square kilometres, which is roughly the size of Switzerland (Bhutan has a population of 700,000). The valleys and mountain slopes of the rich central zone are carpeted with a patchwork of rice paddies and fields of barley, wheat, millet and buckwheat.

Bhutan is situated on the same latitude as Morocco. Its climate is governed by monsoons which contribute to its extraordinary ecological diversity. From south to north, in the space of a mere 130 to 150 kilometres, weather conditions shift from semi-tropical to temperate (in the country's central region) to alpine. With its narrow plain of dense and often impenetrable jungle to the south and the Himalayan barrier to the north, the country has its own natural defences.

Bhutan's central zone is its cultural cradle and the historical heartland of its people. The region is composed of a series of basins, whose inhabitants were totally economically self-sustaining until fifty years ago, and from west to east there is a string of glorious valleys, like reliquaries enshrining the many spiritual and artistic aspects of Bhutanese culture. To the west lie the town of Paro, and Thimphu, the capital of Bhutan, and, to the centre and east, the rich valleys of Bumthang, Trongsar and Lhuntse situated at between 2,000 and 3,500 metres. Further to the east, there are the low-lying valleys of Tashigang, Merak and Sakteng, home to the Sar-chopa, the 'People of the East,' who speak a different language from Dzongkha, Bhutan's national language, which is related to Tibetan.

North Bhutan is a series of peaks rising from 3,000 metres to over 7,000 metres (Jomolhari, the highest peak in Bhutan, reaches 7,326 metres), capped with the eternal snows of the Great Himalaya. Bhutan's semi-nomadic yak-herders live on these northern slopes, enduring the rigours of the Himalayan climate and bringing their herds to graze in spring at between 4,000 and 5,000 metres.

The Tibetan name for Bhutan means 'the southern valley where the medicinal plants grow' and the dense forests of these Himalayan foothills are rich in plant life known for their medicinal properties. The steep slopes shelter a number of rare species such as the Himalayan blue poppy (*Meconopsis grandis*), Bhutan's national flower, as well as a great variety of orchids and rhododendrons. Most of the region – 26 per cent of the country as a whole – has been designated as a national park, a further indication of how highly the Bhutanese government values and respects the environment. Bhutan is home to the snow leopard and the musk deer as well as other species, and even tigers have been photographed here at 4,000 metres. The wealth of Bhutan's flora and fauna, its exceptional forest cover, the abundance of clear-flowing rivers and generous rainfall, and its small population, are all resources that have played an important role in the evolution of Bhutan's culture and represent major economic assets for the country today.

AN UNTOUCHED BUDDHIST CULTURE

In Bhutan, history and spirituality are indissolubly linked. It is said that there, 'the earth is Buddhist and the sky is Buddhist'. The mountains are seen as 'recumbent elephants', 'proudly poised lions' and 'garuda birds taking flight'. The plains are lotus flowers with their eight petals unfolded; the little cut-out pieces of sky in a rock face are *gakyil*, 'circles of joy', or *phurba*, triangular daggers. The lakes are shaped like horns of plenty or cups of ambrosia. The whole landscape is sacred. Every valley is a site of pilgrimage and every rock, cave and river has a history. In one place, a hermit meditated; in another, a spiritual master left his footprint on a rock; in yet another lies the home of a guardian spirit of the earth.

Many of these sites are barely known outside the valley where they are located, while others have a quasi-mythical reputation throughout the world of Himalayan Buddhism. Padmasambhava is said to have concealed a great many spiritual treasures at Taksang, 'the Tiger's Lair,' in the valley of Paro, a cave surrounded by a handful of temples clinging to a sheer wall of rock and one of the most imposing sites in the Himalayas. Kuje Lhakhang, at the heart of Bhutan, is a major pilgrimage site; Mönka Senge Dzong, 'the Fortress of the Lion', another pristine sacred place blessed by Padmasambhava and his female disciple Yeshe Tsogyal, is a platform ringed with rocky peaks and glaciers, located at over 4,000 metres, which takes several days to reach by walking along boggy paths in semi-tropical forests.

The values of Buddhism are deeply embedded in the minds of the Bhutanese people. Some of the larger monasteries, like the one at Thimphu, house more than a thousand monks. Every hilltop has its little temple surrounded by prayer flags fluttering in the wind and the mountain streams keep the prayer wheels turning night and day. There are hermitages scattered throughout the mountains and the forests, where monks, nuns and lay practitioners devote themselves to meditation. The religious calendar is filled with majestic ceremonies and sacred dance festivals and, since the principal monasteries celebrate the festival of the Tenth Day (*tsechu*) at different times in the year, the celebrations tend to be ongoing throughout the country, one after another.

Bhutan has two main religious schools, both derived from Tibetan Buddhism: the Drukpa Kagyu tradition, which is followed by virtually all the state-run monasteries, and the Nyingma tradition, observed by a large section of the population and of the independent monasteries. There have been a number of remarkable spiritual teachers associated with the Nyingma tradition, including Longchen Rabjam (14th century), Dorje Lingpa (14th century), Pema Lingpa (15th–16th century) and, in our own time, Dudjom Rinpoche and Dilgo Khyentse Rinpoche. Bhutan's patriarch, the Je Khenpo, belongs to the Drukpa Kagyu school and holds a spiritual rank that is equal to the king's temporal rank.

Bhutan is an intact Buddhist culture unrivalled in terms of its artistic inheritance. The various traditions of sacred art are still very much alive here and Bhutanese sculptors, who work primarily in clay, are famous throughout the Himalayas for the delicacy and beauty of their creations.

CENTURIES-LONG INDEPENDENCE

Until the 16th and 17th centuries, Bhutan was made up of a collection of small principalities, each one nestling in the valleys of the country's central zone. In the 17th century, Shabdrung Ngawang Namgyal (1594–1651), abbot of Ralung monastery in Tibet, unified Bhutan and established the foundations of the country's theocratic system. Religious power lay with the Je Khenpo and temporal power was exercised by a high-ranking civil dignitary, the Druk Desi. Ngawang Namgyal also divided the territory into administrative regions, each placed under the direction of a governor-prince. When Ngawang Namgyal died, however, conflicts and power battles erupted between the regional governors. This situation continued until 1907, the date at which Bhutan became a hereditary monarchy founded by Urgyen Wangchuck, Bhutan's first king. Under his powerful control, and the continued enlightened rule of his successors, the country has enjoyed unprecedented stability right up to our own time.

In 1953, Bhutan appointed a national assembly and, on the king's personal initiative, in 2008 it took the first step towards becoming a democracy. Bhutan has been a member of the UN since 1971, and manages its own development through revenue generated in large part by hydroelectricity and international aid. The political objectives underlying this development are clear and centred on guaranteeing a better quality of life for the Bhutanese people. This goal led to the idea of 'Gross National Happiness', an index to replace that of Gross National Profit, in which uncontrolled growth can lead to deterioration rather than an increase in quality of life (as is clearly demonstrated by global warming). The concept of GNH, which was first used by King Jigme Sengye Wangchuck at the end of the 1980s, has now been adopted by analysts worldwide.

A PEACEFUL TRANSITION TOWARDS DEMOCRACY

In 2006, His Majesty the king surprised everybody by suddenly announcing that the country would soon be run as a democracy and that he would be abdicating in favour of his eldest son, Jigme Kesar Namgyel Wangchuck, now invested as the country's fifth king, at the head of a constitutional monarchy. The year 2008 has therefore been the occasion for major celebrations: the hundredth anniversary of the institution of the monarchy, the establishment of a democracy, marked by general elections, and the coronation of the fifth king – events commemorating the country's rich heritage and affirming the advent of a new era in which, it is universally hoped, Bhutan will remain a land of serenity far into the future.

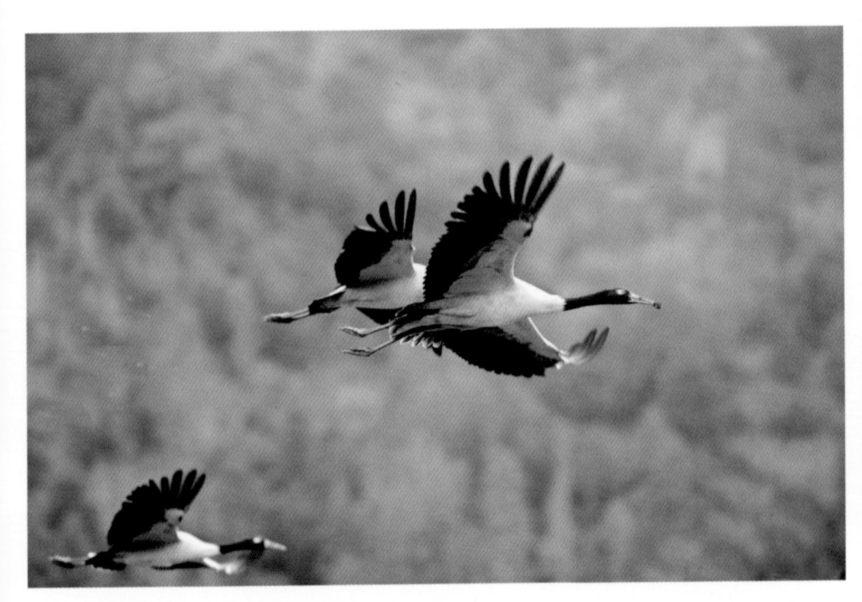

The valley of Phobjika lies at an altitude of 3,000 metres and its inhabitants are proud of the black-necked cranes that winter here between October and March to escape the inhospitable conditions of north-eastern Tibet's high plateaux. This magnificent glacial valley is one of the birds' few wintering grounds and only solar power is allowed here: electrical cables are banned so as not to disturb the birds, which feed in the cultivated parts of the valley and in the low-lying marshes. December 2007.

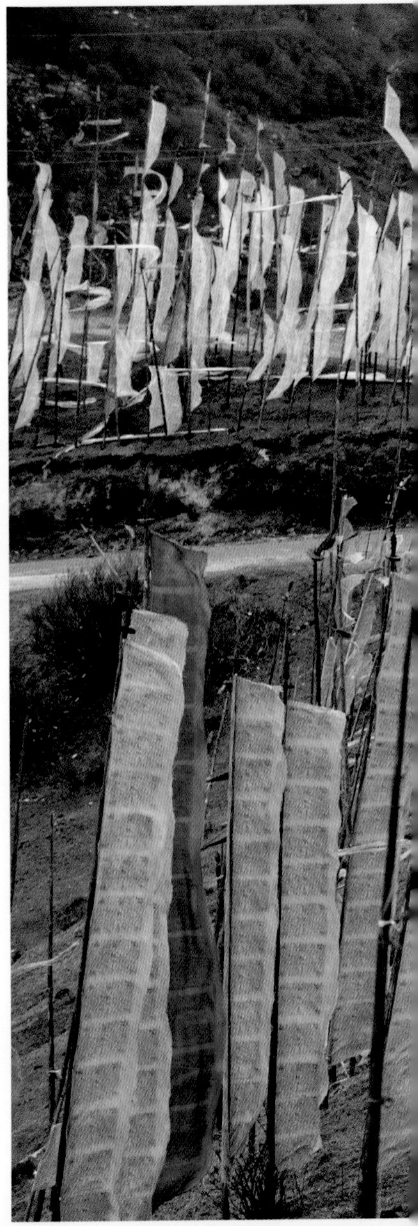

Prayer flags stream in the wind on the Chele-La pass, at 4,000 metres, which separates the valleys of Paro and Ha. 2007.

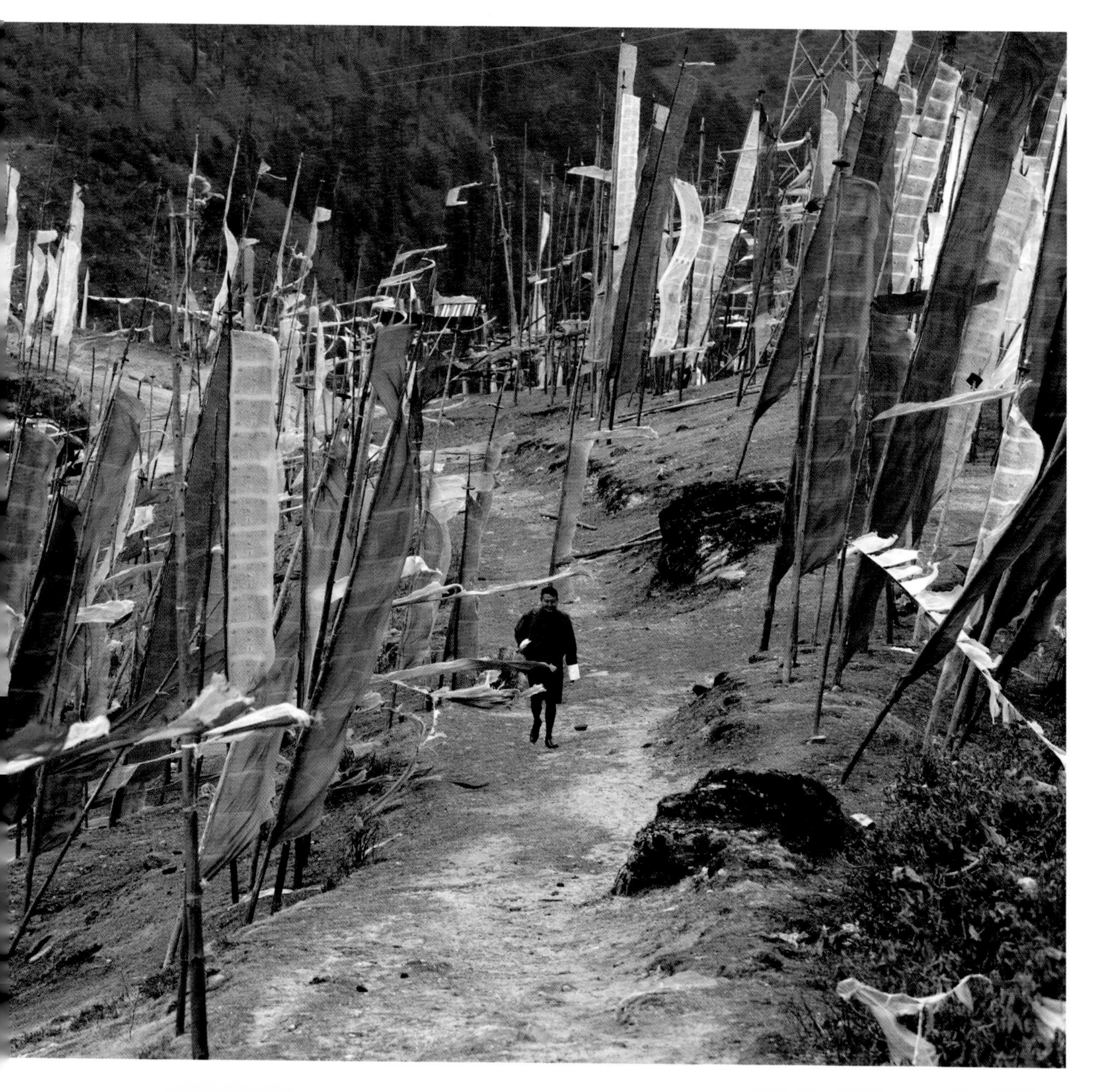

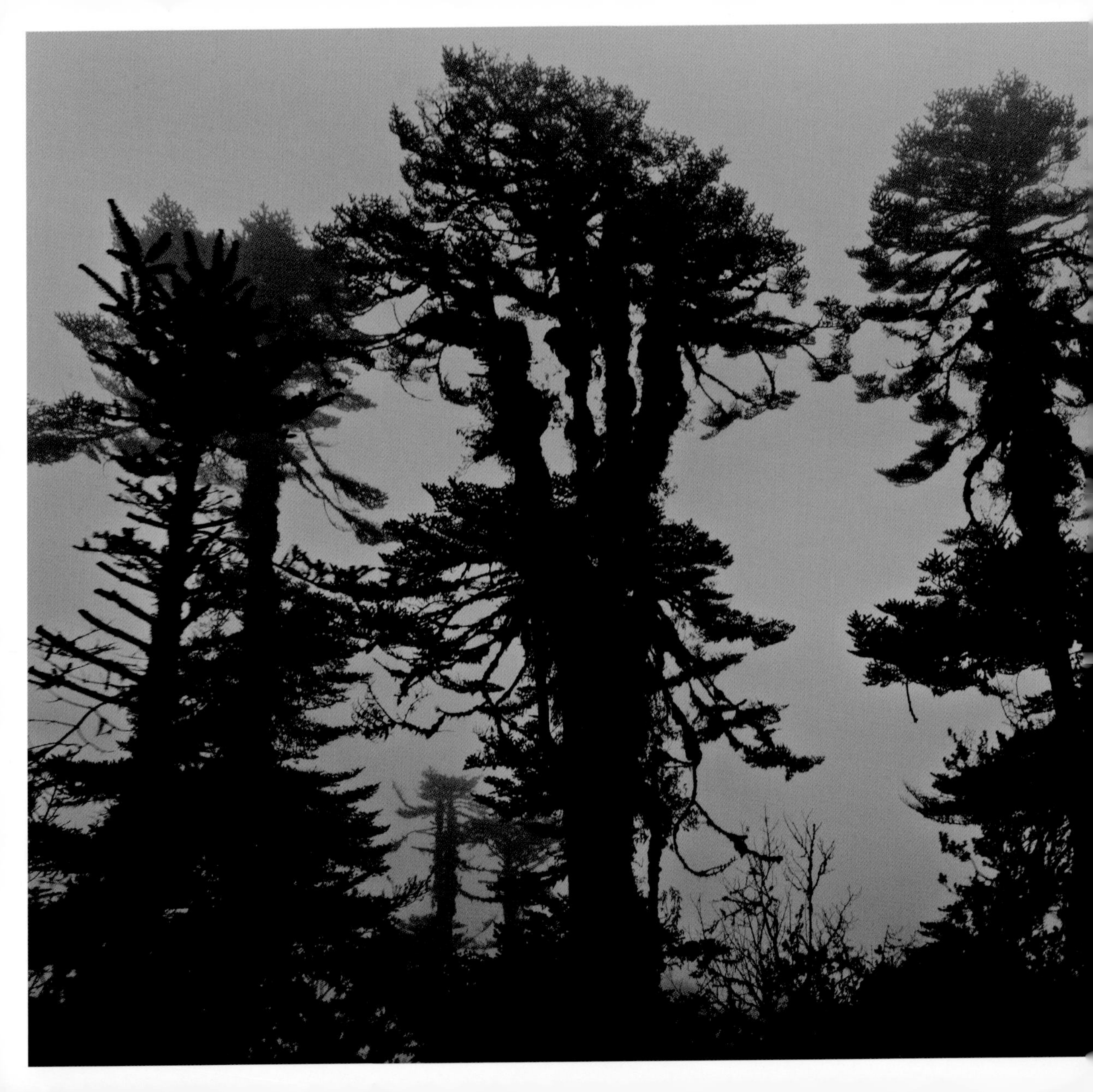

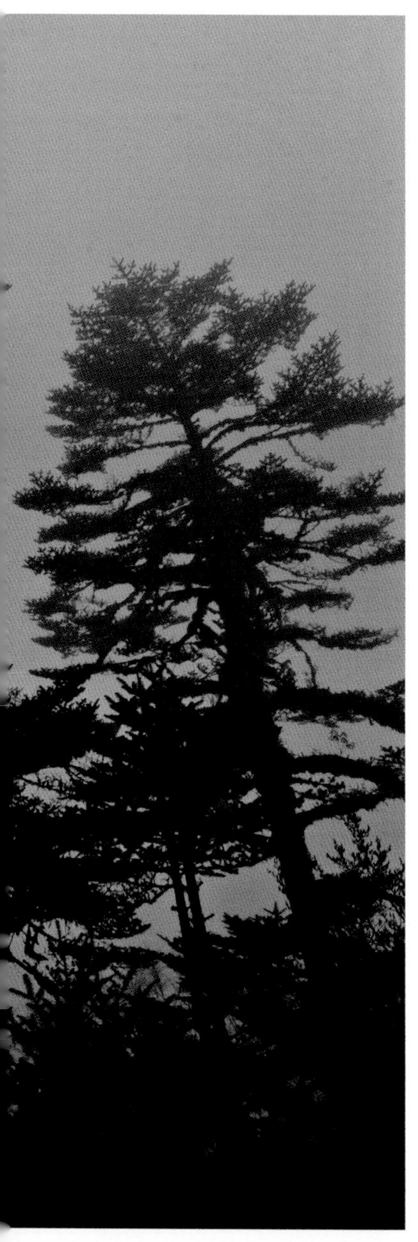

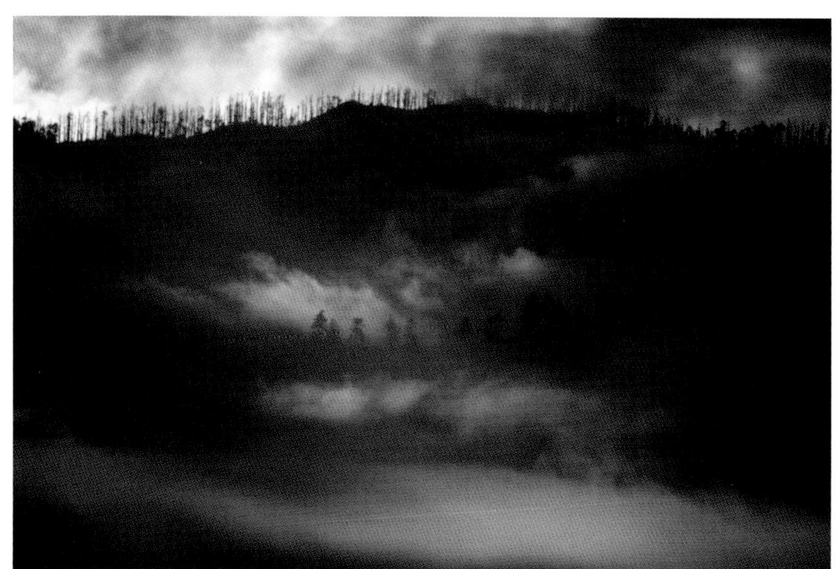

Morning mist in the valley of Paro, 1986.

Magnificent conifers gracing the heights of the 'black mountains' separating west and central Bhutan, near the Pele-La pass (3,300 metres). The trees are several hundred years old. 2006.

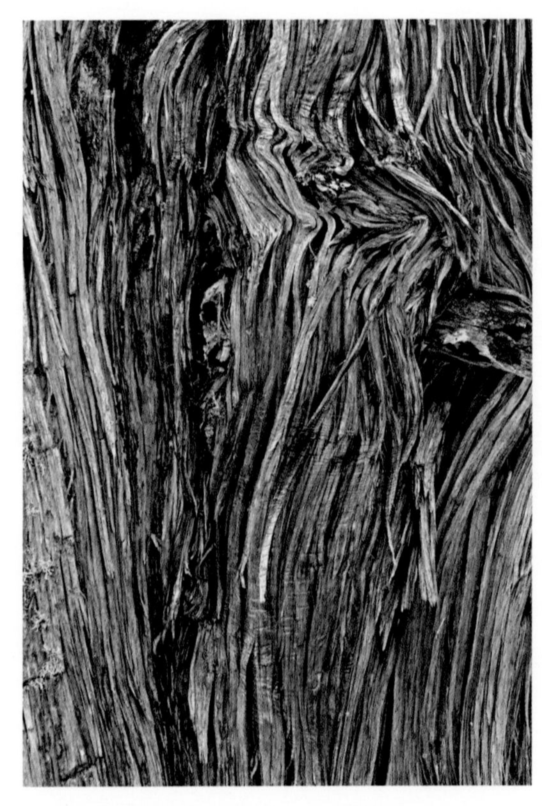

The bark of a large juniper tree growing at an altitude of 3,000 metres.

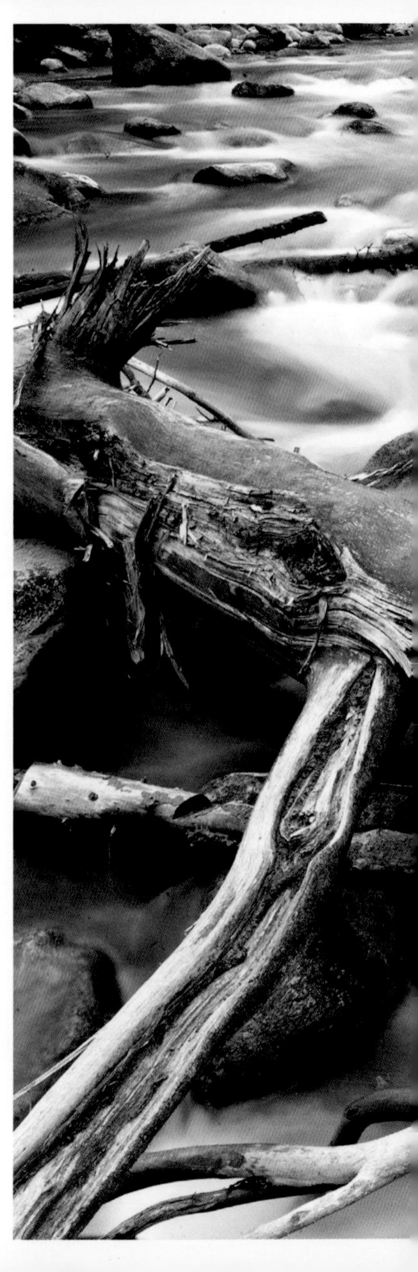

On the way to Jomolhari, a river tumbles down the valley, strewn with rocks and dead branches. 2007.

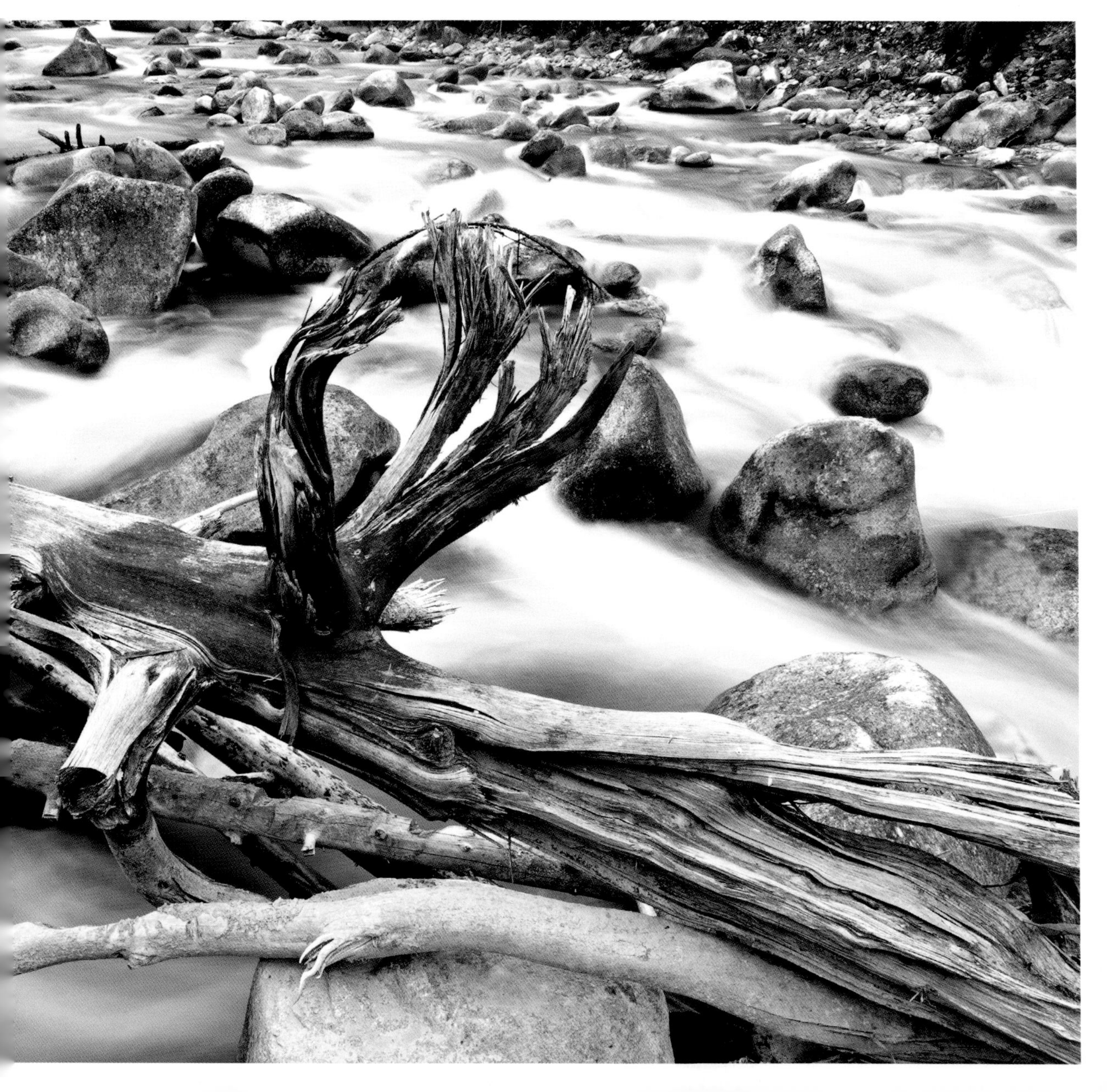

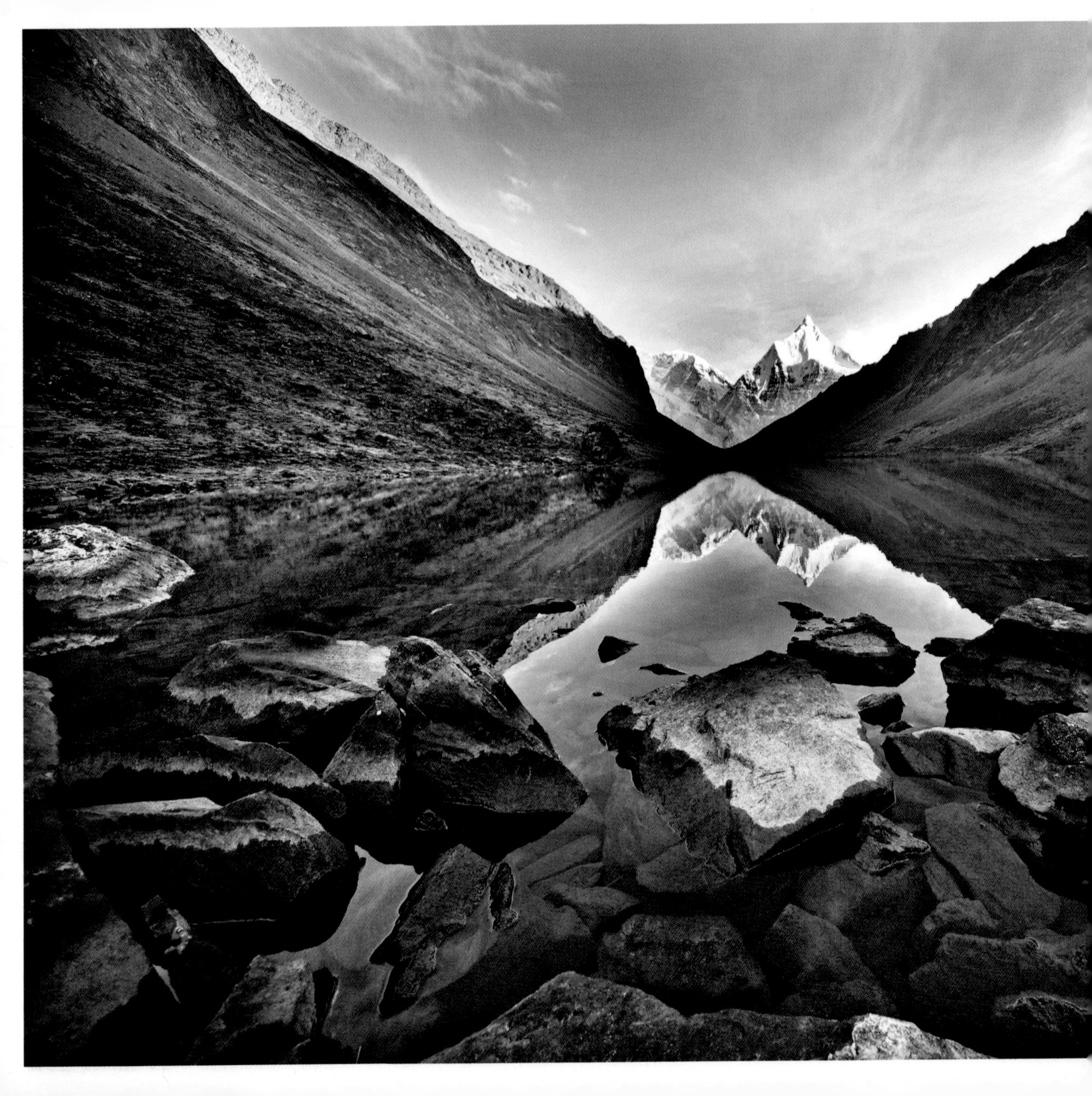

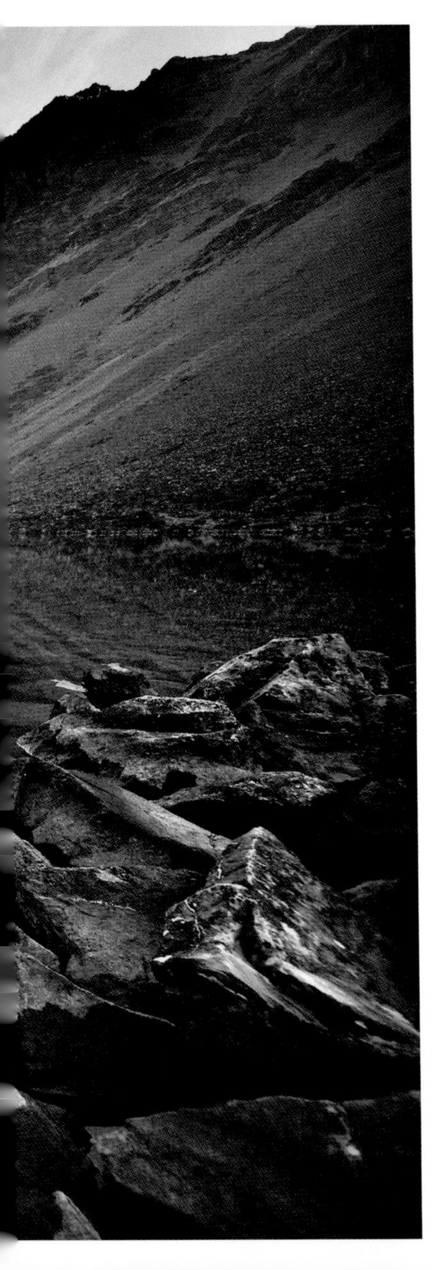

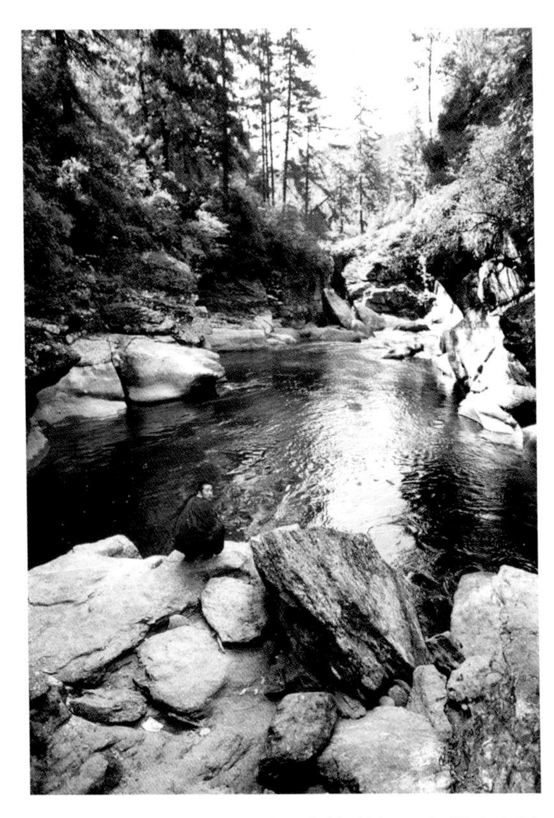

A monk sits on a rock overlooking Mebartso, the 'Blazing Lake', where the great visionary master Pema Lingpa (1450–1521) is said to have revealed a 'spiritual treasure' after diving into the lake with a lighted butter lamp. Bumthang province, 2006.

Jigchu Drake (6,989 m) reflected in the surface of Lake Tsophu (4,350 m) at dawn. May 2007.

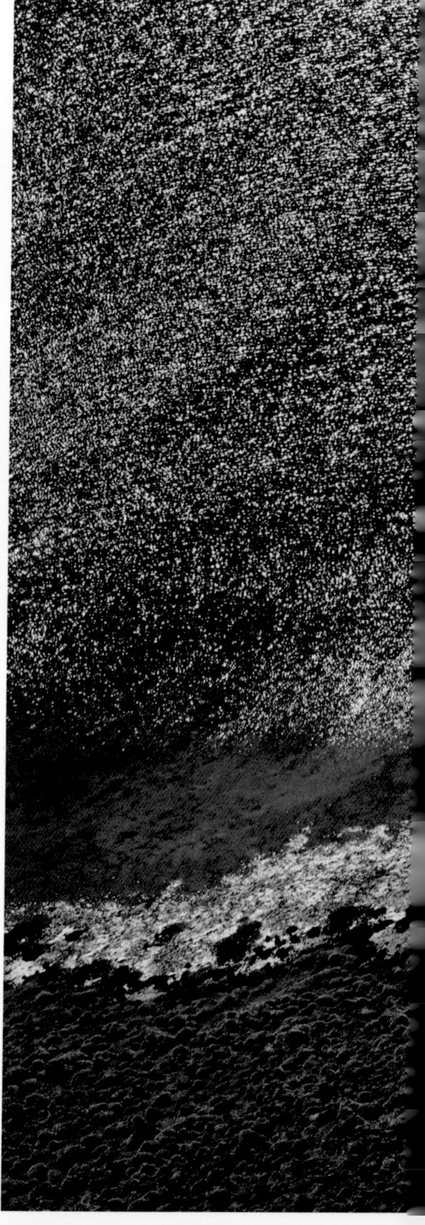

Above and opposite:
Reflections in Lake Tsophu, two hours' walk above Jomolhari base camp.

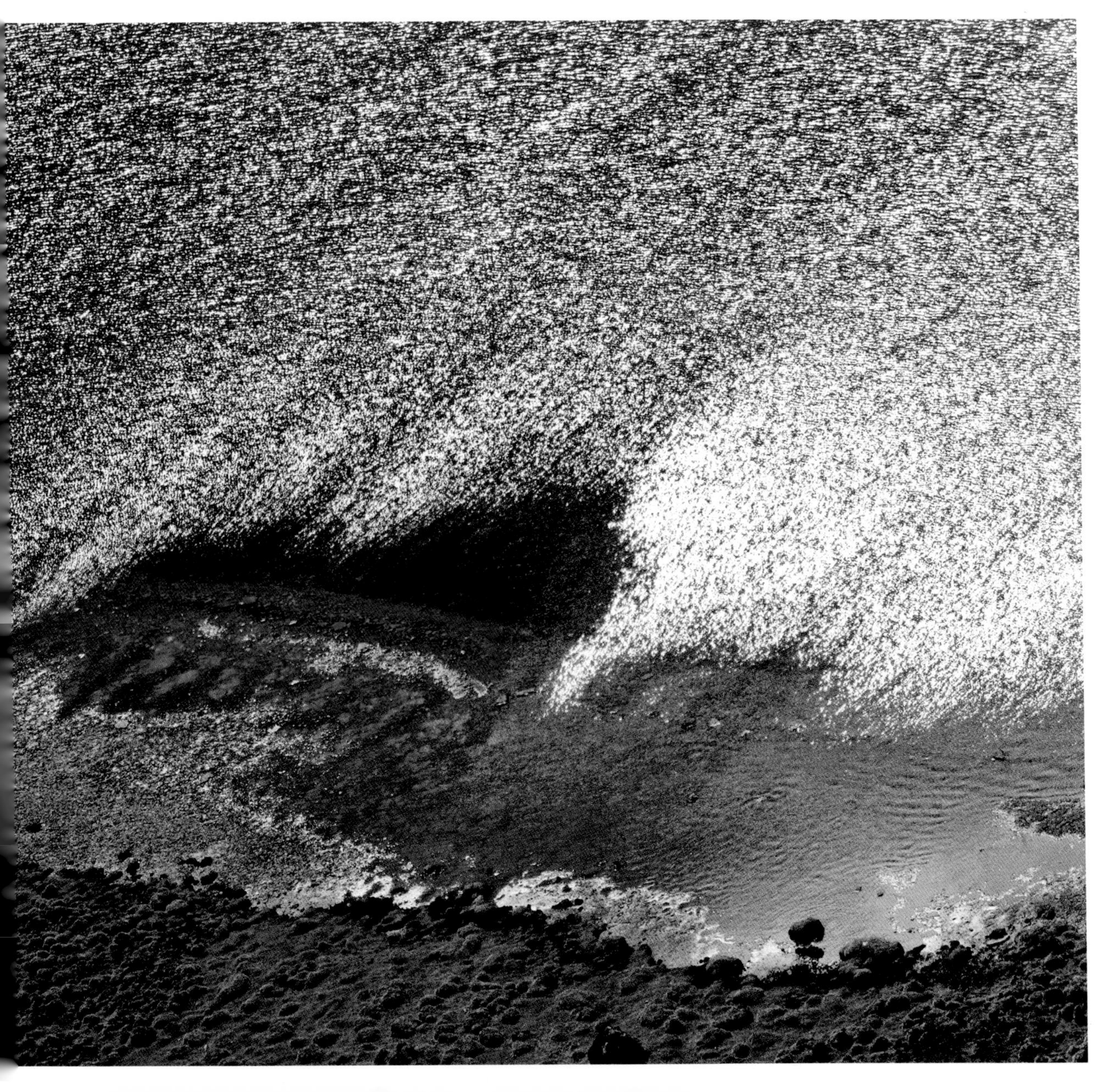

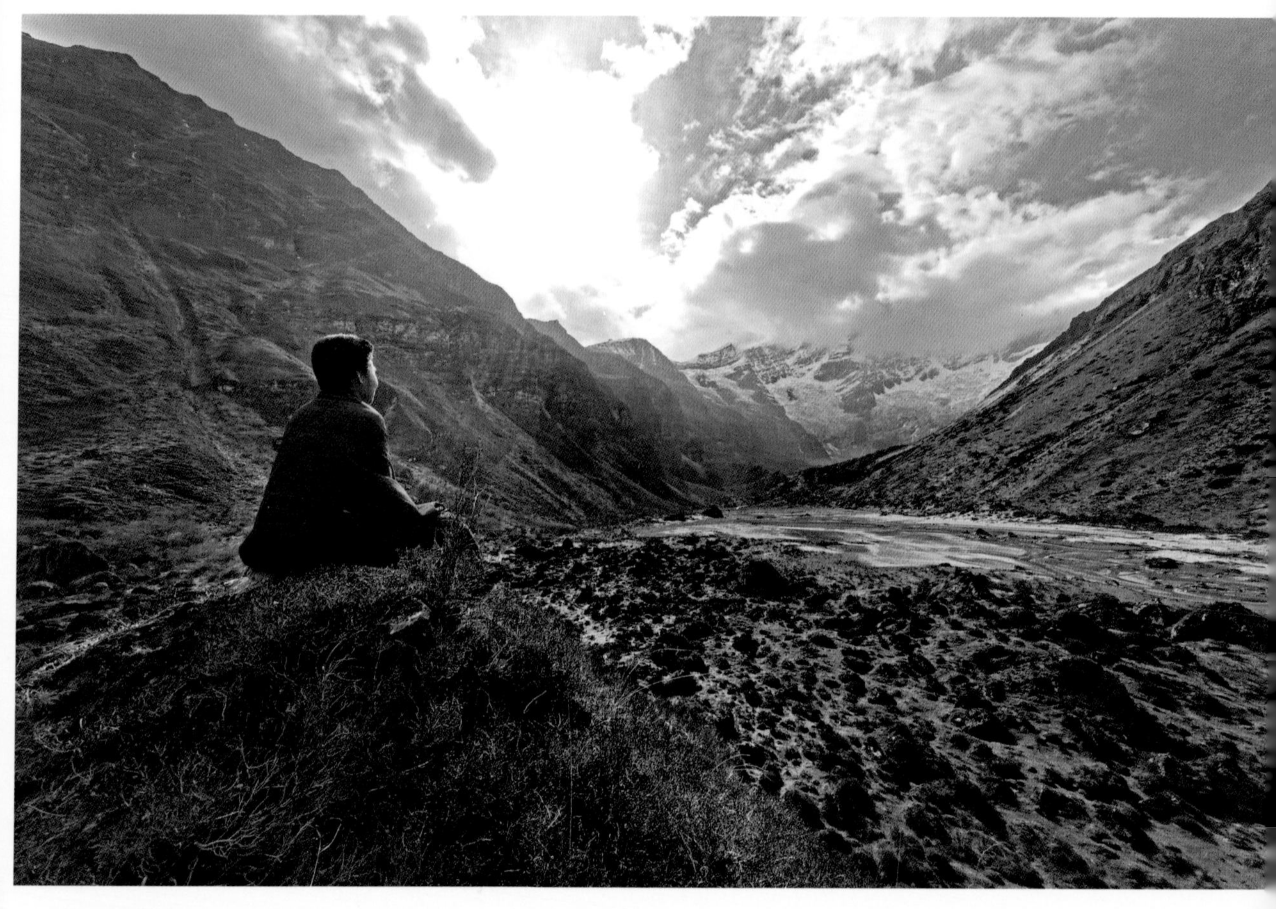

Above and opposite:
Monks meditating, at an altitude of over 4,000 metres, facing the glaciers of Jomolhari (7,326 metres), Bhutan's highest mountain. May 2007.

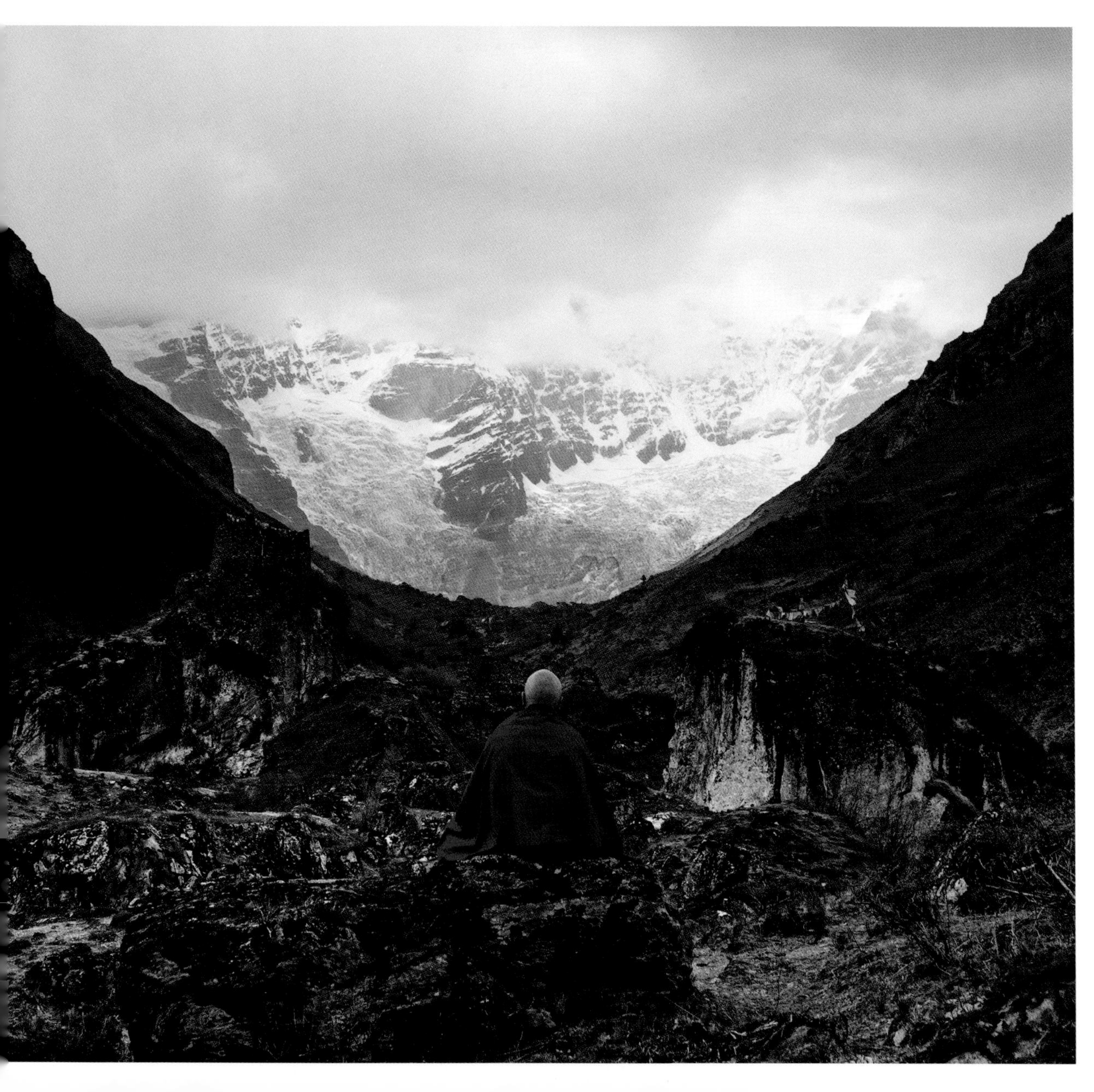

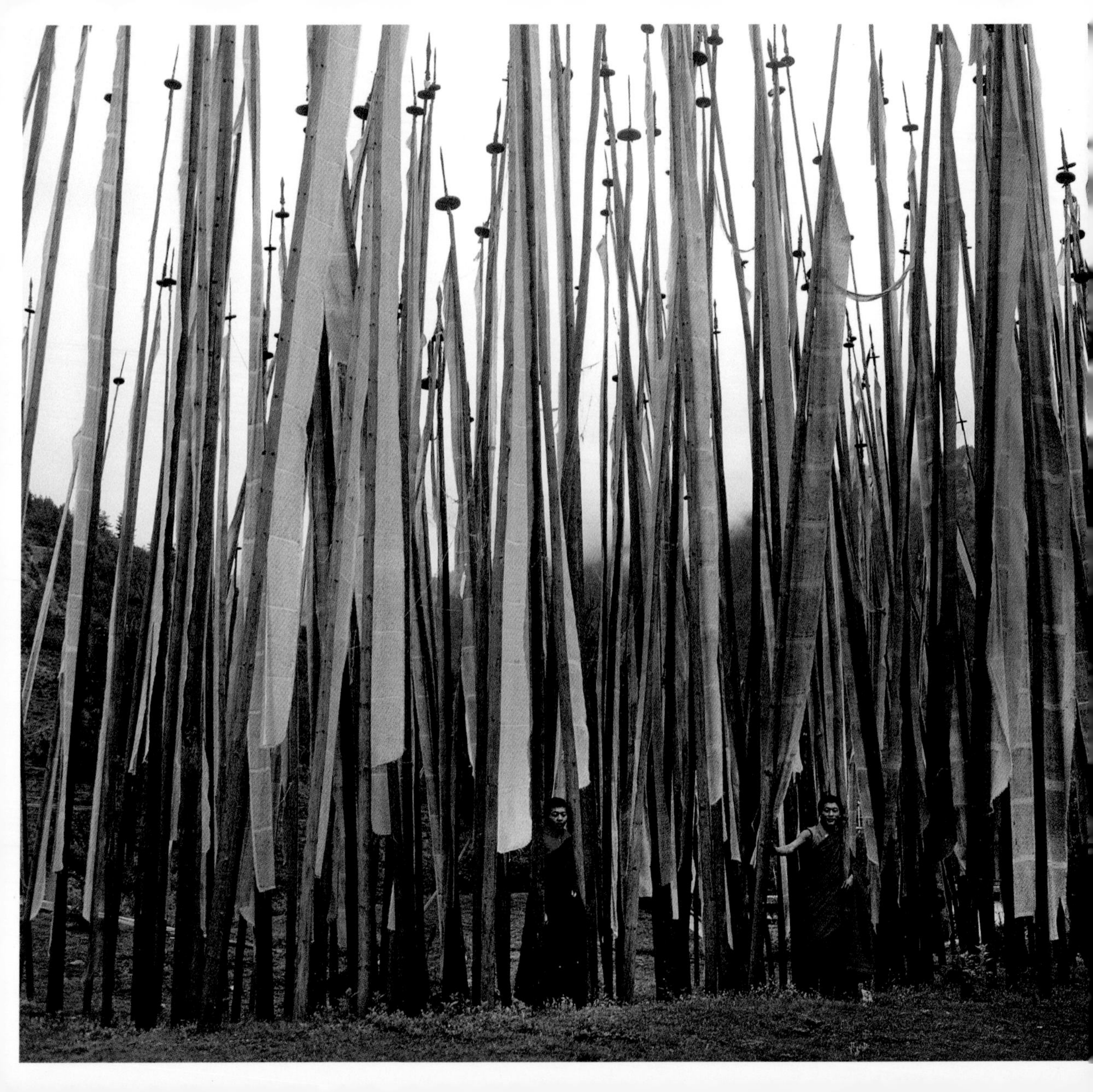

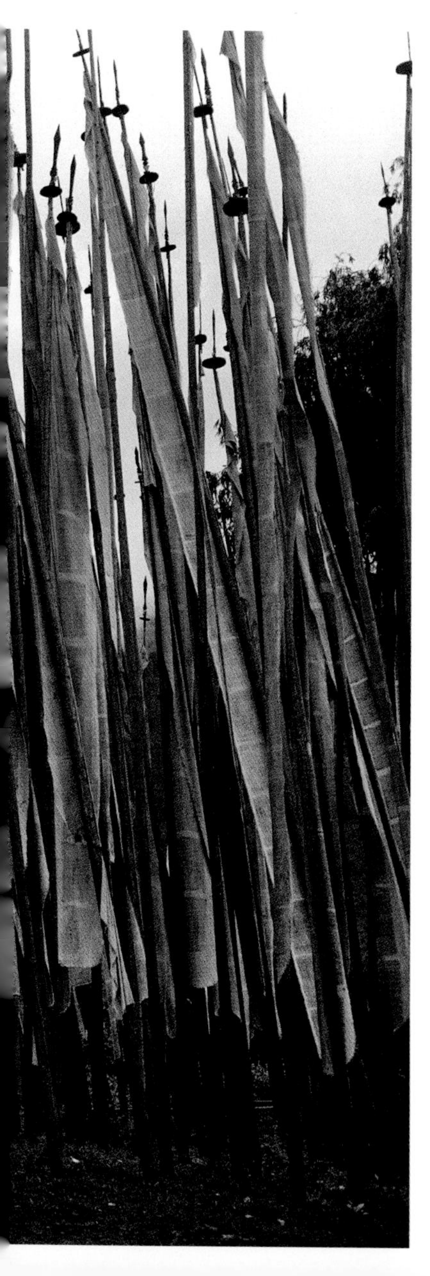

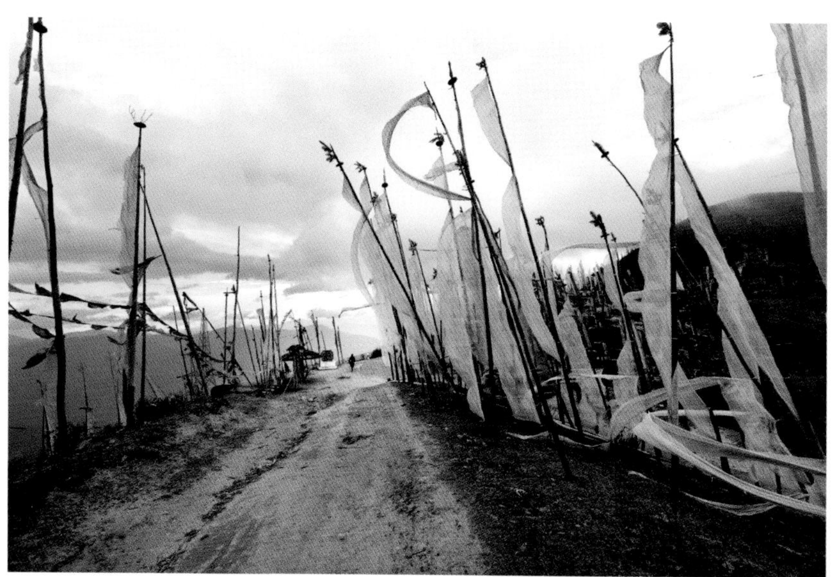

Chele-La pass (4,000 metres), 2006.

A forest of prayer flags near the palace of Dechen Chöling, Thimphu. Prayer flags are everywhere in Bhutan – on hilltops and rocky spurs, in clearings and near temples, or where two rivers meet. 1983.

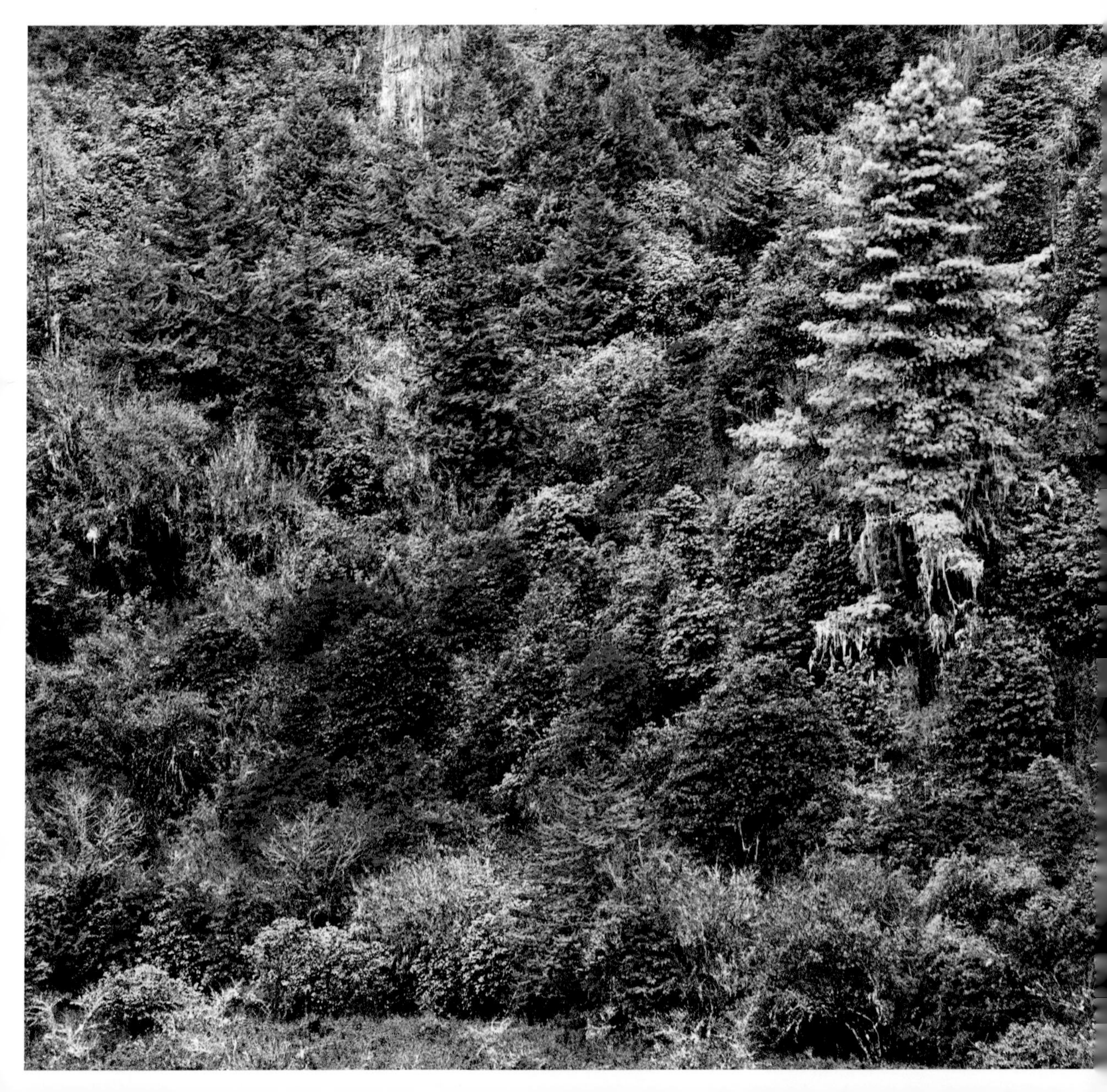

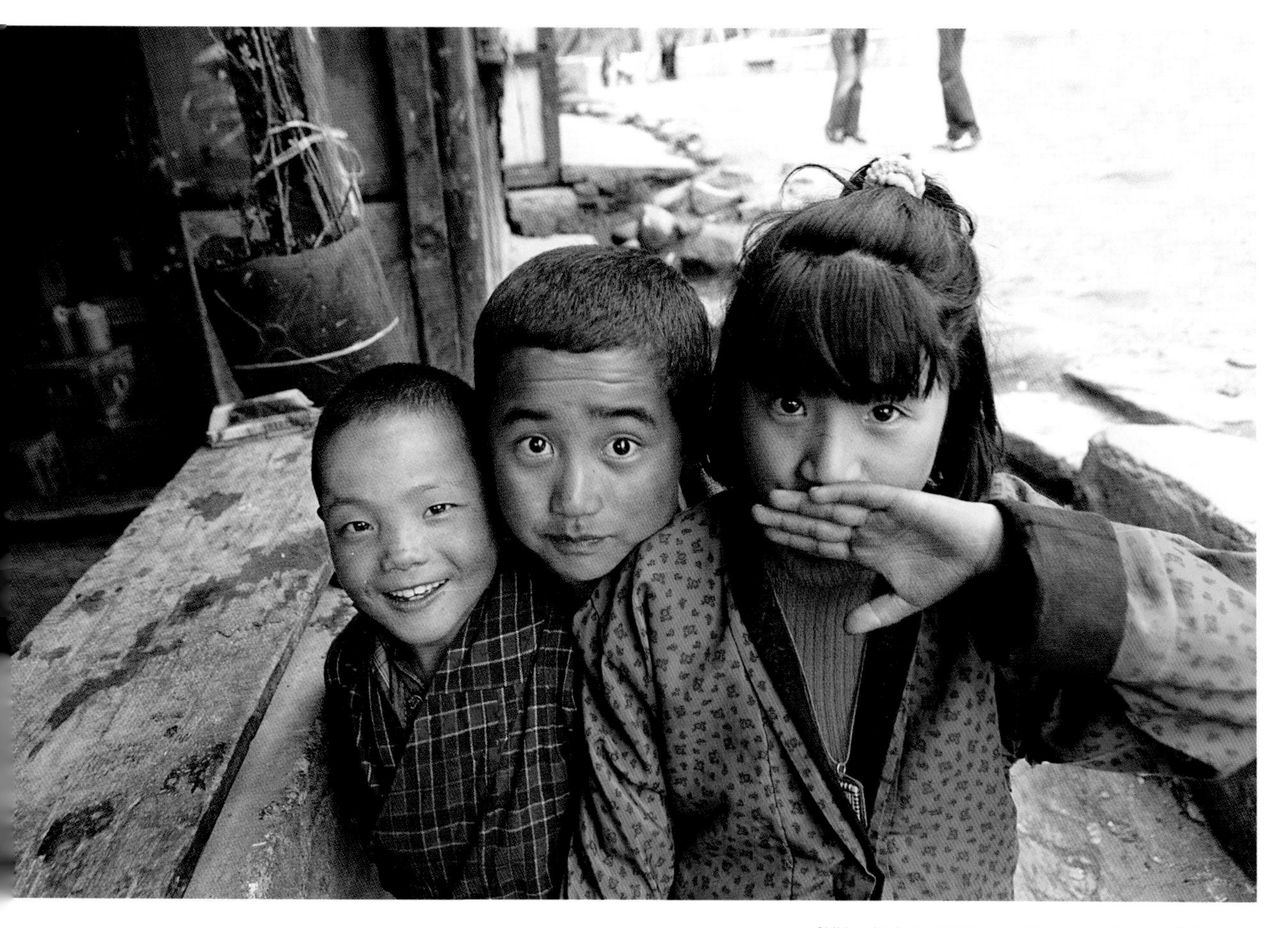

Children by the roadside between Trongsar and Wangdu, 2007.

Rhododendrons flowering at 3,000 metres, below the pass leading to the valley of Phobjika. Late April, 2007.

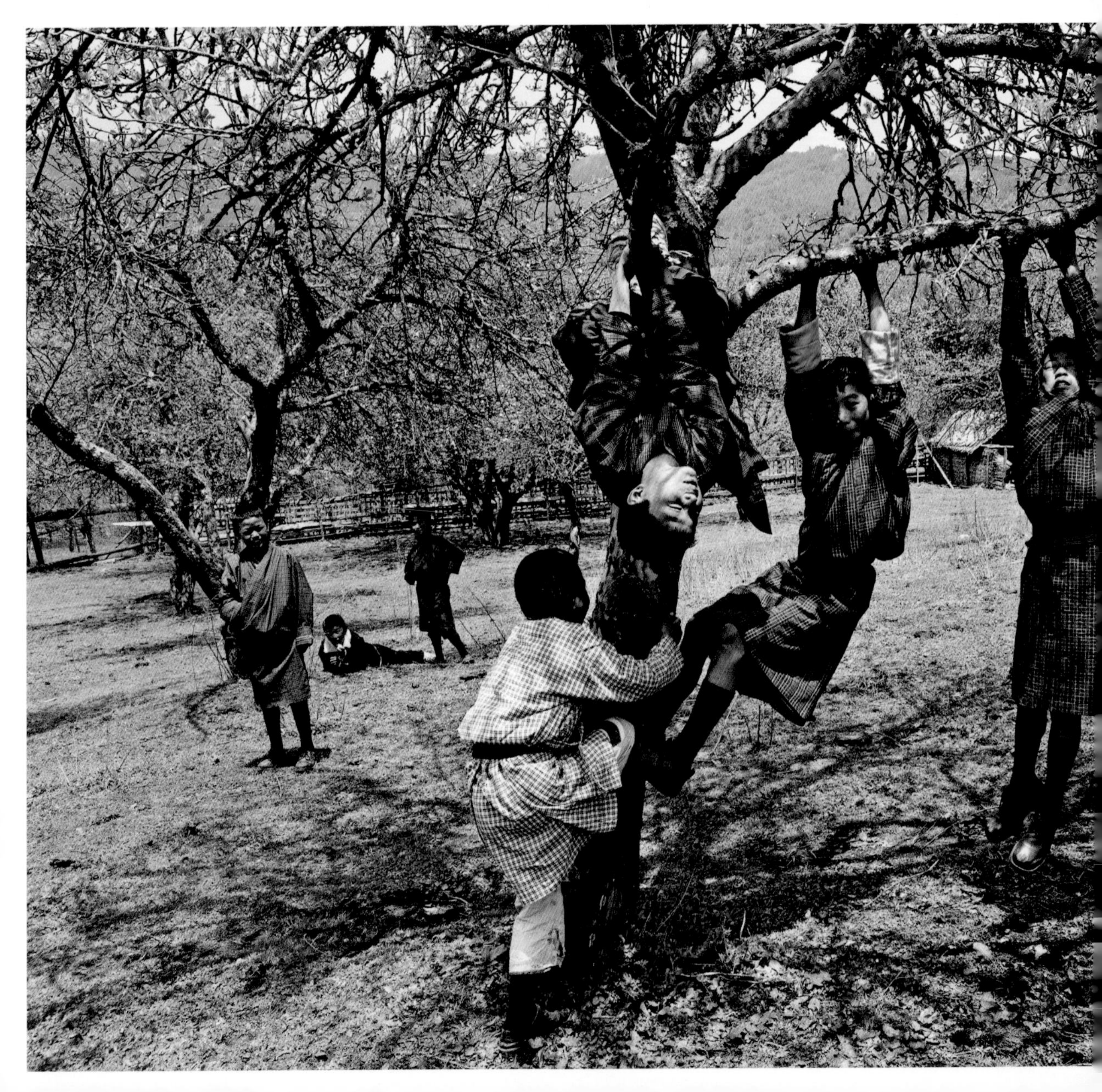

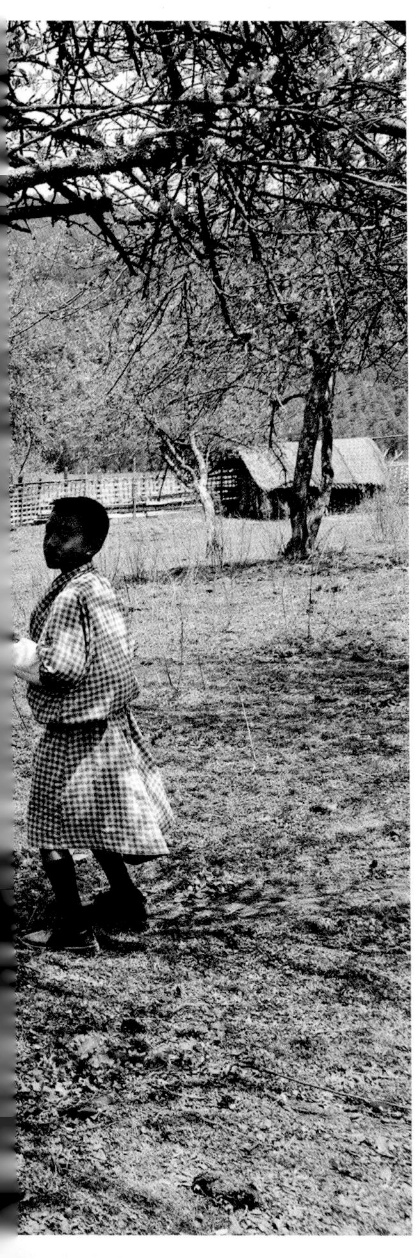

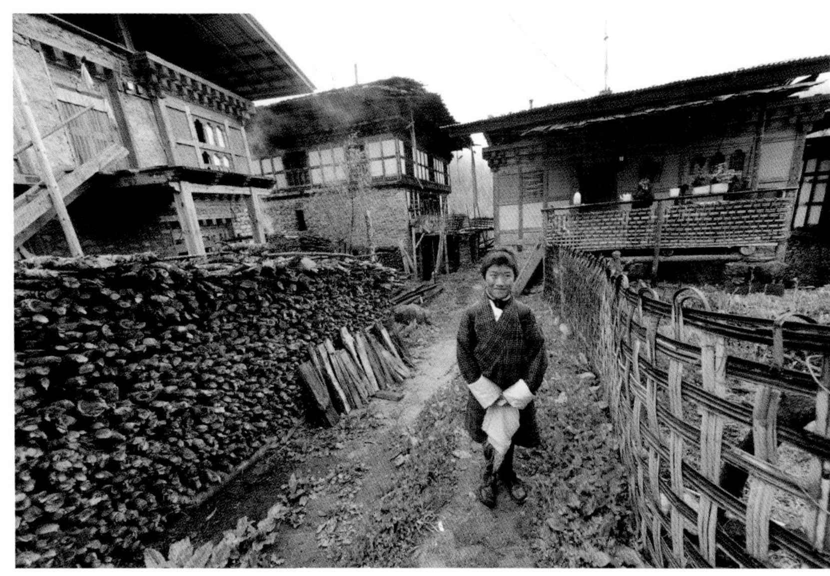

A boy on his way to school in the village of Chumey in the Bumthang valley. The majority of Bhutanese children attend school, and in remote areas they will spend an hour or two walking there and back. 2007.

Young boys playing in an apple orchard. Bumthang province, 2007.

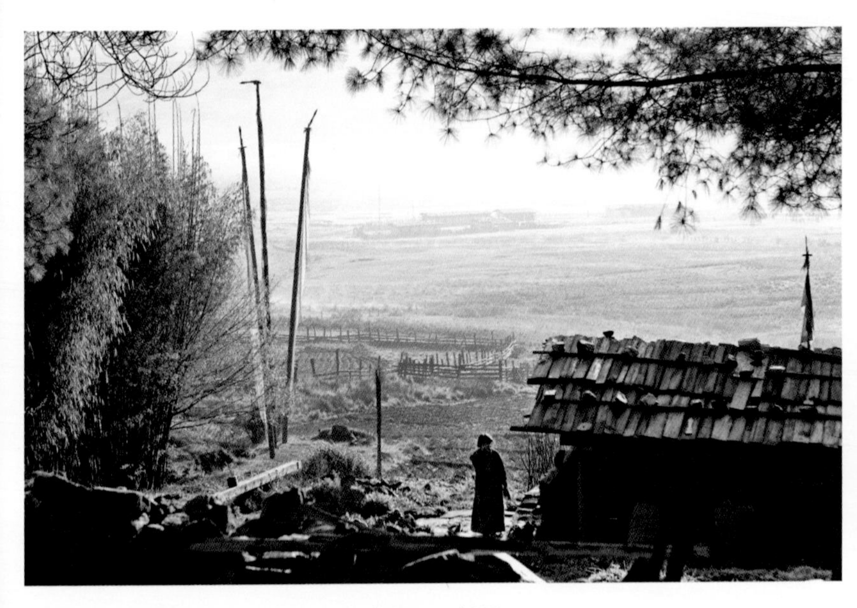

A simple peasant's house in the Phobjika valley (3,000 metres), 2007.

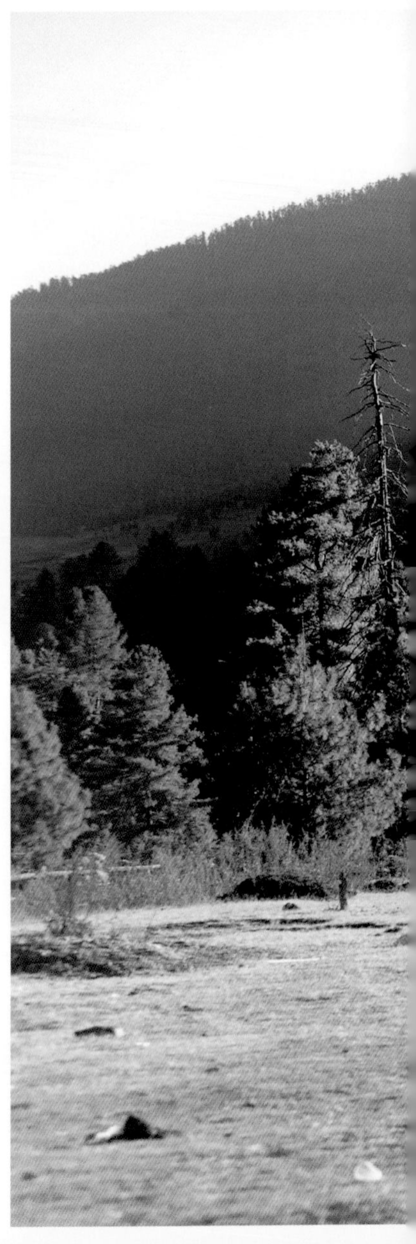

A mother and child in front of Gangtey village and monastery, which dominates the beautiful Phobjika valley. December 2007.

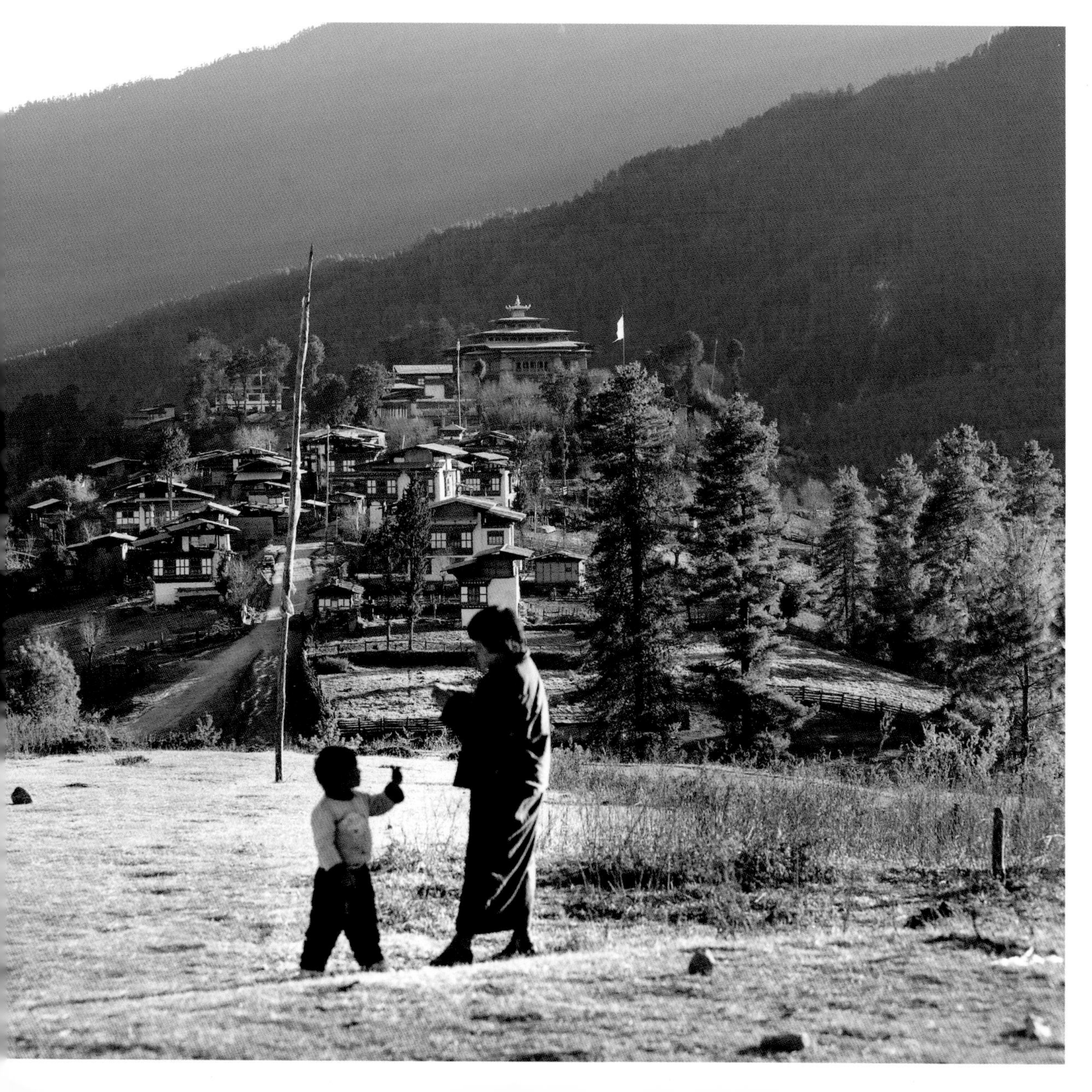

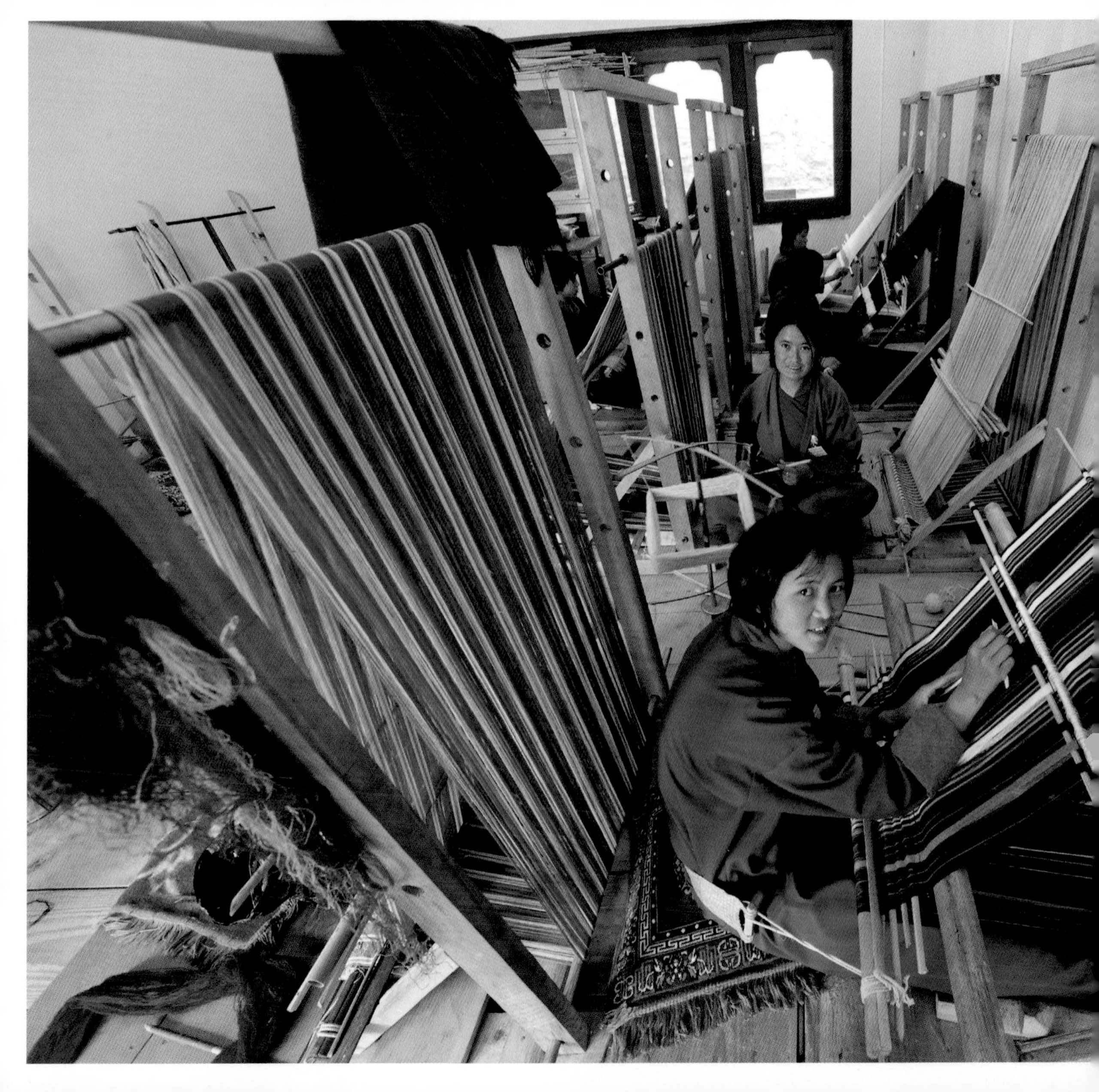

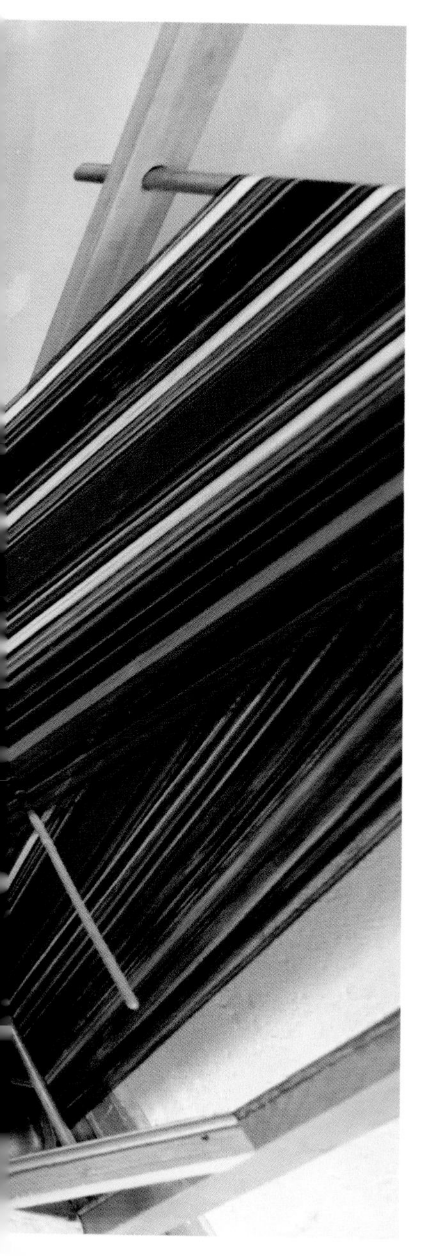

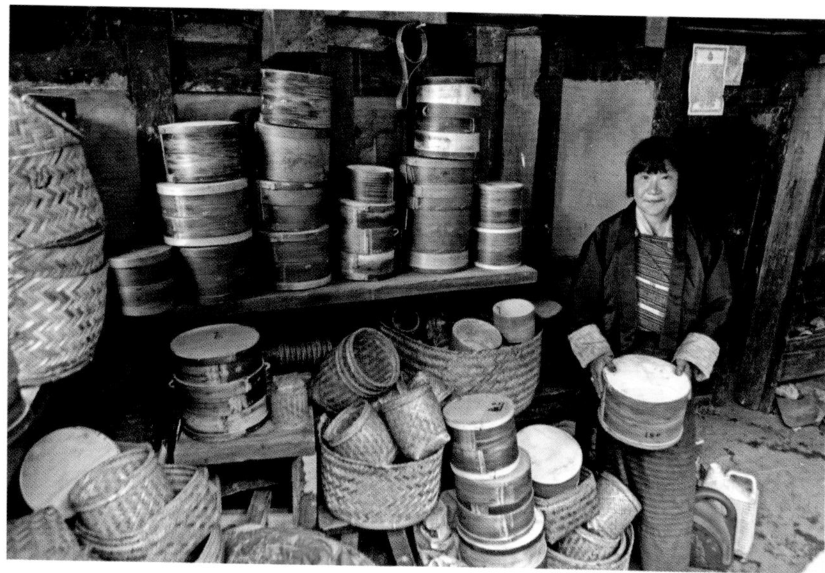

In Sha Jena, on the road between Trongsar and Wangdu, several villages are renowned for the bamboo containers made by local craftspeople. 2007.

Weavers at the Thirteen Arts and Crafts School in Thimphu, where hundreds of apprentices learn the various forms of decorative art traditionally practised in Bhutan. 2007.

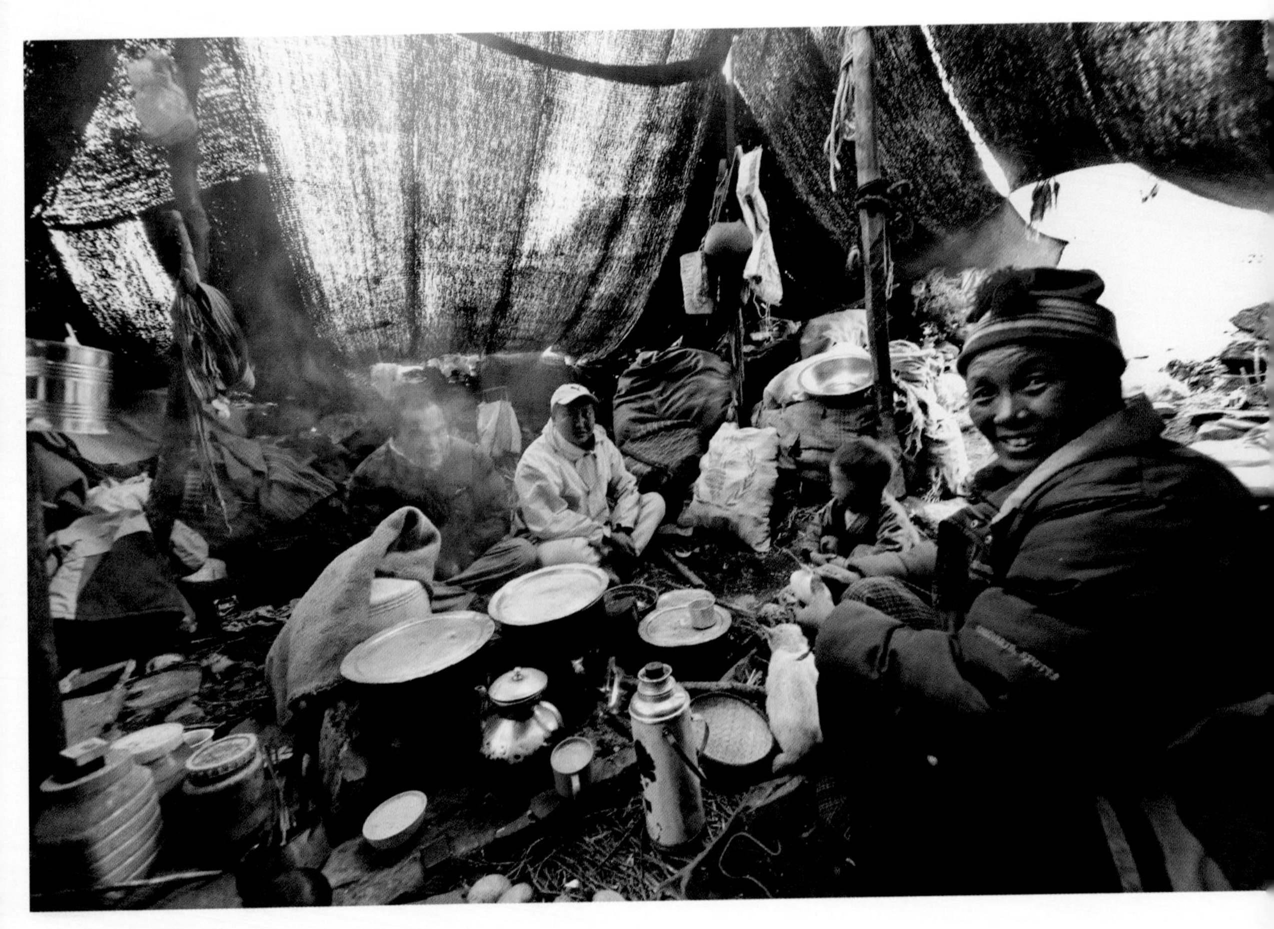

Above and opposite:
A family of nomads camping with their small herd of yaks beside Lake Tsophu, at 4,350 metres.
In the winter, they return to one of the lower-lying villages. May 2007.

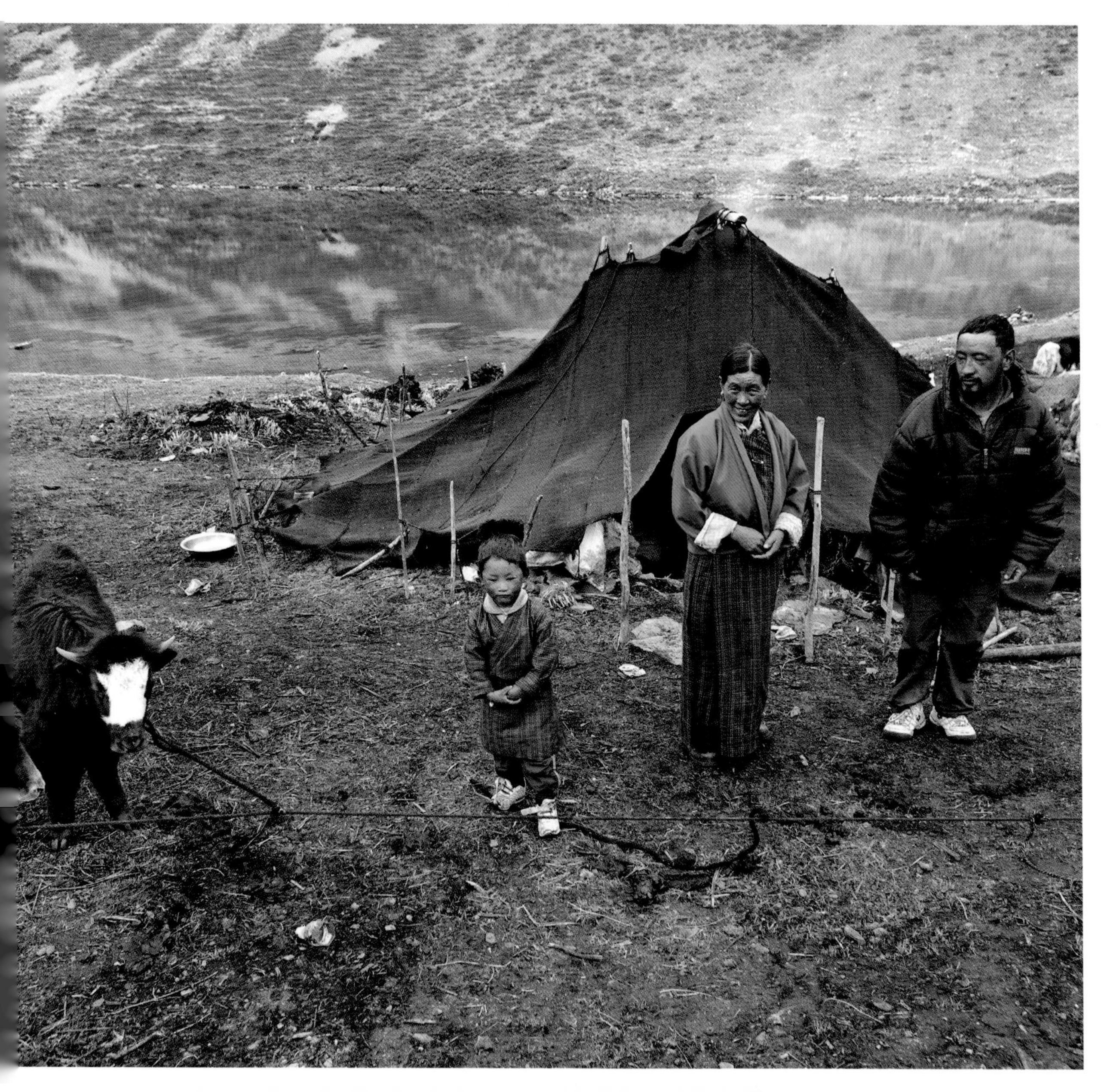

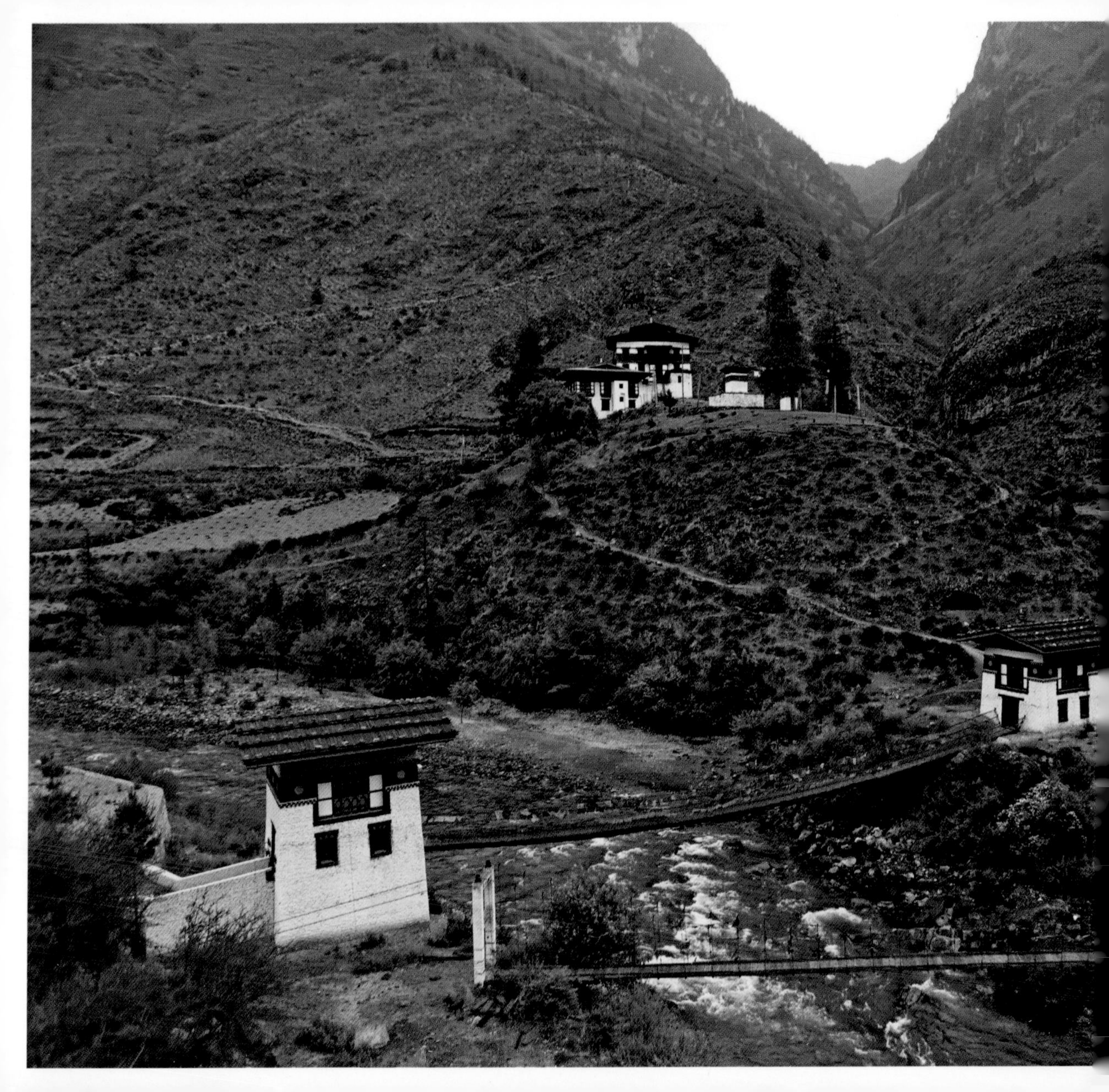

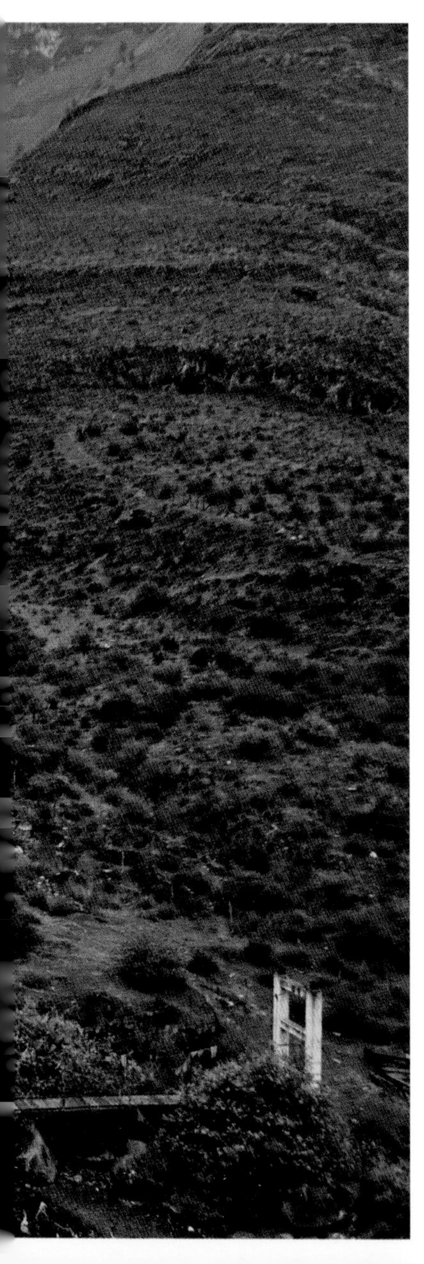

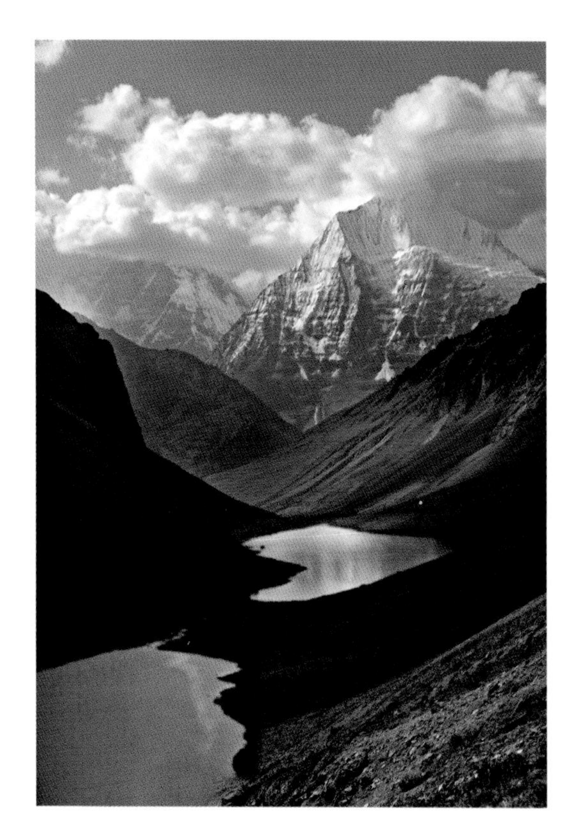

Lake Tsophu with Jigchu Drake (6,989 metres) in the distance. May 2007.

Left:
The bridge over the River Kyichu, near Paro, was built under the auspices of the Queen Mother of Bhutan, Ashe Kesang Choeden Wangchuck, using iron components from a number of other bridges, now in ruins, constructed by the great Tibetan master and bridge-maker Thangthong Gyalpo (1361–*c.* 1485). The huge iron links came originally from Bhutan and Tibet and, although they have been around for centuries, they have never rusted. The building on the hillside, Damchö Lhakhang, was one of Thangthong Gyalpo's residences. 2007.

Overleaf:
An unrivalled view of Everest, the 'Roof of the World' (8,848 metres), from the cockpit of a Druk Air plane. This Bhutanese airline flies between Paro and Kathmandu, the only high-altitude flight immediately south of Everest. 2006.

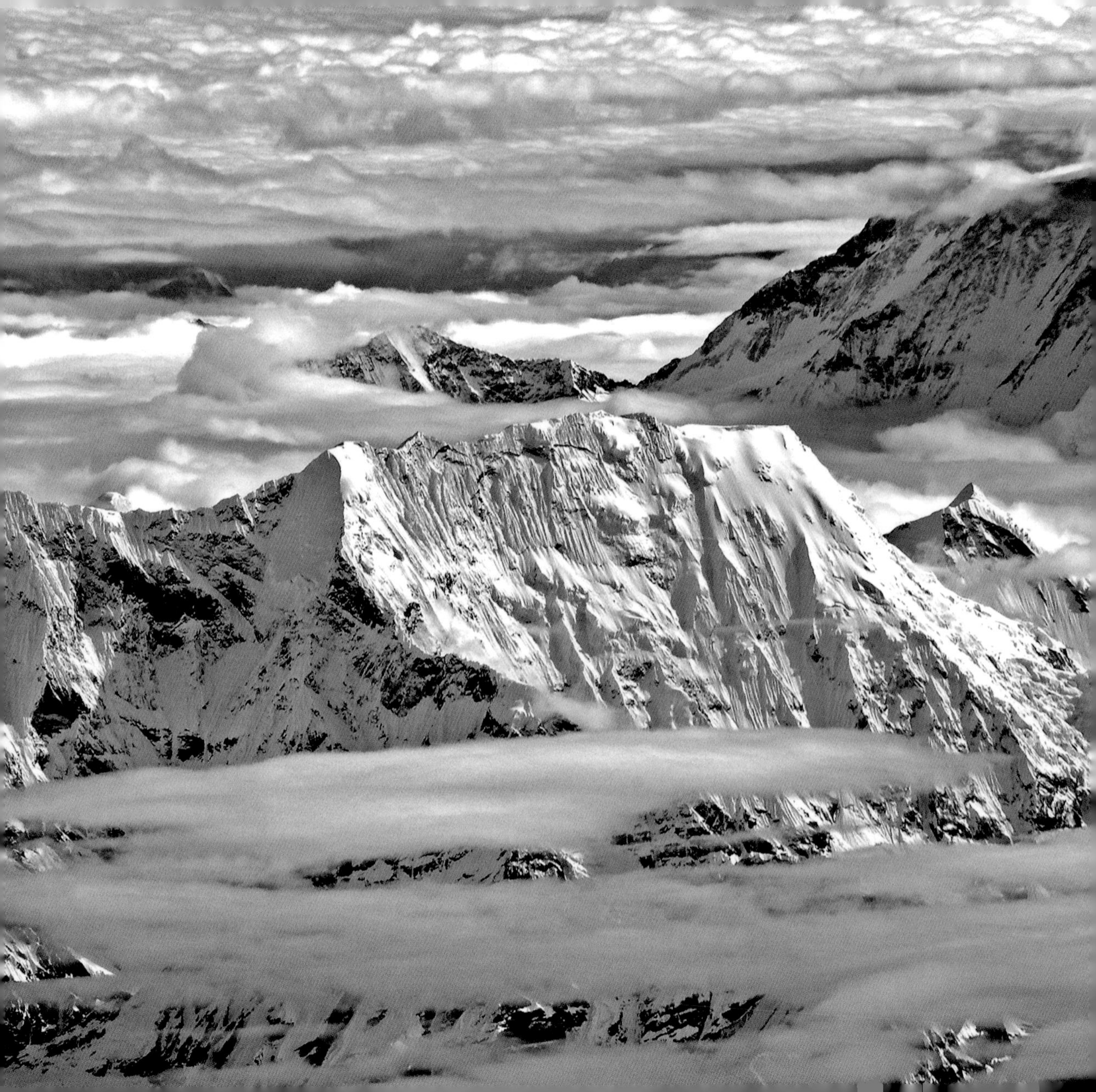

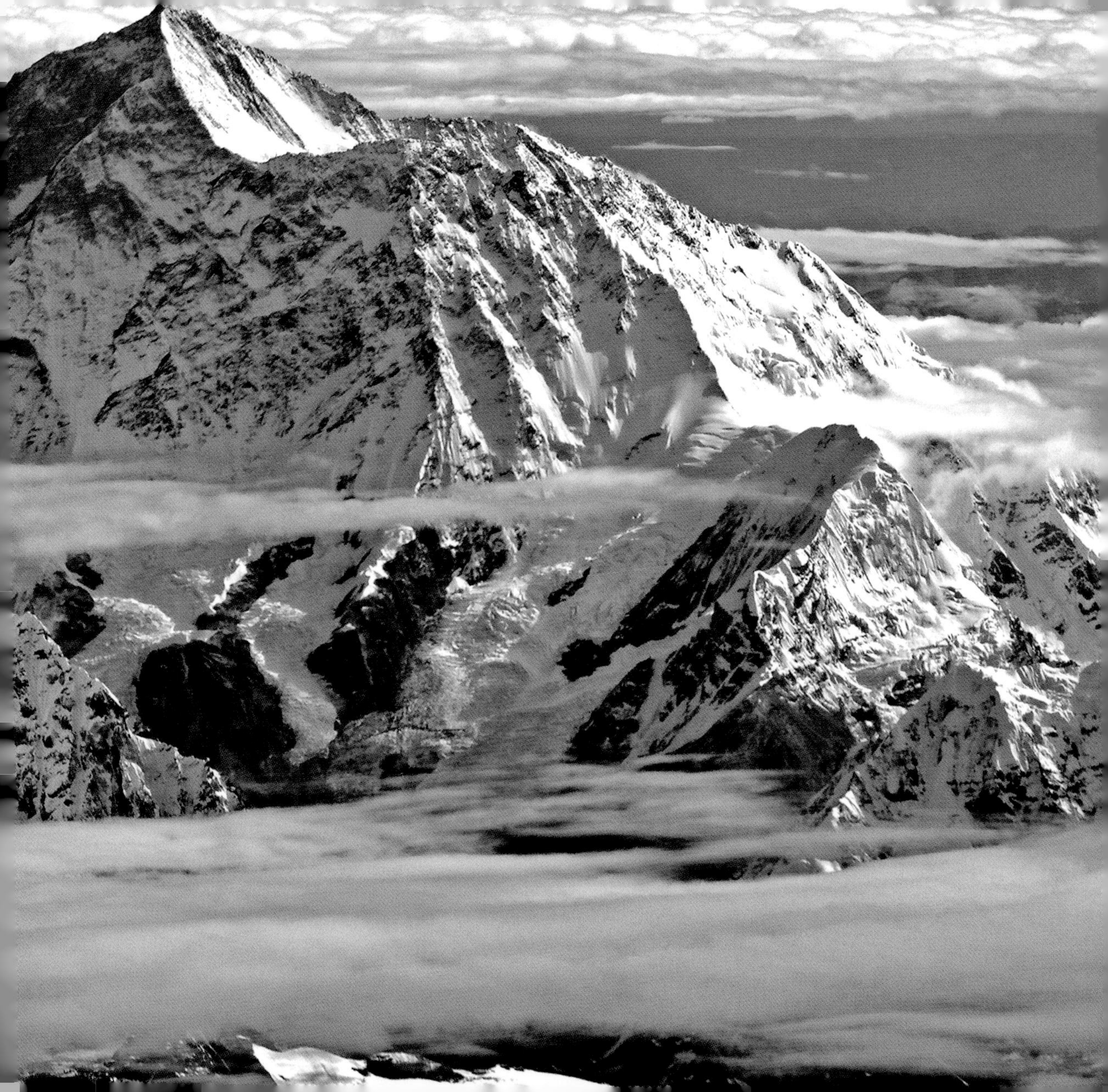

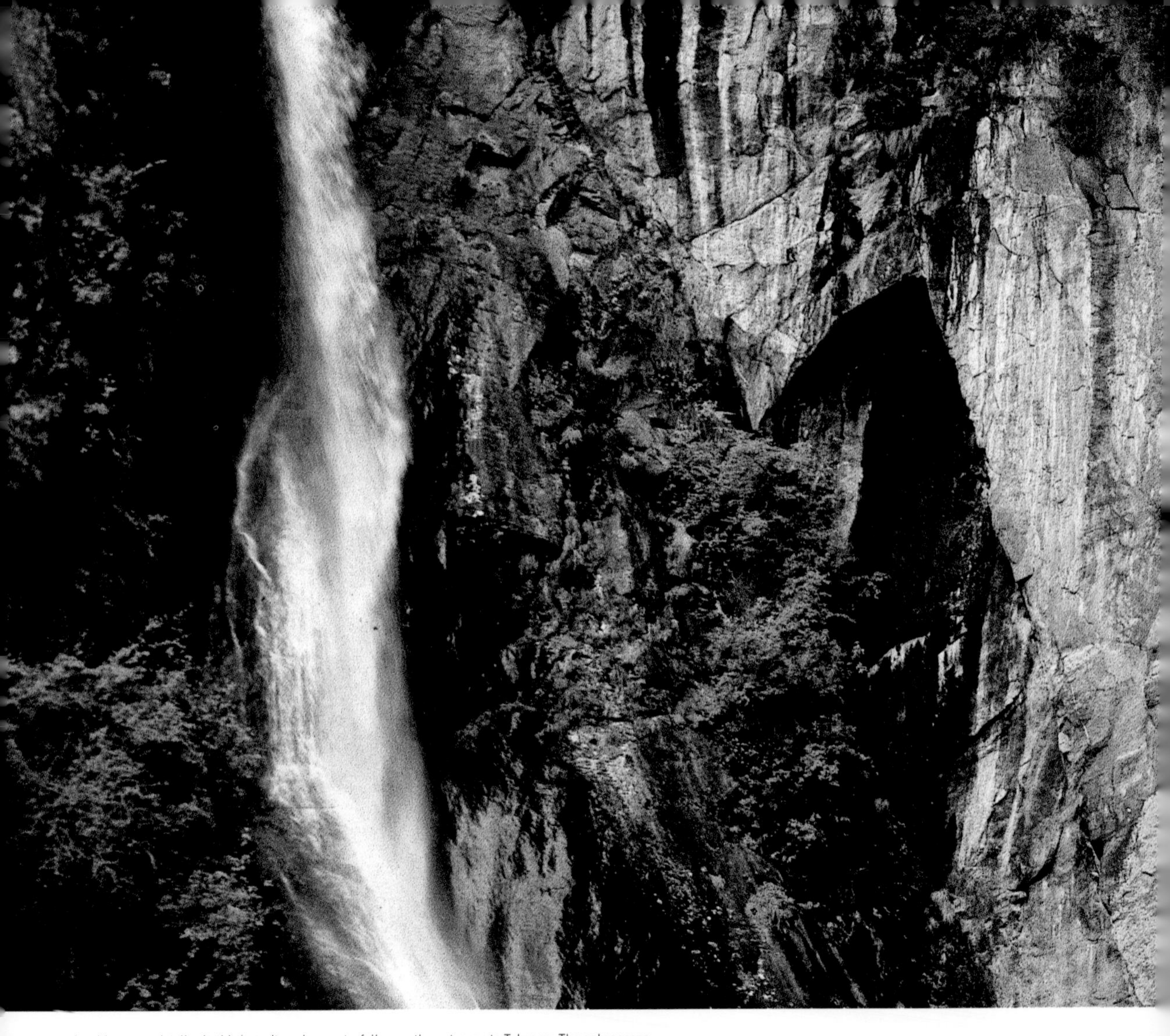

An old nun used to live in this hermitage by a waterfall, near the entrance to Taksang. The only access to it was by a crude ladder made from a tree trunk, leaning precariously against the rock face. 1980.

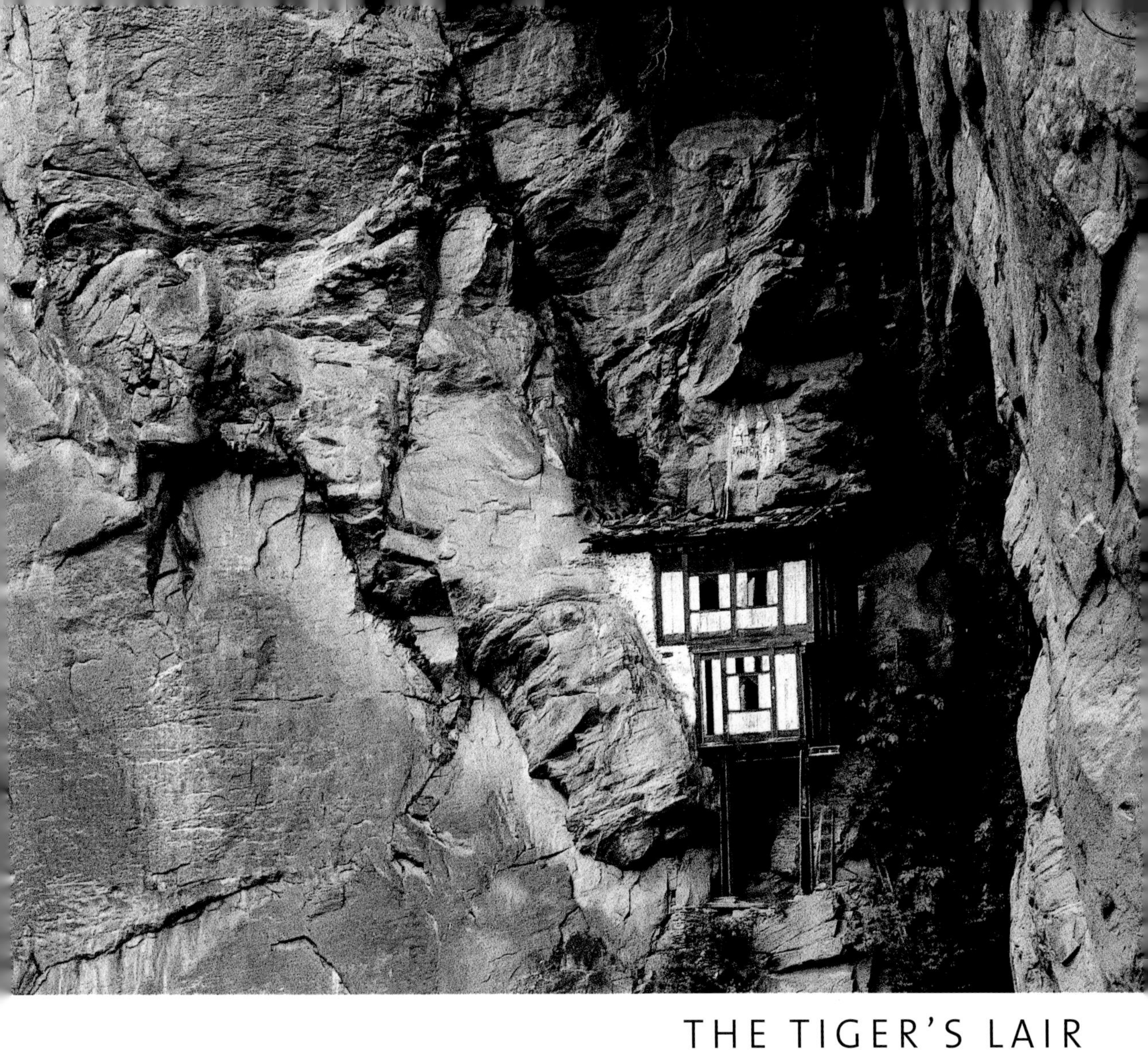

THE TIGER'S LAIR

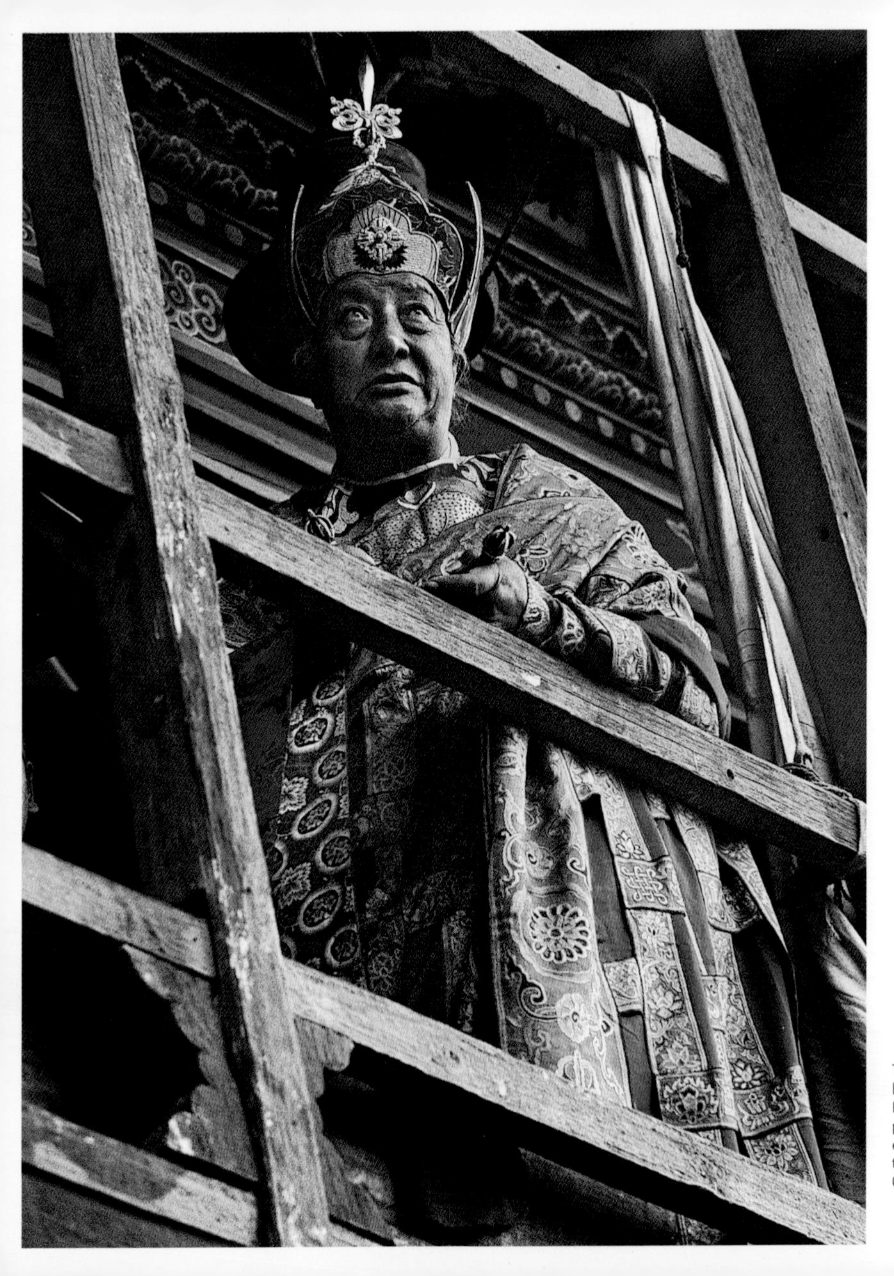

The great Tibetan master Dilgo Khyentse Rinpoche (1910-91) spent several weeks at Taksang, 'the Tiger's Lair', one of Bhutan's most sacred sites. As he was performing a ceremony intended to renew the spiritual energy of Taksang, he stood on a balcony overhanging the precipice, wearing brocade robes and the Lotus Crown, looking out over the landscape. 1980.

The Tiger's Lair

Paro Taksang is one of the thirteen sacred places in Tibet and Bhutan that bear the name 'tiger's lair' and is certainly one of the most impressive sites in the Himalayas. This magnificent chain of mountains has many other cliffs equally sheer and vertiginous, but none where a monastery seems to cling as if by magic, 800 metres above the valley floor, at an altitude of 2,950 metres. When you first see this dark, vertical wall of rock, you wonder how you could ever possibly reach the sanctuary. Padmasambhava is said to have flown there on the back of a tigress – hence the name of the place. And yet there is a path. It winds first through a great forest of centuries-old trees with swathes of pale green moss hanging from their branches: the hair, it is said, of ten thousand *dakini*, celestial deities who 'travel through the sky of the ultimate truth.' After climbing for two hours, you have to follow a zigzag path cut into the rock face opposite Taksang, and then cross in front of a waterfall that begins some two hundred metres higher up and at whose base prayer wheels driven by the current turn day and night. Finally, a steep path takes you up to the entrance to the monastery.

Some visitors are overcome by vertigo when they begin their descent towards the waterfall, but the path is now quite safe. It was a different story before the 1980s, when travellers had to negotiate particularly tricky sections on beams of wood suspended above the drop. A steel rope attached to the rock face along the difficult stretch provided the only support and it was impossible to avoid wondering how old those weather-beaten beams were and how much longer they could support a person's weight.

When you finally emerge in front of the monastery, you feel a mixture of relief and amazement. Stone steps pass under an archway, leading to a complex of temples built into huge overhangs of rock. The external walls of the main temples are vertically aligned with the drop and it is hard to imagine how they were ever built.

When Guru Padmasambhava, the great master who introduced Buddhism to Tibet and Bhutan, came here in the 9th century, all that existed were a few caves where he meditated and imparted spiritual teachings to his close followers, among whom were Langchen Palgyi Senge and his principal female disciple, Yeshe Tsogyal. It is said that he transformed himself into the wrathful Dorje Drollö and, riding a pregnant tiger, concealed various teachings in the form of 'spiritual treasures' (*terma* in Tibetan) in different locations in this sacred place. He hid these teachings so that they would be discovered and disseminated by the future incarnations of his followers when the time was right. Such 'treasures' have supposedly been revealed down the centuries by visionary masters, known as *tertöns*.

In 1980, during the Month of the Monkey in the Year of the Monkey – a combination that occurs once in every twelve years and corresponds to the birth of Padmasambhava – Dilgo Khyentse Rinpoche spent two weeks at Taksang. The monastery, which is usually inhabited by no more than a handful of monks, was suddenly a hive of activity, with a hundred or more of the master's disciples camped out in the communal rooms of Taksang's little temples. A constant stream of people came and went along the monastery's narrow paths, some of them coming up to see Khyentse Rinpoche, others going back down to the valley. On this occasion, Khyentse

Rinpoche gave many teachings to those who had accompanied him and offered 100,000 butter lamps in homage to Padmasambhava. On one of the days of his visit, he stood on a high balcony overhanging the precipice, wearing brocade robes and the Lotus Headdress, and gazing out majestically over the landscape, he performed a ceremony intended to renew the spiritual energy of Taksang.

Phelphug, the 'Glorious Cave' where Padmasambhava meditated, is the heart of Taksang. The first temple was built by Sonam Gyaltsen (1466–1540), a Tibetan master from the monastery of Kathok in eastern Tibet. But the temples that stand today were built from 1692 onwards, under the direction of Gyaltse Tendzin Rabgye (1638–96), fourth governor (*desi*) of Bhutan, who was also a grandson of the 'divine madman', the yogi Drukpa Kunlek (1455–1529). There are nine sacred caves and seven temples at Taksang and in the immediate vicinity. In 1998, a fire, the cause of which remains unknown (the only person who was there that day perished in the flames and the ensuing rock falls), destroyed the majority of the temples, and the debris and spiritual treasures came crashing 800 metres down into the valley. However, one of the major relics, the statue of Padmasambhava, which was located in the temple above Phelphug and is said to have spoken on occasion, survived the disaster almost intact. The temple of Tsepame (*Amitayus* in Sanskrit, the 'Buddha of Infinite Life'), situated to the east, was also spared. Under the auspices of the king and other patrons, all the temples were magnificently restored in a purely traditional style and re-consecrated in 2005.

Every hill around Taksang has its own small temple surrounded by prayer flags that flutter in the wind. The mountains and forests are dotted with hermitages where practitioners devote themselves to meditation, only going back down to the valleys once a year during the monsoon season to receive alms. Every farmer gives them a measure of rice and some dried vegetables, and in the space of a month they receive sufficient donations to be able to spend the remainder of the year in solitary retreat.

Climbing up northwards, near the waterfall, brings you first to the cave of Machik Lapdrön, a famous yogini (1055–1153), who is said to have left her footprint in the rock of her hermitage. Anyone wishing to continue the ascent has to climb for ten metres or so along the cliff using two tree trunks about thirty centimetres in diameter, into which shallow steps have been dug. This is a short climb and child's play for the Bhutanese who seem to have no fear of heights, but more challenging for the passing pilgrim, especially when the steps are slick with rain and the said pilgrim is wearing a backpack and his monk's robes get caught under his feet. It helps not to look down too closely at the drop!

At the top of the cliff, there is a pleasant level area in the middle of which stands the temple of Orgyen Tsemo, with its beautiful wall paintings. From here, it is possible to go back down by a different path that leads to Taksang's eastern temple, Sharma, situated near the cave of Dorje Drollö. The approach to this little temple used to be an extremely narrow ledge carved into the sheer rock, without any kind of handrail – a real source of vertigo! But today there is an easier path.

Behind Orgyen Tsemo, it is possible to climb still higher through a forest of immense trees, passing by the monastery of Öser Gang and emerging in an alpine meadow where the Bumtrak hermitages are located, at 4,000 metres. A famous painter of *thangkas*, Buddhist paintings made on canvas, lived here in seclusion in the 1970s. The name Bumtrak, literally 'the Rock of the Hundred Thousand,' comes from the fact that innumerable marks have been gouged into the rocky escarpment where the hermitages stand, and these are said to be the footprints left by 100,000 dancing *dakinis*, making ritual offerings.

All these places are a powerful source of inspiration for those on the spiritual path. One month spent in meditation in a sacred place like Taksang is said to bring about the same degree of spiritual progress as a year spent in retreat in an ordinary place. But however inspiring it may be, outer pilgrimage must lead to inner pilgrimage – the pilgrimage that leads to Enlightenment.

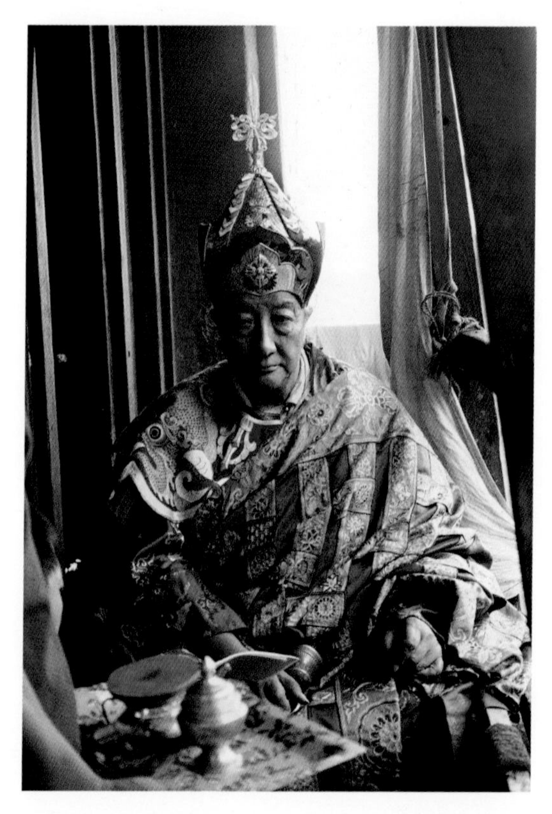

Khyentse Rinpoche performing a ceremony in one of Taksang's temples, 1980.

Right:
View of Taksang. In the foreground are flags printed with prayers for the benefit of all living beings; the prayers are said to be carried on the wind. 2006.

Overleaf, left:
Two monks blowing Tibetan trumpets on one of Taksang's terraces, above the wooded valley of Paro. The trumpets are four metres long. 1980.

Overleaf, right:
The monastery-hermitage of Taksang, perched precariously on the side of the mountain. 1983.

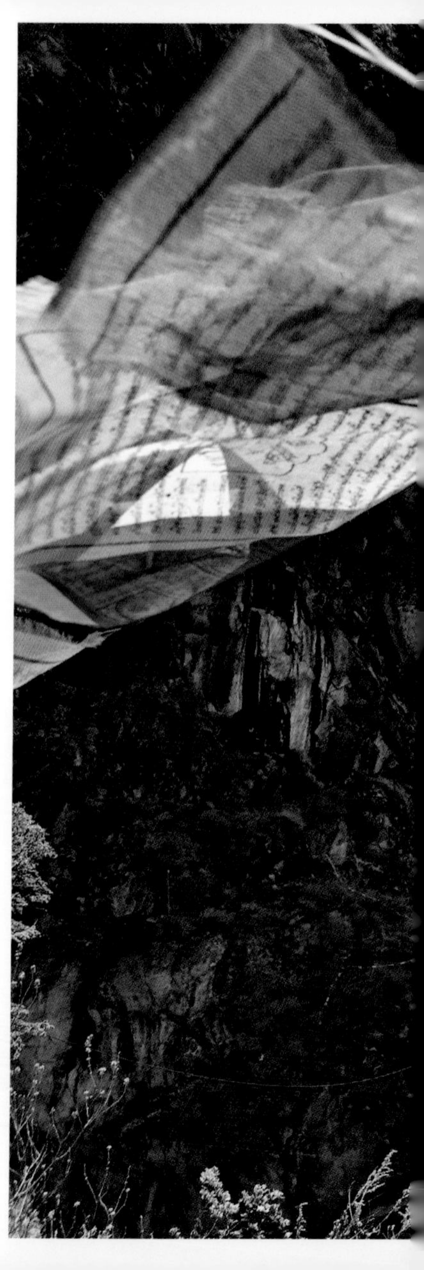

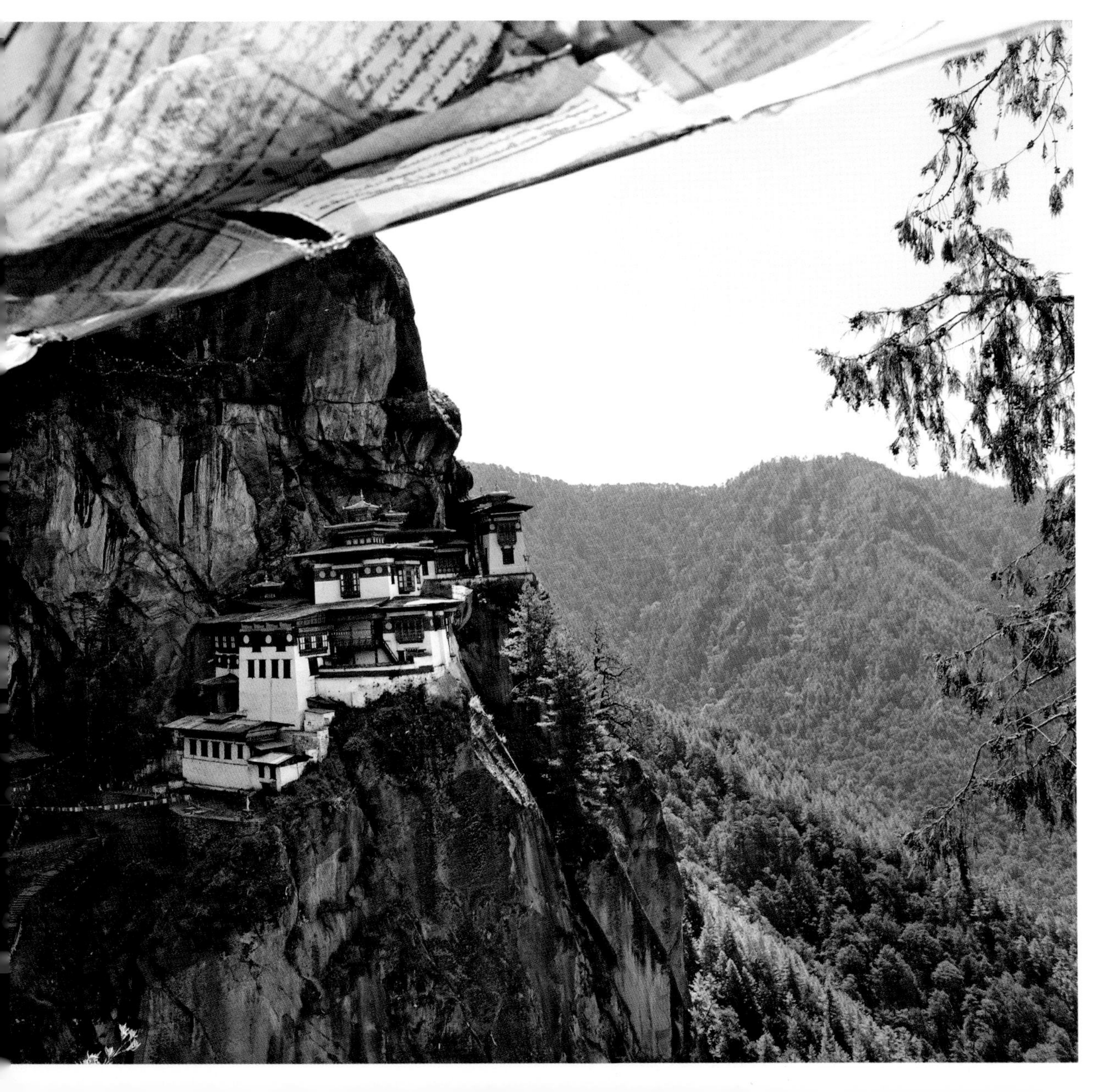

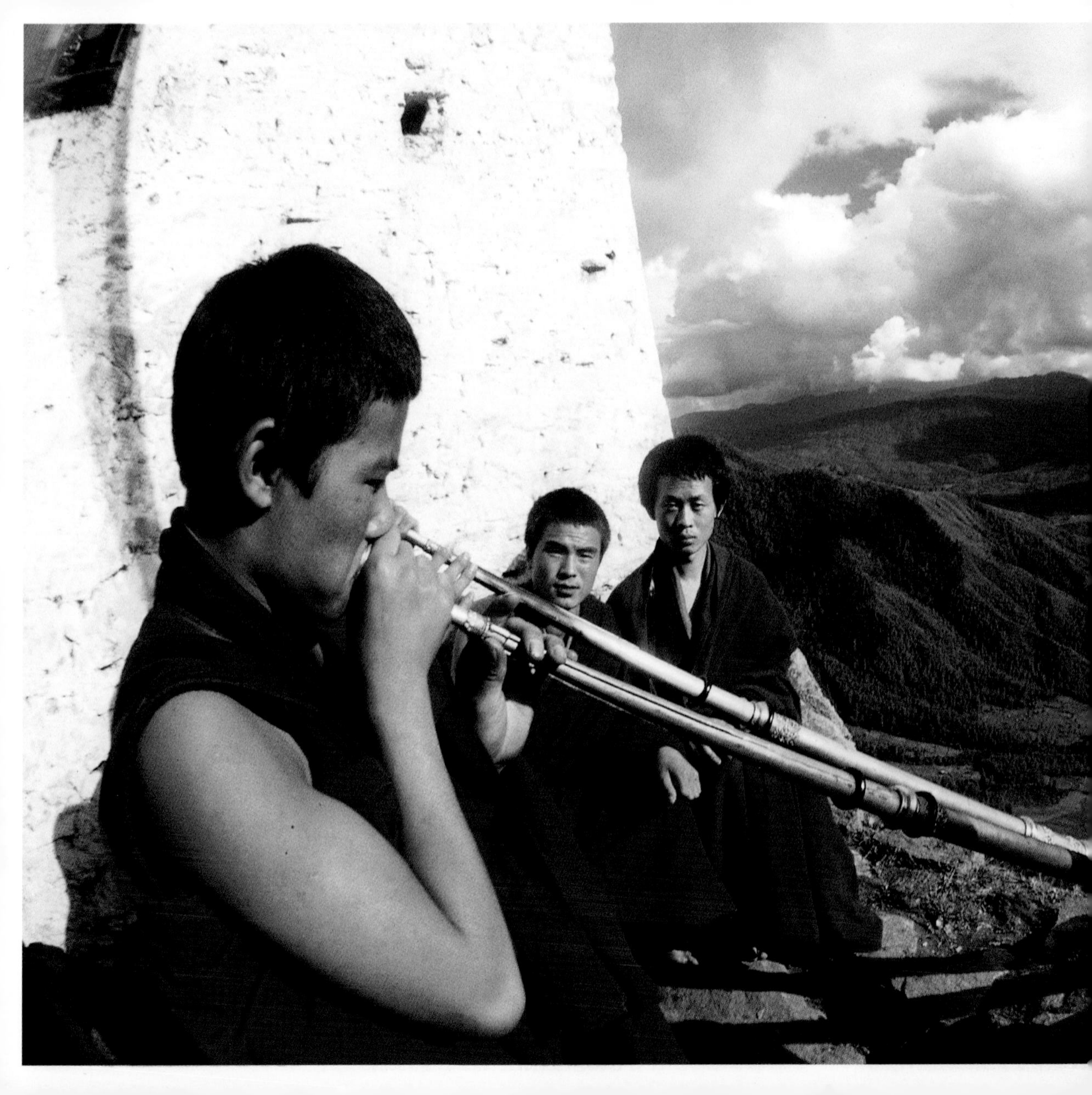

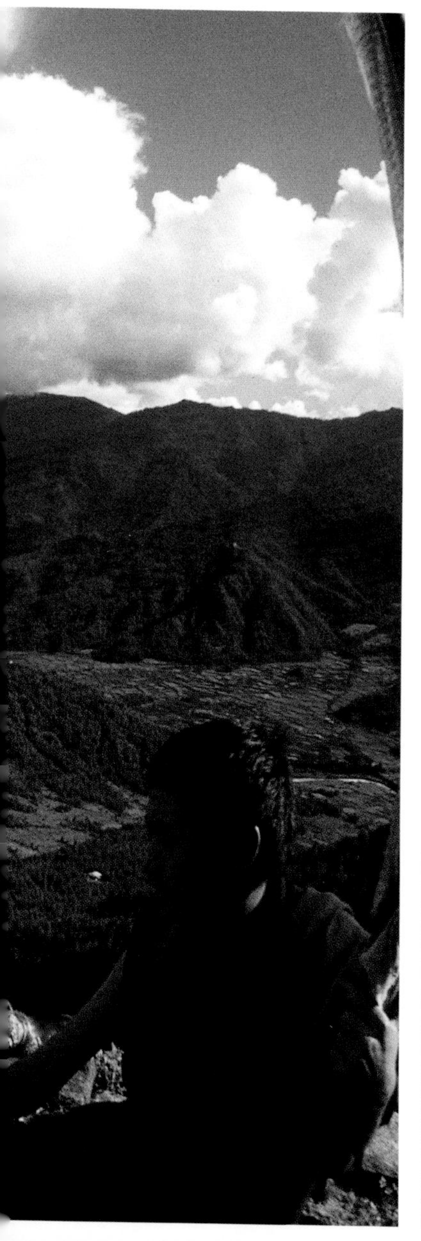
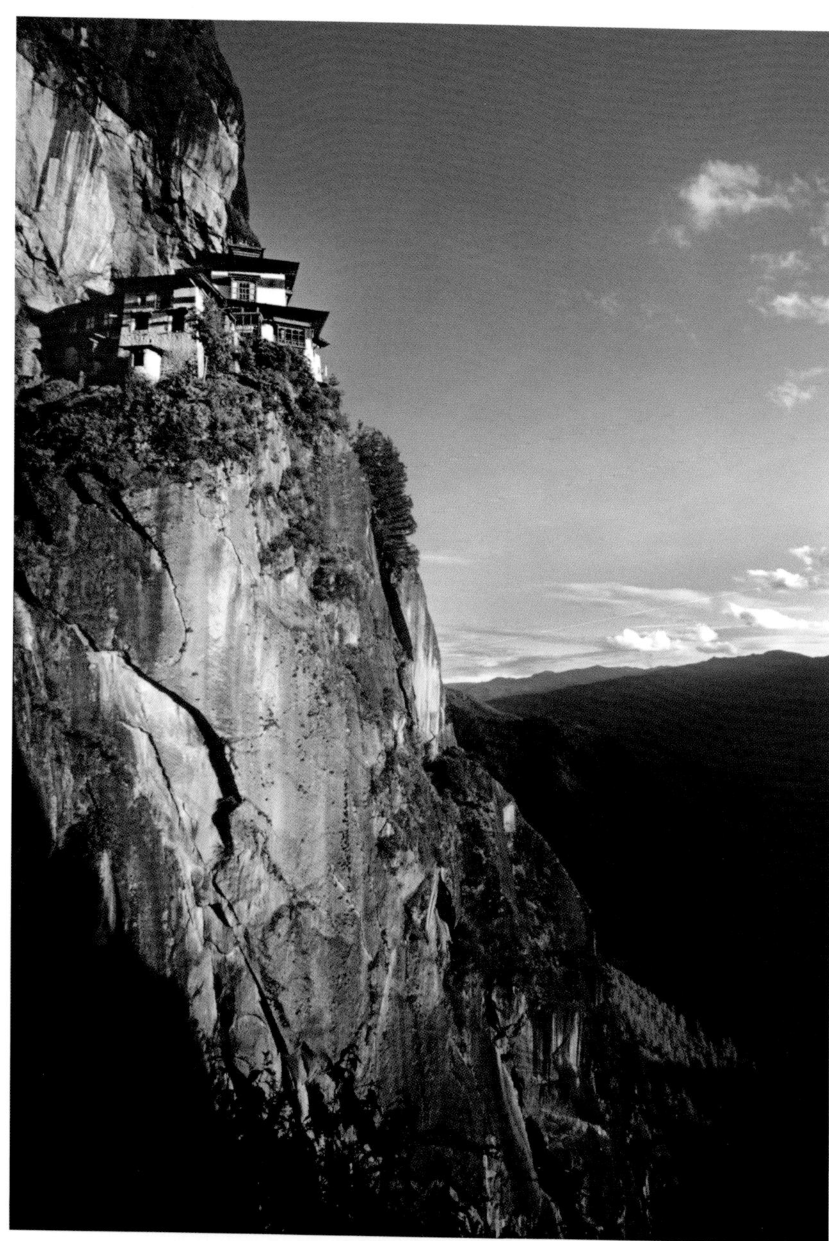

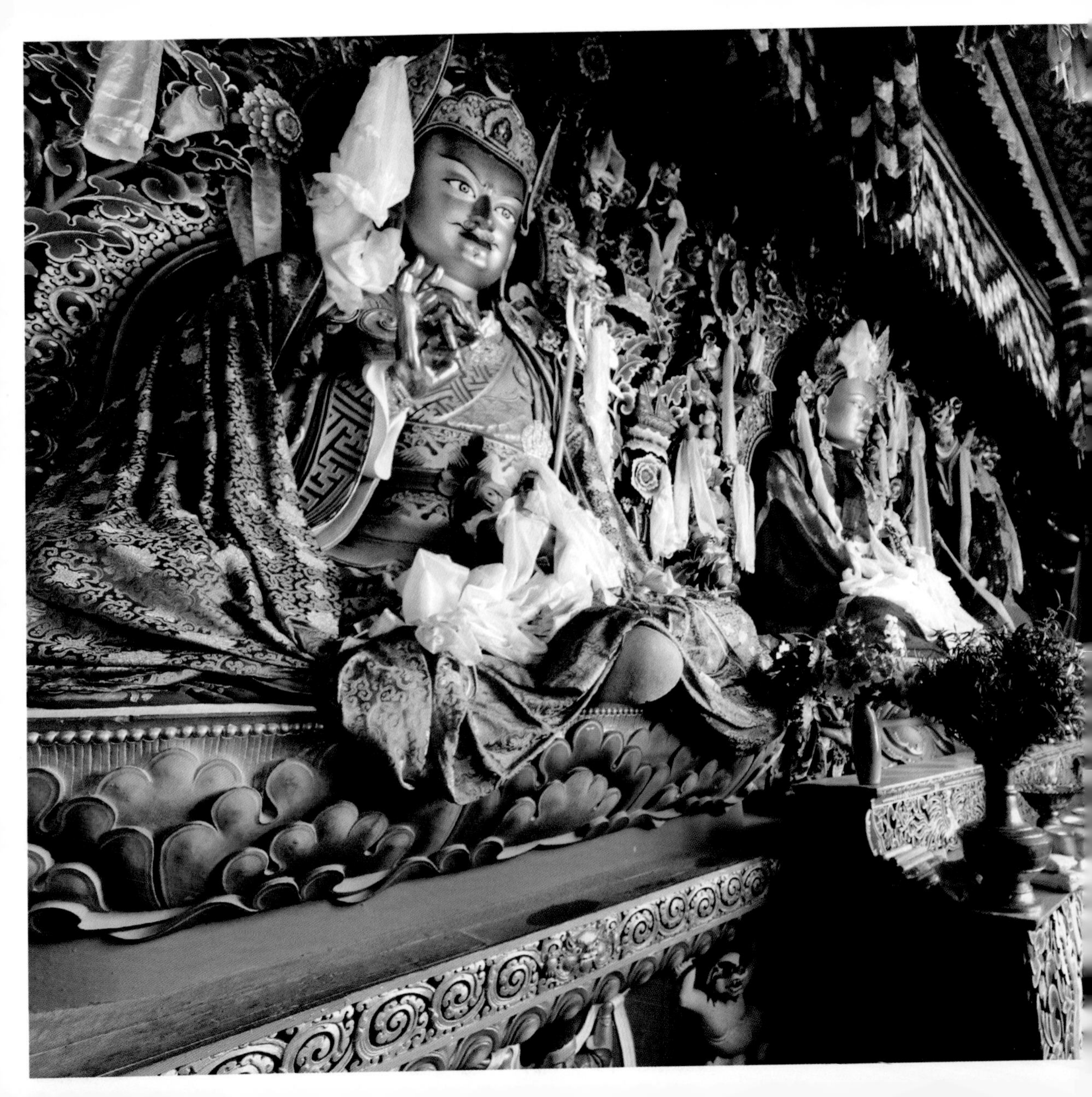

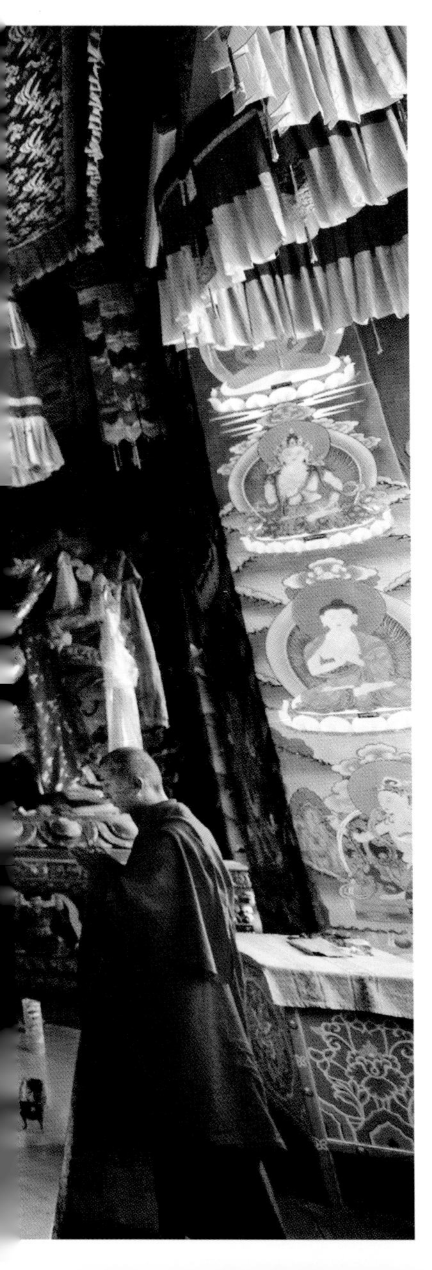

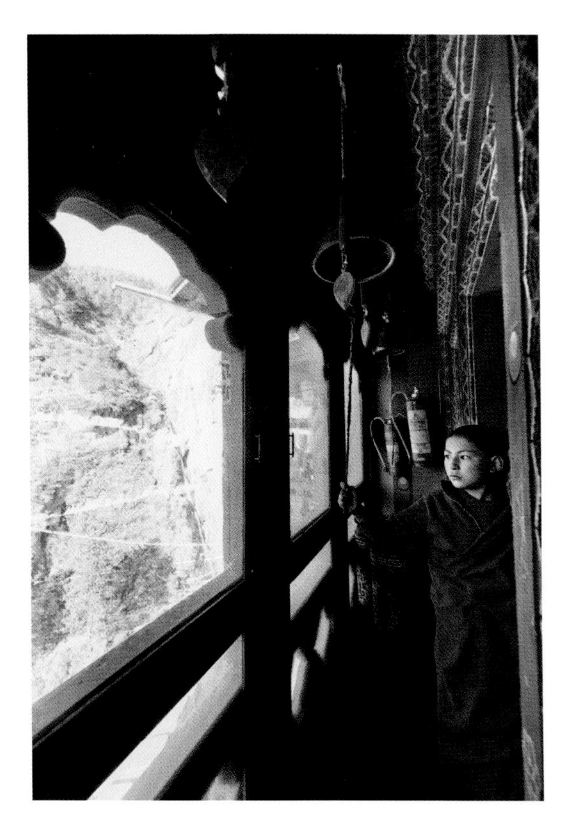

A young monk ringing a bell – a tuneful offering to the Buddha. 2007.

One of Taksang's new temples, magnificently reconstructed following the fire of 1998.

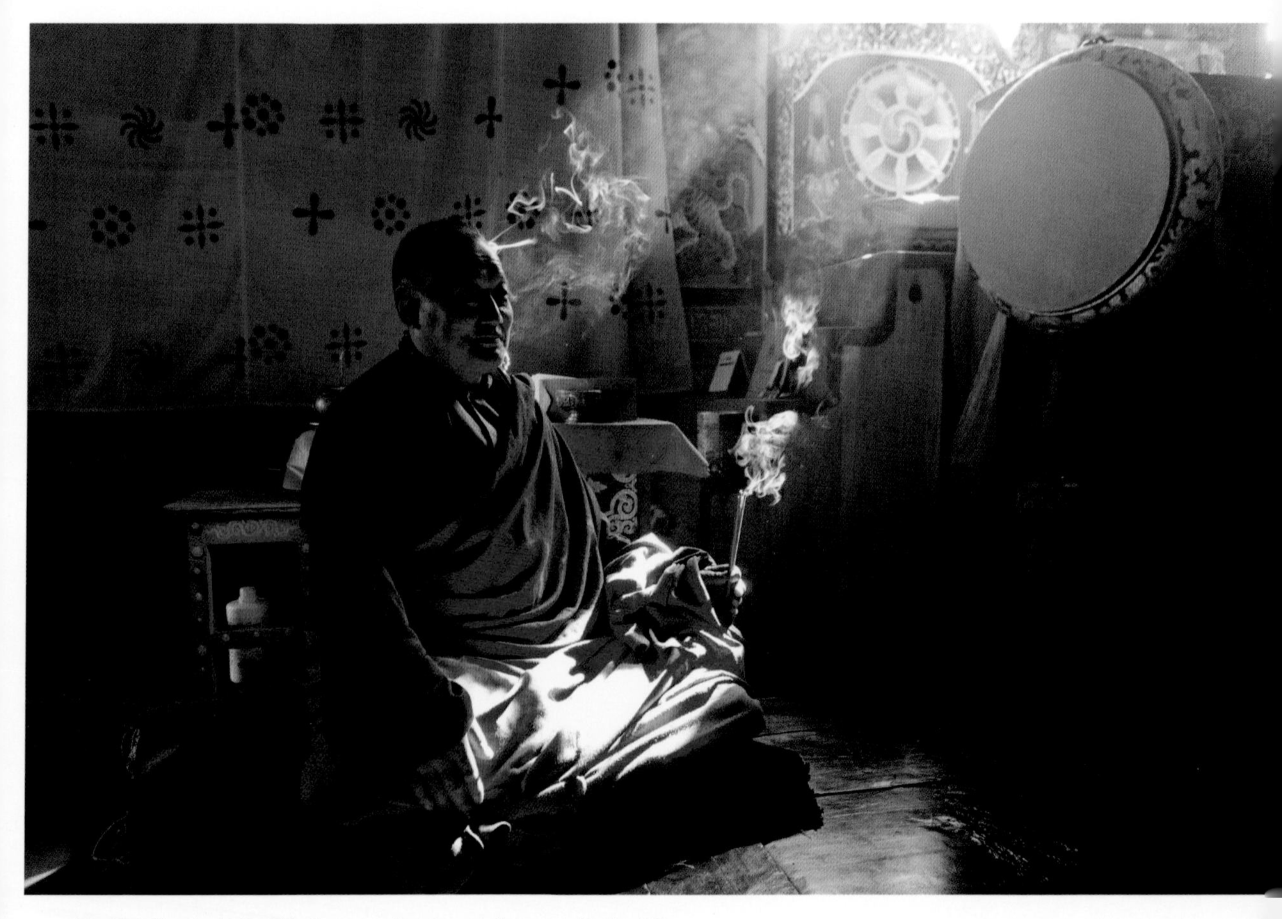

Lama Dorje Wangchuck with a stick of incense, making a fragrant offering to the Buddha. 2007.

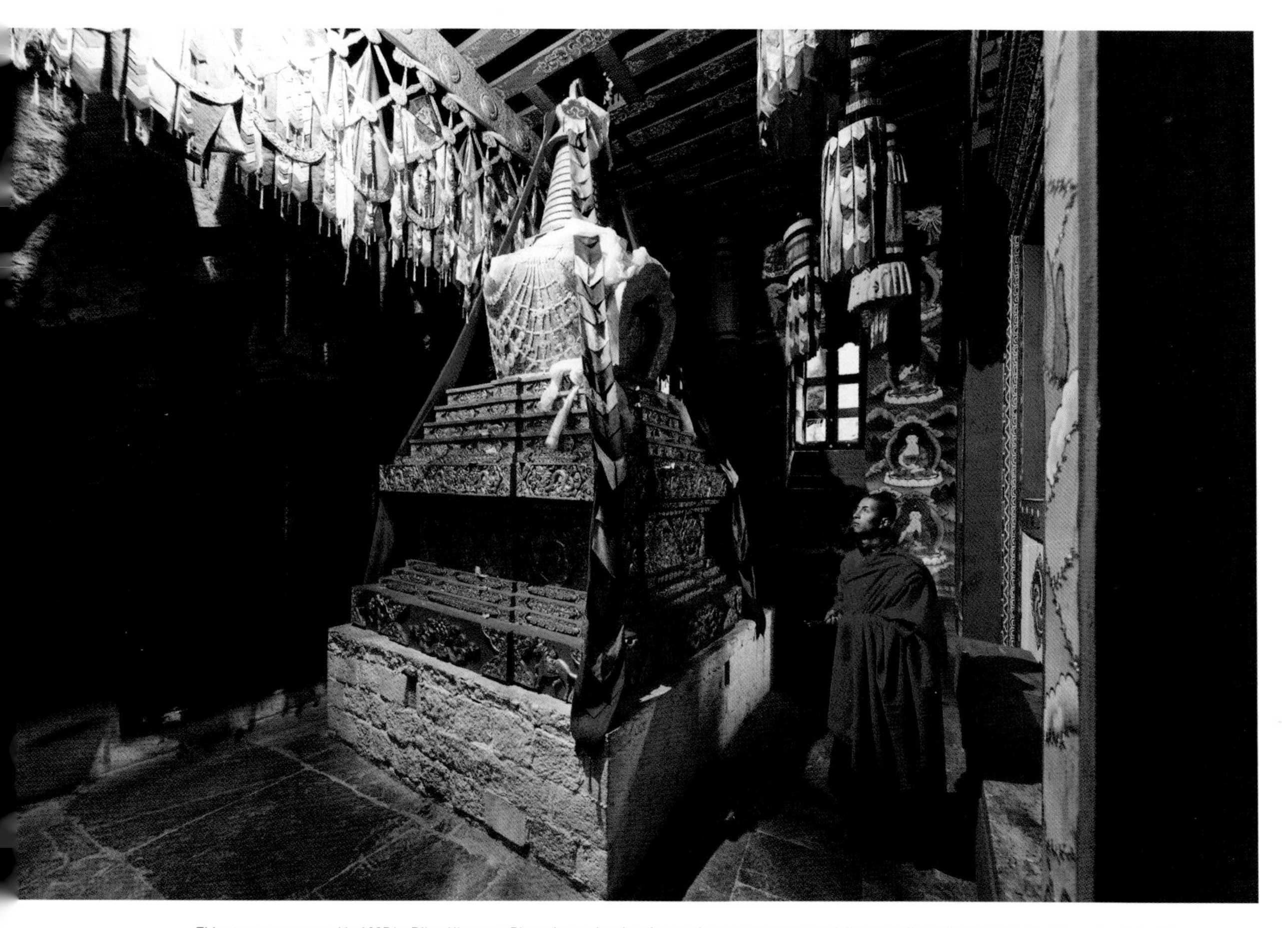

This stupa was erected in 1985 by Dilgo Khyentse Rinpoche on the site of an ancient monument containing the relics of the grand master Langchen Palgyi Senge, a disciple of Guru Padmasambhava who accompanied him on his visit to Bhutan in the 9th century. The stupa was recently restored, following the fire of 1998.

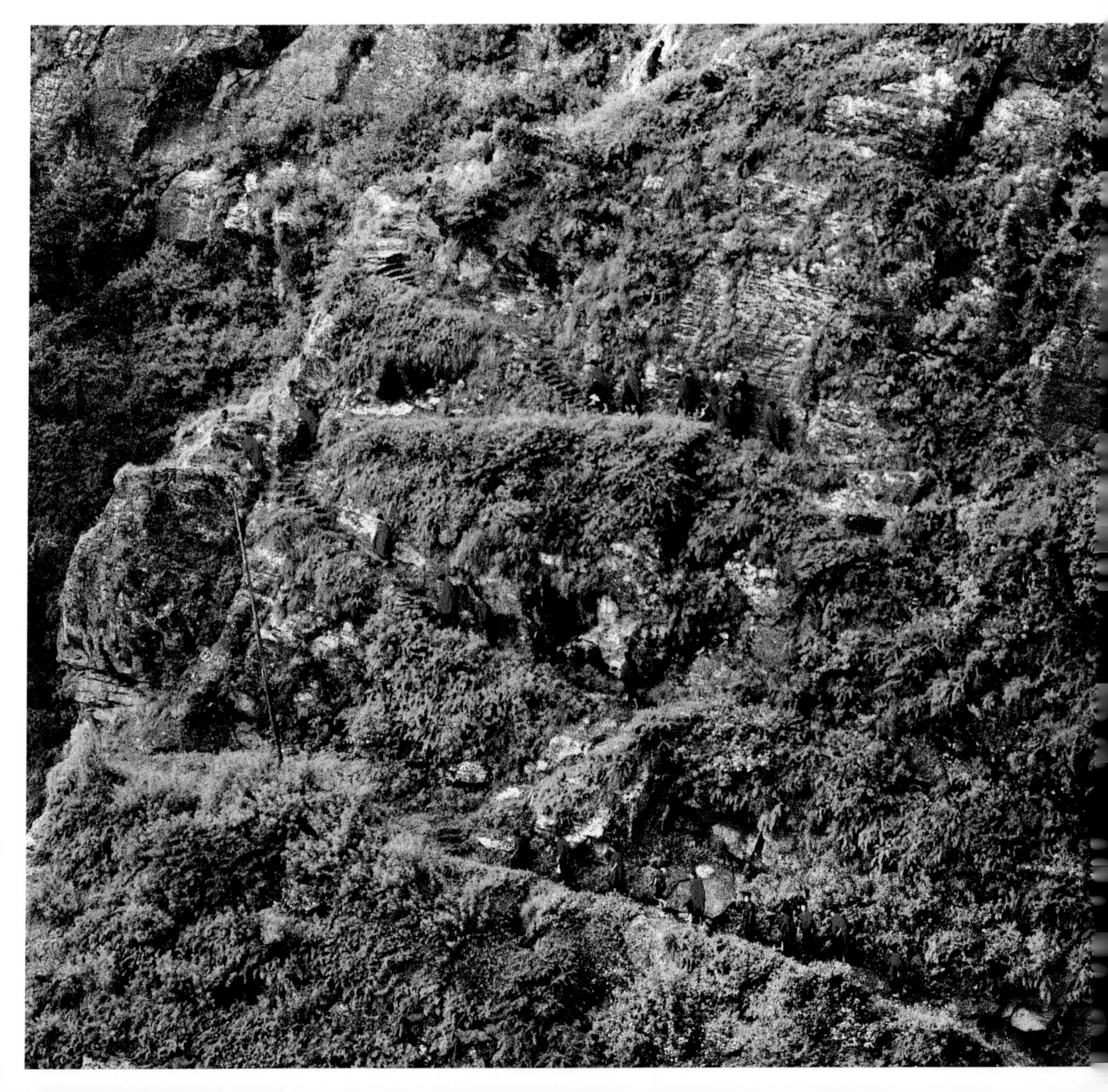

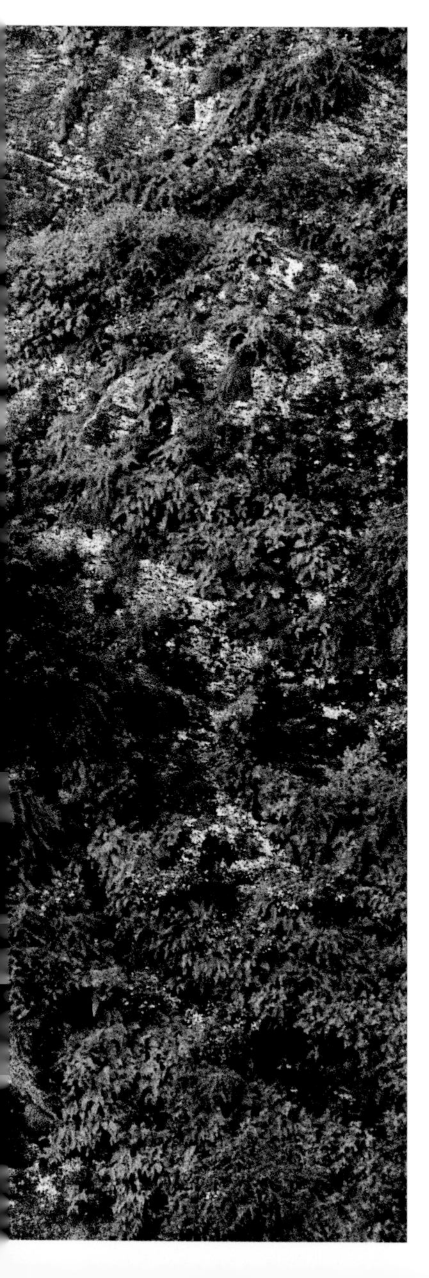

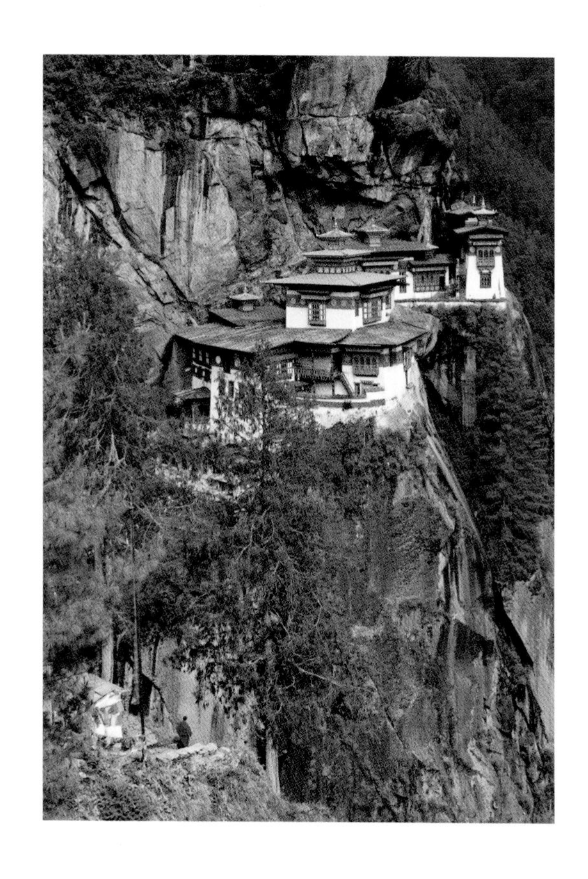

Left and above:
After visiting Dilgo Khyentse Rinpoche, a group of monks make their way back up the zigzag path cut into the rock face opposite Taksang. 1980.

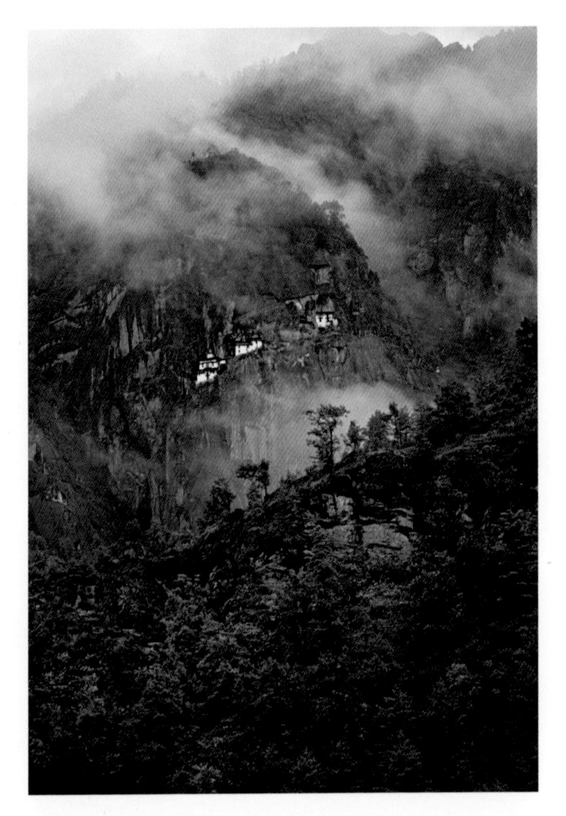

Above and opposite:
Taksang (2,950 metres) is one of the most imposing sites in the Himalayas, clinging to its rock face and suspended 800 metres above the valley floor.

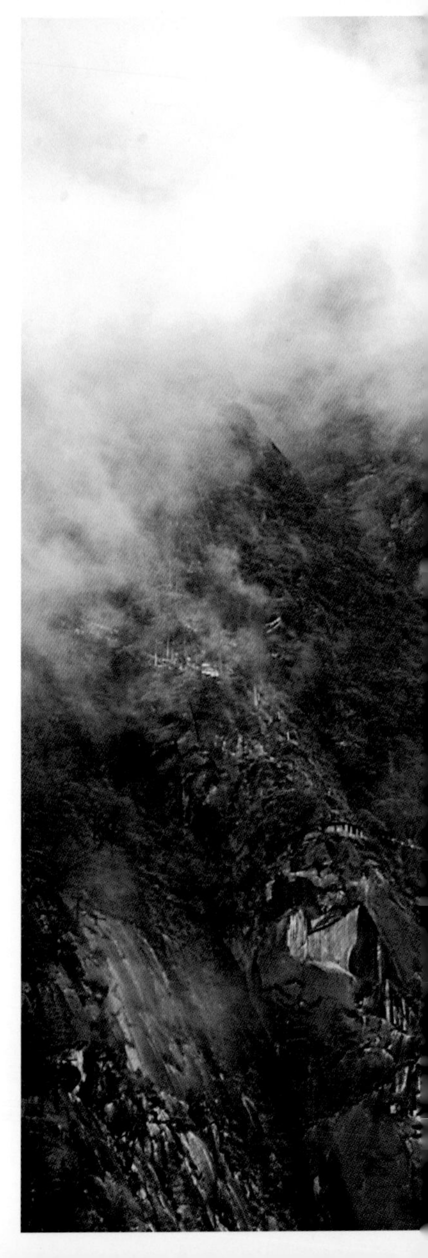

Overleaf:
The temples of Sandokpalri (centre, on its rocky summit) and Taksang (right) emerging out of the morning mist. 2003.

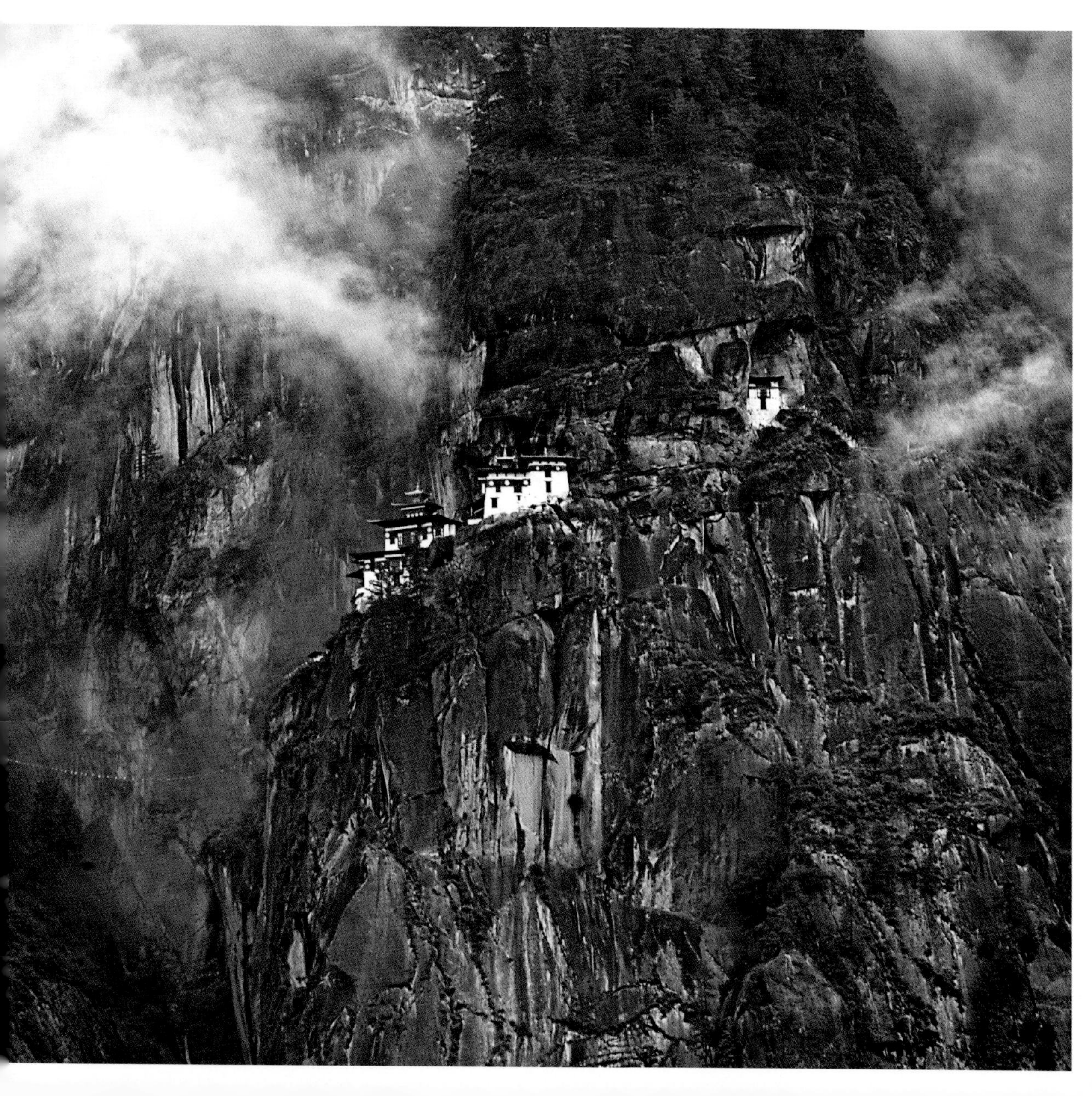

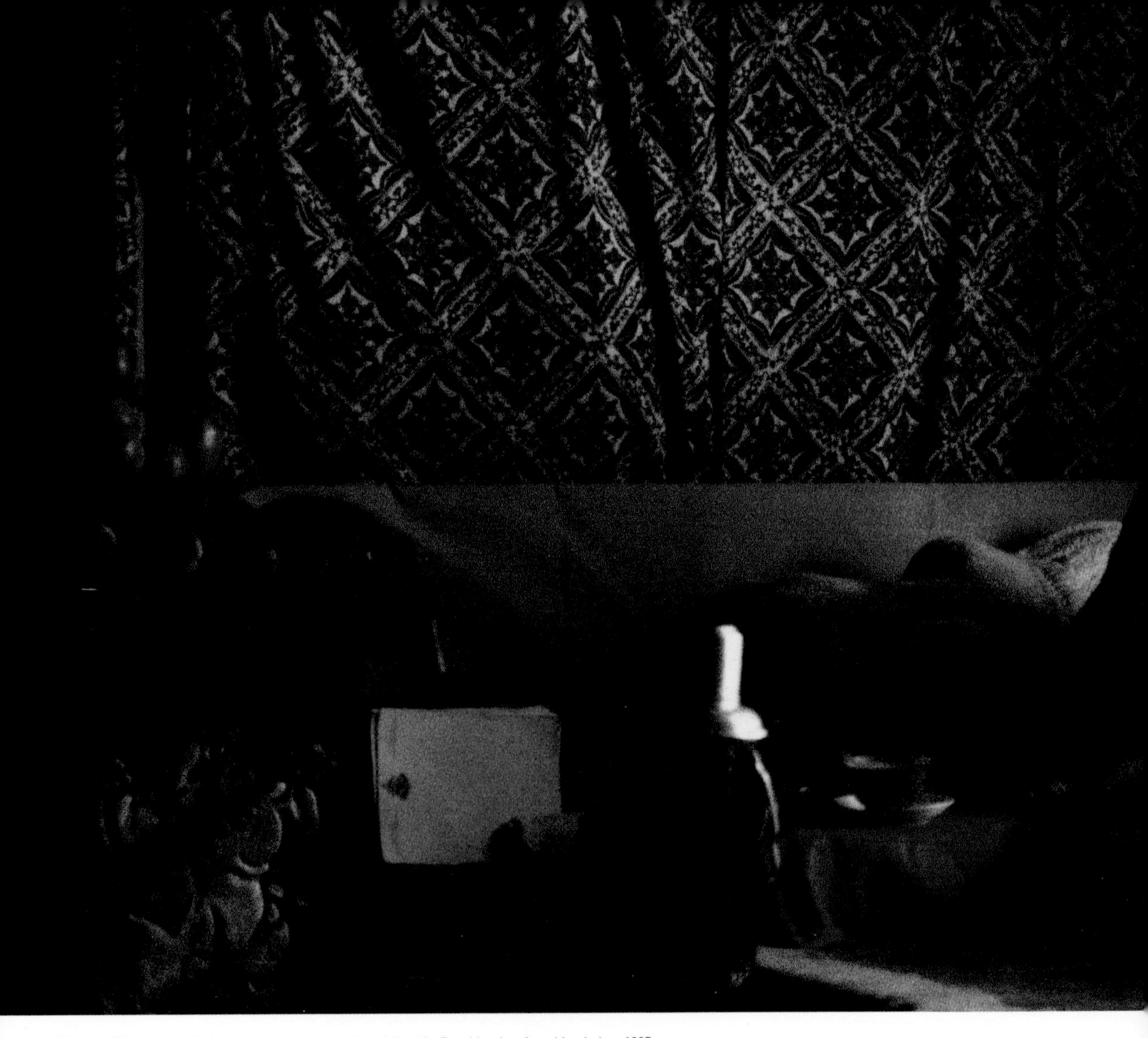

Khyentse Rinpoche during his morning prayers, contemplating the Punakha river from his window. 1985.

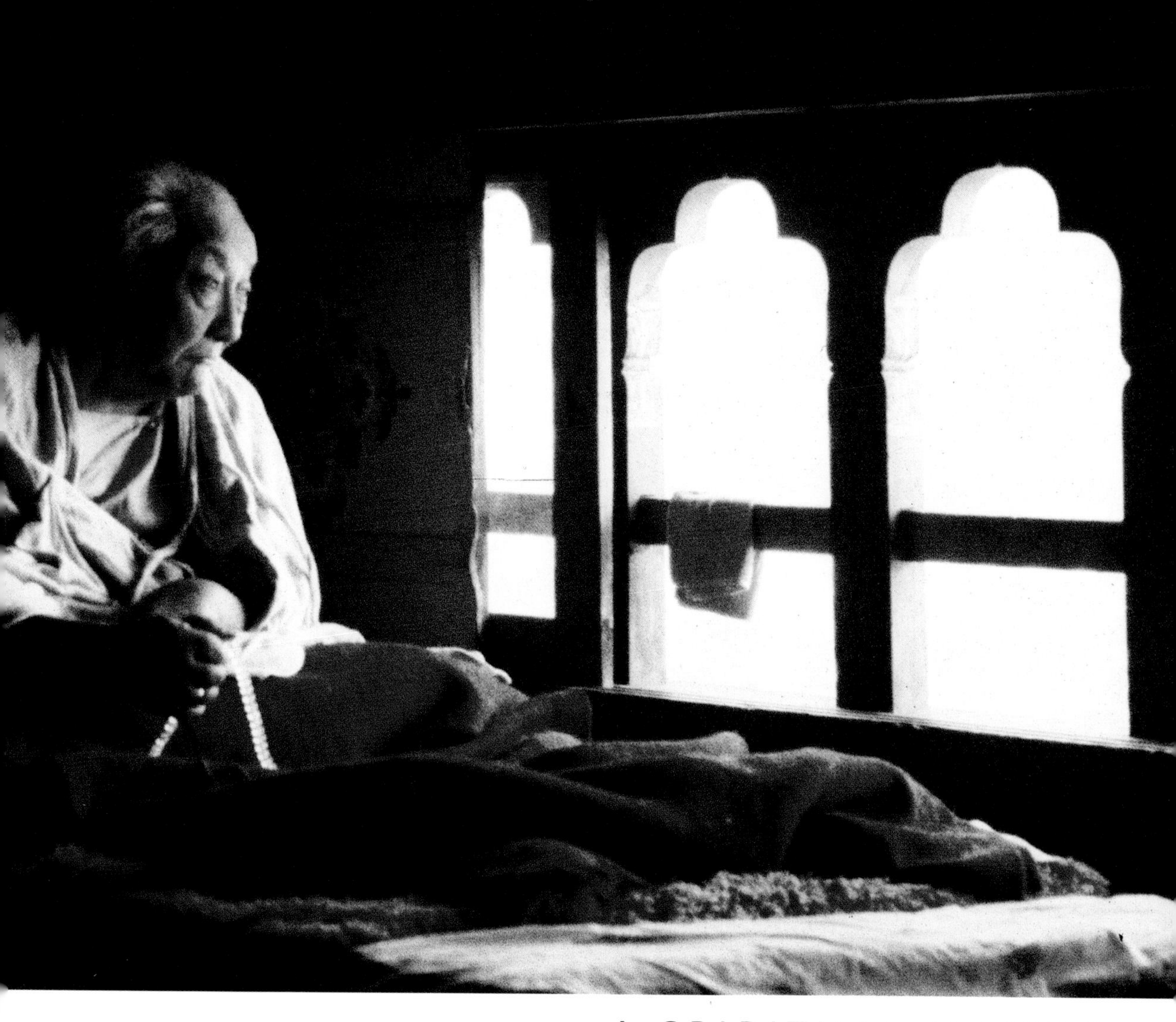

A SPIRITUAL MASTER

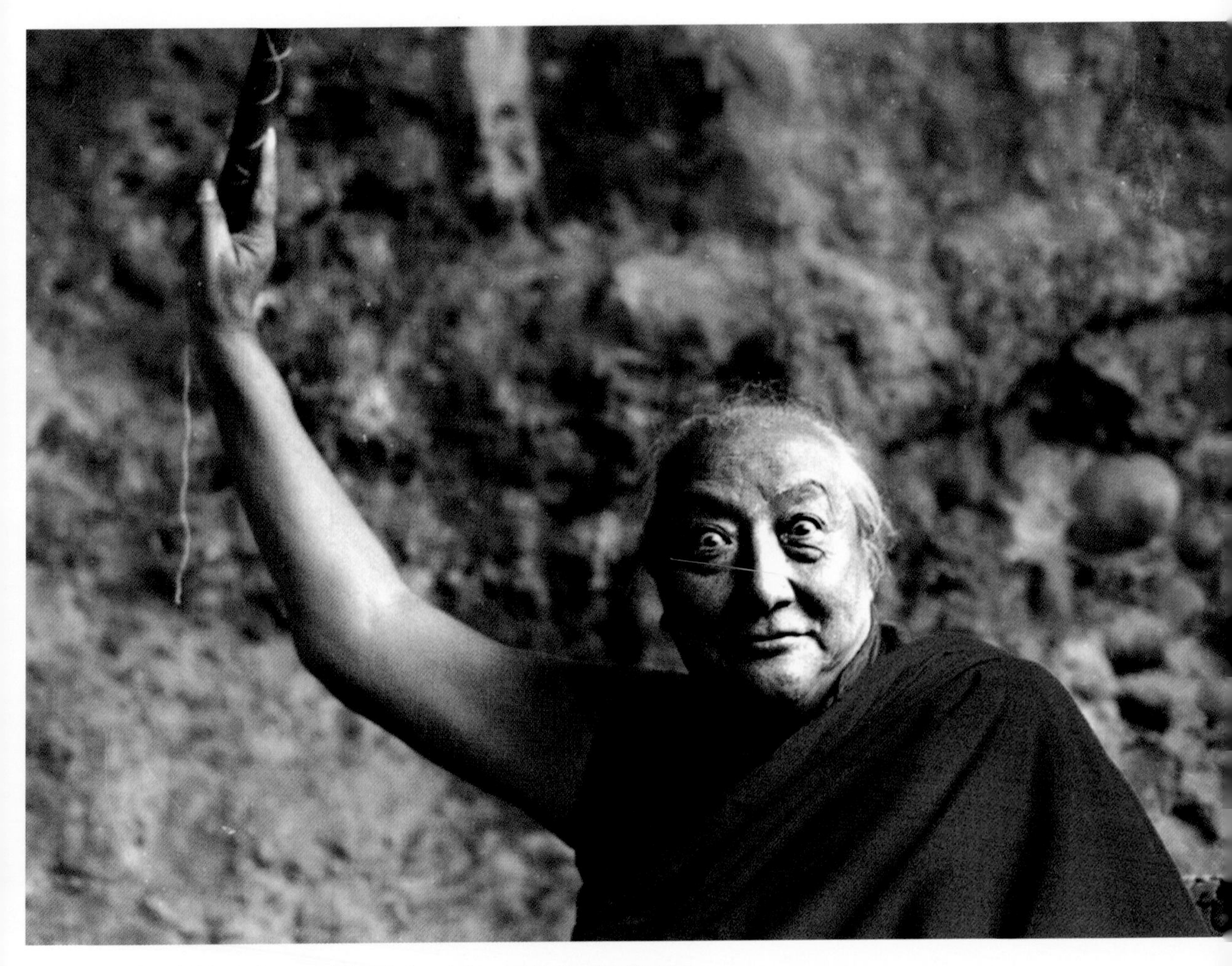

Khyentse Rinpoche joking for the camera during a pilgrimage to the cave, not far from Punakha, where the 15th-century Indian Buddhist master Vanaratna (Nag-Kyi Rinchen in Tibetan) once meditated. 1982.

A Spiritual Master

In the Land of the Thunder Dragon

Dilgo Khyentse Rinpoche was born in 1910, the fourth son of a distinguished family living in eastern Tibet. He felt a strong attraction for the spiritual life from an early age and at thirteen he went to live in a mountain hermitage, a few hours' journey from his native village. He spent the next thirty years in solitary retreat, meditating on wisdom, compassion and loving kindness, and only breaking off at intervals to receive teachings from fifty or so spiritual masters.

The Chinese Communist government had been gradually increasing its stranglehold on Tibet and at the end of the 1950s it imposed a forceful military clampdown on the region. Khyentse Rinpoche, who was then on a pilgrimage near Lhasa, decided to leave Tibet in the company of his family and a group of friends and followers. The journey was to prove an eventful one. A great many other Tibetans were fleeing and the Chinese were shooting on sight, so the party travelled in secret, hiding out by day and walking by night. When they finally arrived at the Mönla Kachu pass, on the frontier with Bhutan, they had almost run out of food, but with the flood of refugees crossing the border, they still had to wait ten days before the Bhutanese government could allow them into the country. They received a warm welcome there and stayed for a while in the beautiful province of Bumthang, before continuing their journey in the face of persistent rain and leech-ridden forests, and finally reaching the capital, Thimphu.

At the request of the royal family, Khyentse Rinpoche took up a teaching post at a school in Simtokha, near Thimphu. He soon attracted a great many followers and as the years passed he came to be revered by people from all walks of life, from the king down to the most humble farmer. The Queen Mother, Ashe Kesang Choeden Wangchuck, was a particularly devoted follower. Khyentse Rinpoche developed a deep affinity with Bhutan and an appreciation of this country where Buddhist culture has been free to flourish and whose people have a spirit that is profoundly imbued with Buddhist values.

No matter where he was, Khyentse Rinpoche would rise well before dawn and spend several hours praying and meditating before beginning an uninterrupted round of activities that continued late into the night and seemed to be effortless. An ordinary day for Khyentse Rinpoche began at four thirty in the morning, when he had tea and opened his book of prayers (over three hundred pages long). At around eight o'clock, devotees from all walks of life who had been queuing at his door would go in to ask him for his prayers for their well-being, and he would put his huge hand on their heads in blessing. He blessed sacred statues or paintings destined for the family temple, met pilgrims who in many cases had travelled a long way to see him, and exchanged news with messengers sent by other lamas. They would offer him rice flakes, roasted barley flour, cottage cheese and fresh butter heaped in round, finely woven baskets of multicoloured straw. When an important ceremony took place, he went to the temple and sat cross-legged in his seat the entire day, even during pauses in the ceremony, at which point he would carry on with his prayers or greet visitors or go back to the texts he was writing at the time.

When Khyentse Rinpoche travelled in Bhutan, it seemed that the whole country knew about it. Every ten miles or so, near a farm or a village, a group of people, sometimes with a few monks, would be waiting by the roadside. A big fire piled with moist juniper branches would send billows of fragrant smoke to the sky as offerings. Sometimes Khyentse Rinpoche would give his blessings from the car, sometimes he would get out and sit for a while to give a longevity blessing to the assembled crowd. Hand-woven woollen carpets would be spread out in front of a wooden table, beautifully carved with dragons, birds and lotus flowers, bearing delicacies and pots of hot tea. The party would stop and be offered refreshments.

When he was going to a larger monastery or village, a long line of monks and local dignitaries would be waiting for him. A slow procession led by monks playing music and holding aloft their brocade banners, sometimes dancing, accompanied him to his quarters. There, the mayor, chief justice and other notables, in ceremonial dress with a sword in its silver scabbard at their waists, would prostrate themselves before him and offer him tea and food. The next day, thousands of people would gather from all around in the courtyard of the monastery, and Khyentse Rinpoche would give them his blessings as they filed past him for hours. When he was older and the crowd was too large he would be carried on a litter between the seated rows of devotees in an open field, scattering consecrated rice among them.

Khyentse Rinpoche was a vastly erudite scholar. His own writings, twenty-five volumes in all, completing and elucidating the works of previous masters, constitute a veritable encyclopaedia of commentaries on the contemplative life. Khyentse Rinpoche also inspired the reprinting of more than three hundred volumes of ancient texts that were in danger of disappearing.

But Khyentse Rinpoche's chief activity was clearly teaching. He taught in every free moment of the day, tirelessly responding to all requests for instruction and spiritual guidance. He would often teach all day for months on end to gatherings ranging from a few dozen to several thousand people. Even after a full day of teaching, he would grant some individual request and teach one person or a small group in his room until late at night. During all-day rituals, while everyone else took their lunch break, he would eat quickly and use every remaining minute before the ceremony resumed to give someone an explanation of a few pages of a meditation text or philosophical commentary. He never turned down any such request. Somehow the subject would always be uniformly covered from beginning to end, in just the allocated time, pitched precisely at the audience's level of understanding. Spoken by him, even a few simple words could open the door to a whole succession of new insights into spiritual life. His immense knowledge, the warmth of his blessings and the depth of his inner realization gave his teachings a quality quite different from those of any other teacher. He was the ideal spiritual guide and became one of the 14th Dalai Lama's principal teachers.

In 1985, after thirty years of exile, the Chinese government finally allowed Khyentse Rinpoche to return to Tibet after the King of Bhutan interceded on his behalf. Accompanying him on this journey was one of the most moving and the most memorable experiences of my life. Wherever he went, he was greeted by crowds of joyful devotees, who had long given up hope of ever seeing their spiritual master again, and few of those who came to greet him and receive his blessing were able to hold back their tears. Khyentse Rinpoche greeted all of them, acknowledging here and there a familiar face, and giving personal advice and teachings.

When he visited central Tibet, Khyentse Rinpoche submitted a petition to the Chinese government asking permission for Samye Monastery to be restored, stressing its importance for the world's cultural heritage. Samye was Tibet's first Buddhist monastery, founded in the 8th century, by Guru Padmasambhava and the Abbot Shantarakshita under the patronage of King Trisong Detsen. Surprisingly enough, the Chinese government agreed. Inspired by Khyentse Rinpoche, the King of Bhutan contributed a large donation to the undertaking.

As Khyentse Rinpoche grew older, his characteristic stamina did not seem to change much. In 1990, he returned for a last time to Tibet, and re-consecrated the newly restored monastery of Samye. However, in early 1991 he began to show the first signs of ill health while teaching in Bodhgaya. He completed his programme there and travelled to Dharamsala where, without apparent difficulty, he spent a month giving important empowerments and transmissions to the Dalai Lama, which the latter had been requesting for many years.

On his return to Bhutan, he decided to go into a retreat near the Tiger's Lair, and later visited several of his disciples who were in retreat and spoke to them of the ultimate teacher, beyond birth and death or any physical manifestation. His condition worsened and on 27 September 1991, at dusk, he asked those who were attending him to help him sit upright; he died in Thimphu, shortly after midnight.

So ended the extraordinary life of Khyentse Rinpoche. He often gave the following advice: 'Never forget that your life passes as swiftly as a flash of lightning or a wave of your hand. While you have the opportunity to practise, don't waste a moment: devote all your energy to the spiritual path.'

At the request of his followers around the world, Khyentse Rinpoche's body was preserved for a year using traditional embalming techniques. Finally, in November 1992, his remains were cremated near Paro, in Bhutan, during a three-day ceremony attended by more than a hundred major lamas, the royal family and ministers of Bhutan, five hundred Western disciples and a huge crowd of over fifty thousand devotees, a gathering unprecedented in the history of Bhutan, which had a population of only 600,000 at the time.

Some of Khyentse Rinpoche's main students became his spiritual heirs and continue his lineage today. One of them, his grandson Rabjam Rinpoche, is abbot of the Shechen Monastery in Nepal and spends much of the year in Bhutan.

After Khyentse Rinpoche's death, his close followers turned to Trulshik Rinpoche, his most accomplished disciple, for help in locating his reincarnation. Trulshik Rinpoche had had dreams and visions clearly indicating the identity of this reincarnation. He kept these details secret until April 1995, when he wrote a letter to Rabjam Rinpoche informing him of the names of the child's parents, his date of birth and the place where he lived. 'Yangsi' (whose name in Tibetan signifies 'he who has returned to existence') was born in June 1993, the son of Chöling Rinpoche and Mayum Dechen Paldrön. The Dalai Lama confirmed: 'I have no doubt that this young child is the true incarnation of Dilgo Khyentse Rinpoche.'

In December 1997, the young Khyentse Yangsi Rinpoche was enthroned at Shechen monastery, an event that attracted almost fifteen thousand people from forty different nationalities and more than a hundred teachers representing all the schools of Tibetan Buddhism. Since then, the young incarnate lama divides his time between his residence at Thegchok Chökyi Gatsel, in the Paro valley, in Bhutan, where he devotes himself to philosophical studies, and Shechen Monastery, in Nepal.

Khyentse Rinpoche performing a ceremony in the courtyard of Punakha monastery. 1984.

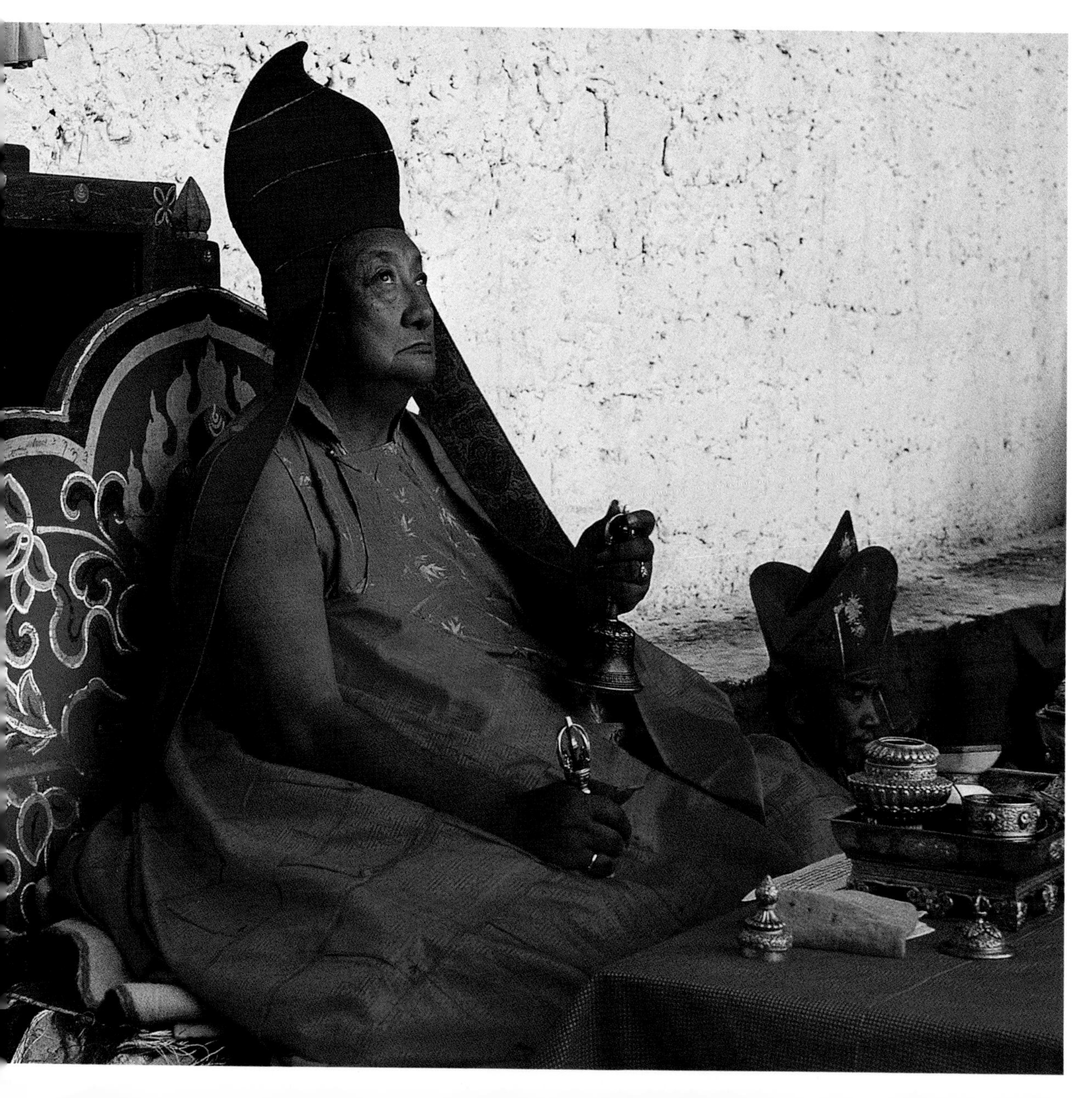

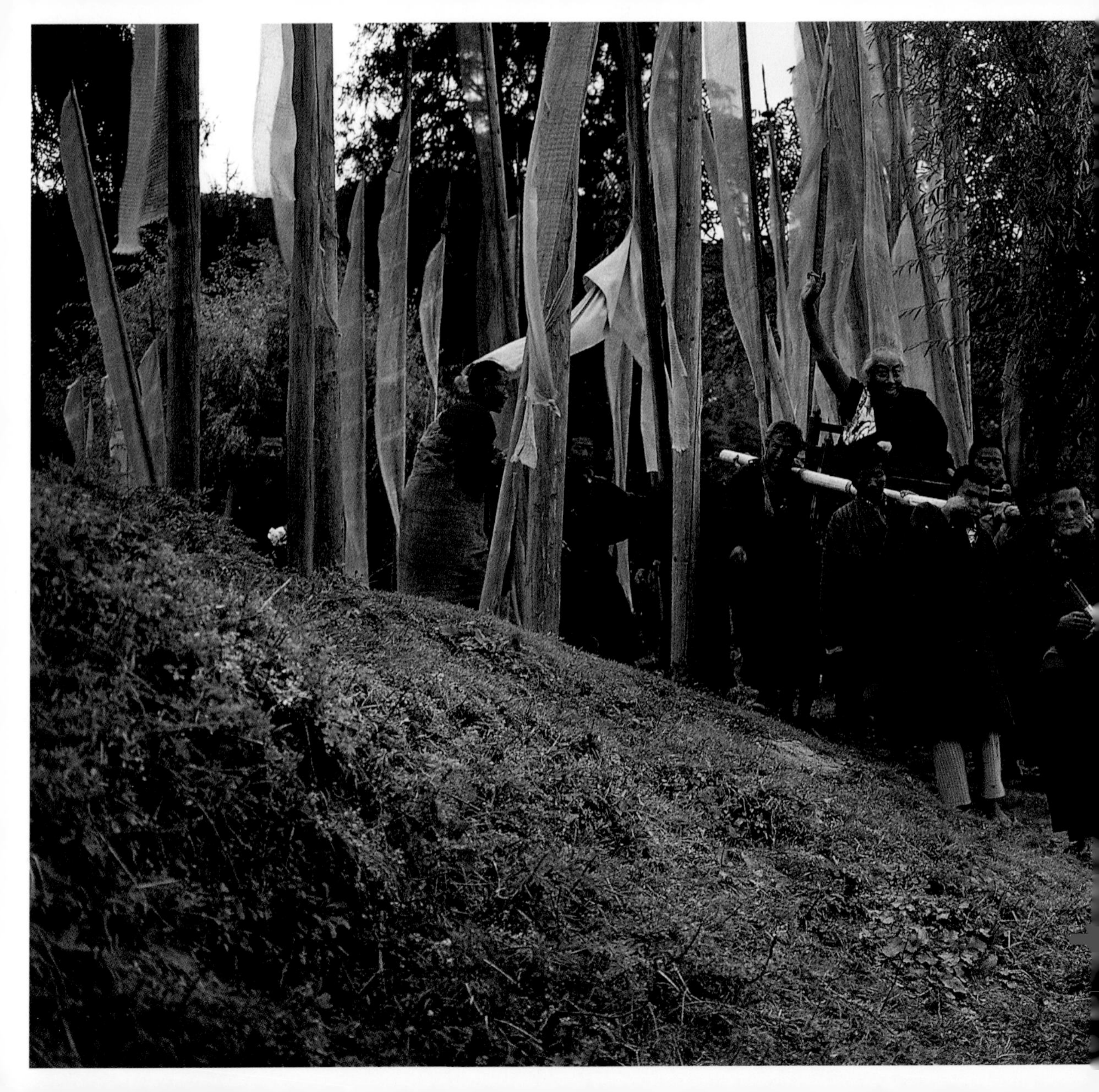

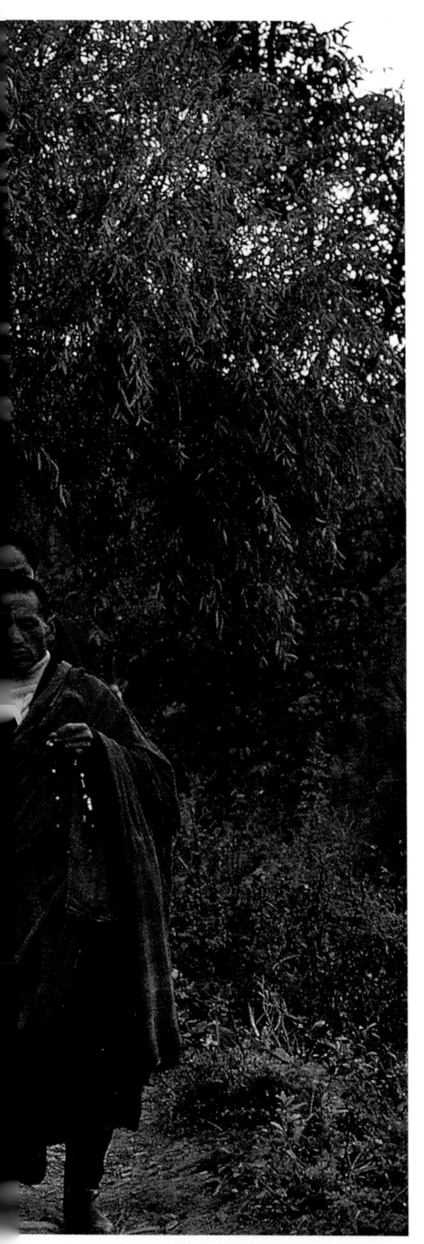

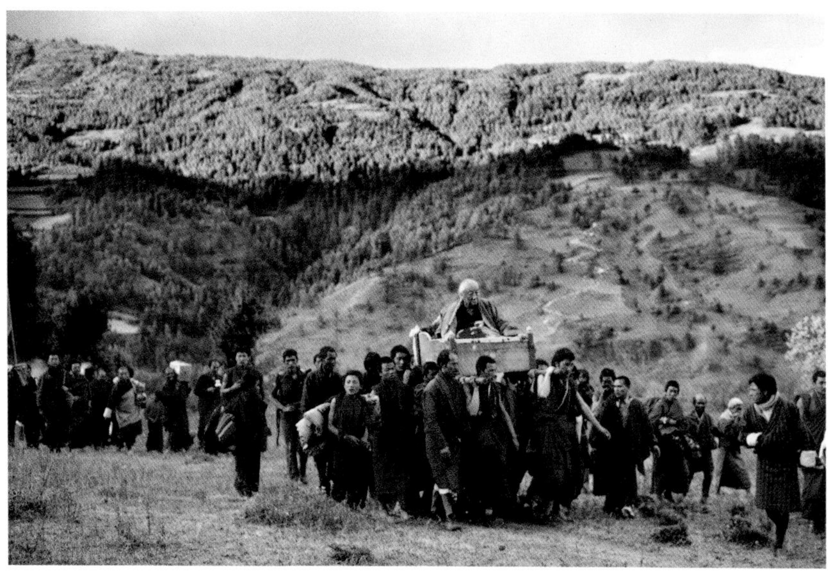

Left and above:
Where there were no roads for cars, the elderly Khyentse Rinpoche often travelled in a litter. Here, he is seen making his way to the monastery of Nyima Lung in Bumthang province. 1983.

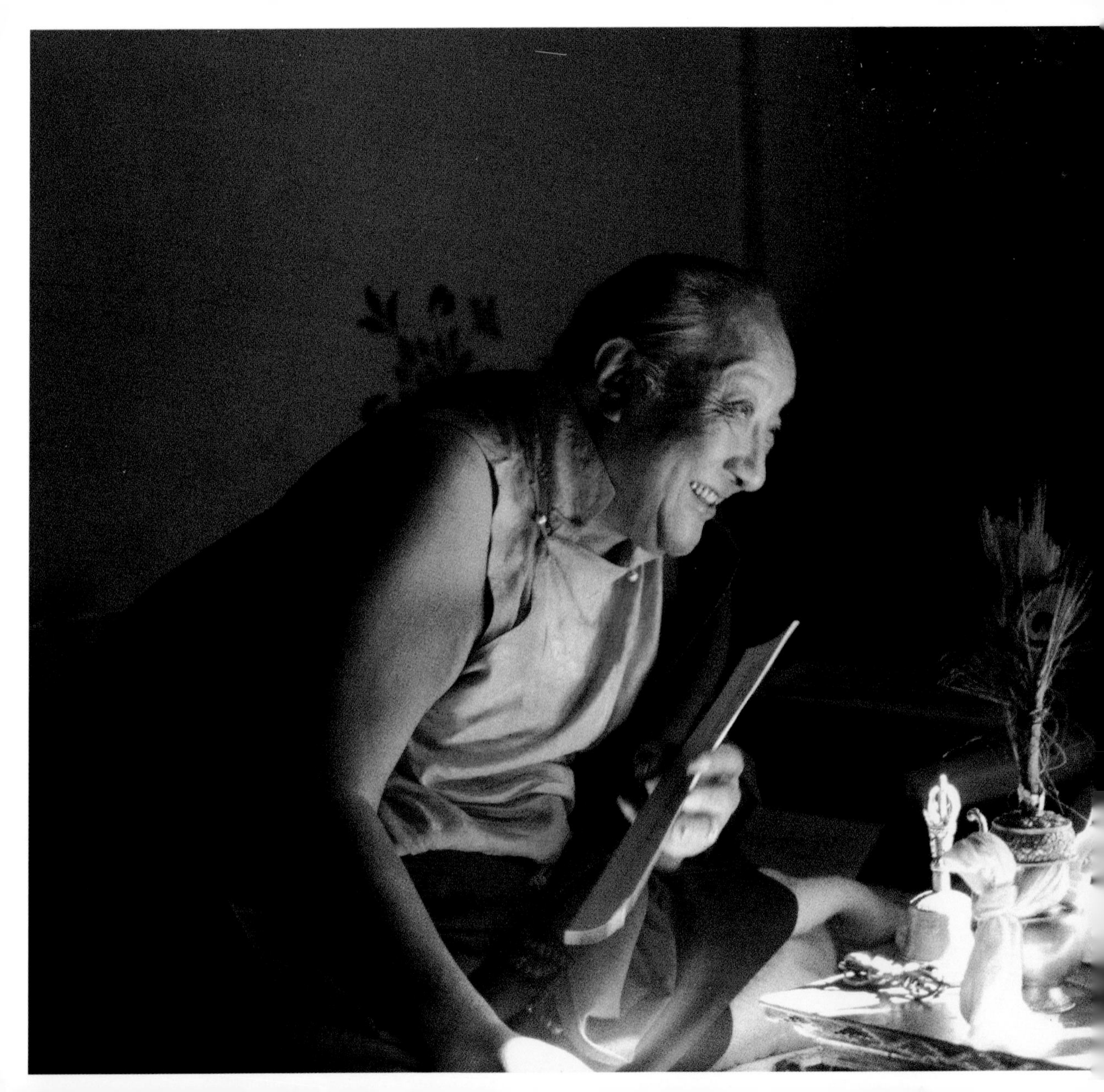

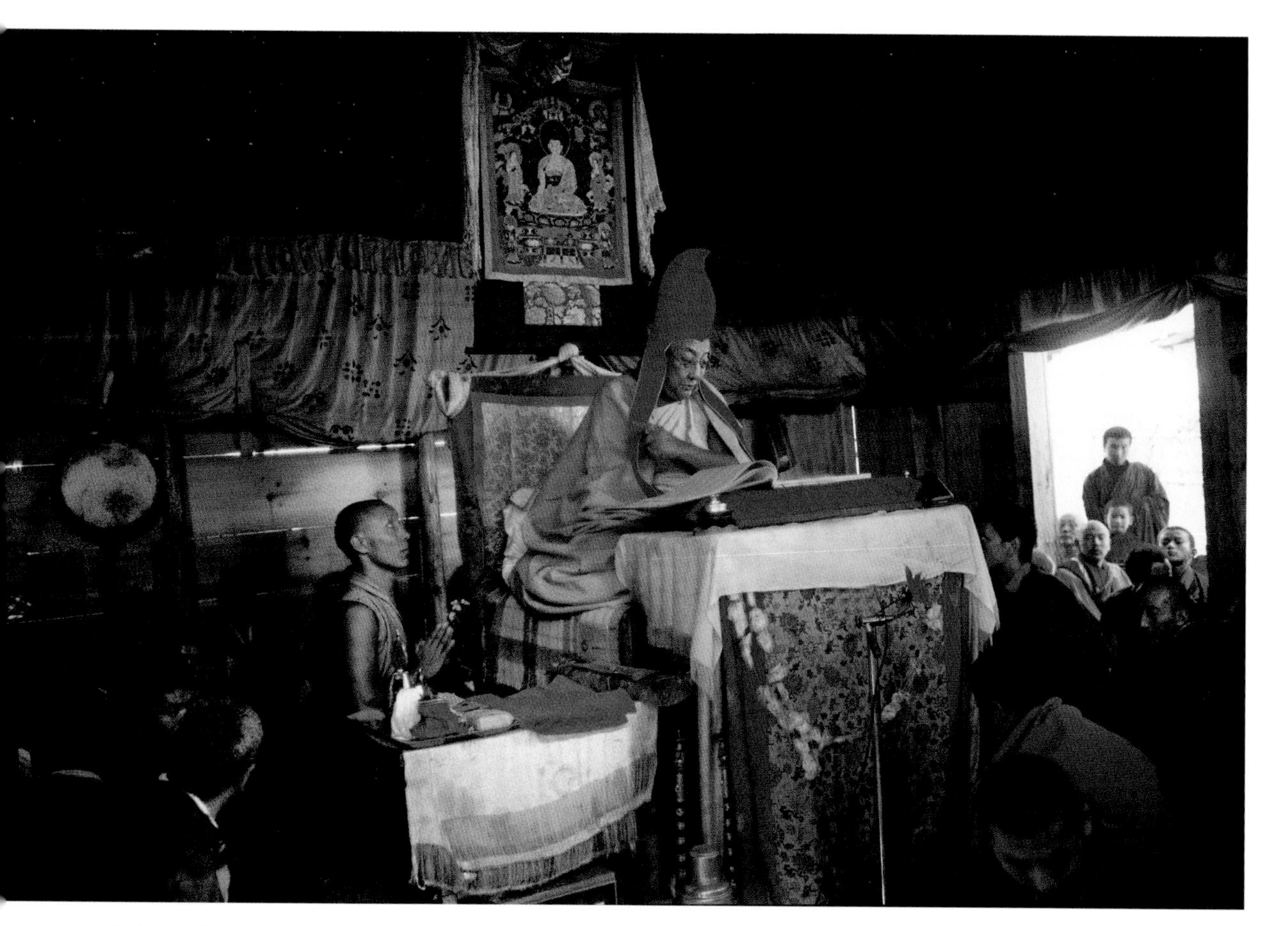

In 1981, Khyentse Rinpoche gave a 'reading transmission' of the hundred and three volumes of the Buddhist canon, the *Kangyur*, or 'Words of the Buddha', at Kuje, in the central Bhutanese province of Bumthang. He was assisted in this task by Sengtrak Rinpoche, seen here sitting on his right, who gave the transmission for part of the volumes.

Khyentse Rinpoche, in his home at Dechen Chöling, Thimphu, 1984.

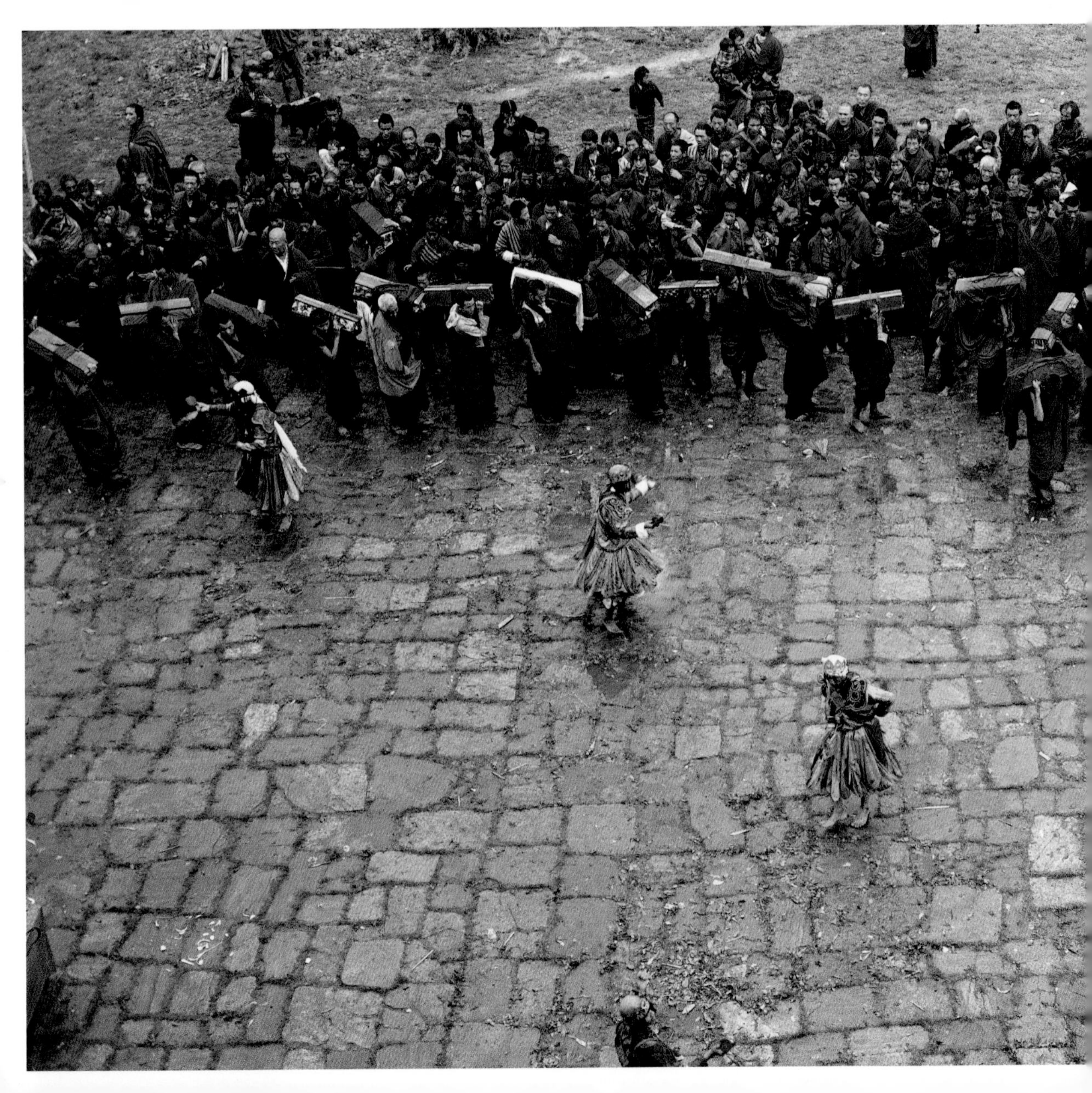

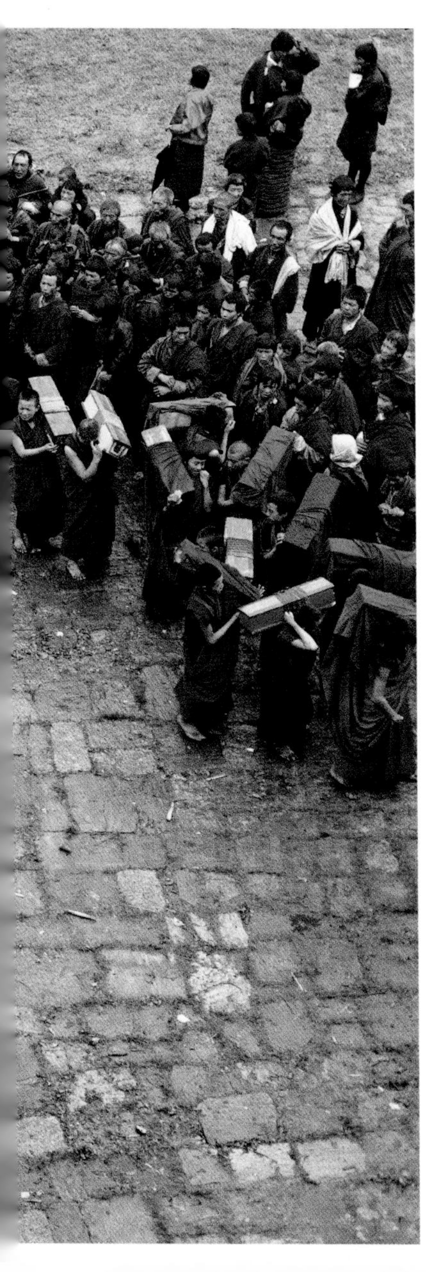

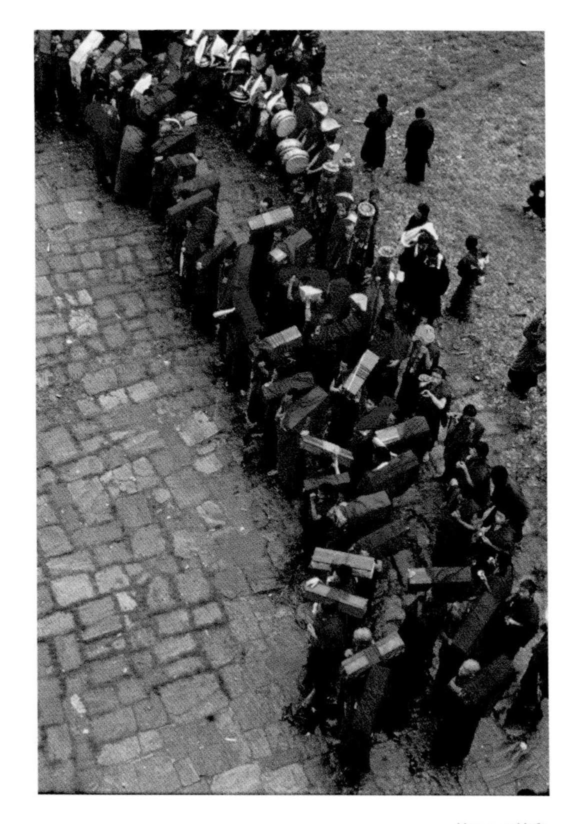

Above and left:
A procession of monks carries the hundred and three volumes of the Buddhist canon, the *Kangyur*, towards a tent erected in the field in front of Kuje monastery. Khyentse Rinpoche read the texts aloud to thousands of followers all day long for three months. Kuje Lhakhang, Bumthang province, 1981.

Overleaf
Left: Monks and riders from Gangtey monastery getting ready to receive Khyentse Rinpoche, 1980.
Right: Under a ceremonial parasol of yellow silk, Khyentse Rinpoche climbs the steps to Kuje's main temple. 1983.

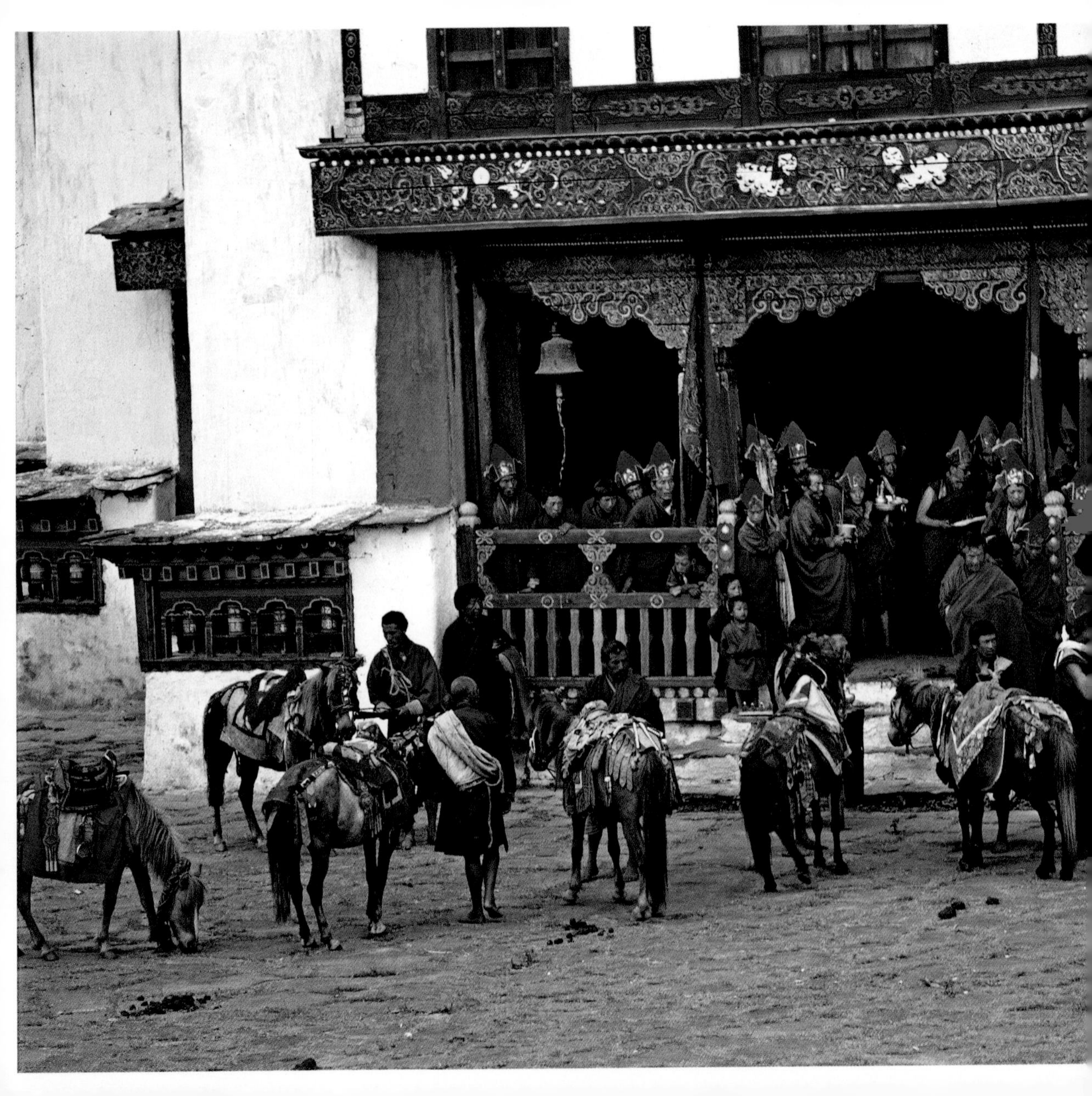

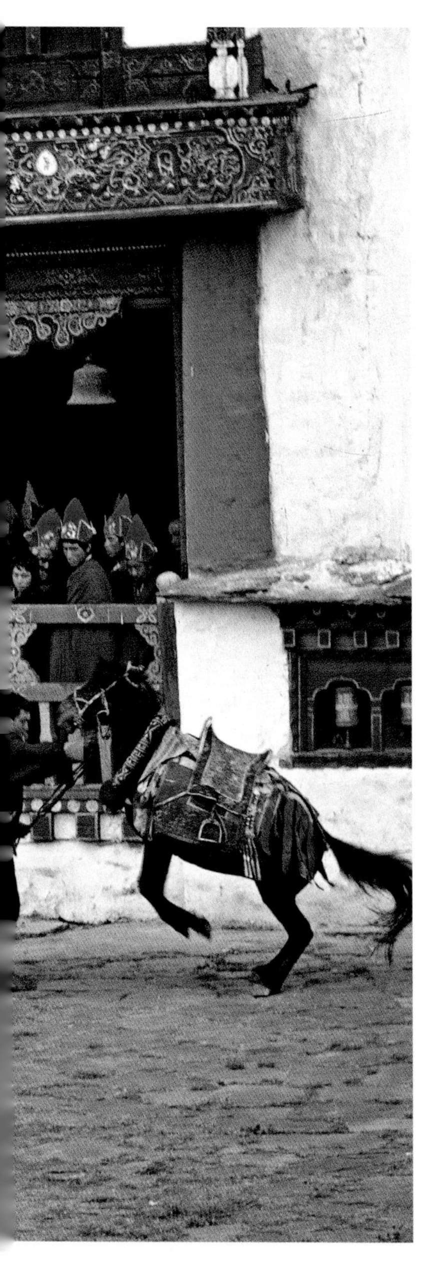
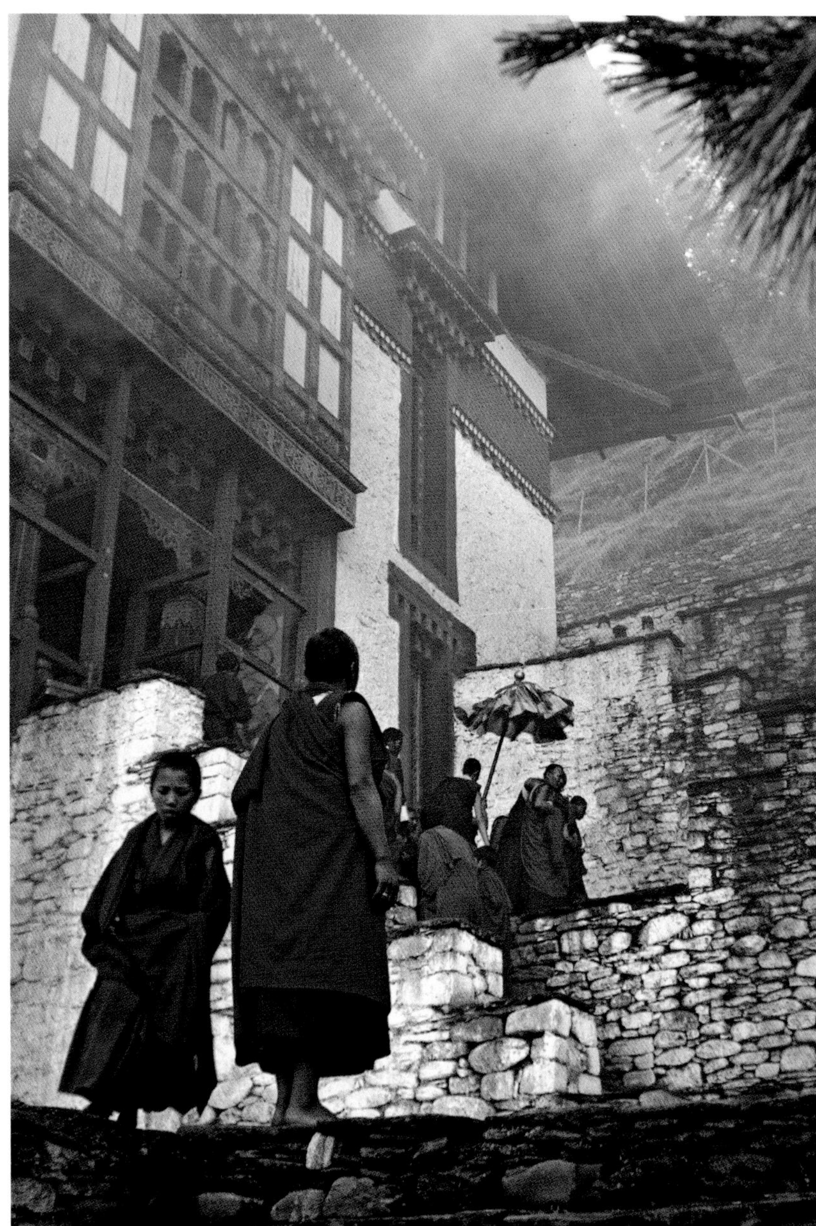

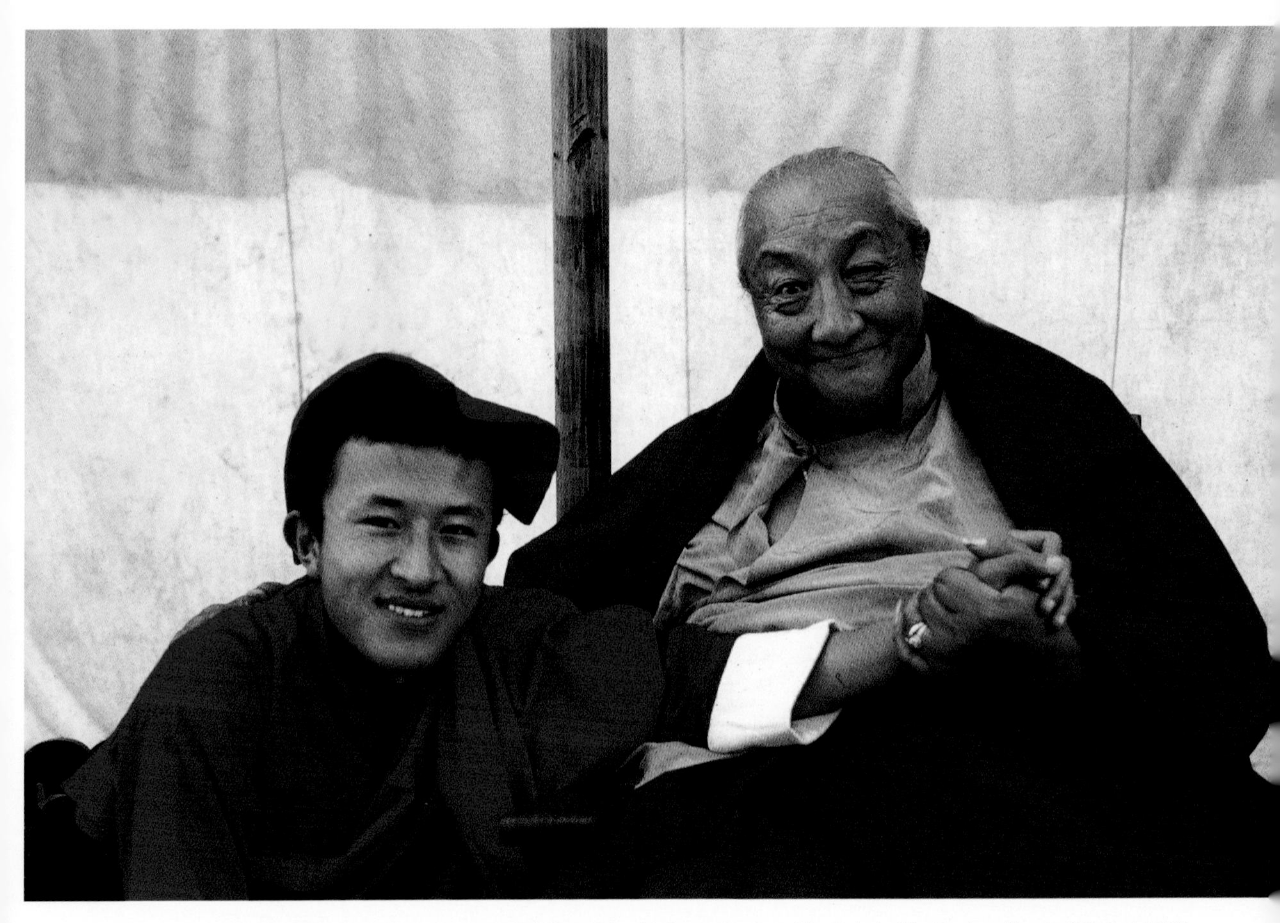

Dilgo Khyentse Rinpoche with Dzongsar Khyentse Rinpoche, who was both his student and the incarnation of one of his principal spiritual teachers, Khyentse Chökyi Lodrö. 1983.

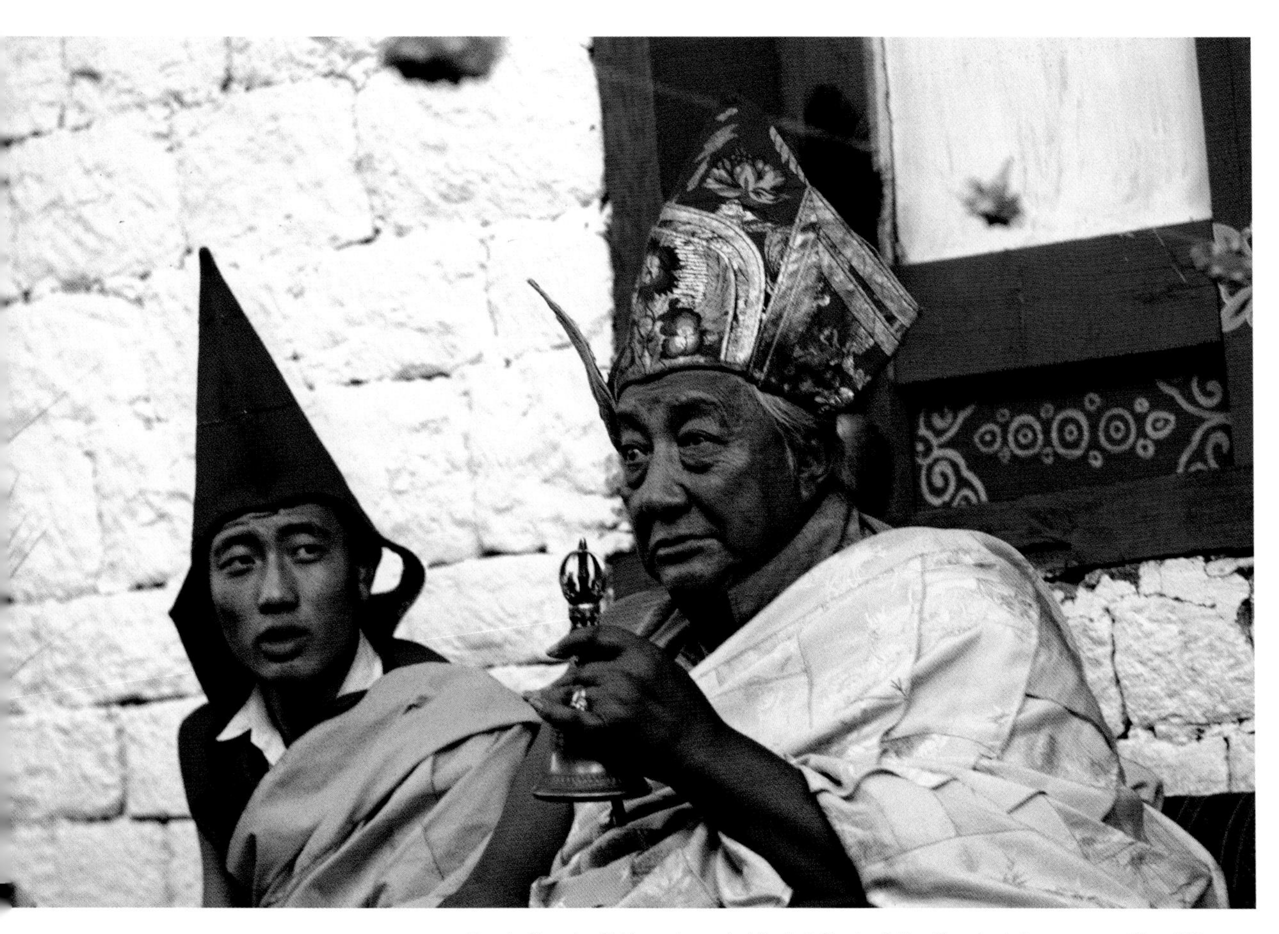

Khyentse Rinpoche with his grandson and spiritual heir, Shechen Rabjam Rinpoche, during a ceremony at Paro, 1983.

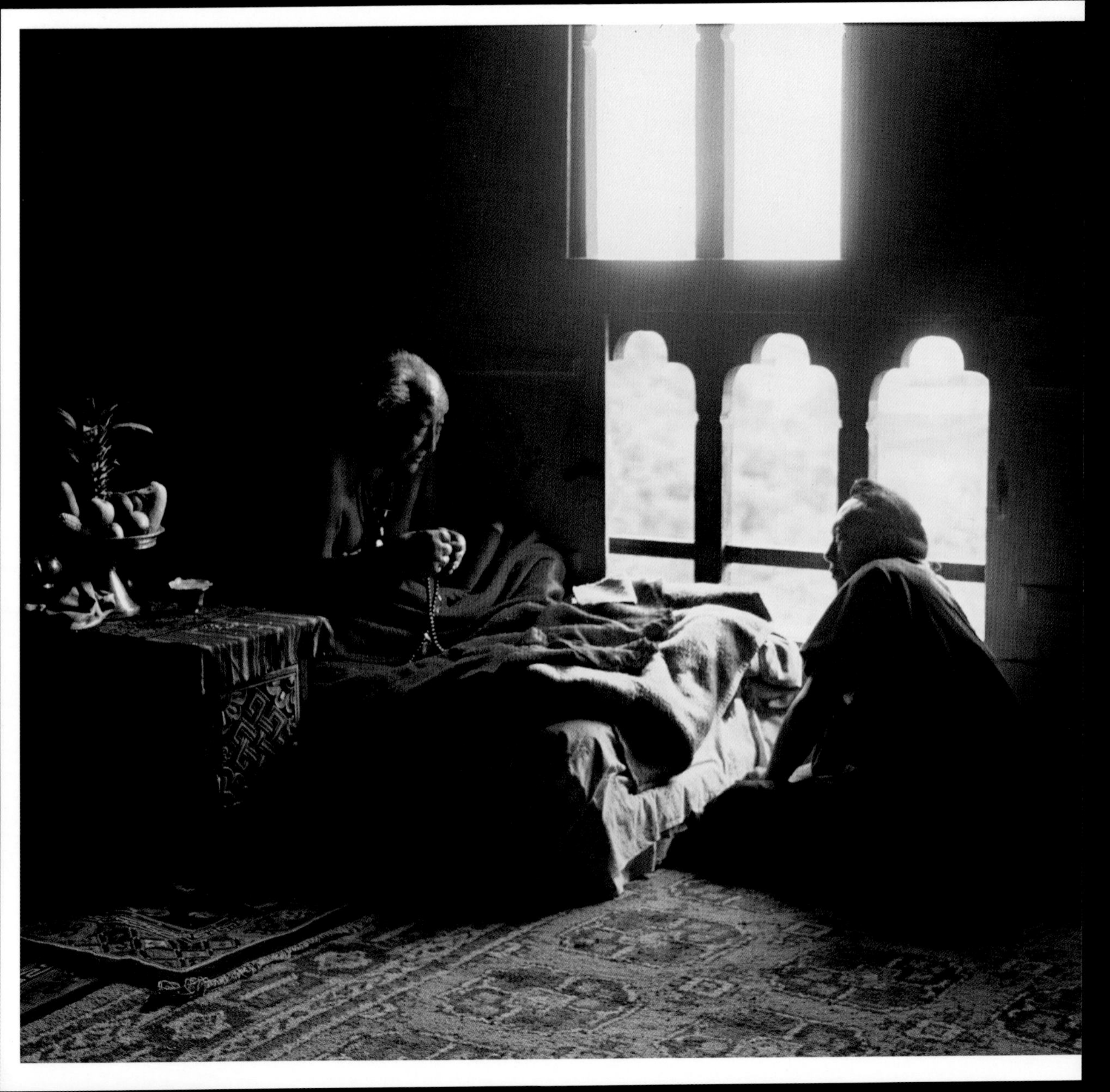

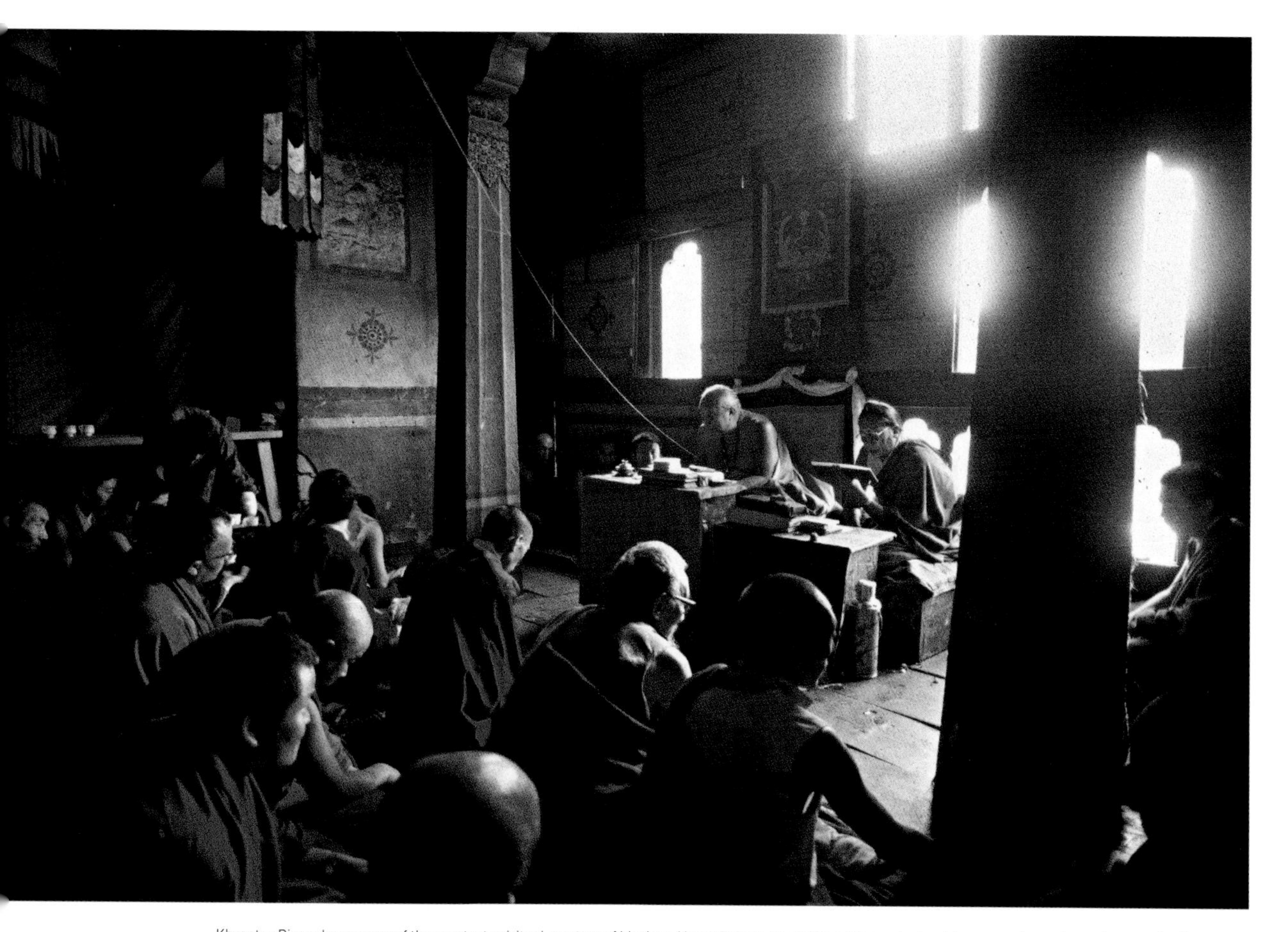

Khyentse Rinpoche was one of the greatest spiritual masters of his time. Nevertheless, he continued to receive teachings even at an advanced age so that he could pass them on to others and ensure their survival. Here we see him in one of the chapels at Kuje Lhakhang, in Bumthang province, with Pewar Rinpoche, a lama recently arrived from Tibet, who is teaching from the writings of an eminent 19th-century spiritual teacher, Jamyang Khyentse Wangpo. 1987.

Khyentse Rinpoche talking to Pewar Rinpoche, a lama from eastern Tibet. Kuje Lhakhang, Bumthang province, 1987.

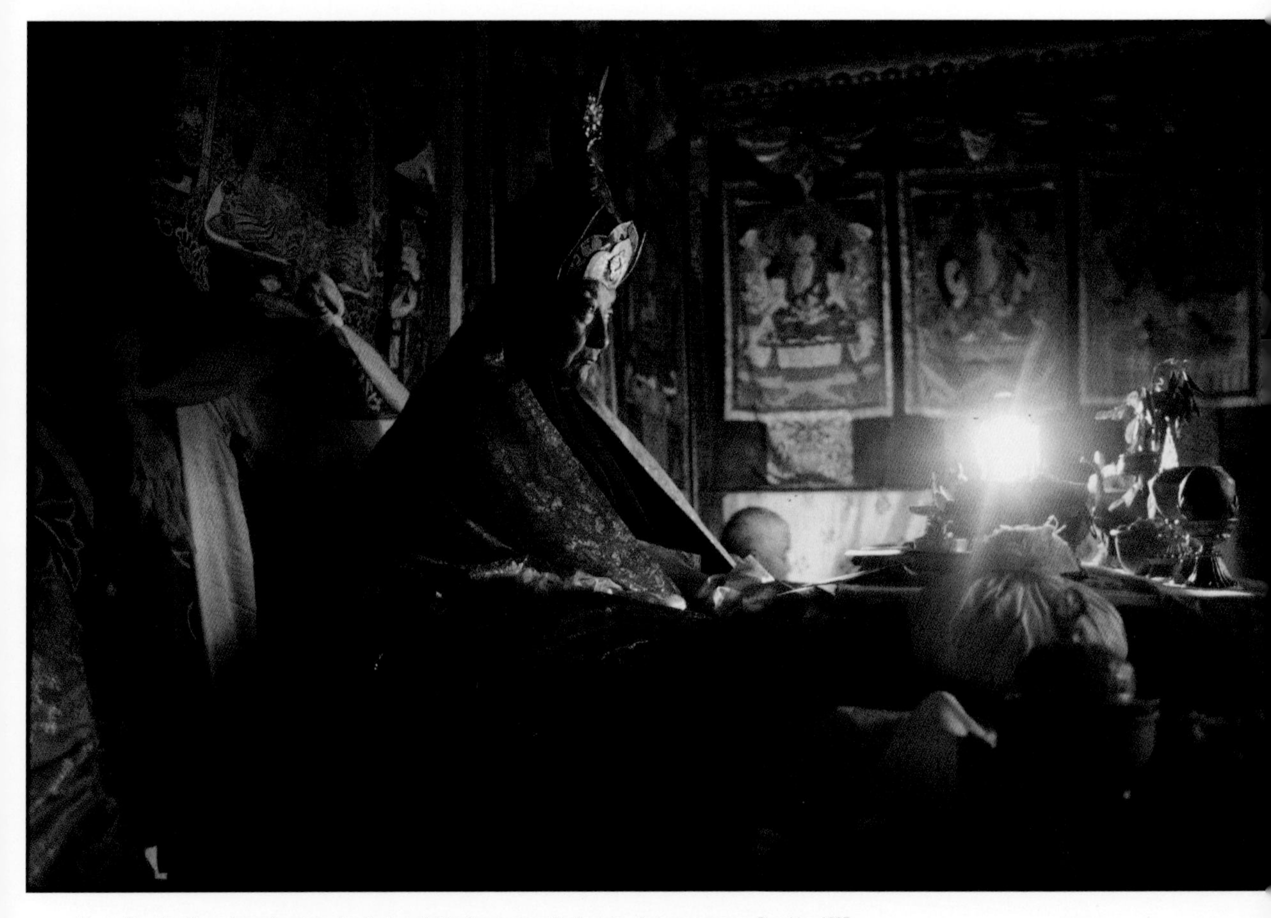

Above: Khyentse Rinpoche performing a ritual by lamplight before dawn on the final day of a long ceremony. Punakha, 1985.

Opposite:
Khyentse Rinpoche wearing the headdress of the great Tibetan master Namkhai Nyinpo. Bumthang, 1981.

Overleaf, left:
Khyentse Rinpoche spent thirty years meditating in a hermitage, produced twenty-five volumes of erudite texts and worked tirelessly to transmit his knowledge to others. He was one of the 14th Dalai Lama's spiritual teachers and a major figure in the struggle to keep Tibet's spiritual heritage alive in the 20th century. 1981.

Overleaf, right:
A group of monks getting ready to form a procession at the temple of Paro Kyichu, during the ceremonies surrounding Khyentse Rinpoche's cremation. 1992.

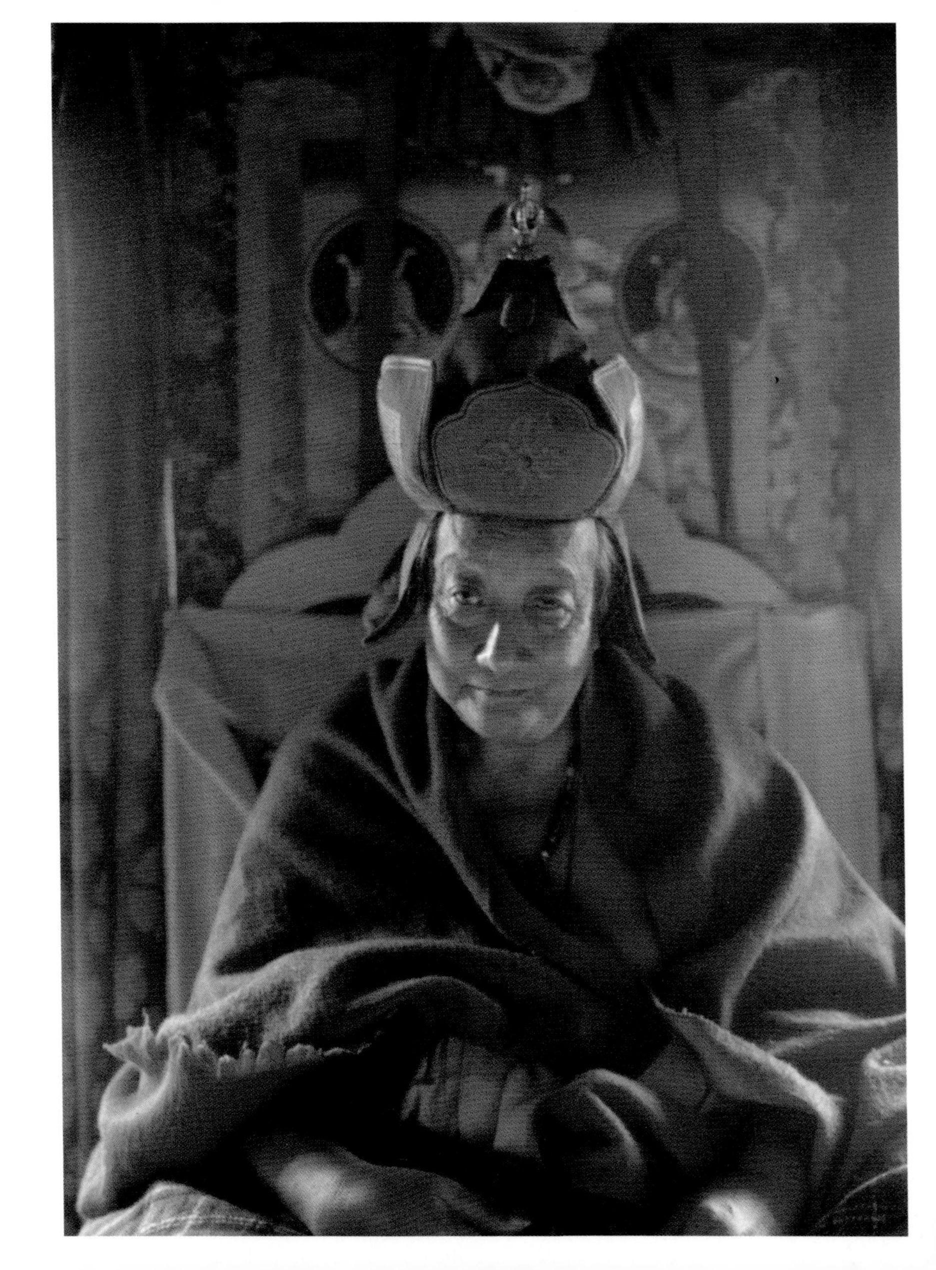

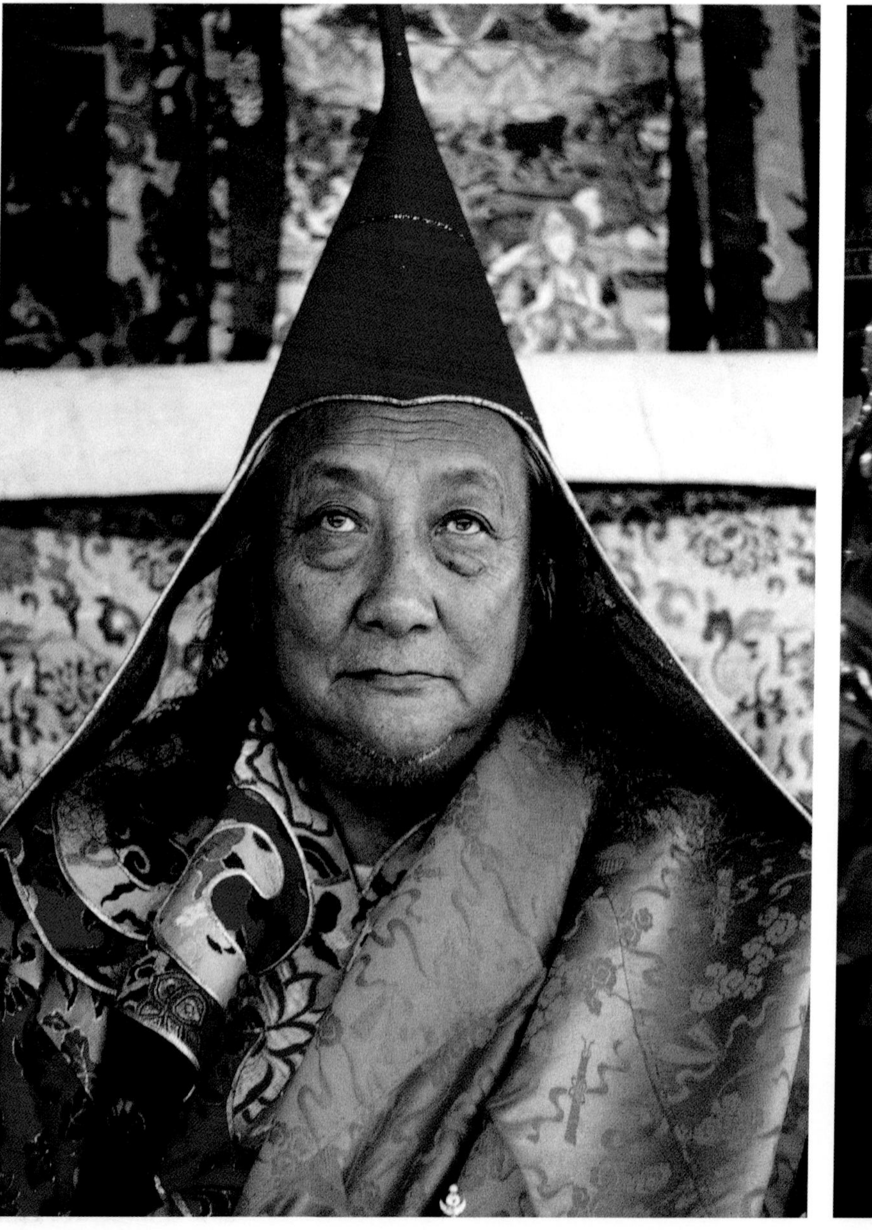
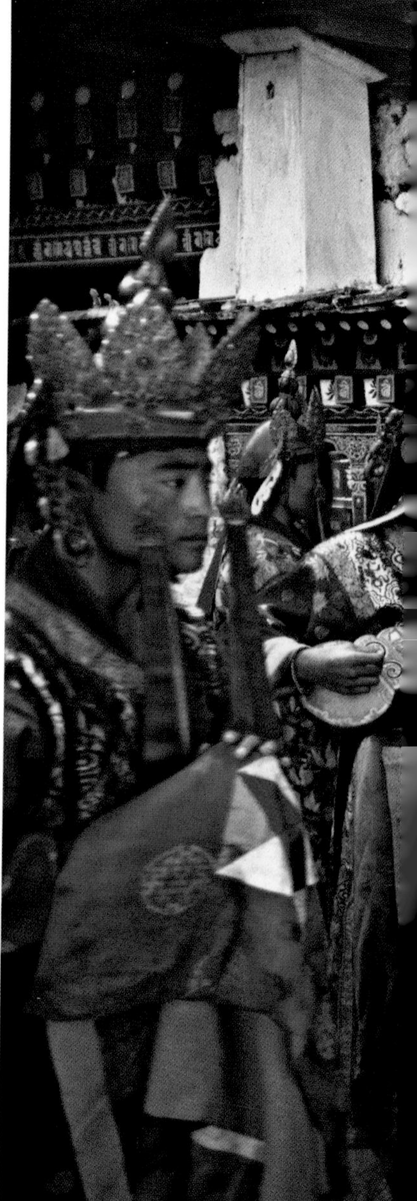

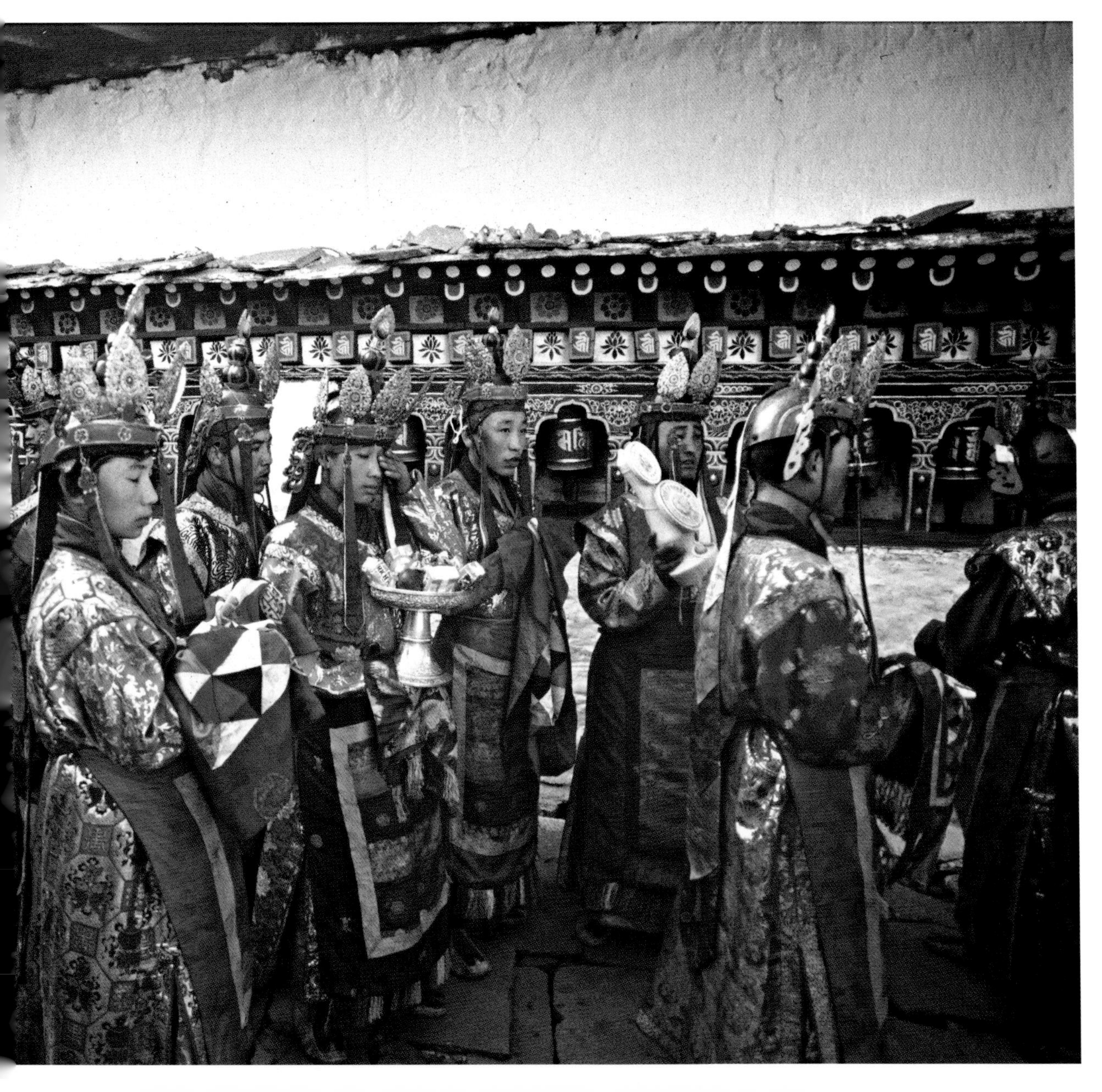

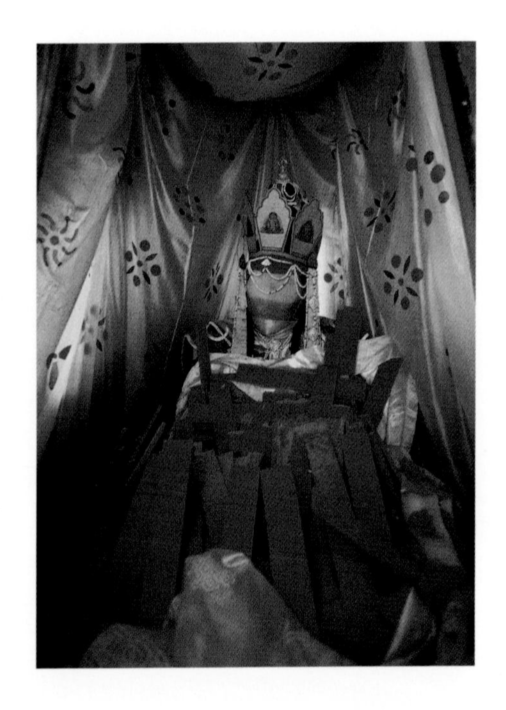

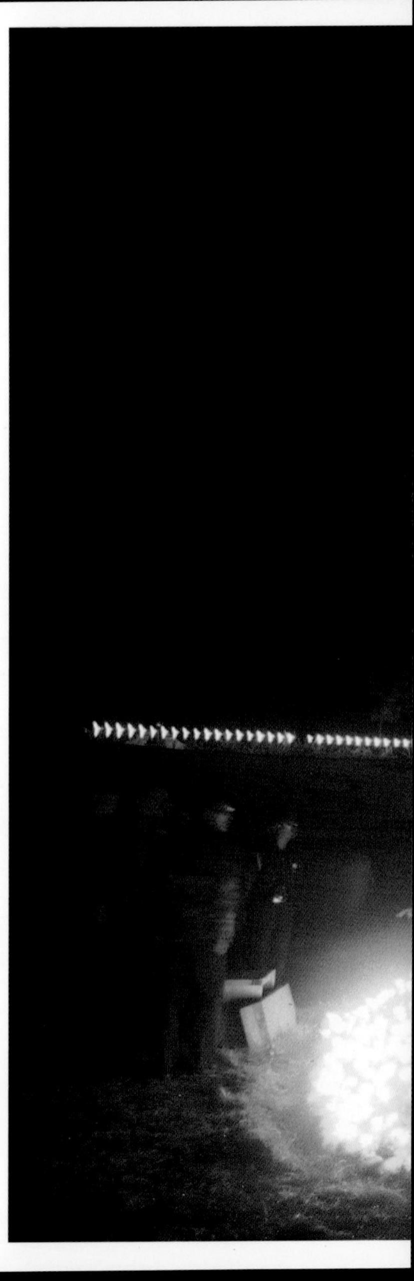

Above: Khyentse Rinpoche died in Bhutan in 1991, but his body was embalmed to give his followers from around the world an opportunity to come and pay their last respects. The cremation took place a year later in the Paro valley, opposite Taksang (the Tiger's Lair). Sixty thousand people, a tenth of Bhutan's population, attended – making this a unique event in the country's history. Here, we see Khyentse Rinpoche's body shortly before cremation, surrounded by sandalwood. His face is covered in yellow silk and he is wearing a diadem, a symbol of Enlightenment. 1992.

Right:
In the evening, countless candles were lit in front of the stupa where the cremation ceremony had taken place. Satsam Chörten, Paro, 1992.

Overleaf:
Khyentse Rinpoche reciting his morning prayers at dawn and contemplating the landscape from his window in the palace of Dechen Chöling, at Thimphu, where he performed ceremonies every year to promote national peace. This is the room in which the fourth King of Bhutan, Jigme Sengye Wangchuck, was born. 1984.

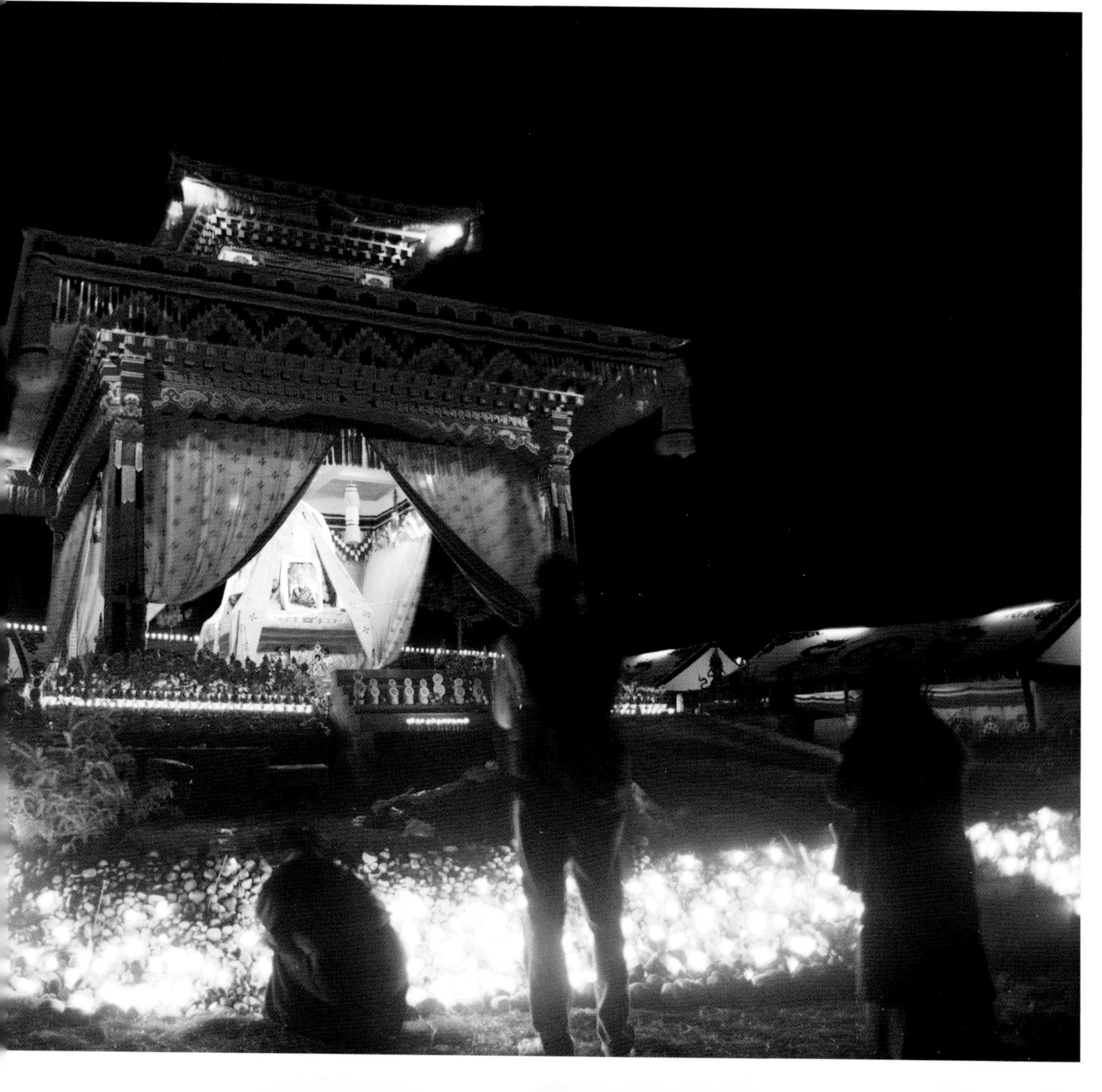

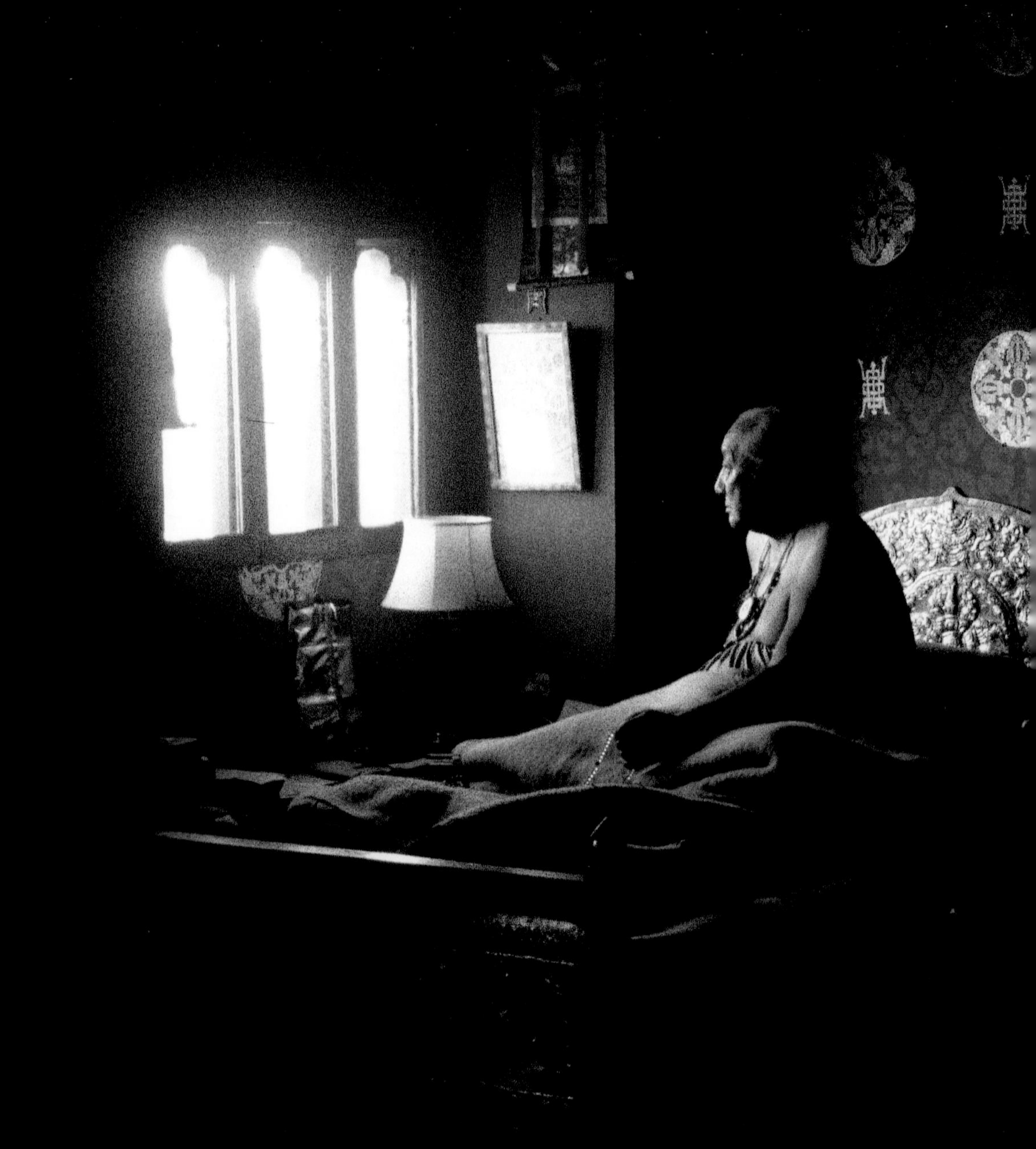

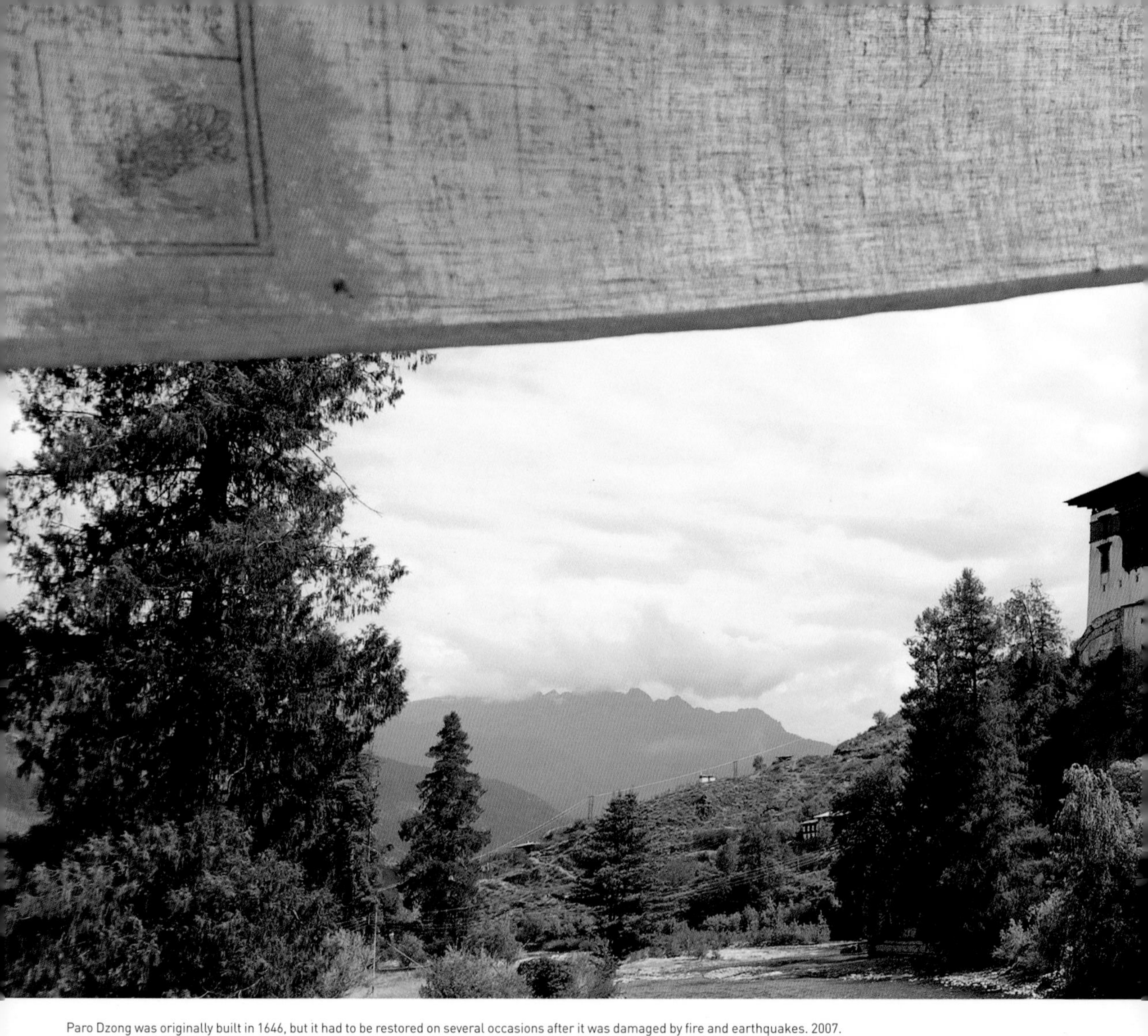

Paro Dzong was originally built in 1646, but it had to be restored on several occasions after it was damaged by fire and earthquakes. 2007.

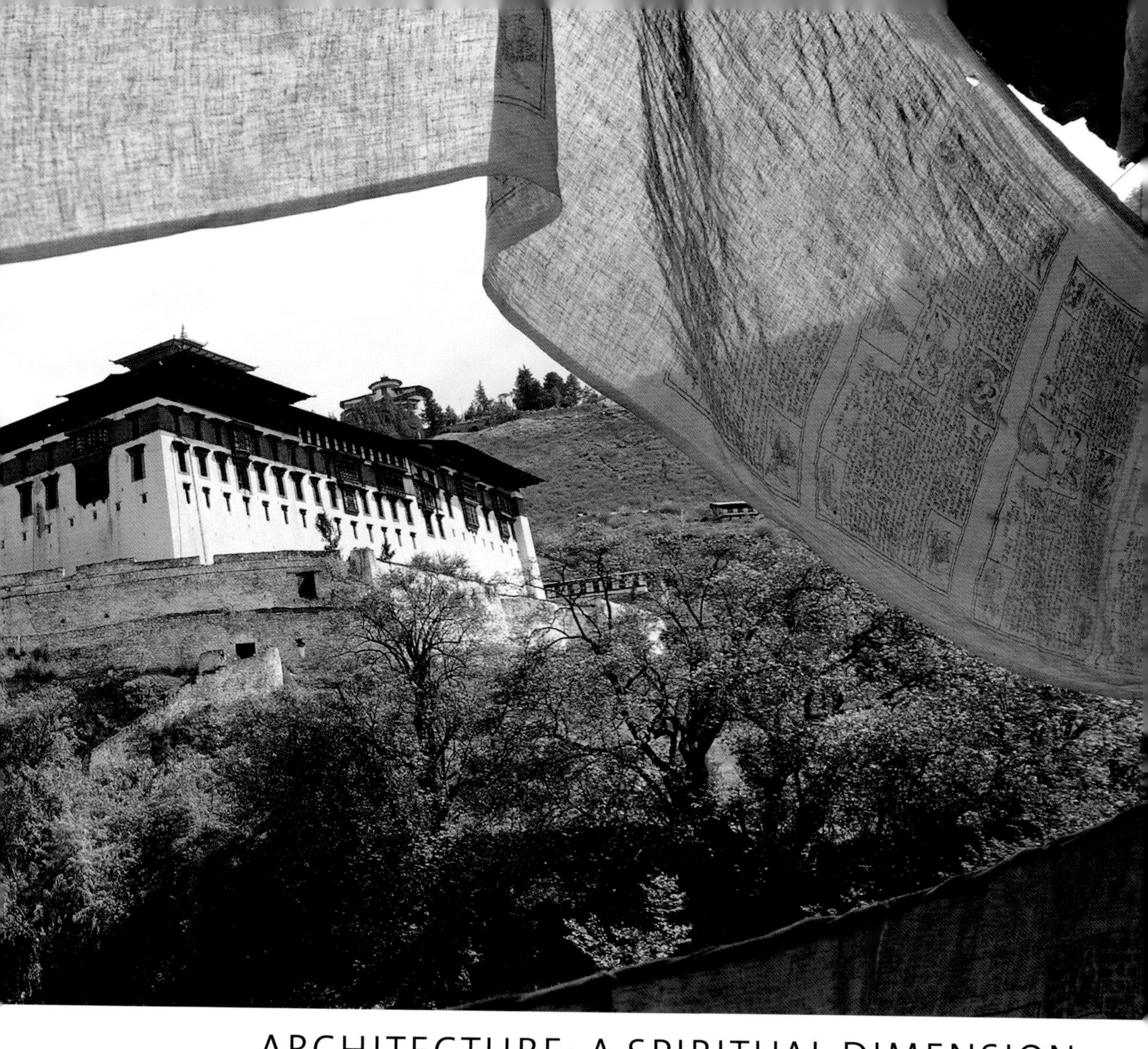

ARCHITECTURE: A SPIRITUAL DIMENSION

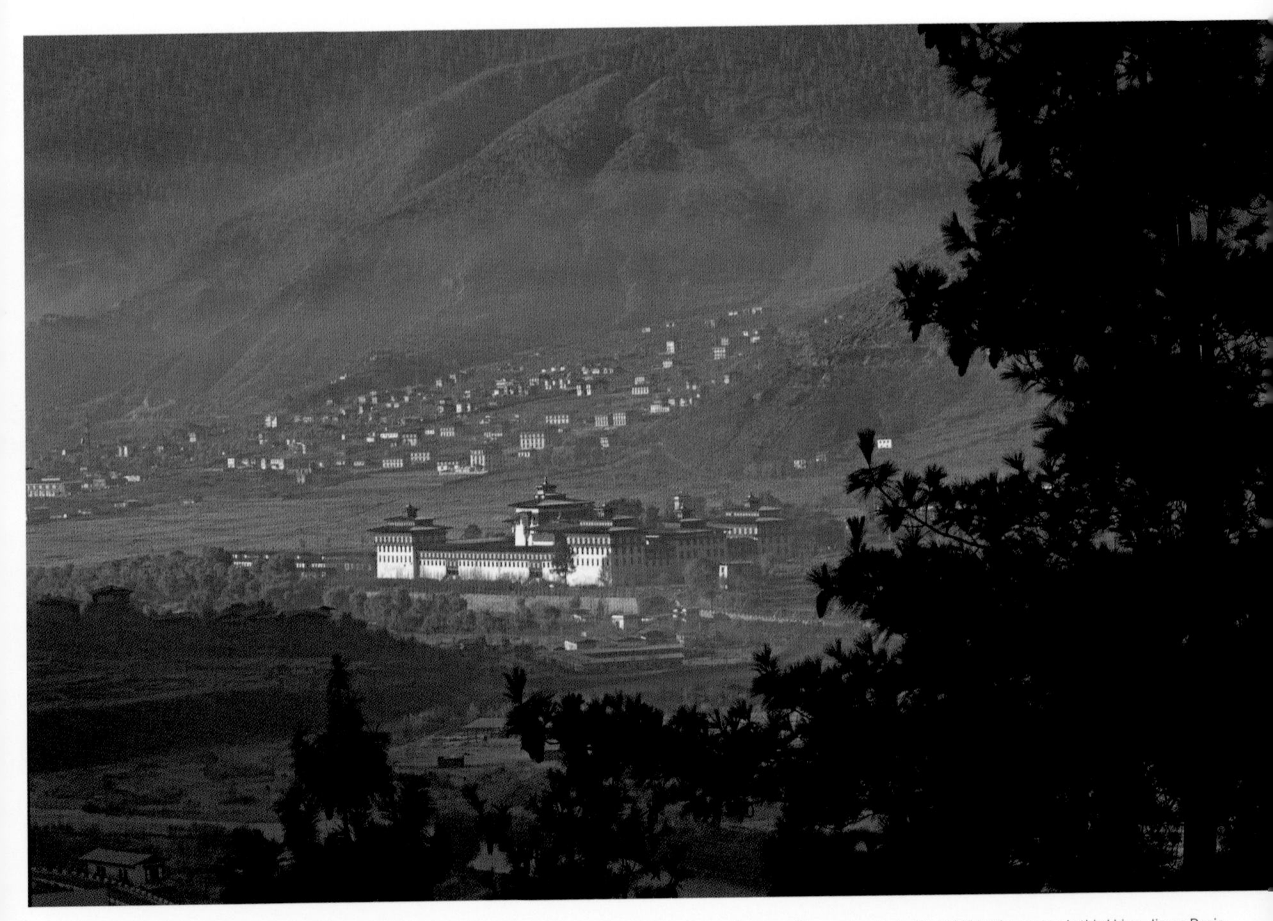

The massive fortress of Tashichho Dzong, in Thimphu, capital of Bhutan, was built in 1641 by Shabdrung Ngawang Namgyal and rebuilt in 1962 by the country's third king, Jigme Dorje Wangchuck. Half the building is occupied by monks (over a thousand in total), the other half by the various government departments and the king's advisory council. The capital is situated in a valley, at an altitude of 2,000 metres. 1985.

Architecture

A Spiritual Dimension

As you enter one of Bhutan's large valleys, the first thing you see is a lush green landscape, within which a dazzlingly white building attracts your eye like a magnet. This is the *dzong*, a magnificent edifice that is always strategically positioned – crowning a piece of high ground, unfurled across the mountainside, marking the confluence of two rivers, protecting the entrance to a valley or majestically enthroned in the heart of the valley. A monastery, a fortress and a seat of local government, these buildings are the nerve centres of the twenty provinces or districts that make up the Land of the Thunder Dragon and a powerful symbol of the country's long independence.

Bhutanese architecture is arguably the best expression of the uniqueness of this nation, both in its quality and its originality. Because of the country's geographical position and its centuries-long isolation from the rest of the world, Bhutan's 'spiritual' architects have developed a style of building that is particular to Bhutan. Each temple and each monastery is a unique creation, and yet wherever you look in Bhutan you also have the sense of a unifying architectural thread. The most notable difference between the buildings of Bhutan and those of central Tibet, for example, lies in the generous use of wood, sourced from the country's extensive forests. Wood was at one time widely used for the double-pitched shingle roofs – a feature of both religious and domestic architecture. This system of roofing, which is vital in a country exposed to the full force of the monsoon, relies on the use of long wooden shingles fixed to a framework of laths and held in place by large round white stones taken from the rivers. There is an open loft space on each side, immediately beneath the roof. These days, however, the traditional roofing system has almost universally been replaced by roofs of corrugated iron, painted in red or yellow.

Wood tends to be used for the openings in a building, including doors, doorframes, lintels and heavily carved and painted three-part windows. Sometimes the upper storeys of a *dzong*, monastery or temple are entirely constructed from wood, as is the case at Paro, and until recently no nails were used at all in this joinery work, only wooden dowels. In addition to wood, whitewashed stone is used to build the high walls of the most prestigious *dzong*, monasteries and *chörten* (stupas), and monastery courtyards are paved with large slabs of stone. The walls of smaller *dzongs* and monasteries are made of dried mud, which is then whitewashed.

The *dzongs* are the spiritual and temporal guardians of a town or village, and not ordinary buildings at all. Despite their often monumental size and complex construction, they were built, without detailed plans, under the direction of spiritual teachers. These visionary architects drew their inspiration from their meditative experiences and from texts describing the geomantic configurations that must be present at a site for such a construction to be auspicious and ensure the security and prosperity of the country. Strategic considerations also entered into the calculations, since the *dzong* was also designed to serve as a refuge in the event of invasion – a rare occurrence in a country that has benefited from a long and peaceful history.

The majority of *dzongs* were built in the early 17th century, under the auspices of Shabdrung Ngawang Namgyal, who decided where the buildings should be constructed on the basis of his own meditative visions. However, recent research indicates that the first *dzong* was in fact that of Dobji Dzong, built in 1531 on a cliff top overlooking the gorge where the Wangchu flows. This *dzong* was constructed for purely spiritual purposes and marked the site where Ngawang Chögyal, brother of the famous yogi Drukpa Kunlek, '...followed a spring that gushed forth beneath the spot where Jetsun Milarepa had meditated, at Druk Ralung, because he was looking for the right place to build a centre for the propagation of Buddhist teachings in Bhutan.'

The *dzong* is divided into two parts. One is the seat of the provincial government and the other serves a purely religious function. The civil and religious buildings are separated by a central tower (*utse*), which generally houses a number of temples. The religious wing consists of a monastery comprising the monks' living quarters, the rooms reserved for the abbot, the main temple (*kundrel*, pronounced *kunre*) where the monks gather, various chapels (*lhakhang*), study rooms, libraries and kitchens.

The coexistence of these two worlds is imbued with an atmosphere of mutual respect, characteristic of Buddhist tolerance. The notion of interdependence, moreover, is a cornerstone of Buddhist philosophy and here we see its practical application in the cultural life of Bhutan. The religious authorities refrain from interfering in government affairs, but Buddhism is omnipresent in Bhutan.

The walls of the *dzong* are sometimes as much as two metres thick at the base and frequently four to five storeys high, and they incline gradually inwards as they rise, decorated just beneath the roof by a broad band of red. The austere exterior of these monastery-fortresses (which abandoned their defensive role a long time ago) is lightened at the upper levels by brightly painted projecting wooden balconies, and the decorative theme continues inside with richly ornamental woodwork. The monks' living quarters extend over two or three storeys, opening onto inner courtyards through a series of galleries and elegant three-part windows decorated with flowers and painted cartouches highlighting the building's lines of force.

The various internal buildings are accessed by steep stairs cut into thick wooden beams, their edges slippery with constant use. The young monks run down these steps with tremendous agility, but anyone unused to them is at risk of descending them faster than he or she intended – a bit like sliding down a bumpy road on a toboggan. Groups of monks are regularly to be seen coming and going, at the end of a ceremony or a study session, scattering in all directions over the paved courtyards. The youngest sleep in the great study rooms on mats which they unroll each night and roll up again in the morning.

Bhutanese temples and monasteries are generally smaller than the mighty *dzong*. But like the temple of Guru Padmasambhava at Paro Kyichu, which was consecrated by Dilgo Khyentse Rinpoche, these buildings are imbued with a great feeling of stillness. The

English writer C. S. Lewis spoke of certain buildings where 'the inside is larger than the outside'.

Although they are sometimes integrated into a *dzong*, Bhutanese temples and monasteries are usually built in isolated spots – on a rocky spur or a remote hillside, for example – that are particularly conducive to meditation. A large monastery generally has three main sections. The monastery proper is where the various ceremonies and sacred dances and other events of monastic life occur; it is also the place where novices receive basic instruction. Next to the monastery, there is sometimes a monastic college designed for the pursuit of philosophical studies, lasting from nine to twelve years. Finally, the monastery usually has a retreat centre, situated a little apart from the main buildings, further away in the mountains, where those who choose to can engage in a life of meditation, the culminating point of their spiritual training.

Stupas, or *chörtens* in Tibetan, are the landmarks that punctuate the Bhutanese landscape, cropping up in the centre of a town (like the monumental Thimphu *chörten*), in the neighbourhood of a monastery, at the bottom of a valley, on a hillside or the top of a pass. They originated in India, where they were built to preserve the relics of the Buddha and great Buddhist masters. Bhutanese *chörten* serve as receptacles for the ashes of major spiritual teachers. They appear in a variety of shapes and sizes and, essentially, symbolize the Buddha's mind and wisdom.

DOMESTIC ARCHITECTURE

Thimphu, the capital of Bhutan, has a population of 70,000. There are barely any other large towns in Bhutan, but there are a great many villages, large and small, and hamlets of beautiful whitewashed houses whose painted decorations are designed to bring good luck and confer on the buildings a typically Bhutanese character. Domestic architecture uses the same materials as religious architecture: beaten earth in the west and freestone in the wealthier centre and east of the country, together with wood for the doors and windows, projecting balconies and roofs – although corrugated iron, coated with paint, is more often used for roofs these days.

Eighty per cent of Bhutan's landscape is rural and settlements are scattered. A village tends to be a cluster of sturdily built farmhouses, situated beside a river or on the sunny slope of a mountain surrounded by rice fields. Not infrequently, you also come across remote hamlets, small stone-built farmhouses tucked away in a deep coomb or shrouded in mist on a mountain. Although there are local variations, in general a farmhouse is two storeys high, three in the case of the wealthier ones. The ground floor serves as a stable (and is also where the store is located in larger villages), and a steep staircase carved from a tree trunk leads up to the living area on the first floor. This is the main family room: the kitchen where meals are prepared and eaten and the room where relatives and neighbours are received, and where the family sleep on mattresses laid on top of mats, which are rolled up against the wall during the day. It is also the principal source of warmth and a welcome refuge during the bitter Himalayan winters.

A second staircase – more of a ladder – leads up to the loft, a small, low room under the roof where meat, seasonings and some vegetables are dried and stored. Most houses have a small private sanctuary, the most highly decorated room in the house, situated on the top floor. A prayer flag (a square of coloured cloth printed with prayers) is always erected on the roof to protect its inhabitants and send blessings of peace and compassion to the four corners of the earth:

As long as space endures
And as long as sentient beings exist,
May I too continue to exist
To dispel the suffering of the world.

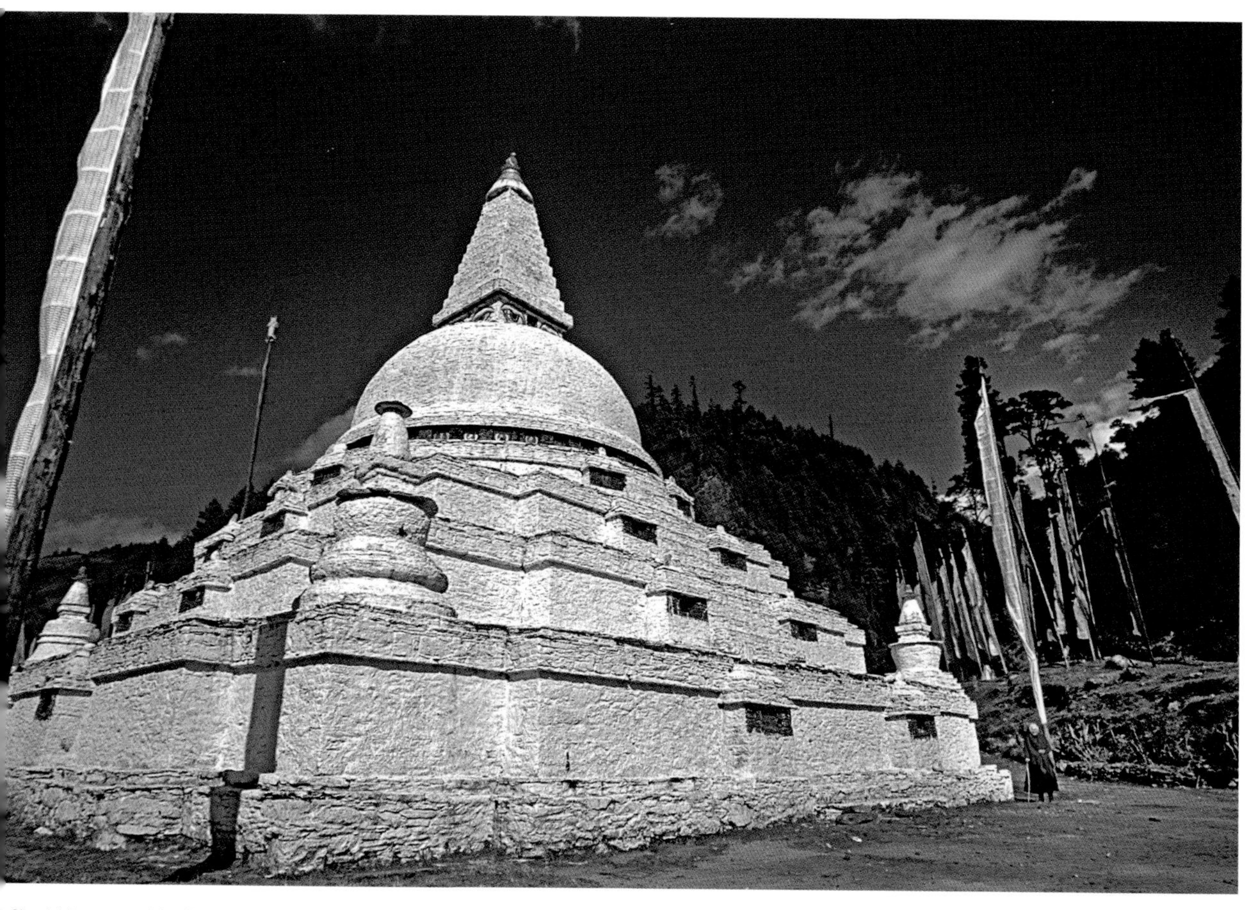

Chandebji stupa stands beside a river on the Bumthang road in eastern Bhutan. Built by a Tibetan lama in the 18th century, it is modelled on the Bodhnath stupa in the Kathmandu valley. 2004.

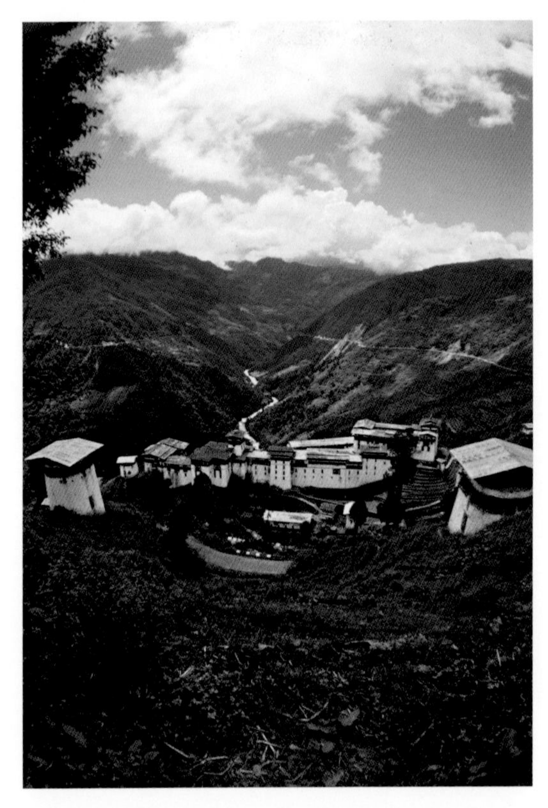

Trongsar monastery is situated on the side of a deep valley, at an altitude of 2,000 metres, and is home to three hundred monks. 1983.

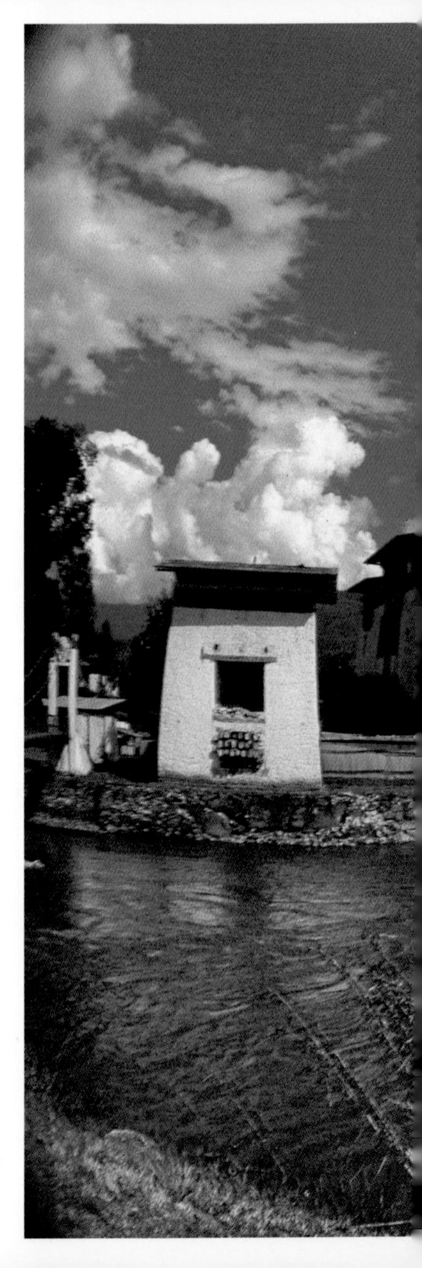

Punakha monastery was built in the 17th century and is situated at the confluence of two rivers, the Pochu and the Mochu, in central Bhutan. It serves as winter quarters for the thousand monks of Thimphu Dzong, who formerly made the three-day journey from Punakha to Thimphu on foot. 1980.

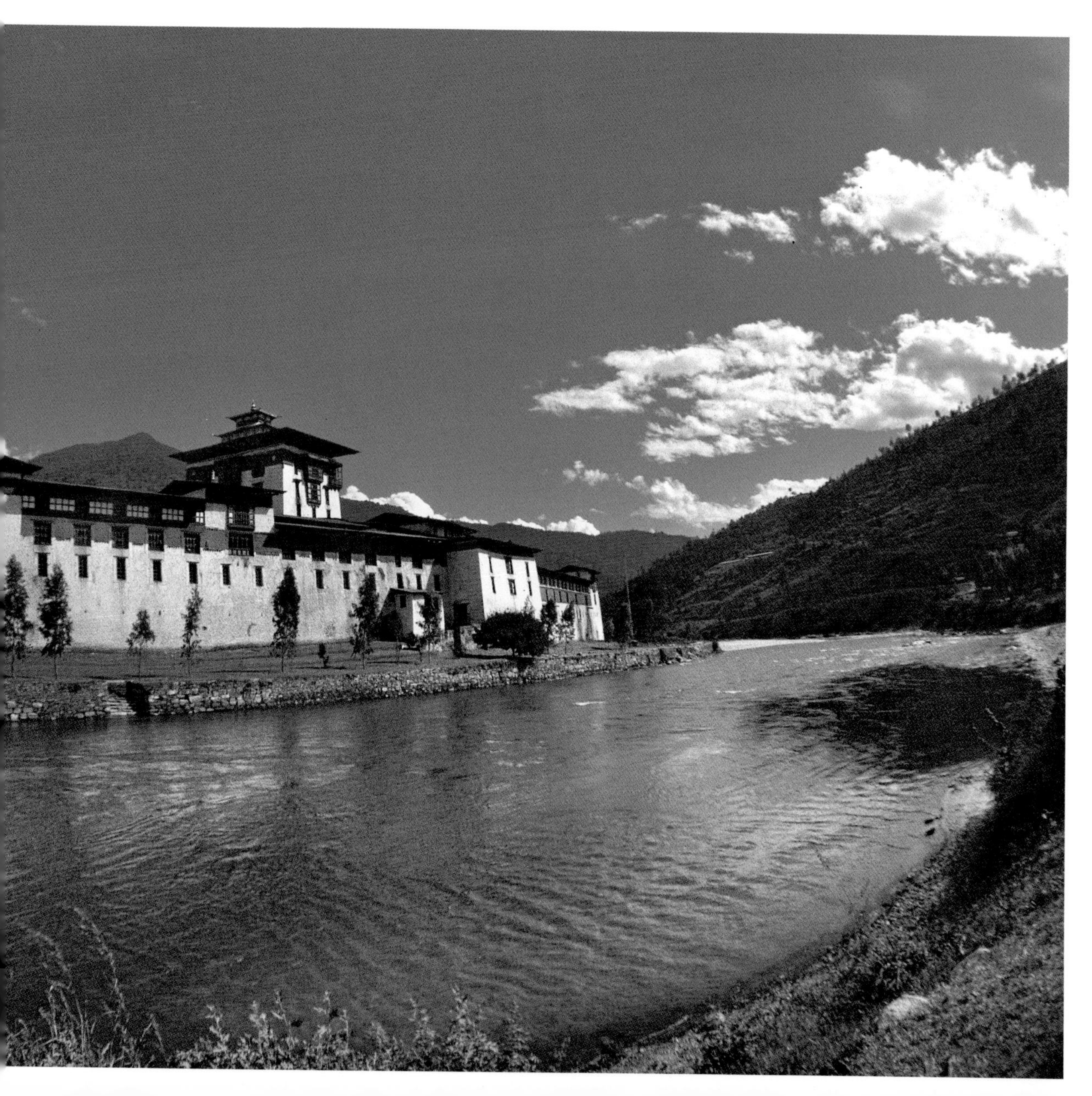

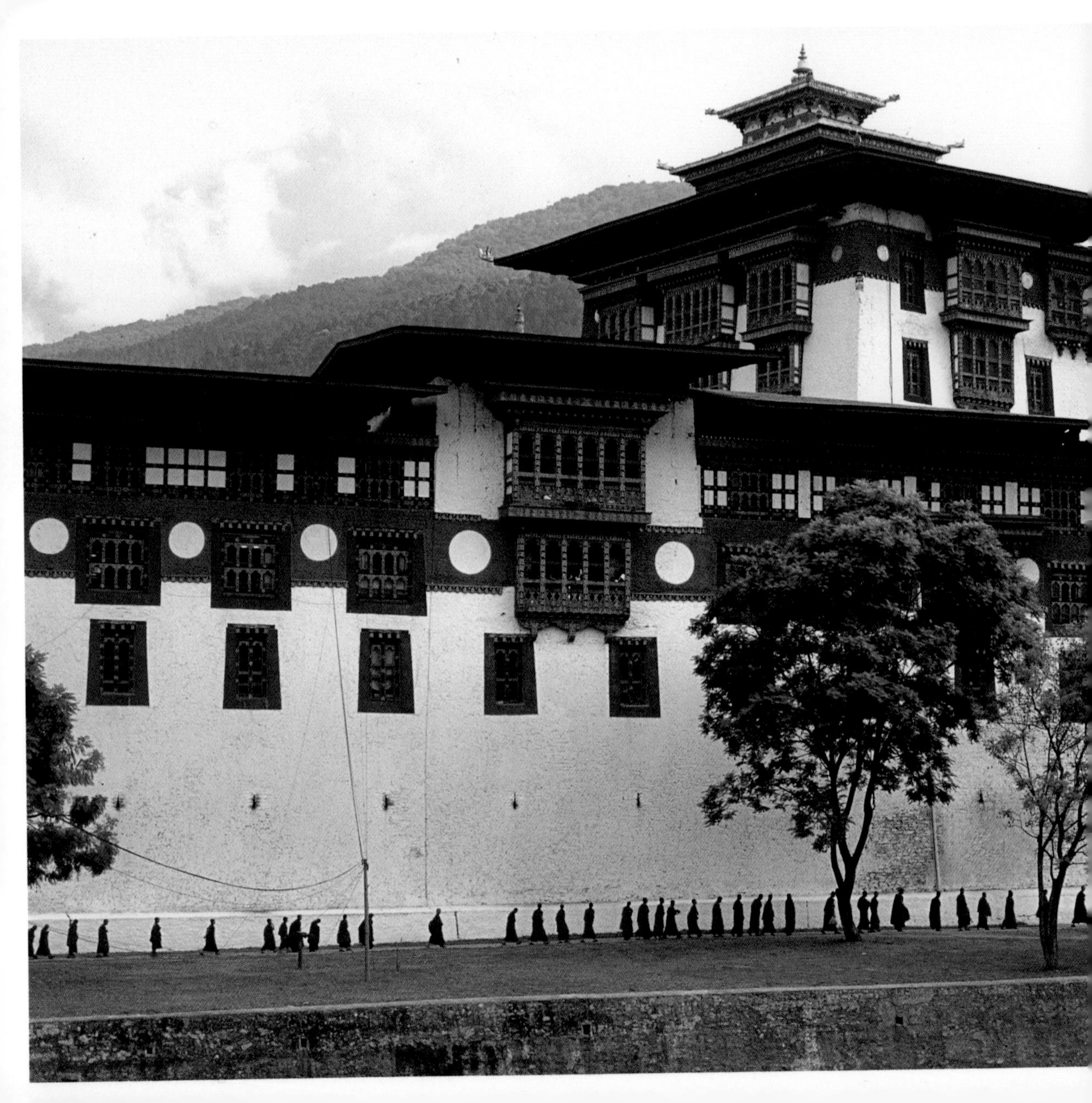

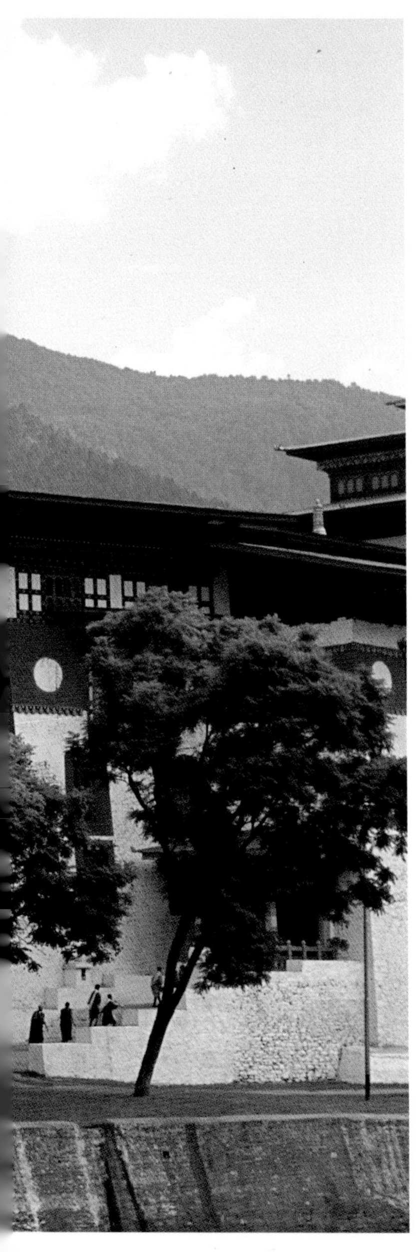

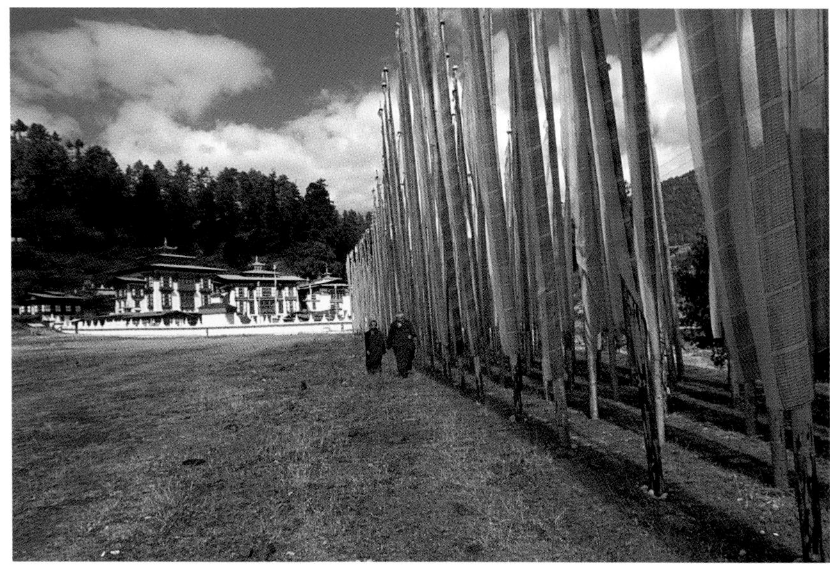

Monks and prayer flags in front of Kuje monastery in Bumthang. The monastery was built around an imprint of Guru Padmasambhava's body left in the rock in the 9th century. 2004.

Punakha monastery was badly damaged by fire in 1986, then again in 1994 when a dam burst at the head of a glacial lake. Bhutan's fourth king had the building magnificently restored using traditional materials and techniques. 2004.

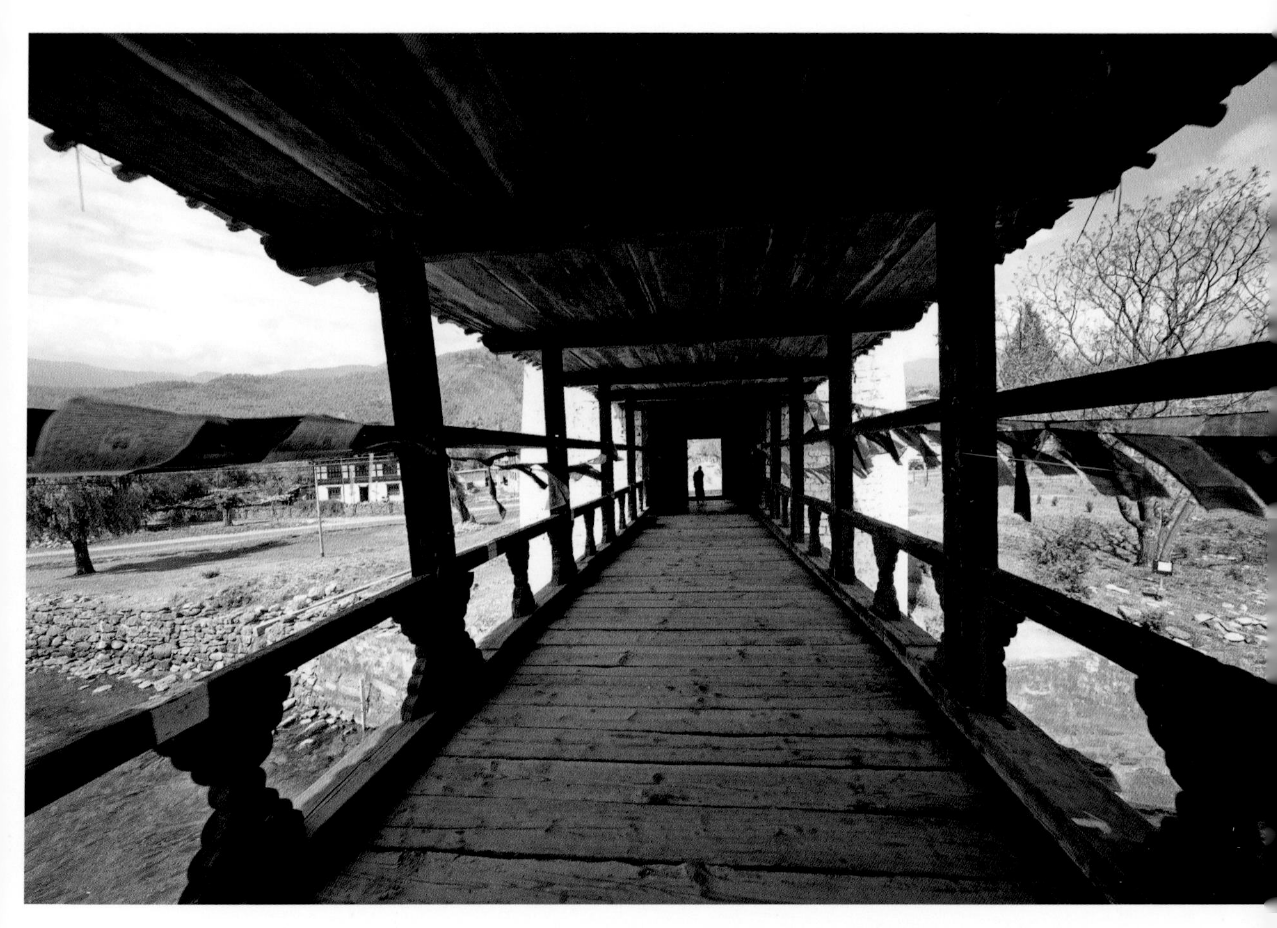

This covered wooden bridge at the foot of Paro Dzong has been preserved and restored and is one of the few old structures of its kind. The Paro bridge is now designated a historic monument. 2007.

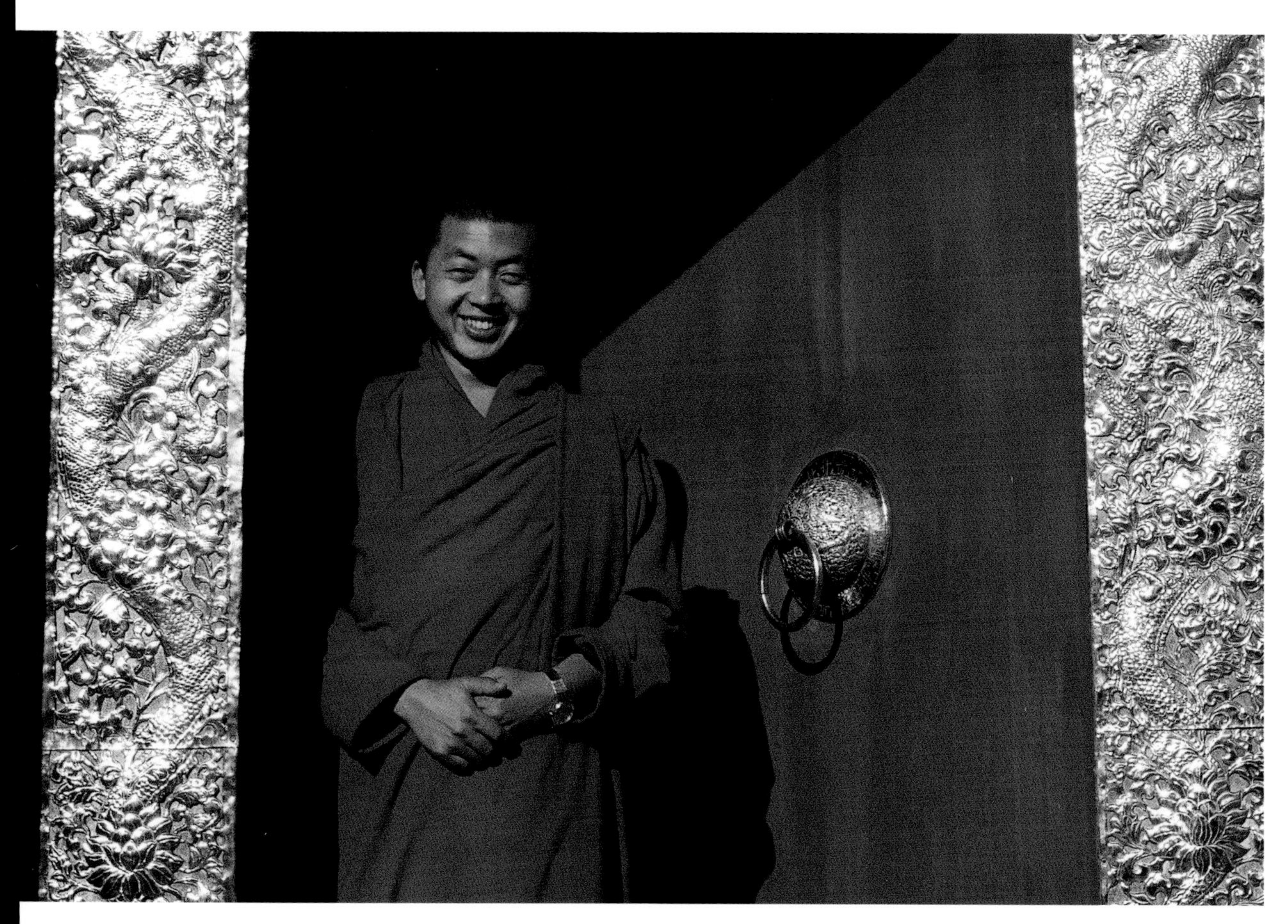

A Bhutanese monk in front of temple doors made of beaten copper, 1990.

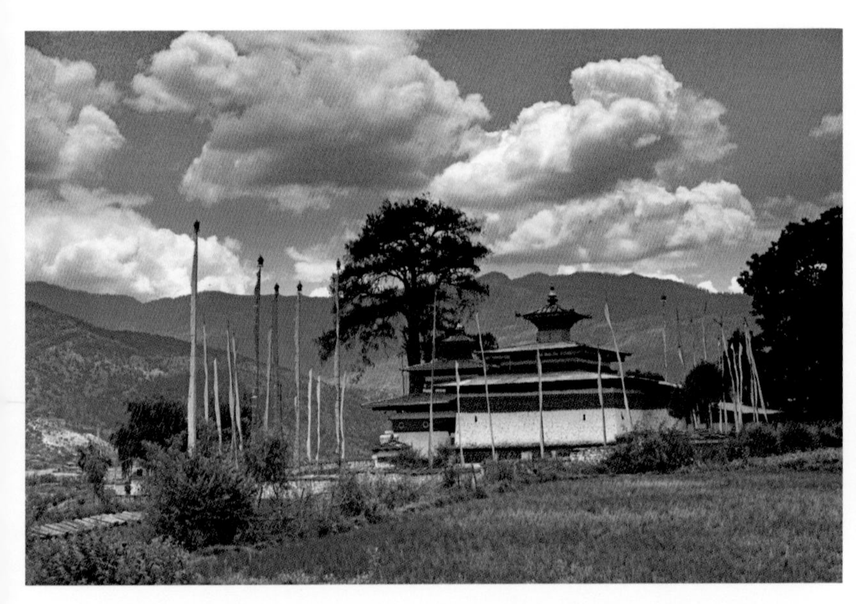

The temple of Kyichu, at Paro, was founded in the 7th century by Songtsen Gampo, Tibet's first Buddhist king, and is one of Bhutan's great treasures. It has an ancient chapel where a crowned Buddha sits enthroned and a more recent chapel housing a majestic sculpture of Padmasambhava commissioned by Bhutan's Queen Mother, following the advice of Khyentse Rinpoche. 1983.

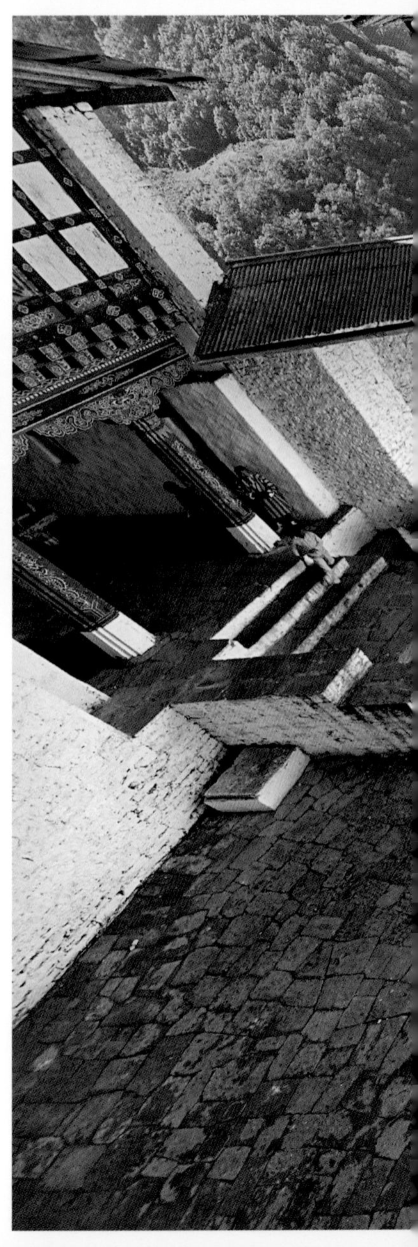

One of Trongsar Dzong's courtyards, 2007.

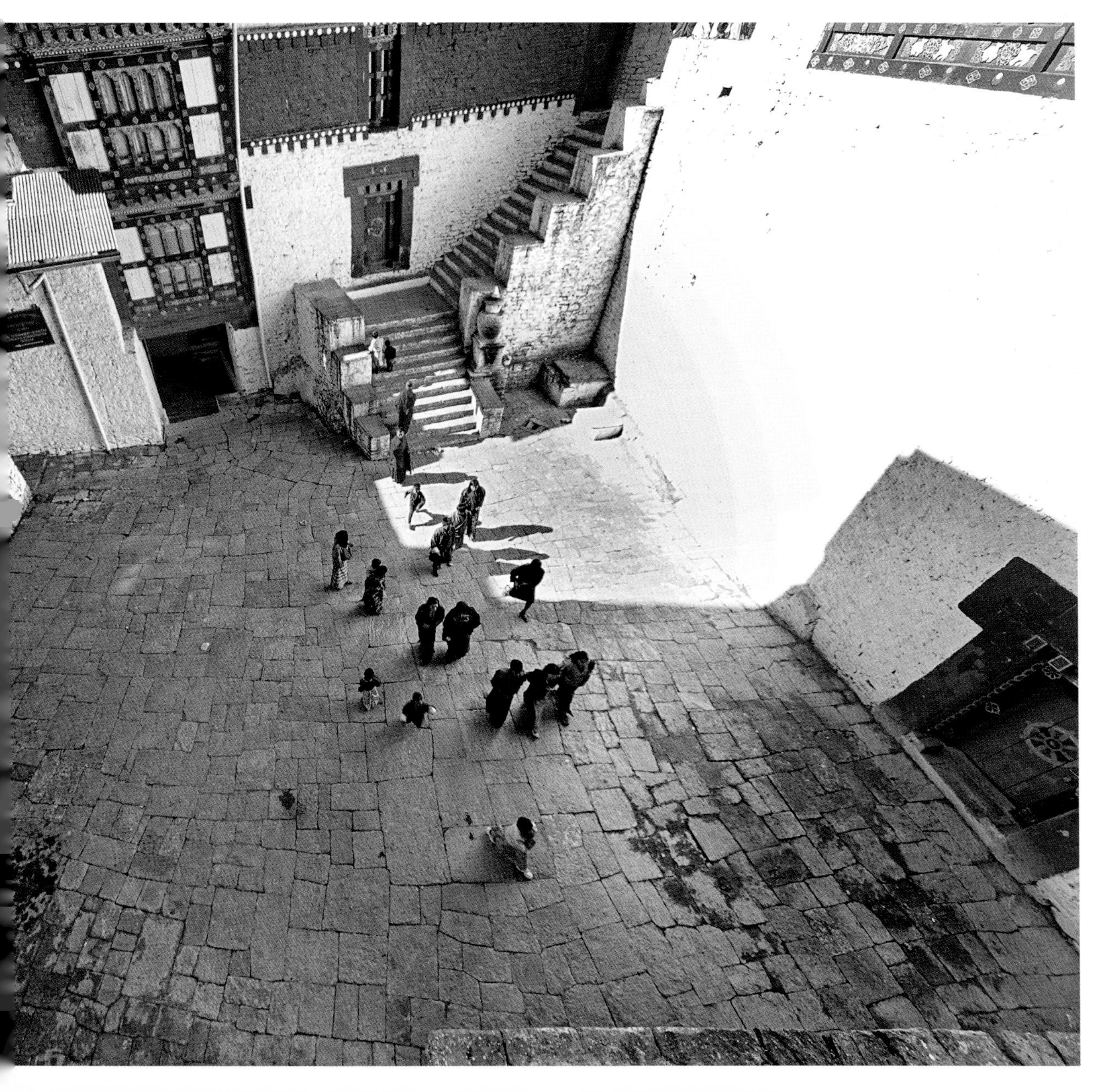

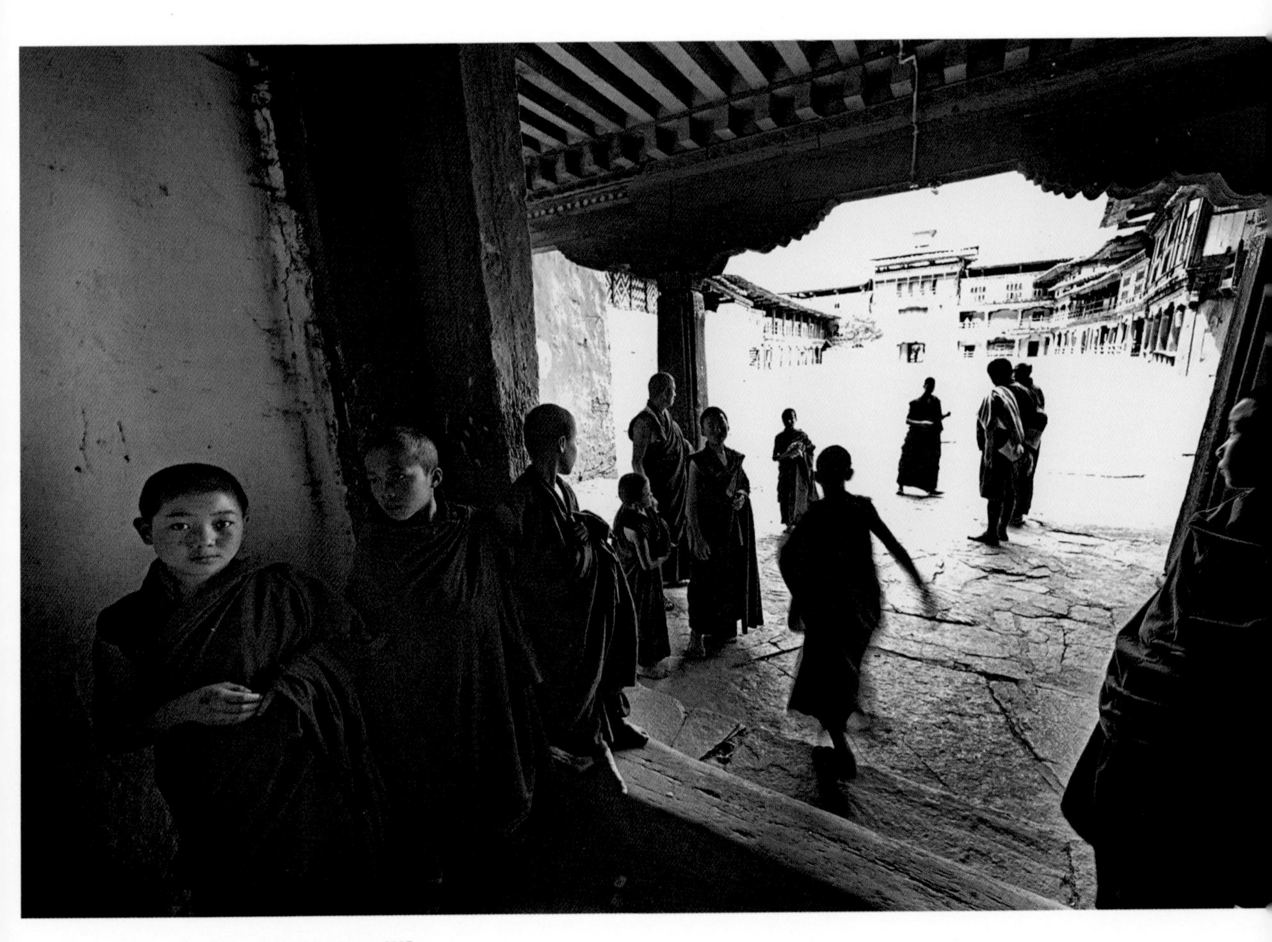

Young novice monks at Wangdu Phodrang Dzong, 2007.

The rich and complex architecture of Kuje temple, in Bumthang province, 2006.

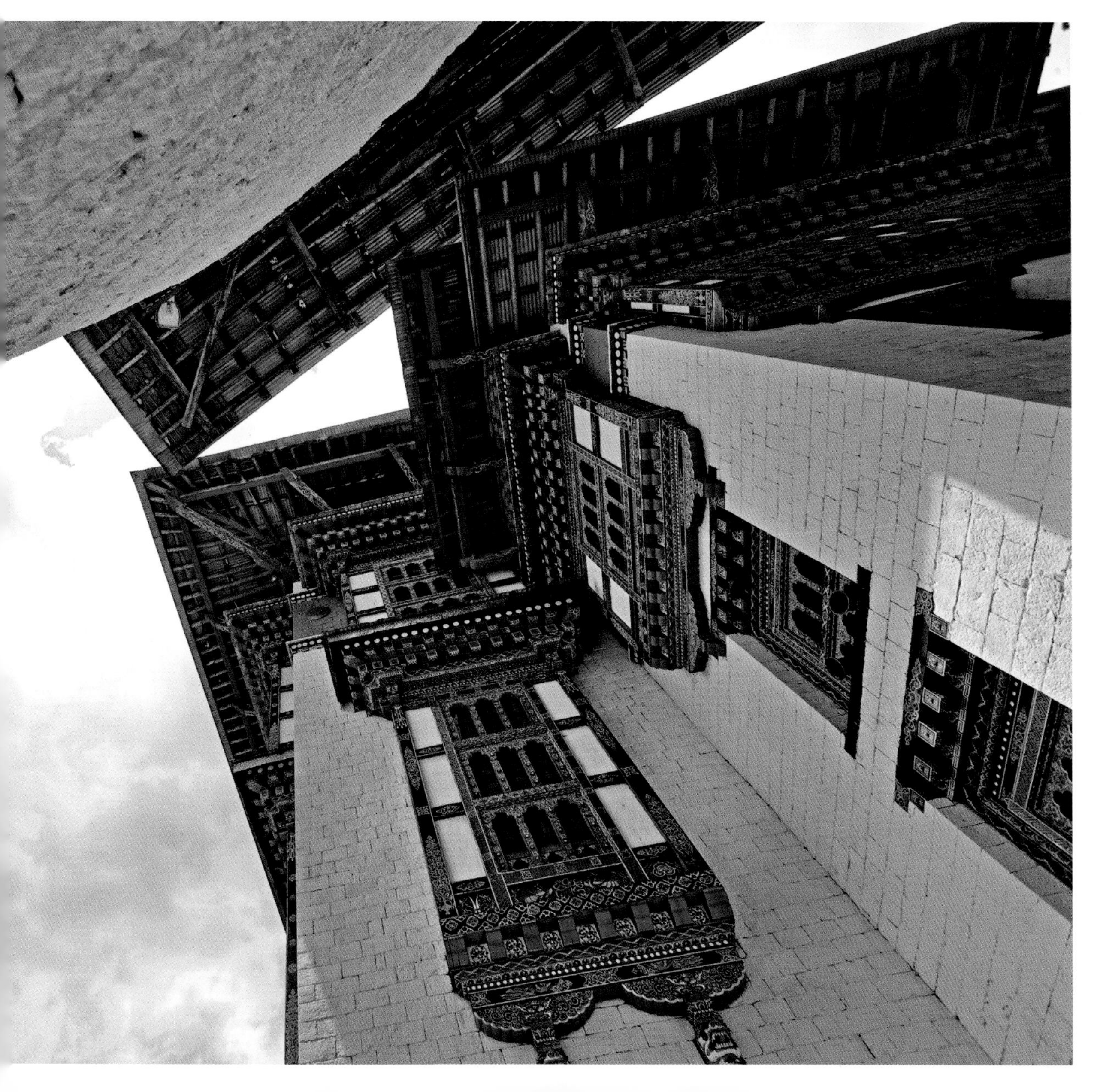

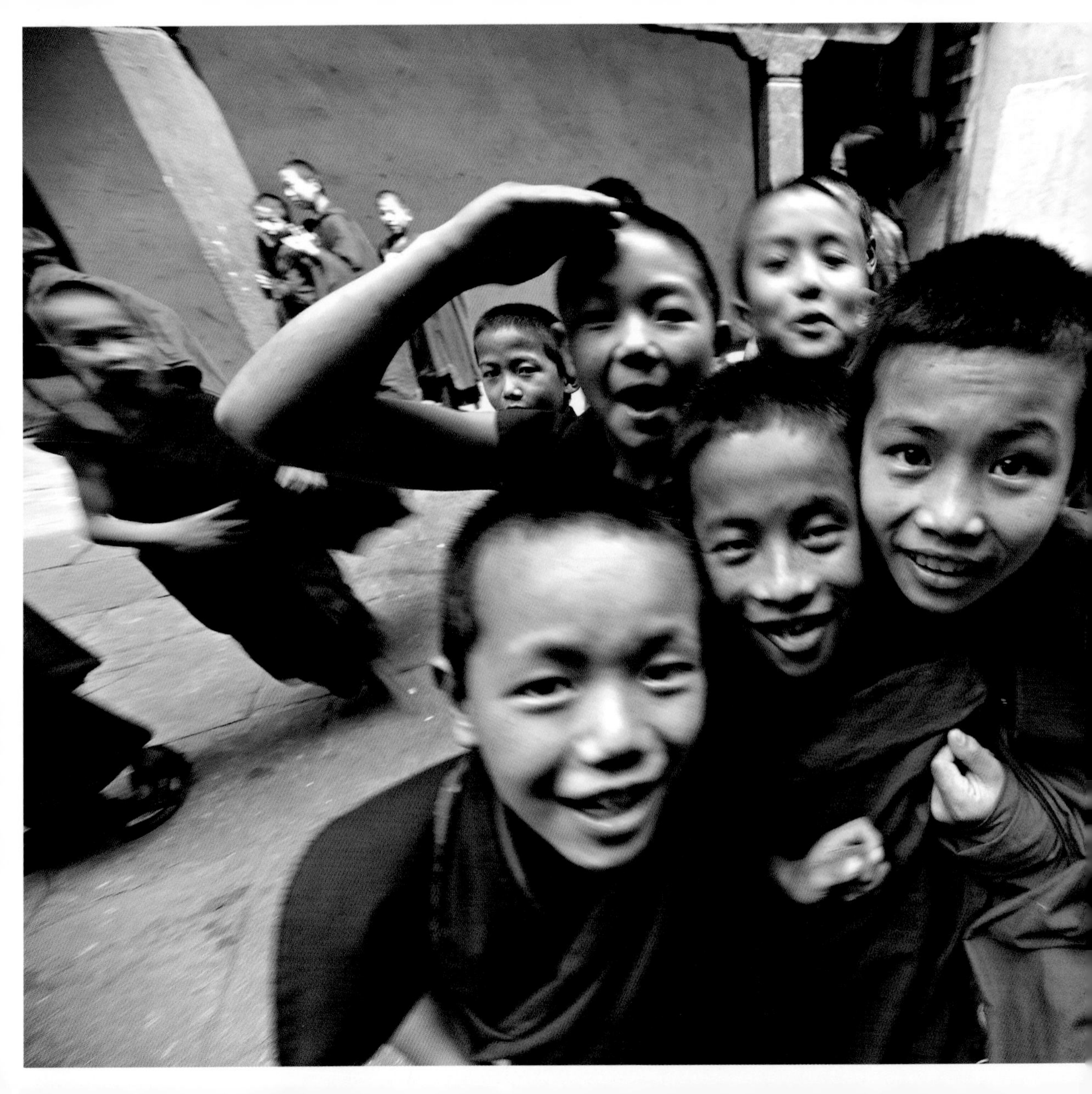

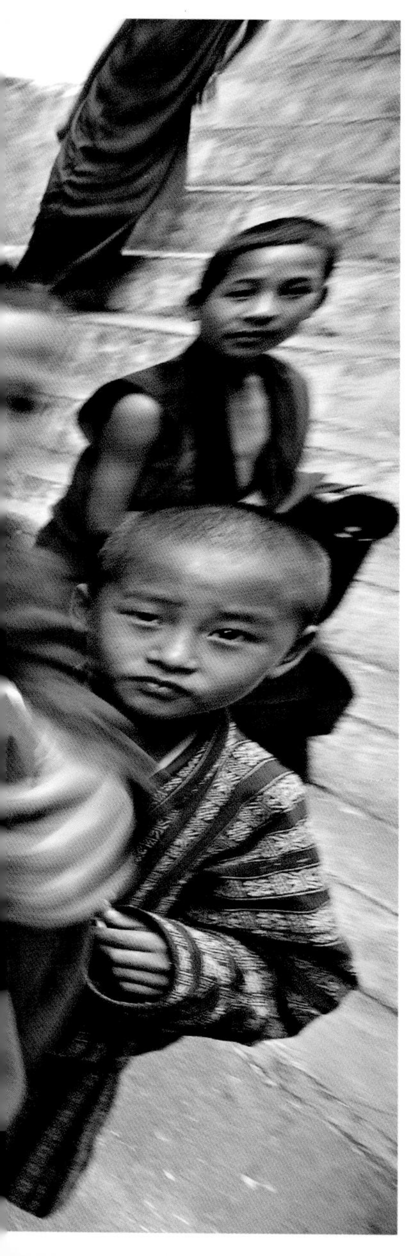

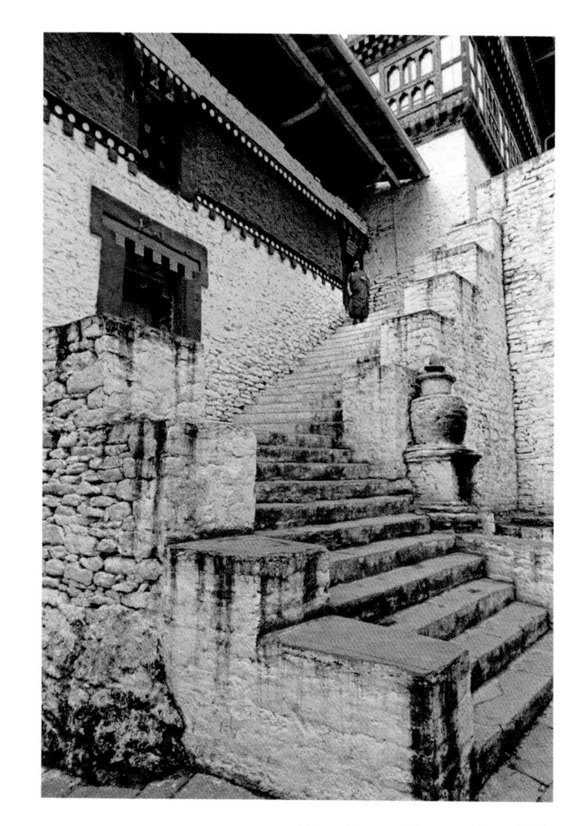

Stone staircase at Trongsar Dzong, 2007.

Left:
Mischievous young monks in the courtyard of Wangdu Phodrang Dzong, 2007.

Overleaf, left:
Two monks looking out of Paro Dzong's ornate windows, 2007.

Overleaf, right:
The lower courtyard of Paro Dzong, where the monks' quarters are located, 2007.

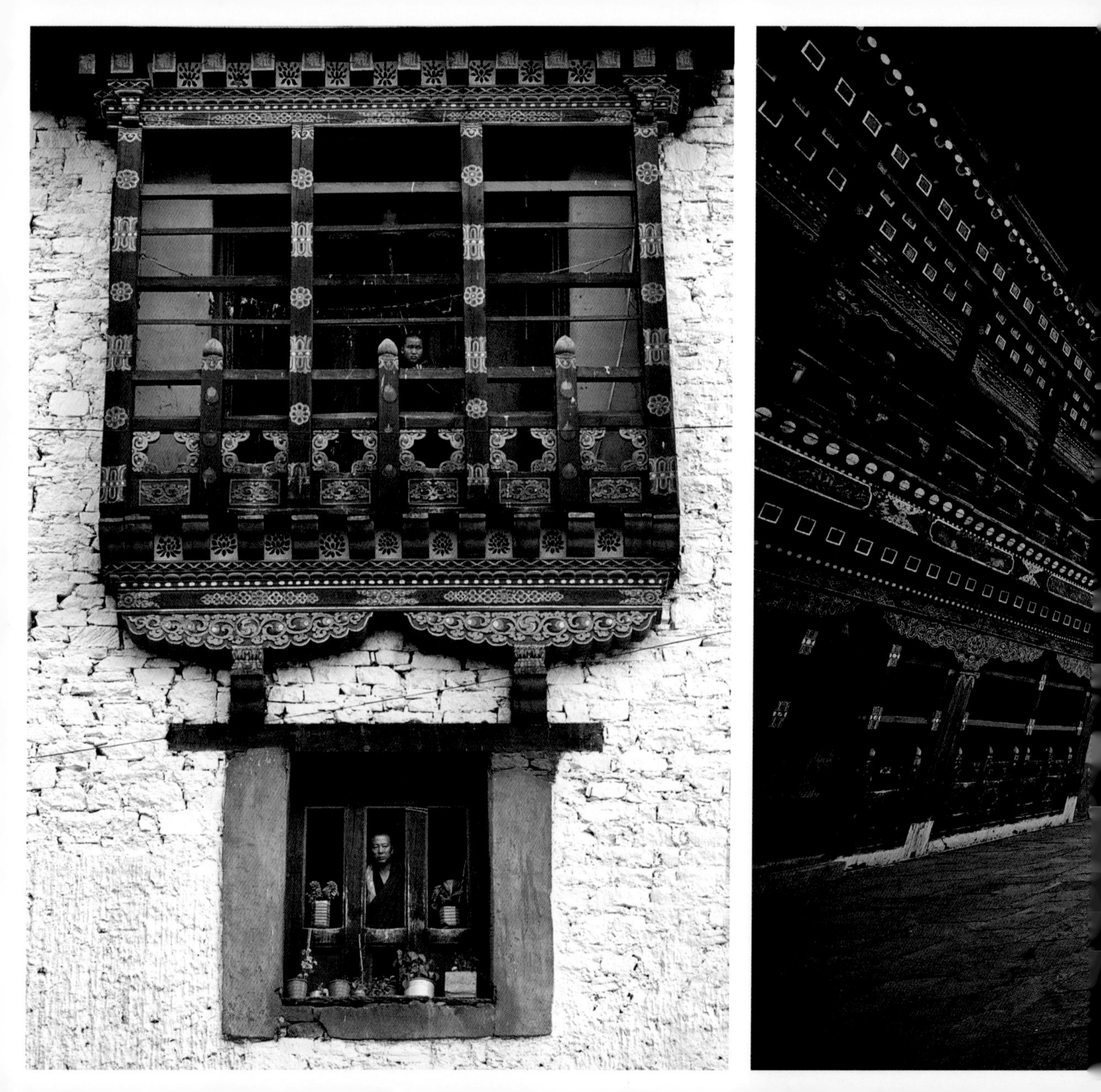

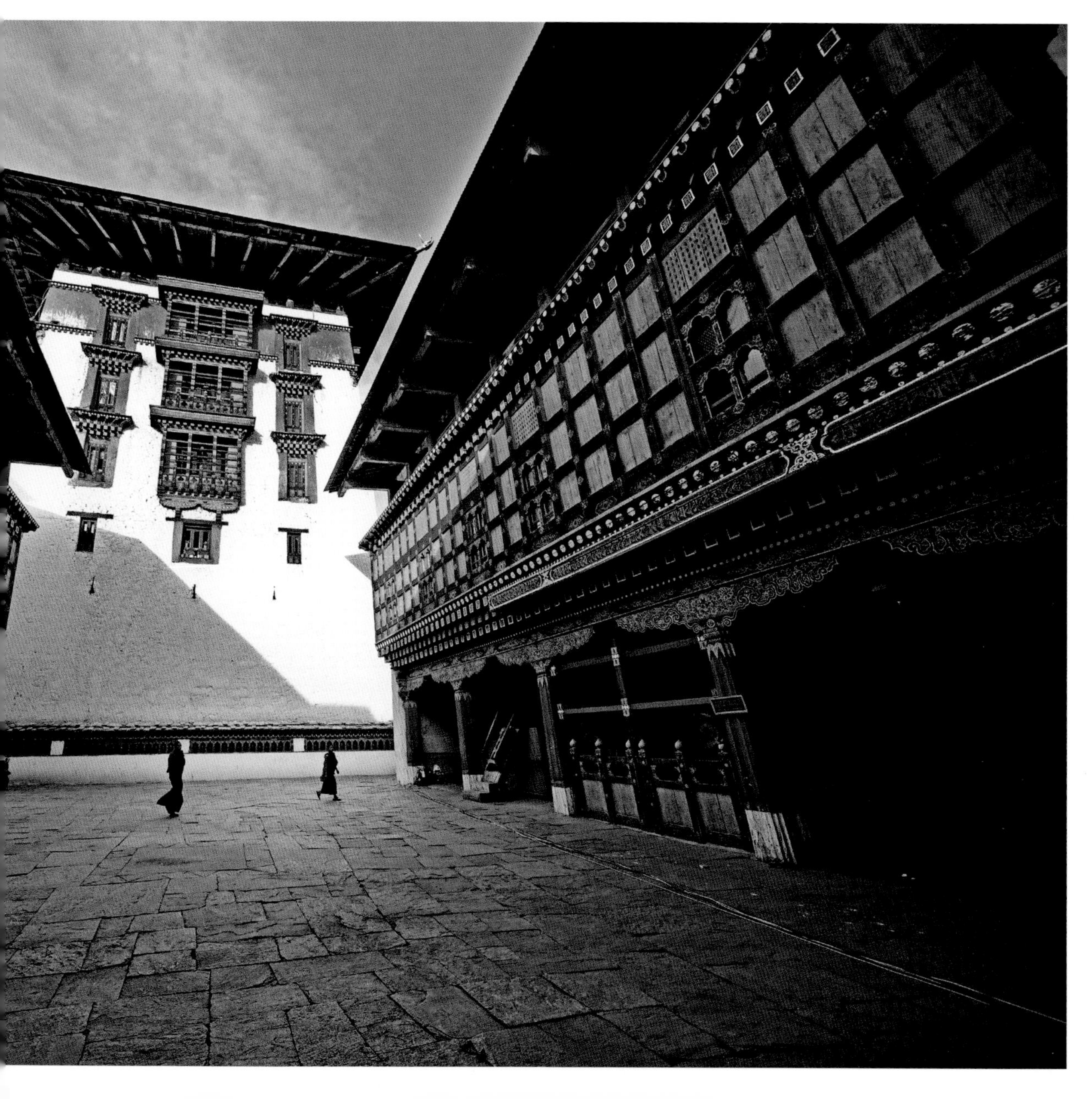

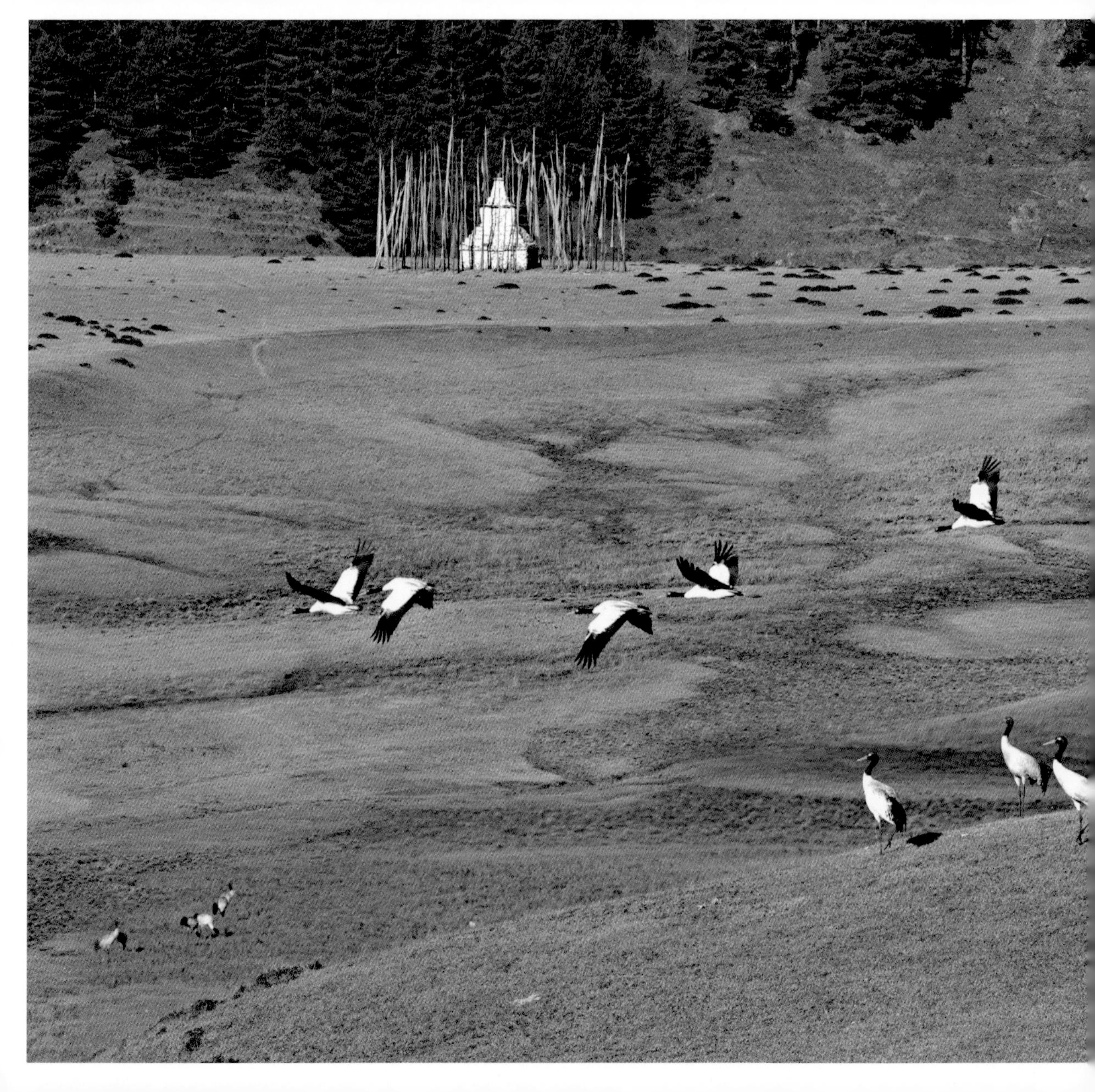

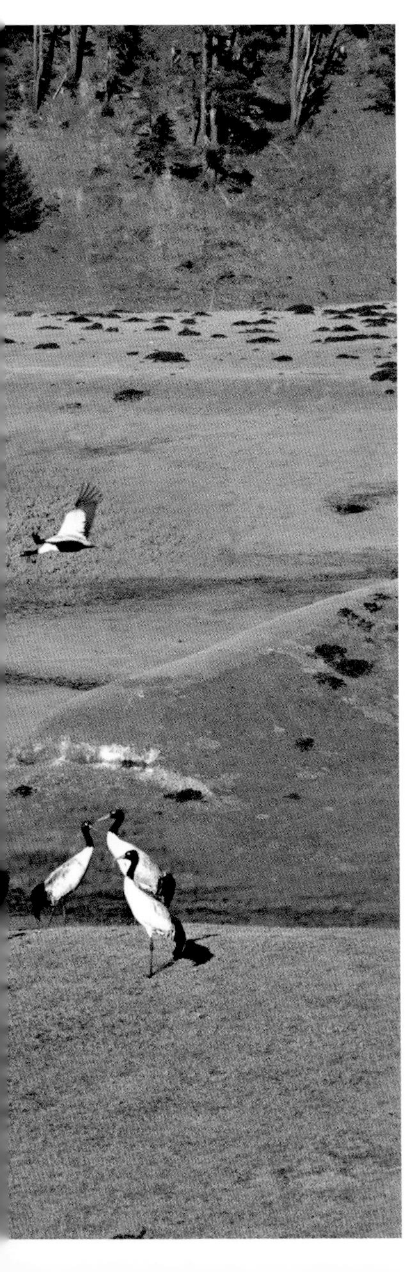

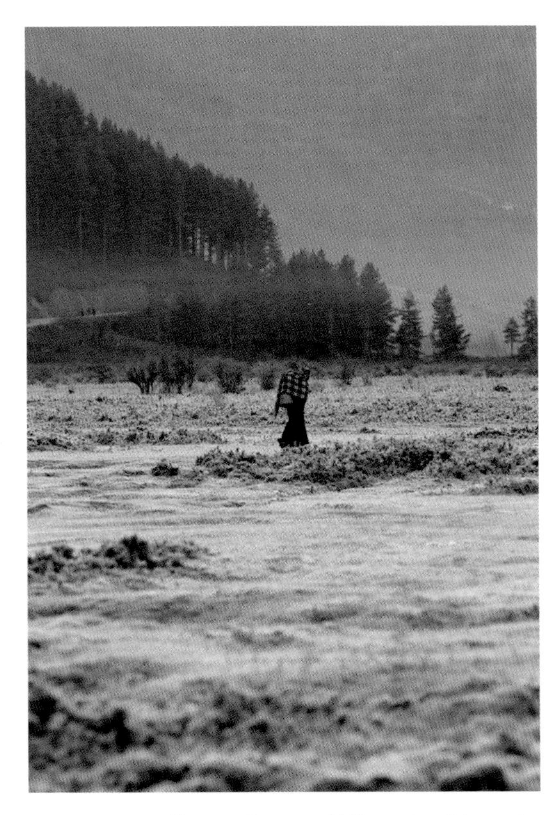

A woman walking across frost-covered fields on a clear winter morning.
Phobjika valley, December 2007.

Cranes flying over the marshes of the Phobjika valley, with a stupa and prayer flags in the background. December 2007.

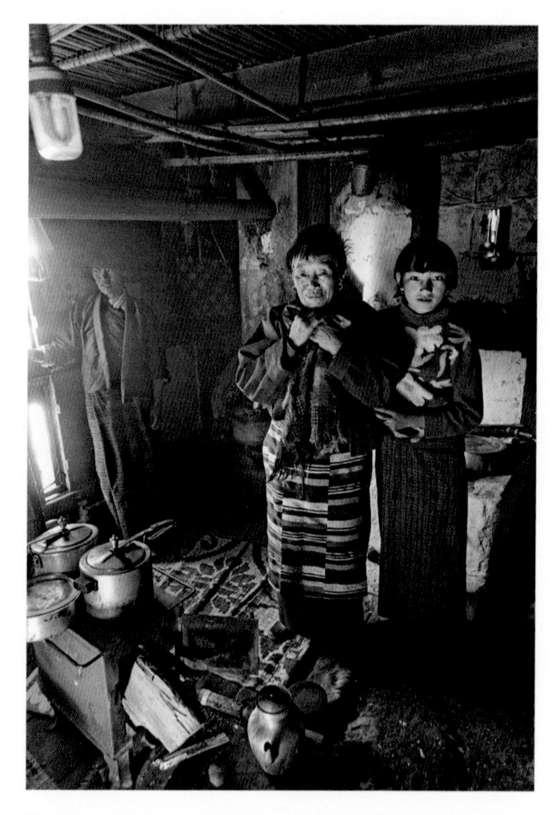

Three generations of women in a house in the village of Dur, Bumthang. The family generally gather in the kitchen, which is the only part of the house that is heated. December 2007.

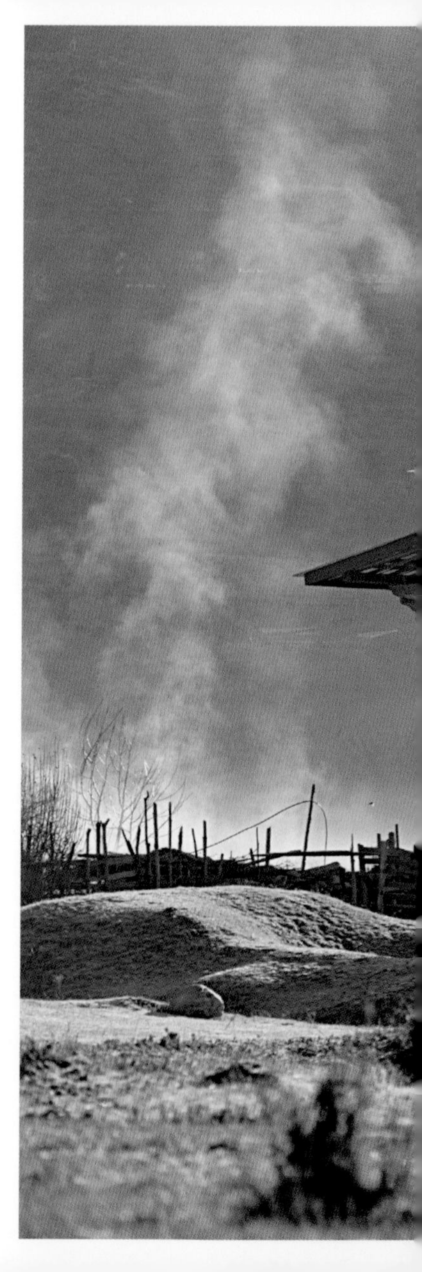

House built of mud and wood, typical of Bhutan's high-altitude regions. Phobjika valley, 3,000 metres, December 2007.

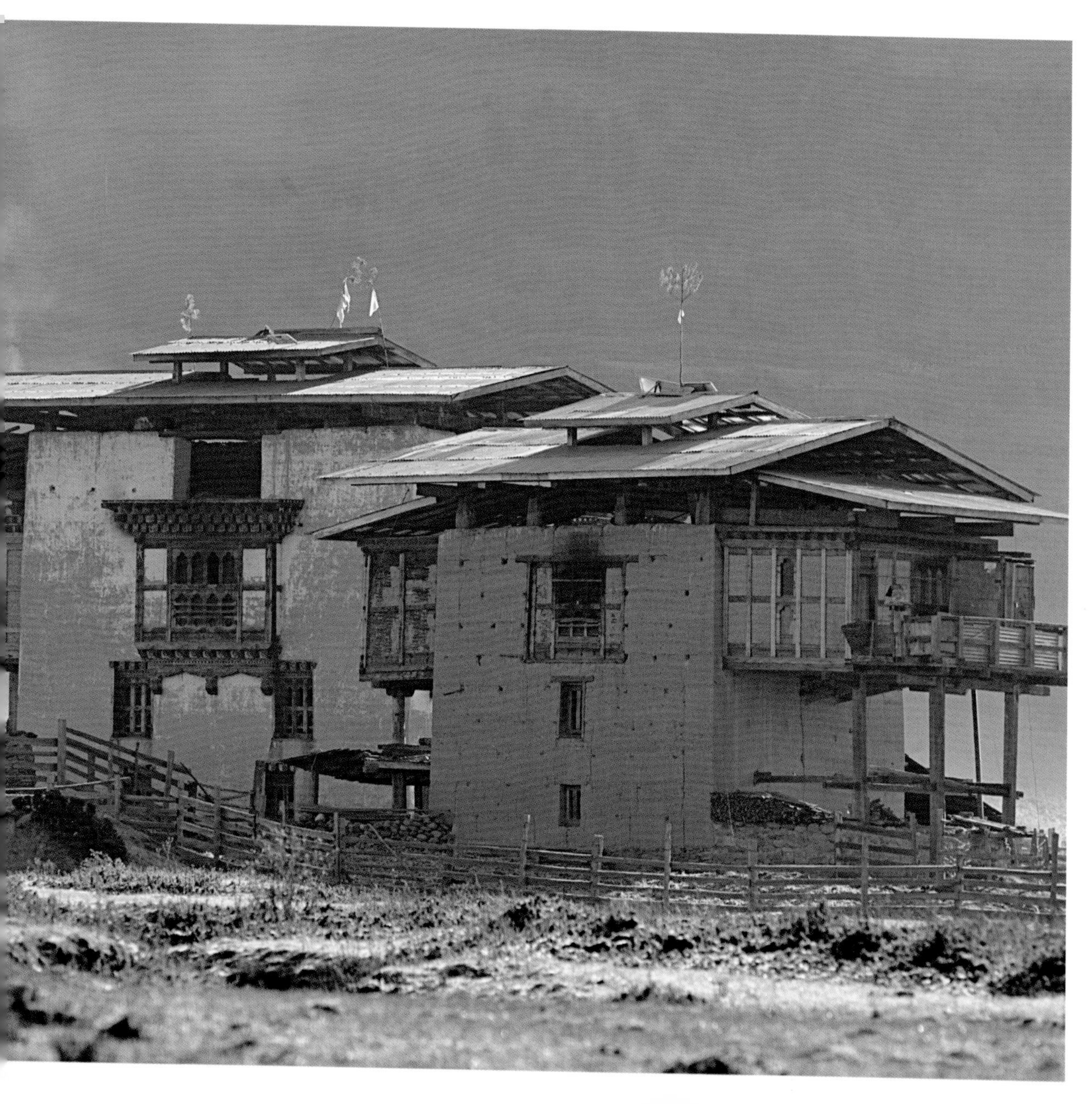

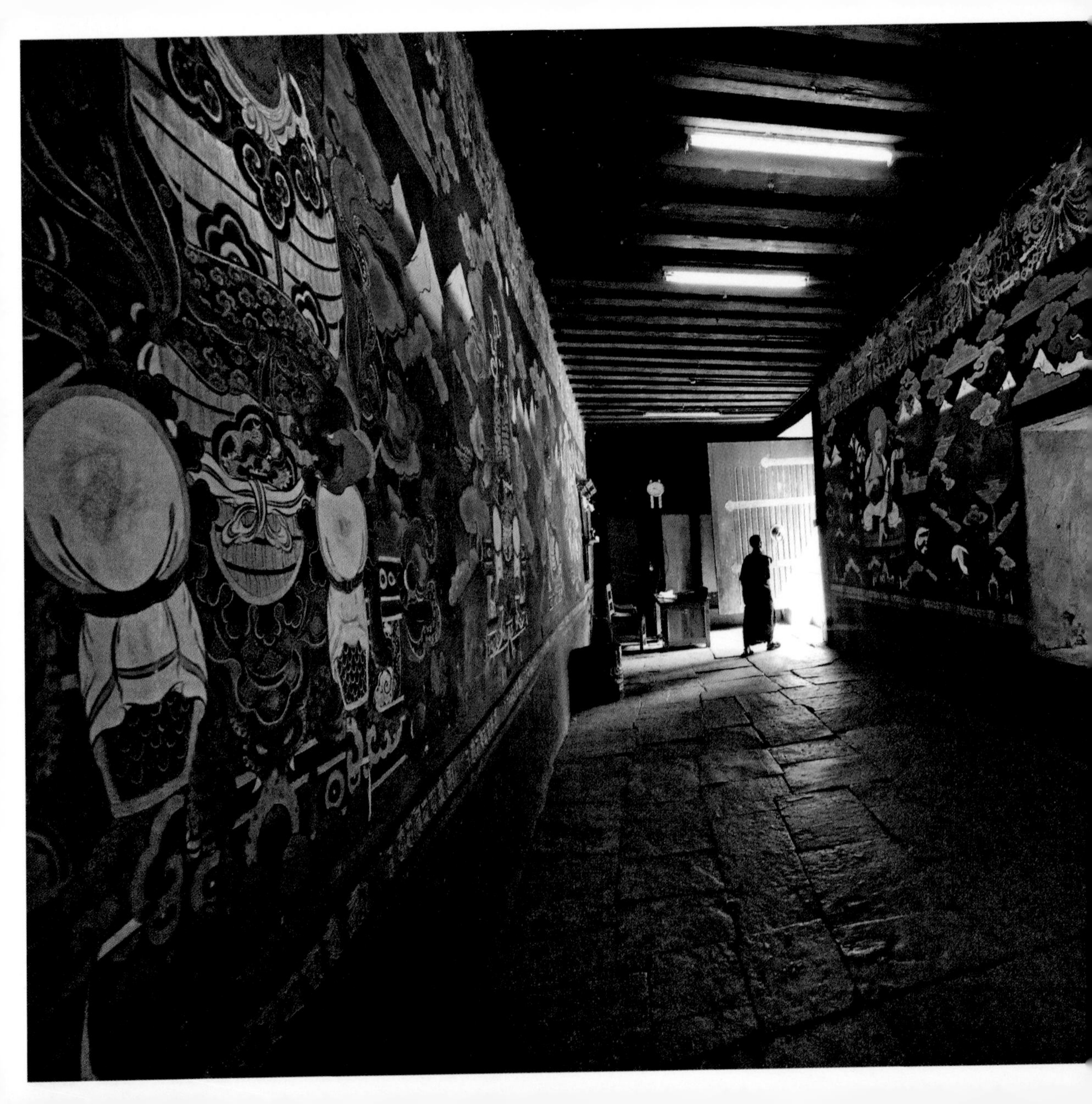

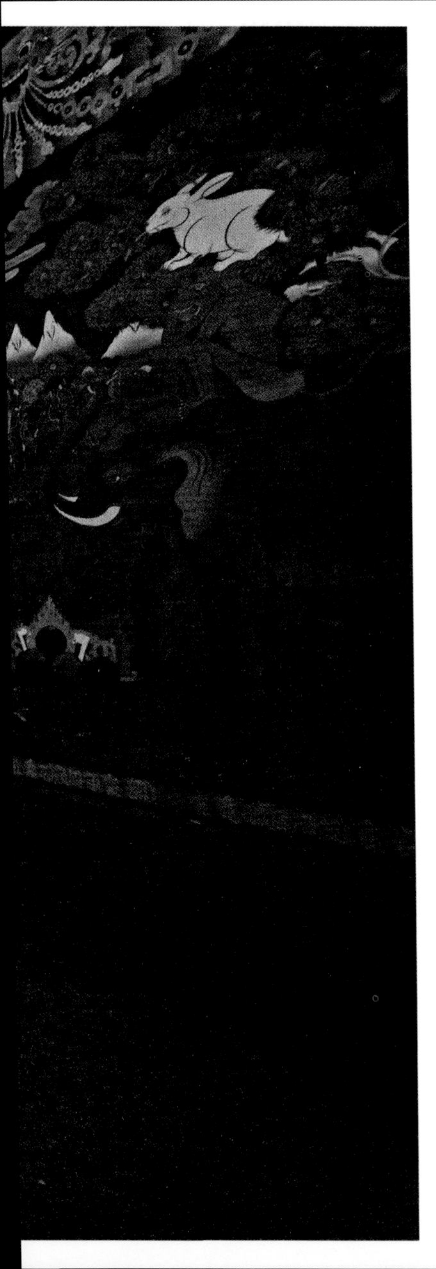

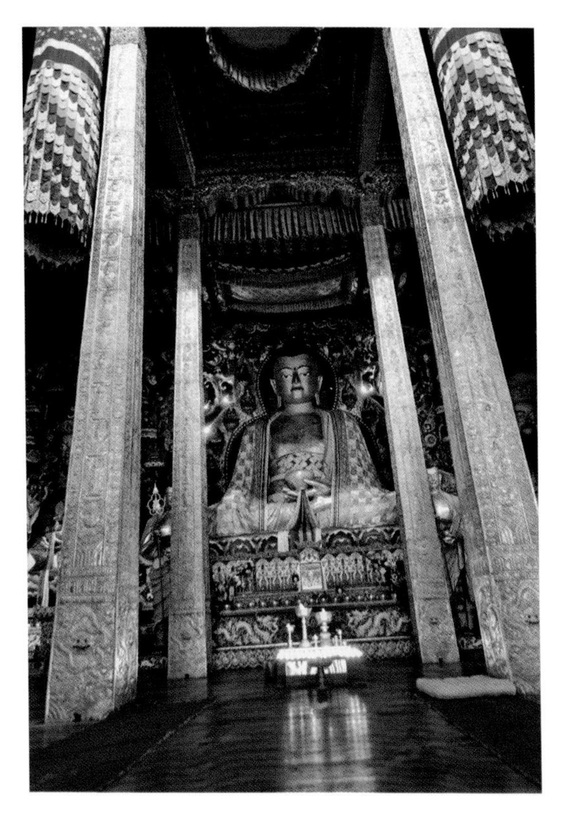

A monumental statue of Buddha Shakyamuni in Punakha monastery's main temple. This sculpture is painted with real gold and was erected during the recent restoration of the *dzong* following the 1996 fire.

The dark corridors at the entrance to Paro Dzong are decorated with brightly coloured wall paintings. 2007.

Overleaf
Paro's monumental *dzong* seen at dusk, 2007.

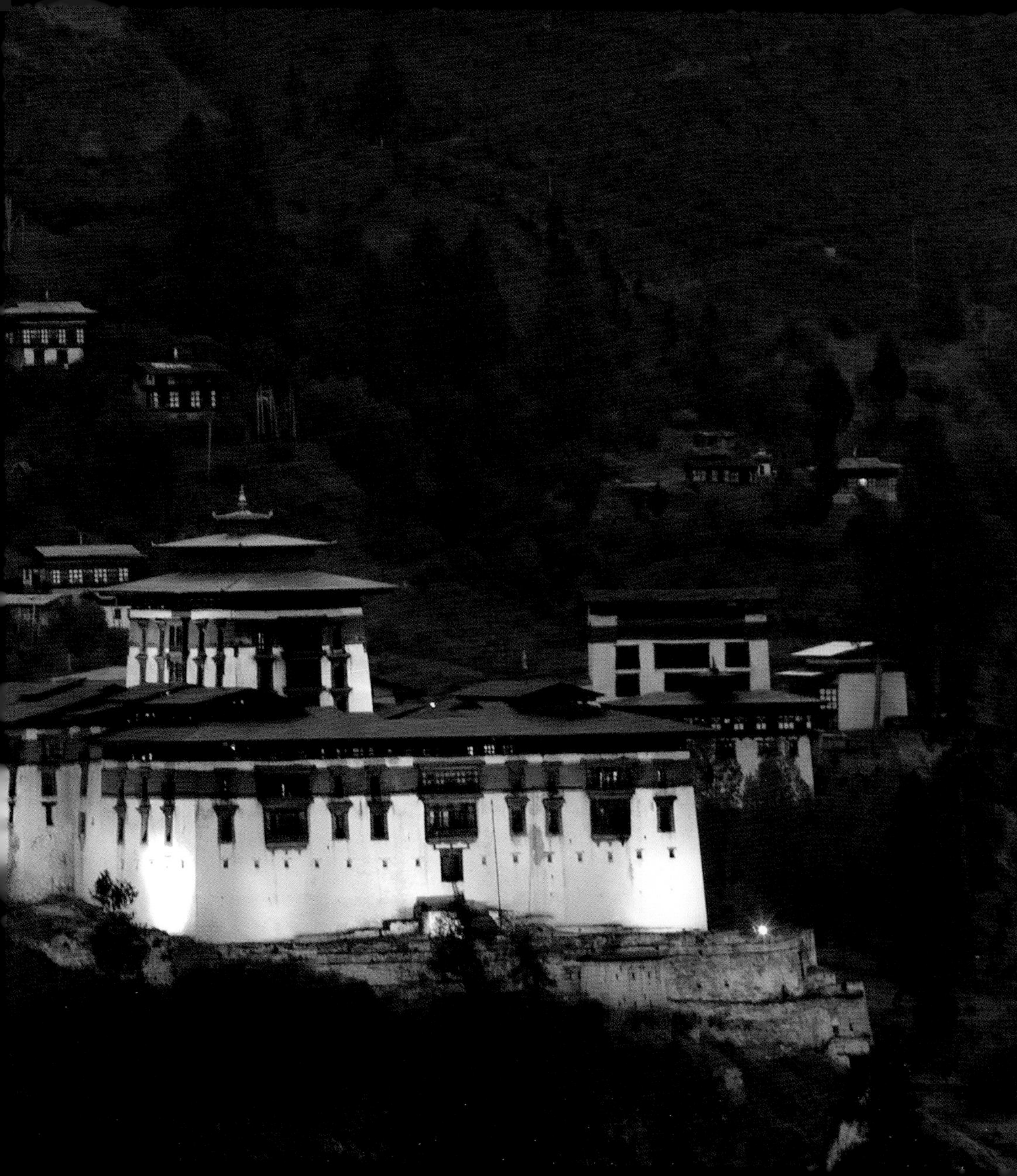

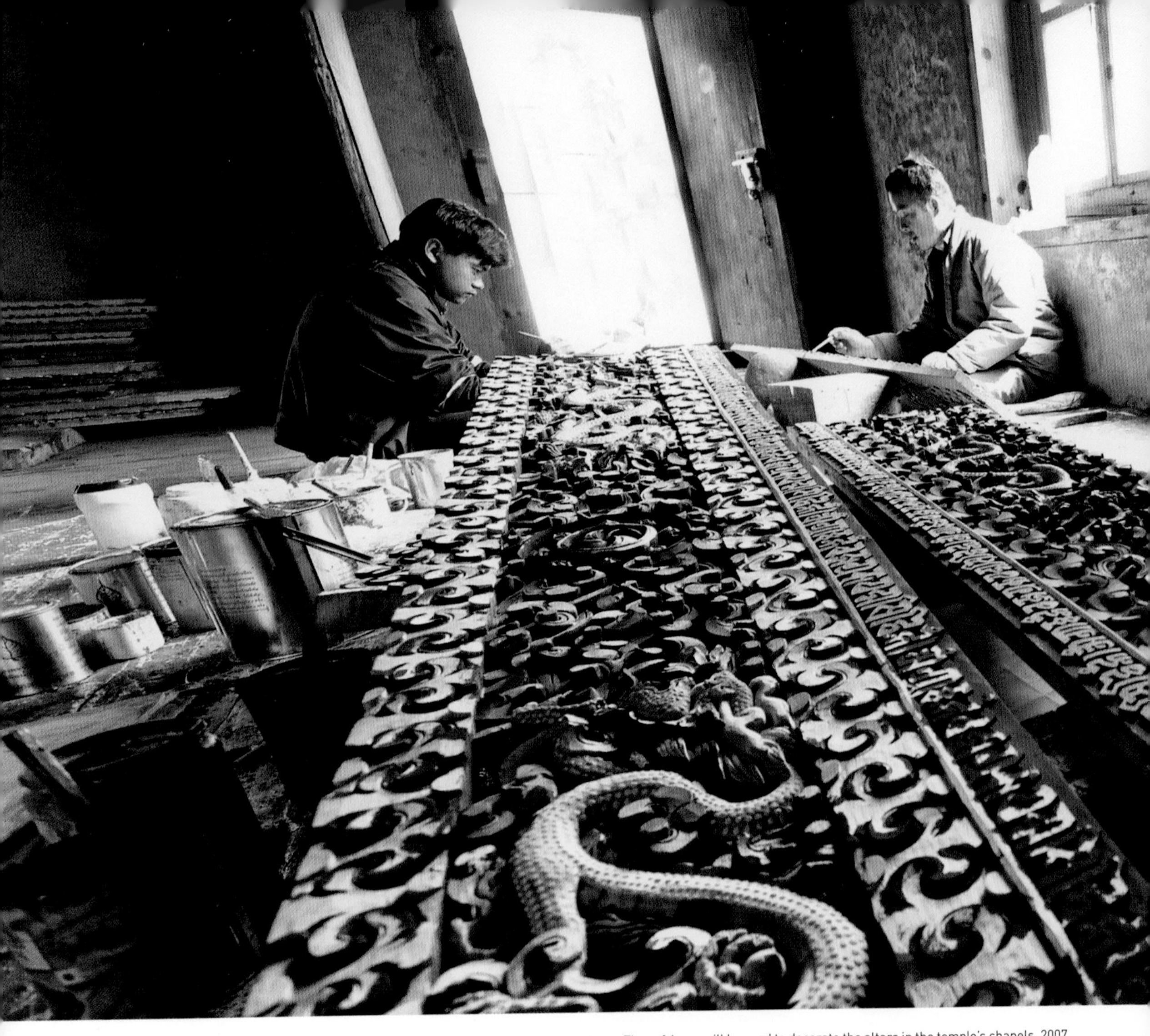

Artisans painting carved wooden friezes in the new temple of Sandokpalri, near Kuje, Bumthang. These friezes will be used to decorate the altars in the temple's chapels. 2007.

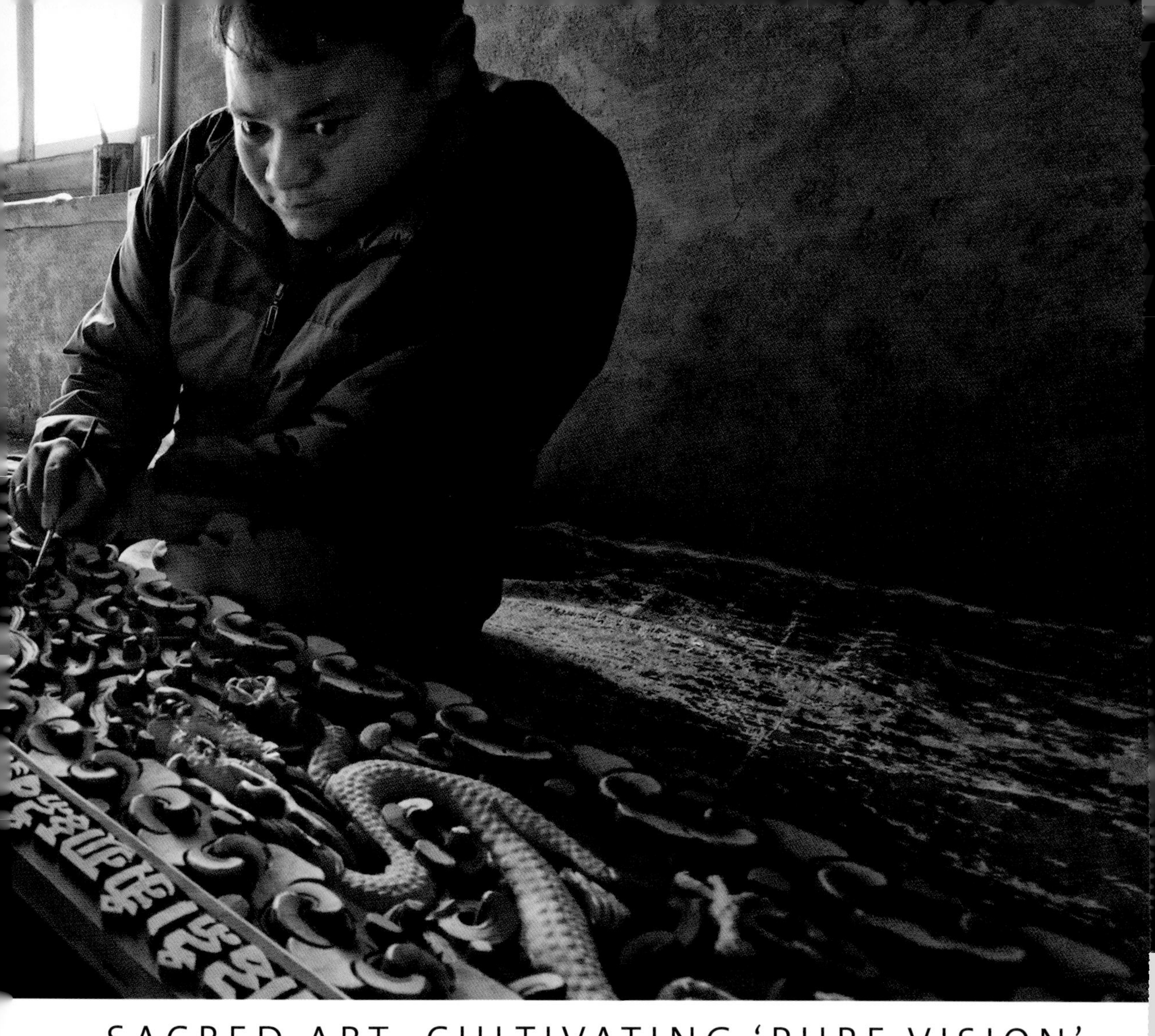

SACRED ART: CULTIVATING 'PURE VISION'

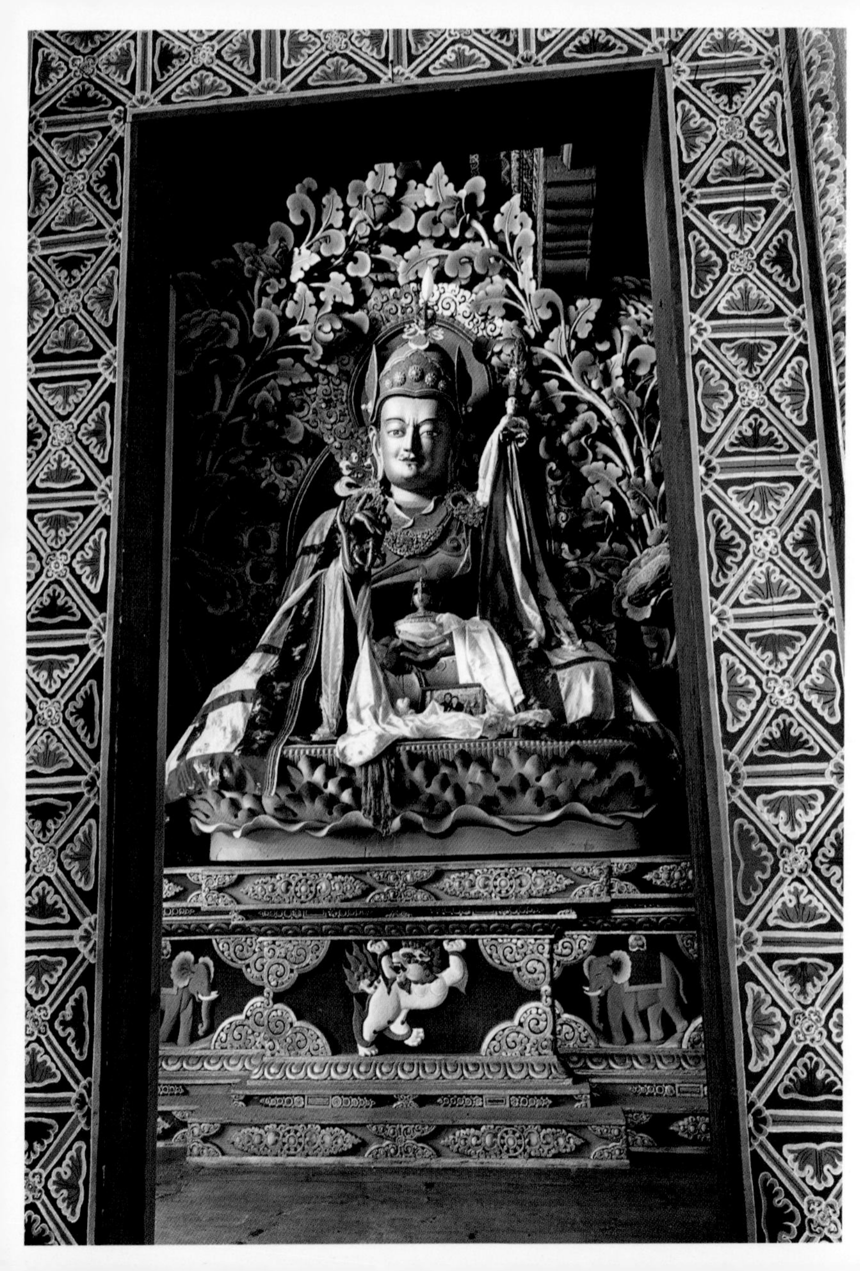

Statue of Padmasambhava in the temple of Phurba Lhakhang, Satsam Chörten, Paro, 2007.

Sacred Art

Cultivating 'Pure Vision'

Although the purpose of art is often to create an imaginary world, Buddhist art helps us to penetrate the nature of reality and bridge the gap between the contemplative life and the active life. It is not merely an illustration of symbols or ideas; it is a direct experience of inner peace, free from attachment to the illusory reality of the ego and of the world of phenomena. Rather than stirring the passions, it calms them. The painter, for example, establishes a correspondence between forms, symbols and an awareness of the spiritual path. The musician links the universe of sounds to the resonance of prayer and mantra. The contemplative writer and poet teach us the essential truth of non-attachment, which unravels the ties of avarice; of discipline, which eschews actions liable to cause suffering; of patience, which tolerates adversity and triumphs over anger; of diligence, which facilitates dedication to practice without distraction; of concentration, which dominates disturbing emotions and mental chatter; and finally the truth of wisdom, which reveals the ultimate nature of reality, united with infinite and unconditional compassion.

Sacred art can be seen, more particularly, as another way of meditating on 'pure vision', in other words the perception of the primordial purity of all phenomena, both animate and inanimate. This perception, or pure vision, is a quality of the Vajrayana, the Diamond Vehicle of Buddhism. It involves recognizing the Buddha-nature present in every being and the 'original purity' of phenomena. The expression 'primordial purity' or 'original purity' signifies that sentient beings and phenomena have no separate existence of their own and no intrinsic properties such as permanence, beauty, ugliness, pleasantness, unpleasantness, and so on. The Buddha taught that every being is imbued with the essence of Buddha-nature, just as a sesame seed is pervaded with oil. Ignorance is simply being unaware of this fact. We are like a beggar who does not know that a nugget of gold is buried beneath his hut. To follow the path of the Buddha is to regain possession of that lost treasure.

PAINTING AND SCULPTURE

Thangka and wall paintings are central to Bhutanese art. *Thangka* are painted on specially coated cloth canvases that are hung by cords from a wooden frame. Natural pigments are generally used and these are mixed with water and glue and applied like tempera. The appearance of the various deities is determined by precise iconographic rules and the proportions of the image are governed by a 'grid', which varies from one deity to another. Despite these restrictions, there is plenty of scope for individual artistic expression: the general style of the picture, the background and the subtle differences in terms of posture and expression are all opportunities for a painter to make his particular mark. The finished painting is then framed by brightly coloured brocade borders.

Bhutanese statues are almost always made of clay mixed with what is sometimes called 'rice paper' (but is in fact made from fibres extracted from the bark of two different shrubs, *Daphne* and *Edgeworthia*) for a more dense texture. These statues are hollow and carefully filled with the relics of spiritual teachers and small rolls of paper printed with prayers and mantras. The finished statues are painted and the face (in some cases, the entire statue) is covered in a fine layer of gold paint. Each area of the Himalayas has its particular sculptural expertise: Bhutanese craftsmen are regarded as the best sculptors in clay; the Nepalese have perfected the technique of bronze casting using the lost wax method, and the Tibetans excel in beaten copper work.

There is a complex symbolism associated with the many deities represented on temple *thangka* and wall paintings, and altar statues. Padmasambhava, the Lotus-Born, wears nine garments representing the nine *yana*, or vehicles, of Buddhist teaching. His face represents the one ultimate truth; his two arms symbolize the union of wisdom and compassion, and his two legs represent the sameness of samsara and nirvana in ultimate reality. His eyes are wide open and gaze straight ahead into space, indicating that he is always aware of the absolute nature. He sits in the posture called 'royal ease', his right leg slightly extended and his left bent, signifying that all the worlds of samsara are obliged to follow his instructions, which are those of the king of wisdom. His right hand holds a five-pointed *vajra*, symbol of the transmutation of the Five Poisons – desire, hatred, ignorance, jealousy and pride – into the Five Wisdoms. In the palm of his left hand, which rests in his lap in the gesture of equanimity, he holds a skull filled with nectar, surmounted by the vase of immortality, symbolizing that the wisdom of Padmasambhava is beyond birth and death. His yellow monastic robe symbolizes mastery of the Fundamental Vehicle; the blue robe symbolizes mastery of the Great Vehicle, the way of the bodhisattvas; and the brocade cape symbolizes mastery of the secret teachings of the Diamond Vehicle.

Padmasambhava wears a lotus hat whose five petals represent the five Buddha families (Buddha, Vajra, Ratna, Padma and Karma). On the crown of the hat are a sun and a moon, symbols of means and of wisdom and topped by a white vulture's feather, which represents the ultimate view of Great Perfection. In the crook of his left arm, he holds a trident, or *khatvanga*, whose three prongs symbolize the empty nature of all things; its expression is clear light, and its nature is omnipresent compassion. Padmasambhava has no tangible, material body, made of flesh and blood and bones, but a body of light, clear and translucent like a rainbow radiating in the ten directions of space.

SACRED MUSIC

Music and song play an important part in Buddhist rituals. Playing music is an apprenticeship in 'pure vision' in which all sounds are perceived as mantras whose ultimate nature is emptiness. In this sense, sacred music is a form of aural liberation and contributes to the process of spiritual elevation.

The dull, muffled sound of the great drums provides a counterpoint to the bright tone of the cymbals, which play a key role in the structuring of musical rhythms, and accompany singing, chanting and ritual dances. At intervals in the ritual, other instruments are introduced: the *dungchen*, a spectacular telescopic metal trumpet three to four metres long, and the *gyaling*, a reed instrument similar to an oboe.

All the schools of Himalayan Buddhism rely on musical instruments, and each of these has symbolic significance. The bell and the small drum, for example, express the union of wisdom and means, corresponding respectively to the understanding of emptiness and compassion.

HANDICRAFTS

An important aspect of the various crafts and art forms practised in Bhutan is that they enjoy the patronage and support of all classes of society, from the king and the monasteries to the simplest peasant who commissions a little wooden or painted clay Buddha. Bhutanese tradition distinguishes thirteen artistic categories, including woodcarving and weaving, *thangka* painting, sculpting in stone or clay, metal casting, goldsmithing, masonry, leather work and embroidery. The Zorig Chusum, or 'Thirteen Arts and Crafts School', in Thimphu, was set up by the government to provide training for hundreds of young apprentices, both male and female, in these various crafts under the direction of experienced masters.

TEXTILE ART

Textile art is the one craft from those thirteen that is exclusively practised by women, and Bhutanese skill in this field is unrivalled throughout the Himalayas. Textiles play an important social role in Bhutan: they are elements of a strict social code and until the late 1950s served as a form of currency. The weavers of the north-eastern districts (Lhuntse, Tashigang and Bumthang) are especially renowned for the quality and complexity of their silks and cottons. In addition to traditional garments like the *kira*, a long band of cloth draped around the body and worn by women, and the *go*, a full knee-length tunic that fastens at the waist and is worn by men, they also weave rich brocades for use in the monasteries. The complexity of the designs and the number of colours employed demonstrate the quality of the workmanship and also the social status of the wearer. Over their *go* and their *kira*, men and women wear a ceremonial scarf, a compulsory item of clothing when going to the *dzong* or attending major religious ceremonies. There are strict rules (which are still obeyed today) governing the colour and the width of the scarf, and also the embroidered designs. Men wear a broad white scarf over their *go* and women wear a red narrow scarf magnificently woven or embroidered with complex patterns in a range of shimmering colours. Provincial governors, the *dzongdag*, and other officials wear a long scarf made from raw silk in varying colours depending on their rank, with a large sword in a crafted silver sheath attached to their belt.

The bright colours used in the various types of weaving are obtained from natural pigments – red from madder roots and blue from indigo, for example – although chemical dyes from India are now coming to replace their vegetable equivalents. Bhutanese textiles (which are found as far afield as Ladakh) used to be exchanged for carpets in Tibet and until 1959 were one of the main products used in commercial exchanges, alongside rice, medicinal plants and paper. The principal motifs used in Bhutanese weaving are also to be found, with variants, in Arunachal Pradesh and Burma and as far away as Laos.

Detail of a *thangka* showing Padmasambhava initiating his principal disciples in the Chimphu cave, above Samye – the first such initiation in Tibet. Next to him is the mandala of the 'Eight Herukas'.

Overleaf:

Some of the founding masters of the Nyingma school, the most ancient Buddhist tradition in Tibet and Bhutan. From left to right: Jampel Shenyen (Manjushri Mitra in Sanskrit), Padmasambhava, Yeshe Tsogyal (Queen of Tibet and Padmasambhava's main disciple) and the great Bhutanese master Pema Lingpa.

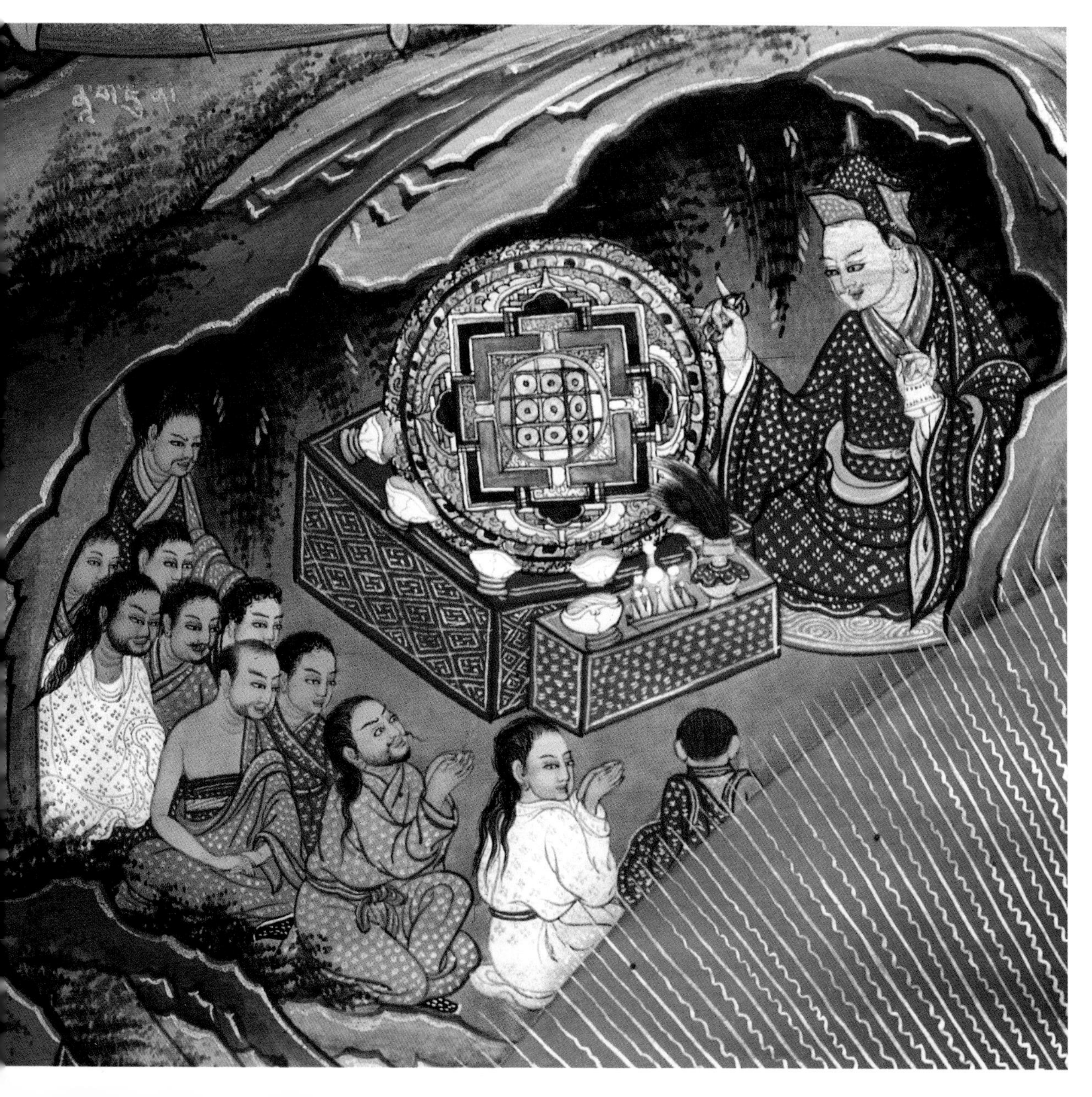

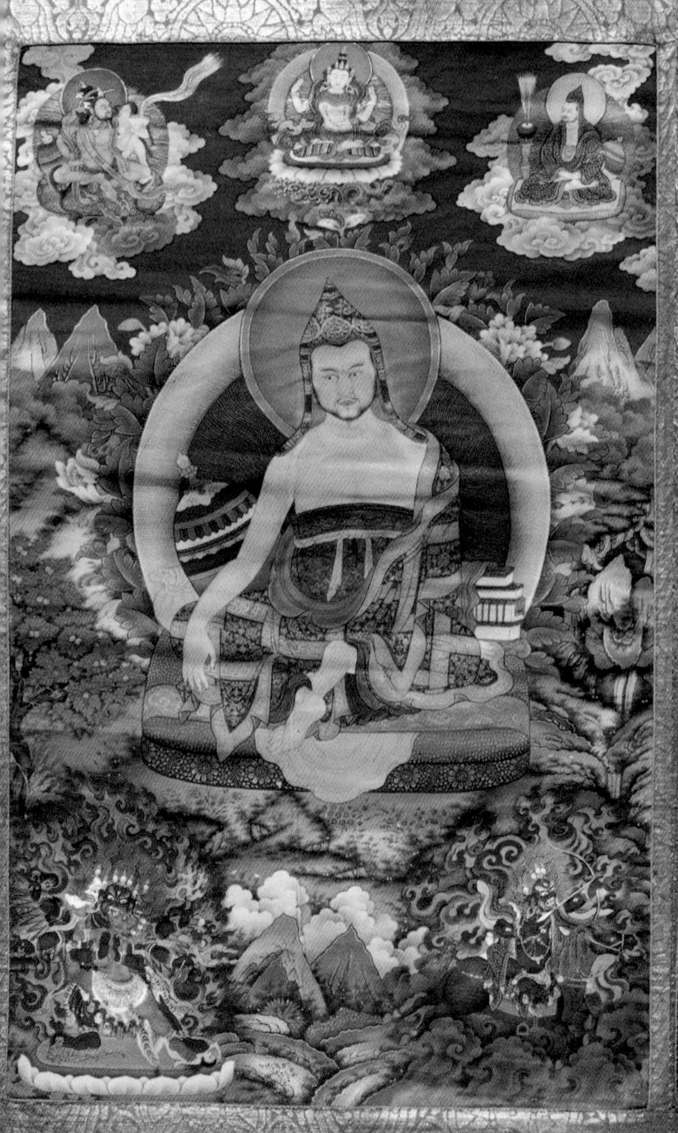

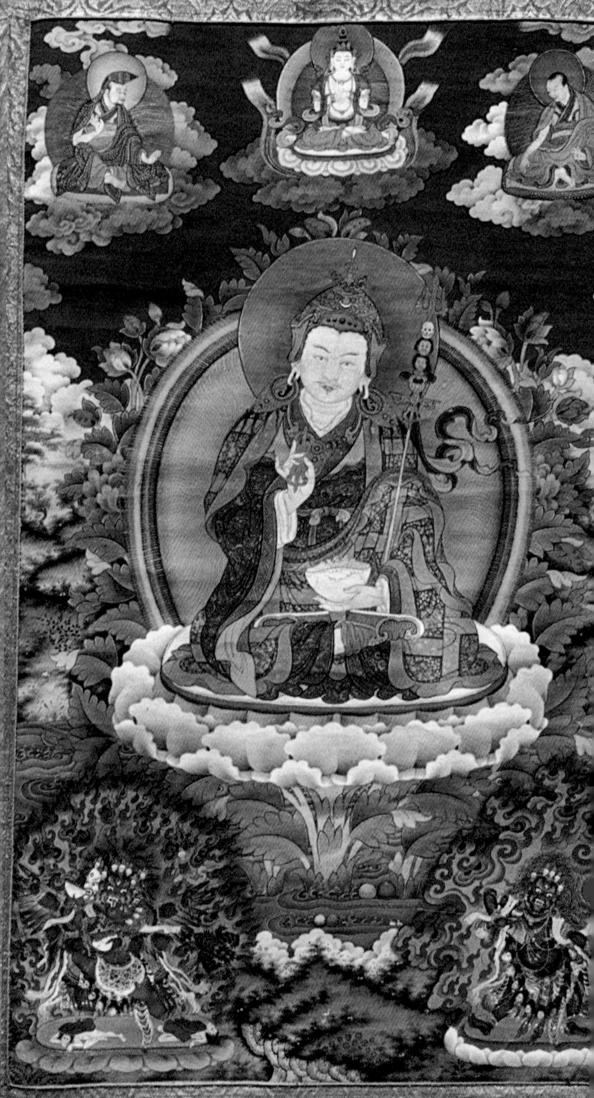

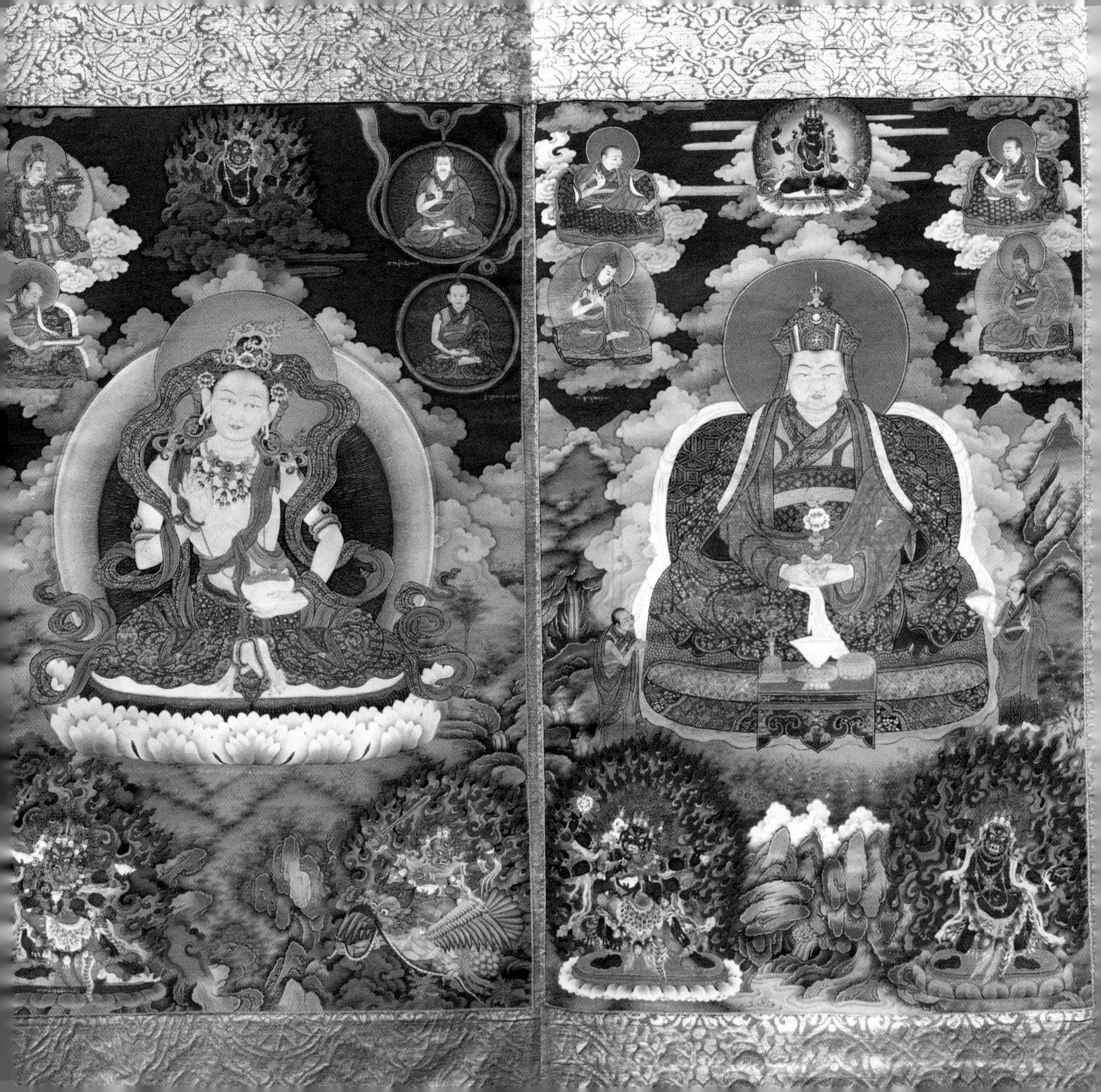

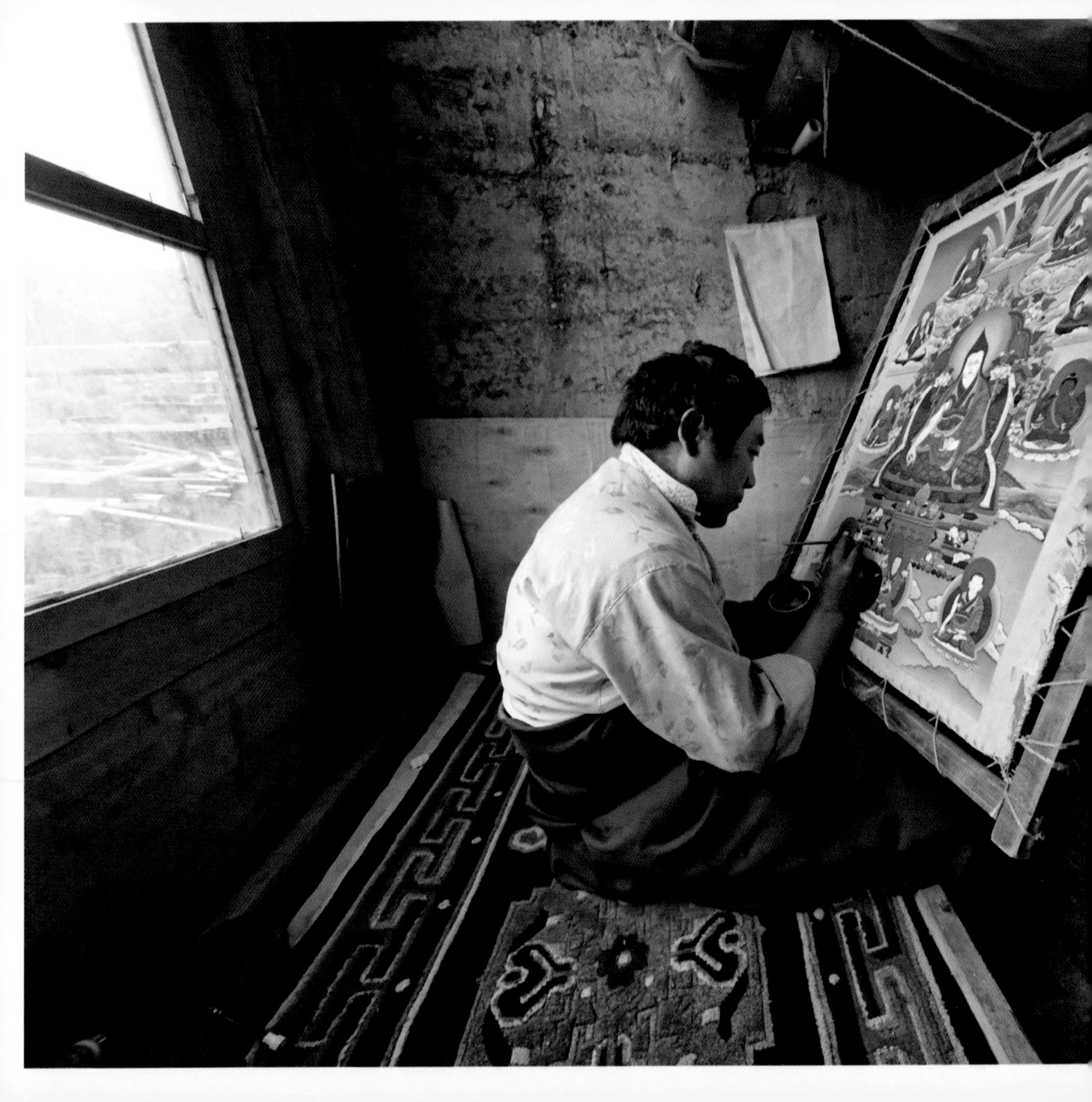

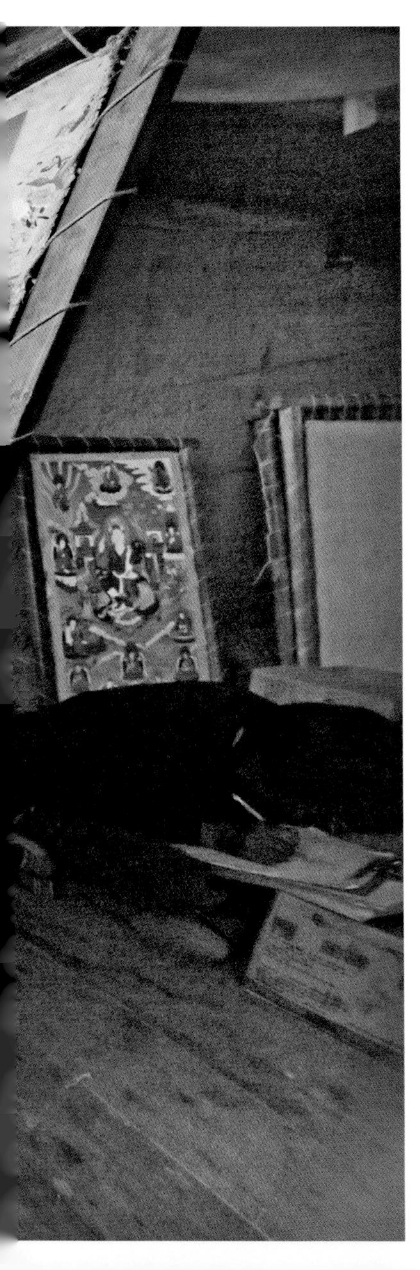

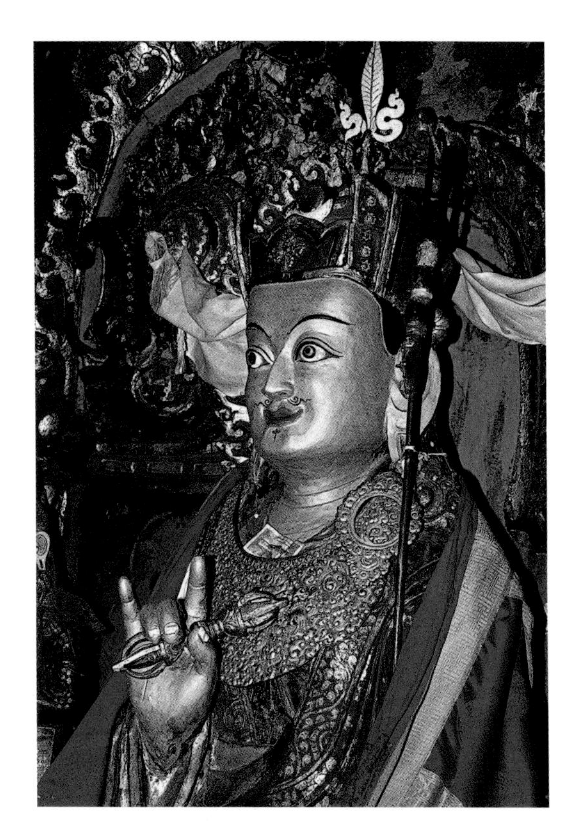

Statue of Guru Padmasambhava sculpted, partly in clay, by the famous Bhutanese visionary master Pema Lingpa (1450–1521). Tamchin monastery, Bumthang province. 1983.

A *thangka* painter from Dzongsar monastery in Tibet, working on a painting showing the spiritual lineage of Khyentse Wangpo, Dilgo Khyentse Rinpoche's predecessor. 2007.

Overleaf:
The first four of Guru Padmasambhava's 'Eight Manifestations'. From left to right: Padmasambhava, Tsokye Dorje, Loden Choksey and Pema Gyalpo.

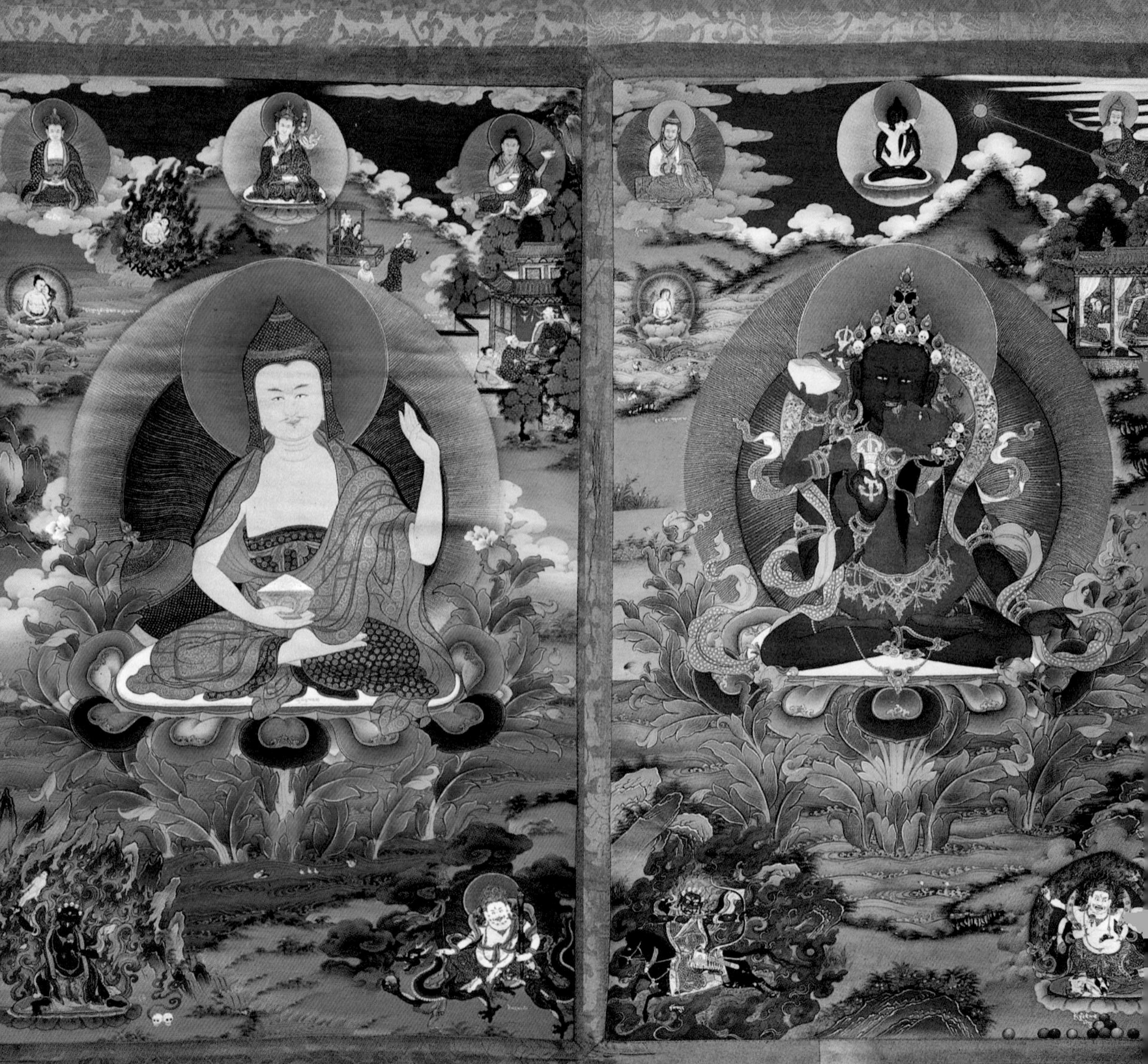
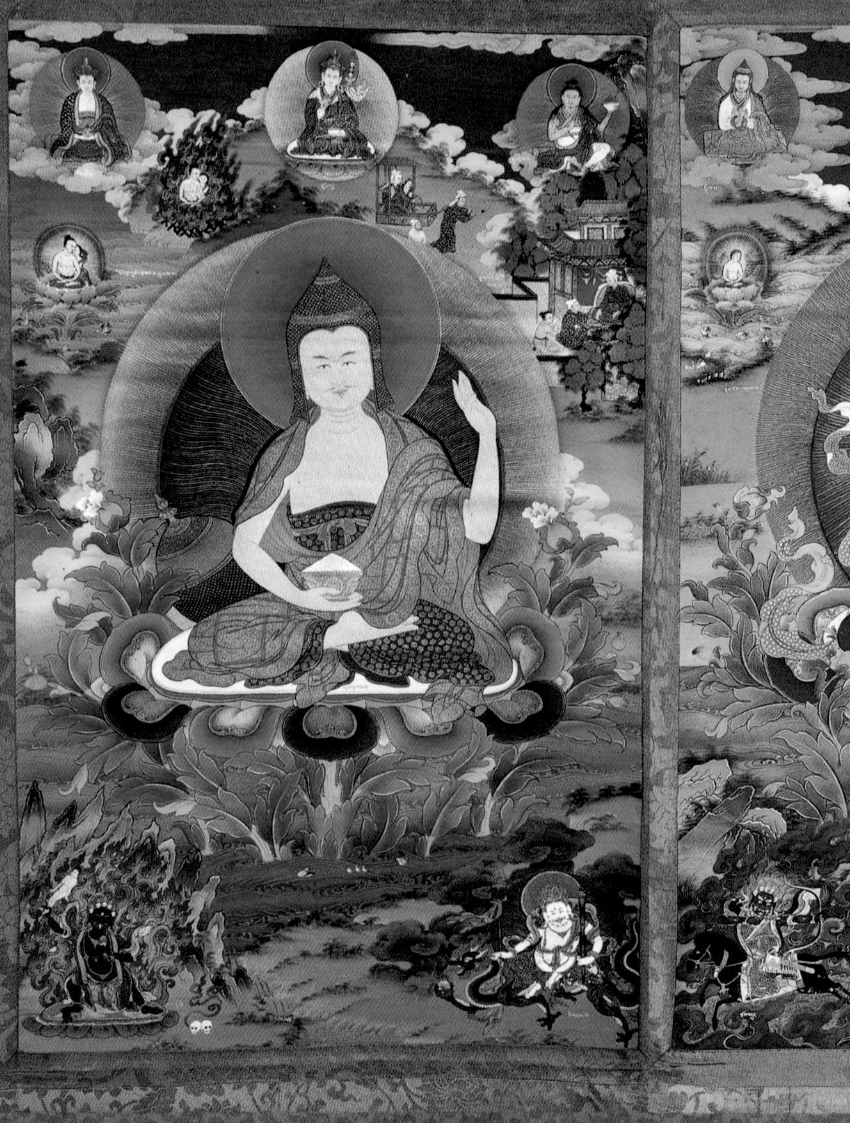

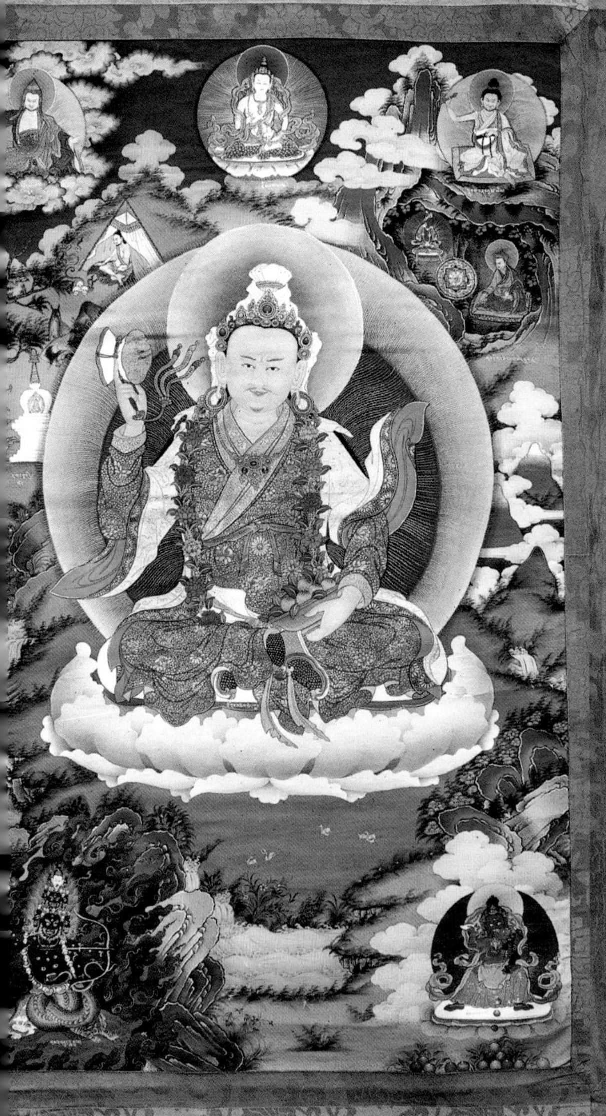
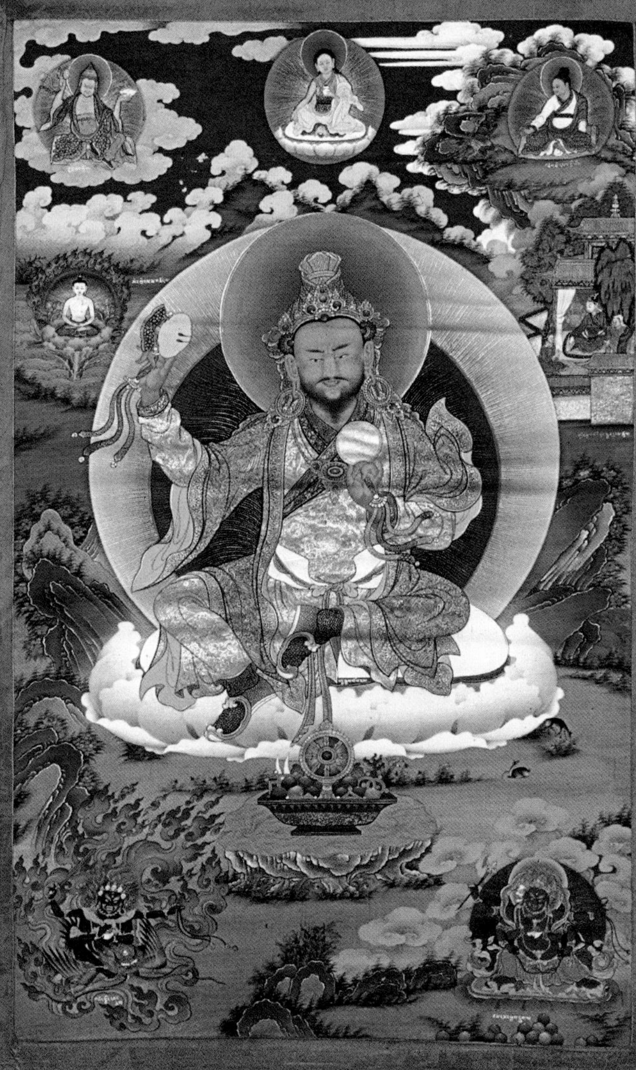

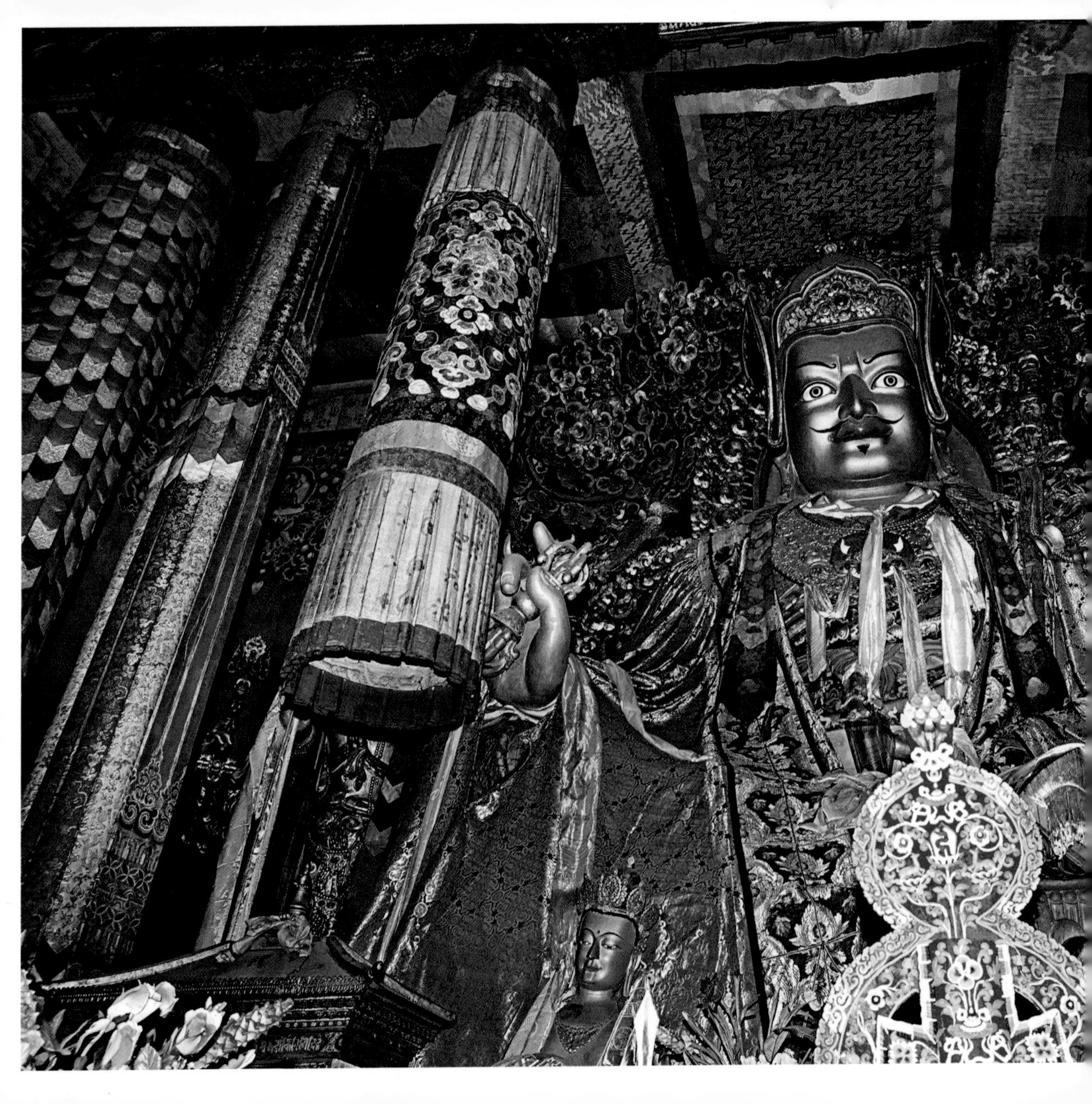

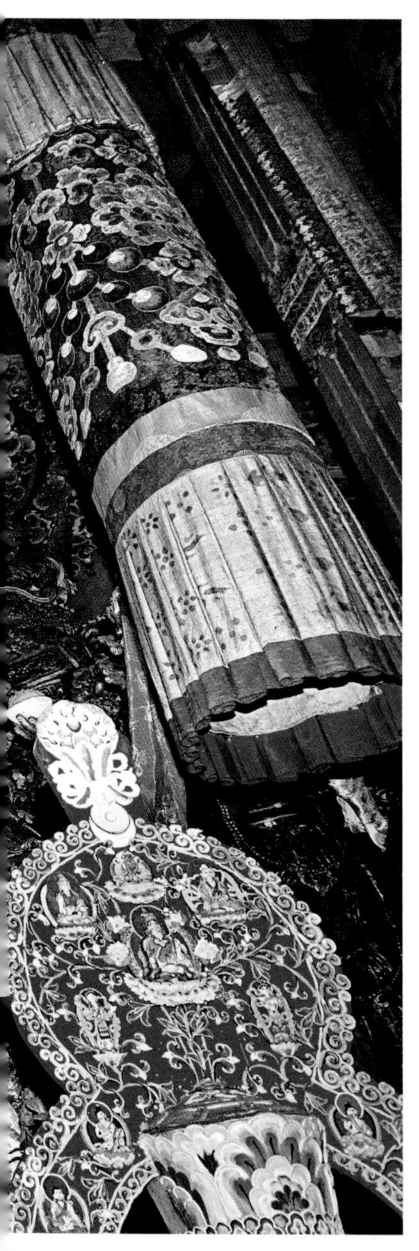

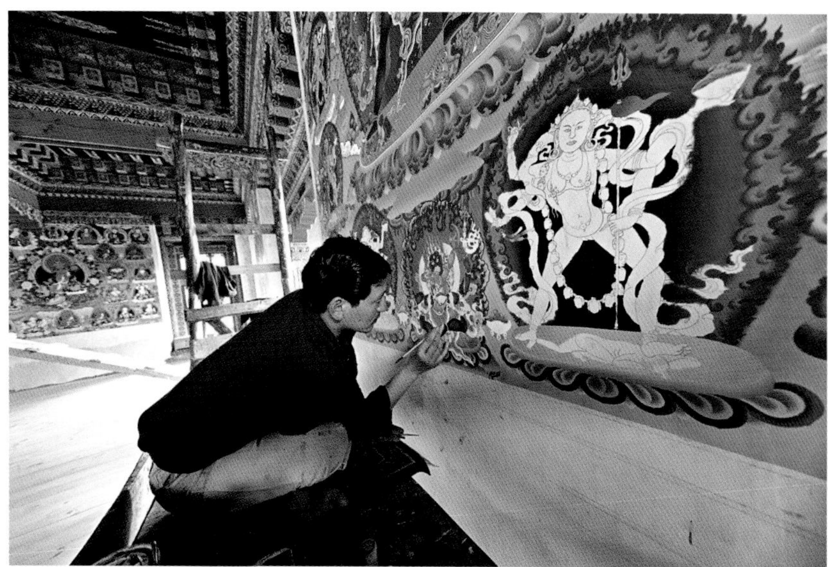

An artist working on a wall painting in the new temple of Sandokpalri, 'the Glorious Copper Coloured Mountain', which was completed in 2008 near Kuje temple in Bumthang. The temple was built under the patronage of Her Majesty the Queen Mother, Ashe Kesang Choeden Wangchuck, in memory of her mother, Rani Chönyi Dorje, who died at the age of ninety-nine, and its decoration has been entrusted to Bhutan's best artists. 2007.

The monumental statue of Guru Padmasambhava, three storeys high, in a chapel at Kuje temple-monastery. Bumthang province, 2006.

Overleaf:
Four of the 'Eight Manifestations' of Guru Padmasambhava. From left to right: Sakya Sengye, Nyima Öser, Senge Dradrok and Dorje Drollö.

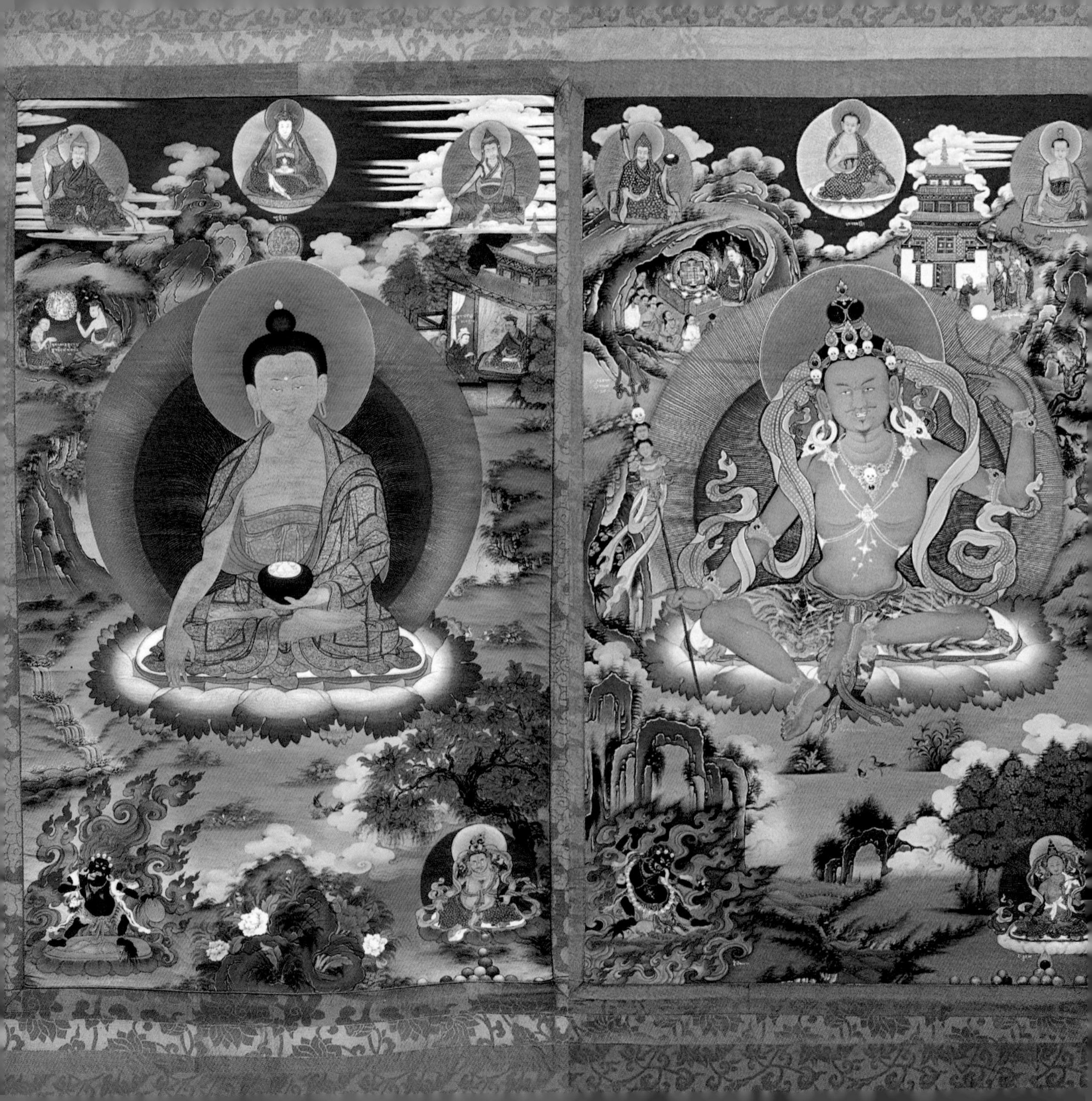

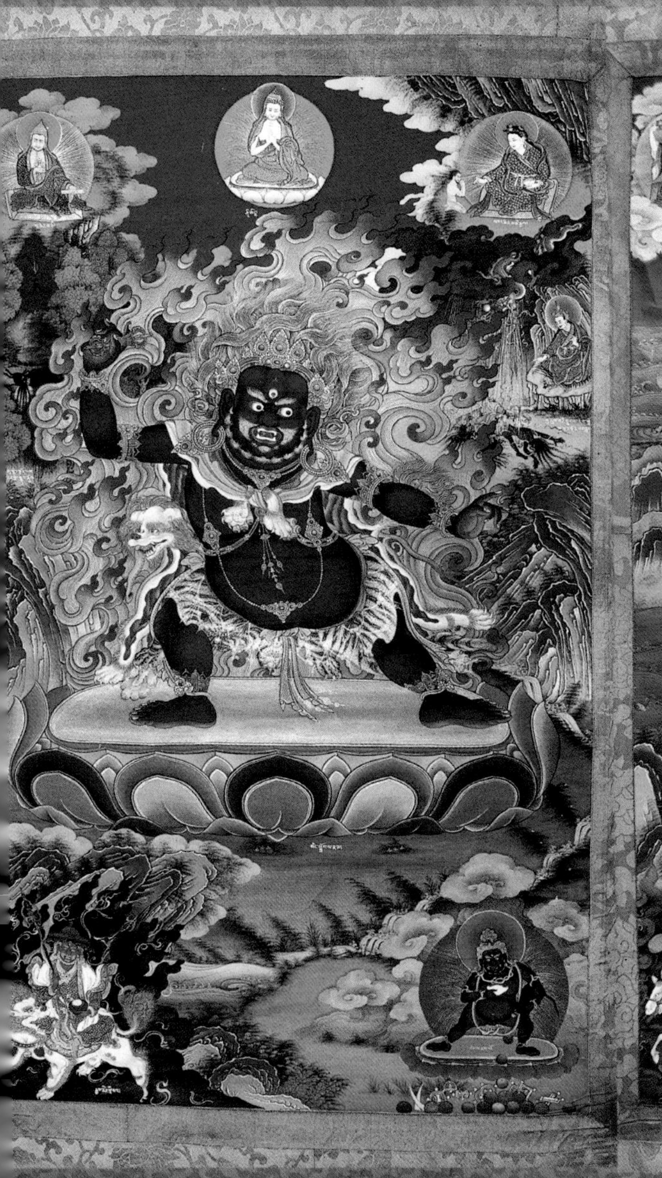
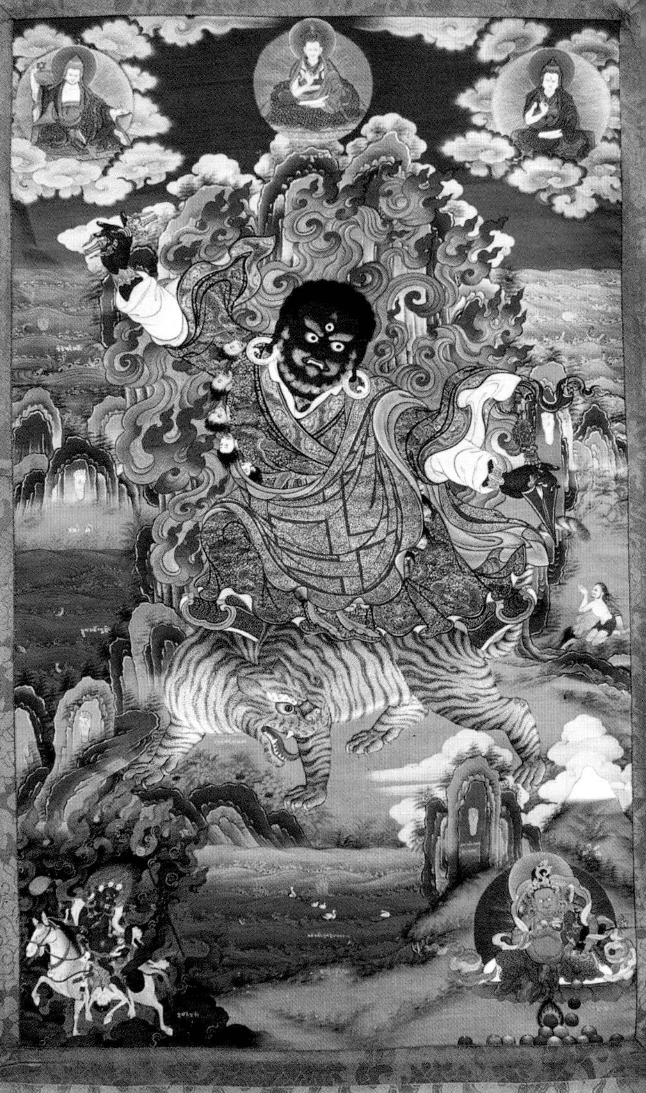

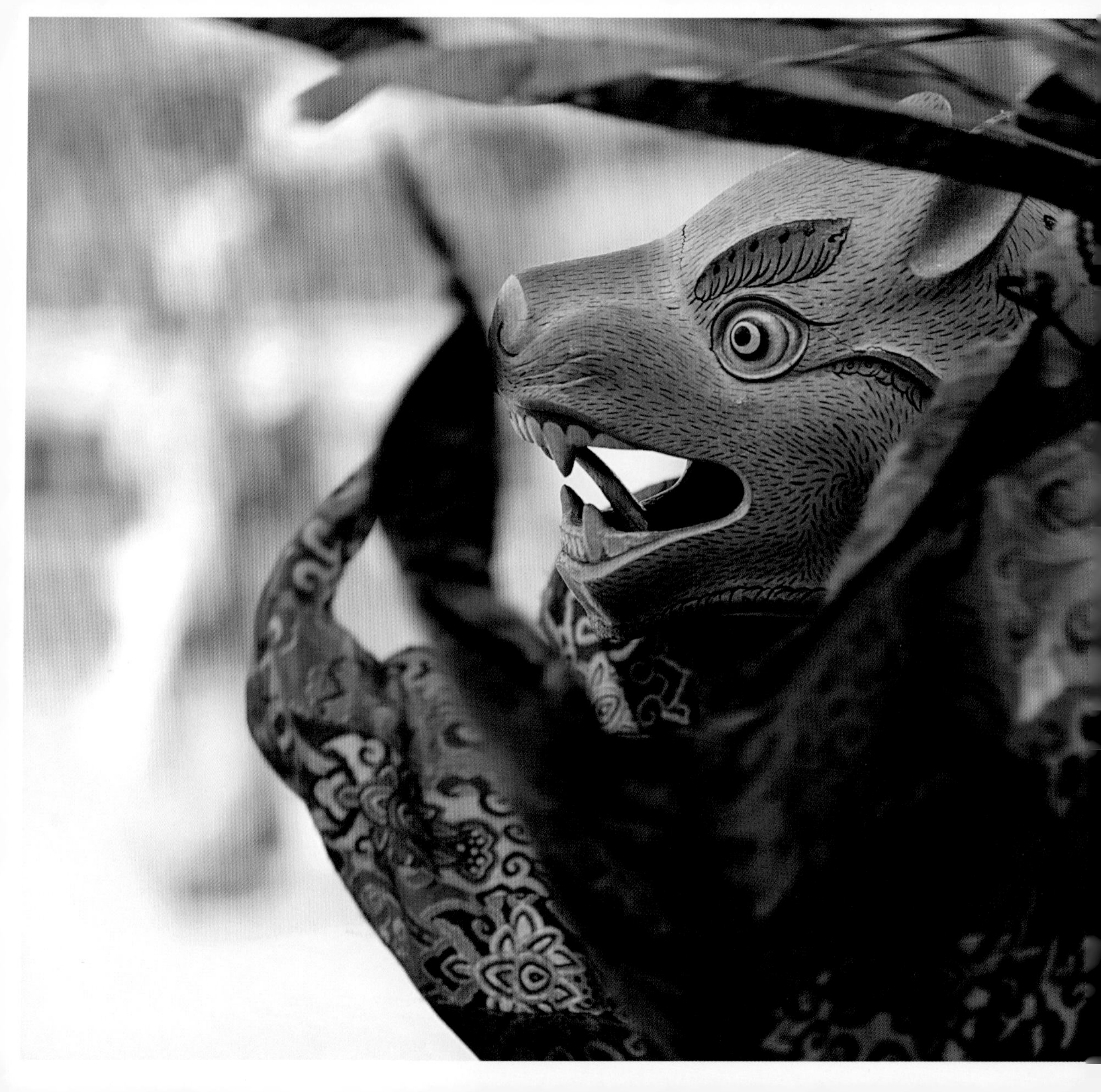

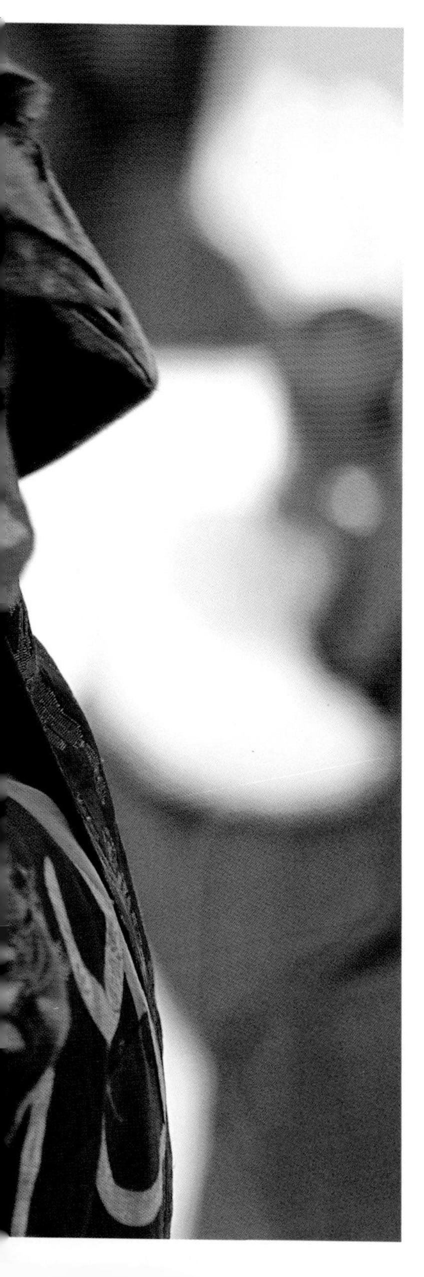

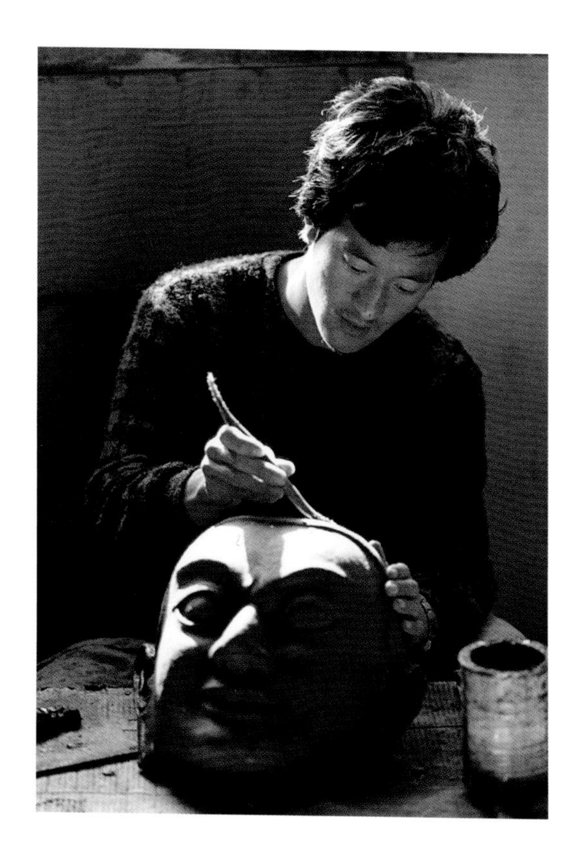

Left and above:
Bhutanese sculptors are among the most skilful makers of masks used during sacred dances. The finest masks are made from several layers of glued fabric applied over a shaped clay mould. When the mask is dry, the mould is withdrawn and the features are refined and accentuated with iron spatulas, heated until they are red hot. Then the mask is painted, and hair or ornaments are sometimes added.

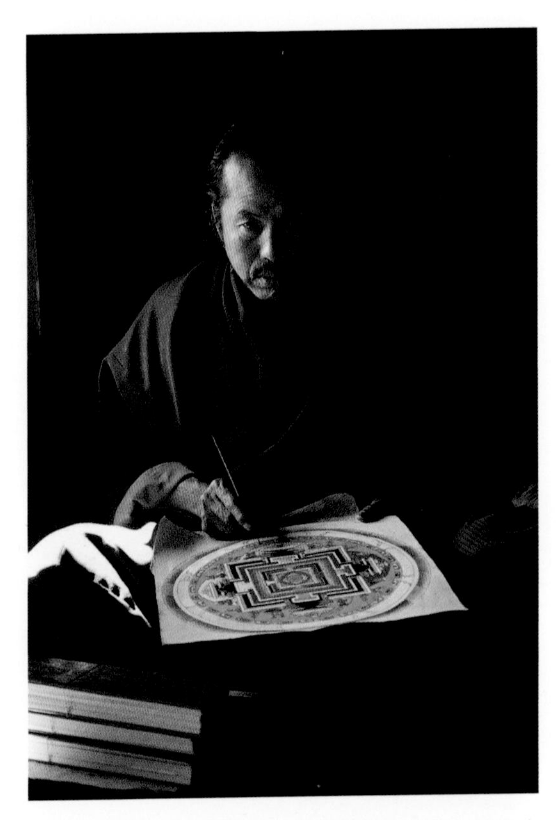

This Bhutanese hermit spends most of his time living in seclusion. Here, he is painting a mandala for a fellow practitioner. Bhutan, 1983.

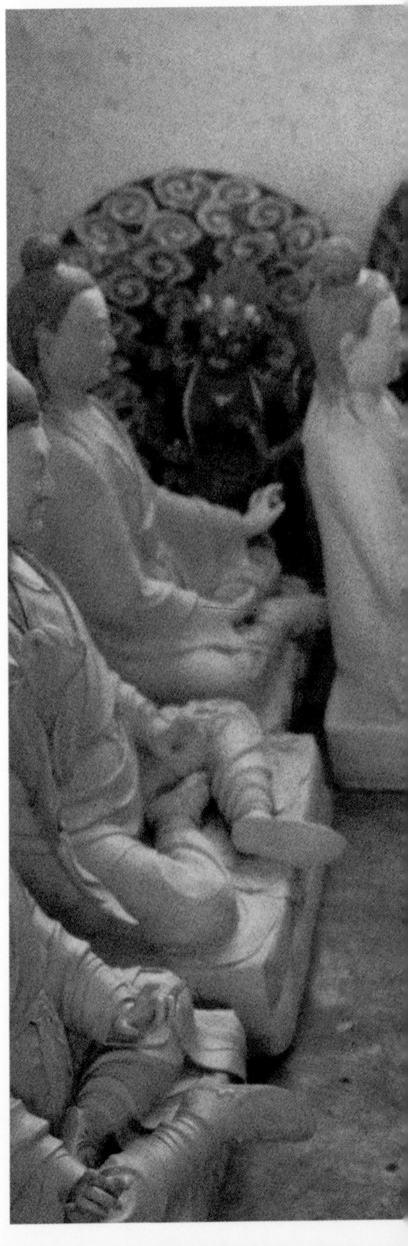

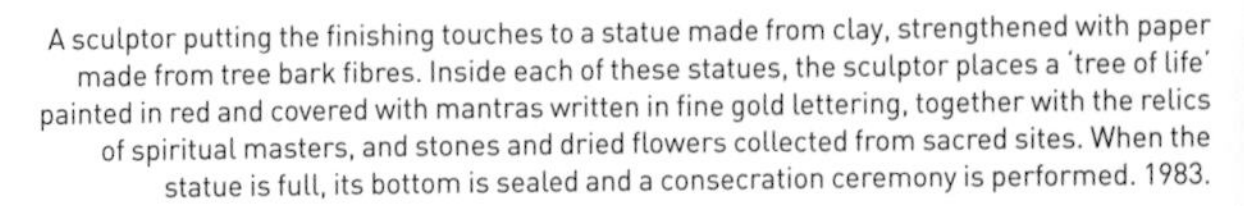

A sculptor putting the finishing touches to a statue made from clay, strengthened with paper made from tree bark fibres. Inside each of these statues, the sculptor places a 'tree of life' painted in red and covered with mantras written in fine gold lettering, together with the relics of spiritual masters, and stones and dried flowers collected from sacred sites. When the statue is full, its bottom is sealed and a consecration ceremony is performed. 1983.

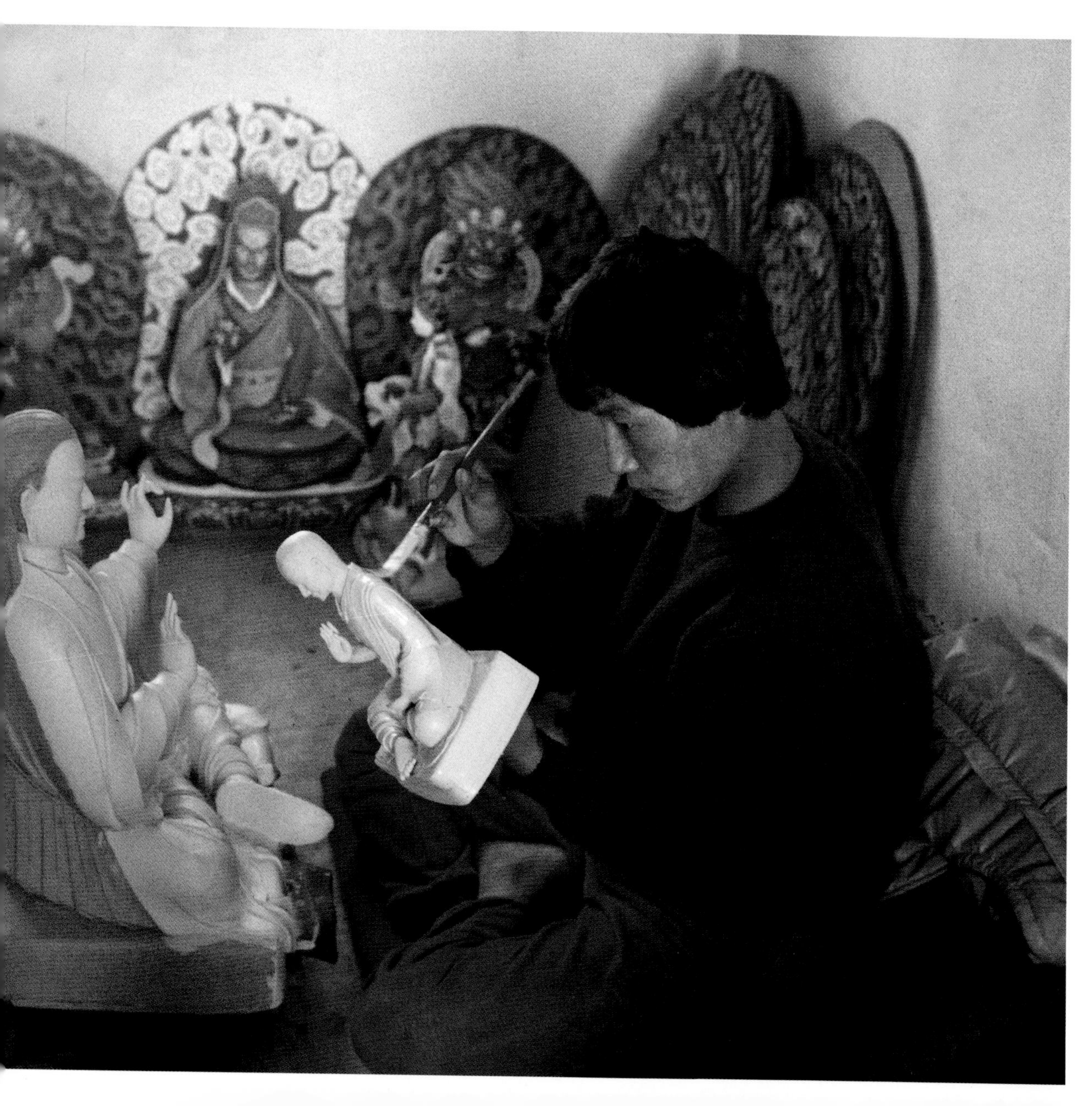

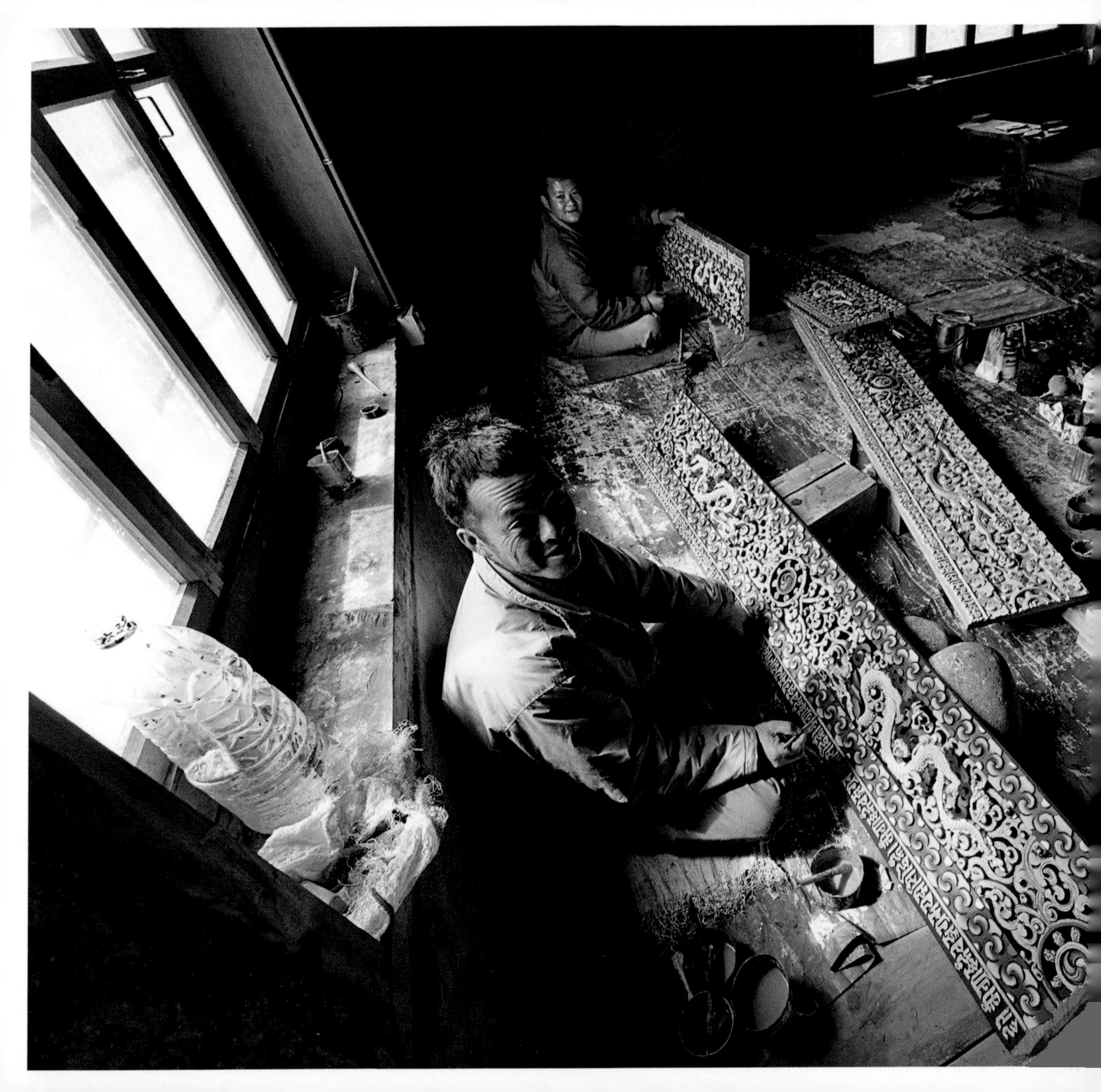

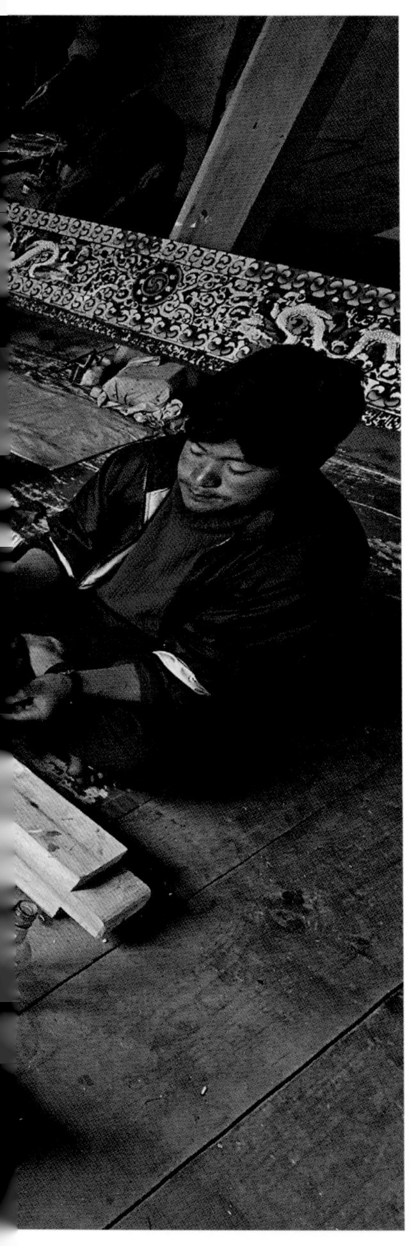

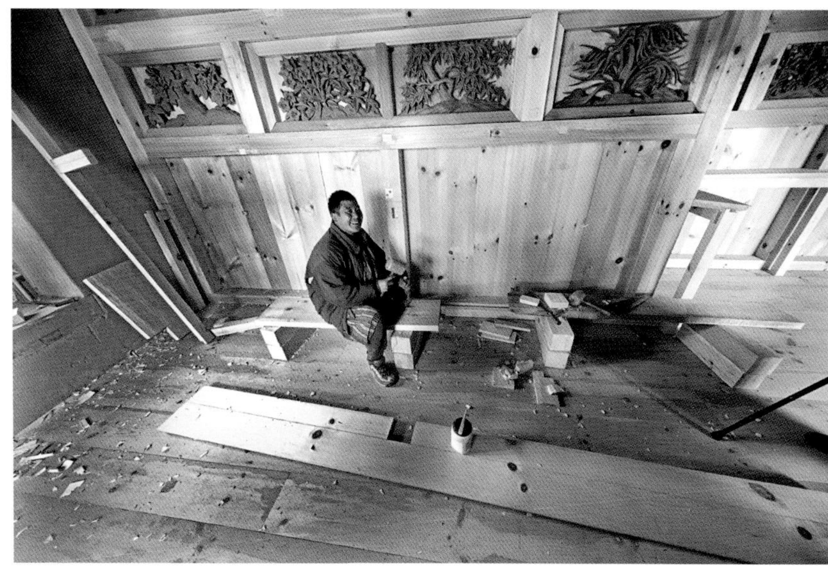

A master cabinet-maker working in the temple of Sandokpalri. 2007.

Carved wooden friezes being painted. These will be used to decorate the chapel altars in Sandokpalri temple, near Kuje, Bumthang. 2007.

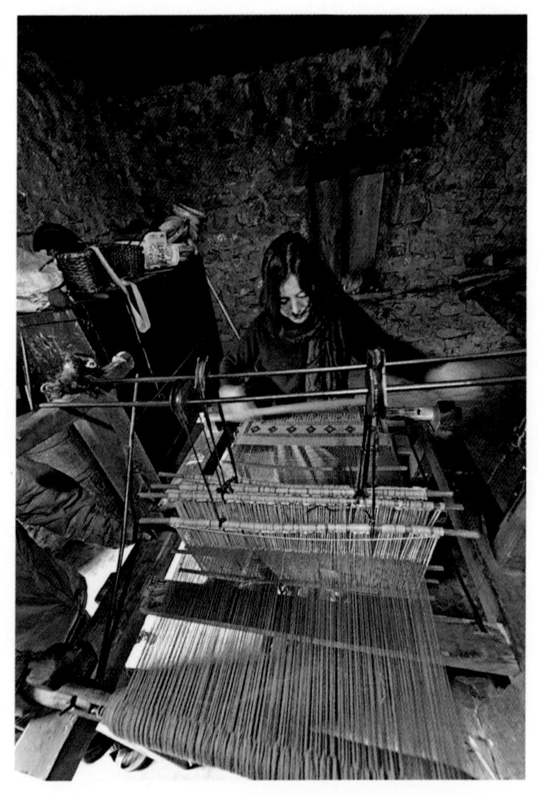

Above and right:
Many women weave in the village of Chumey in Bumthang valley. Weaving is a highly prized craft in this central province of Bhutan, and almost every home here has its own loom. 2007.

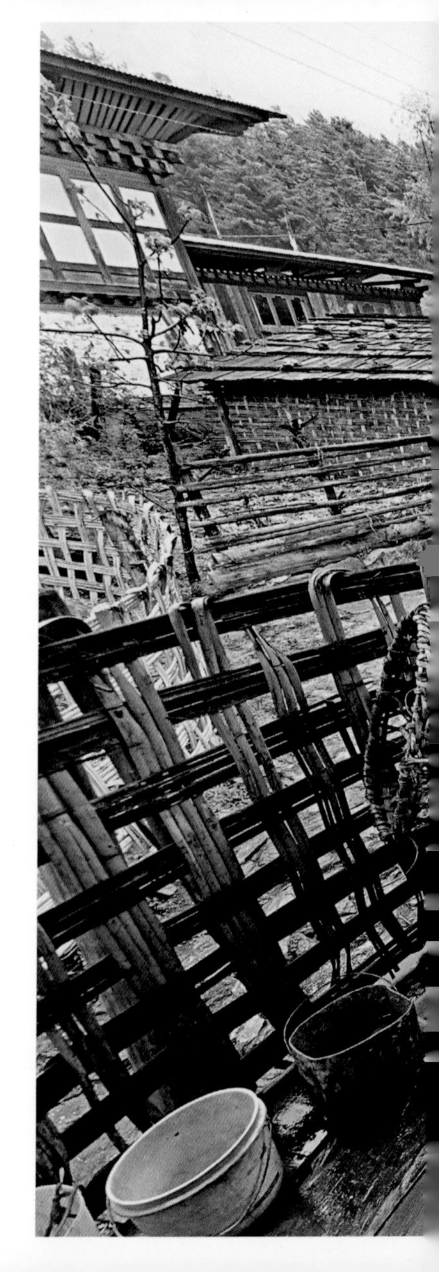

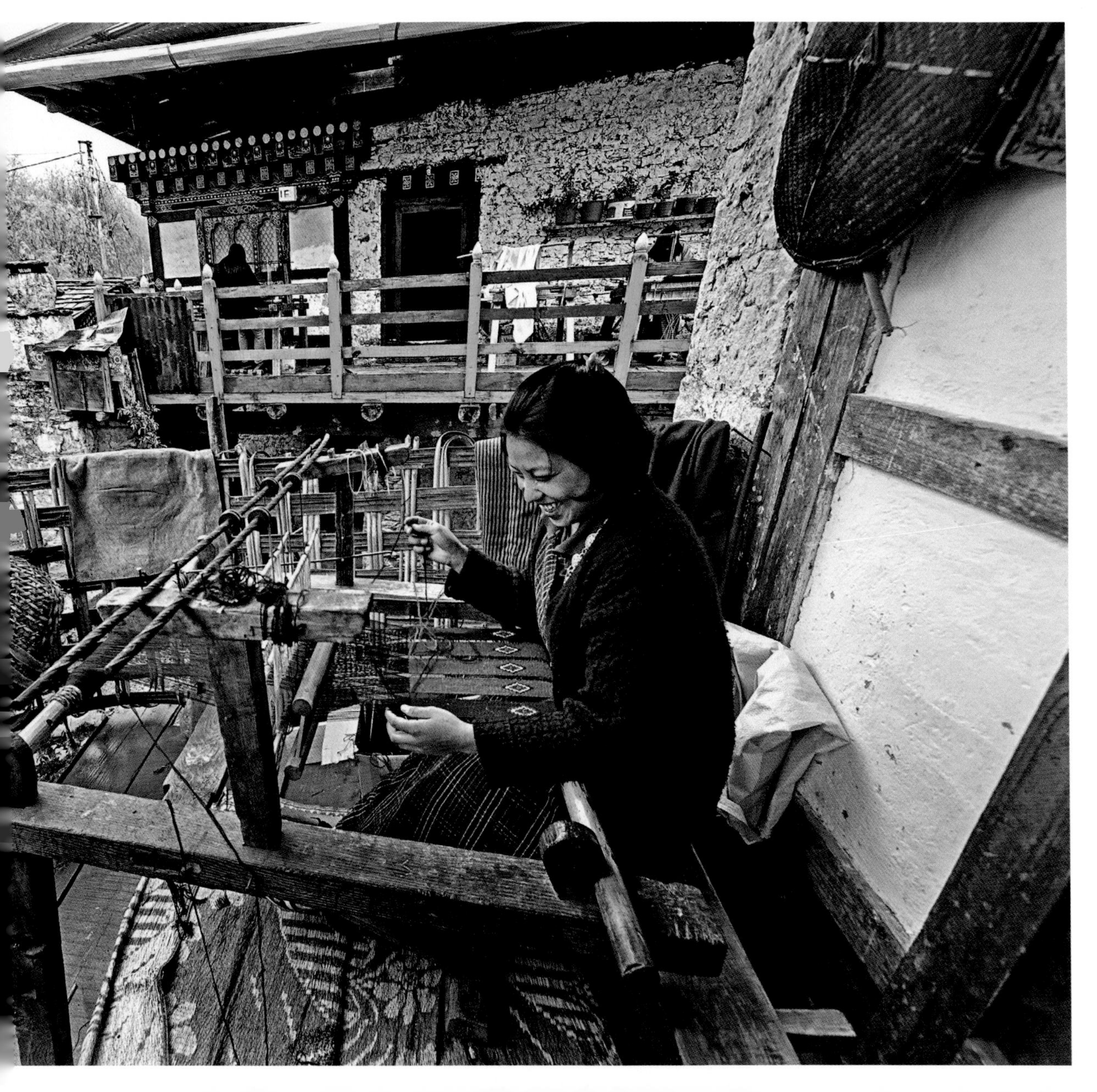

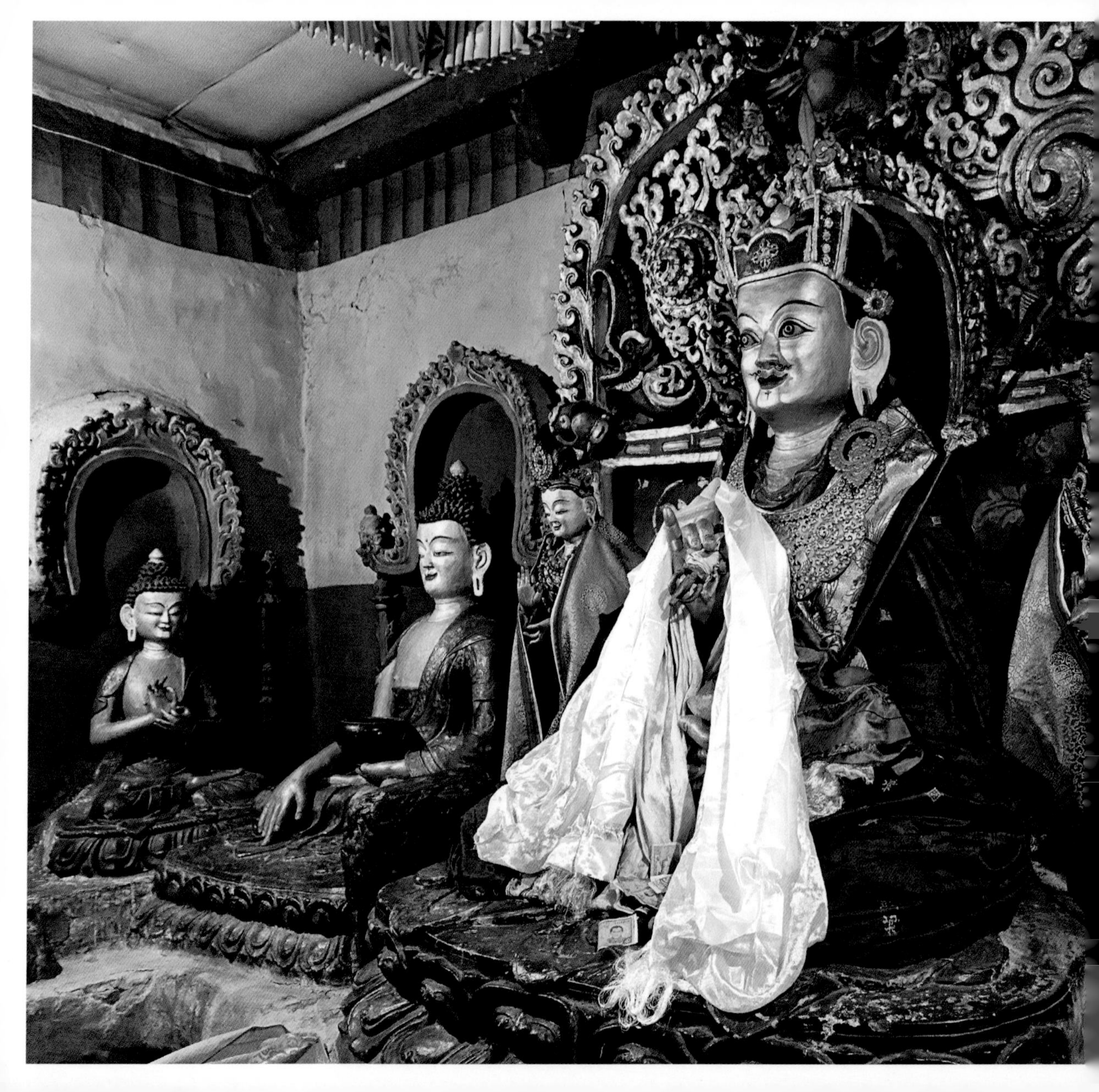

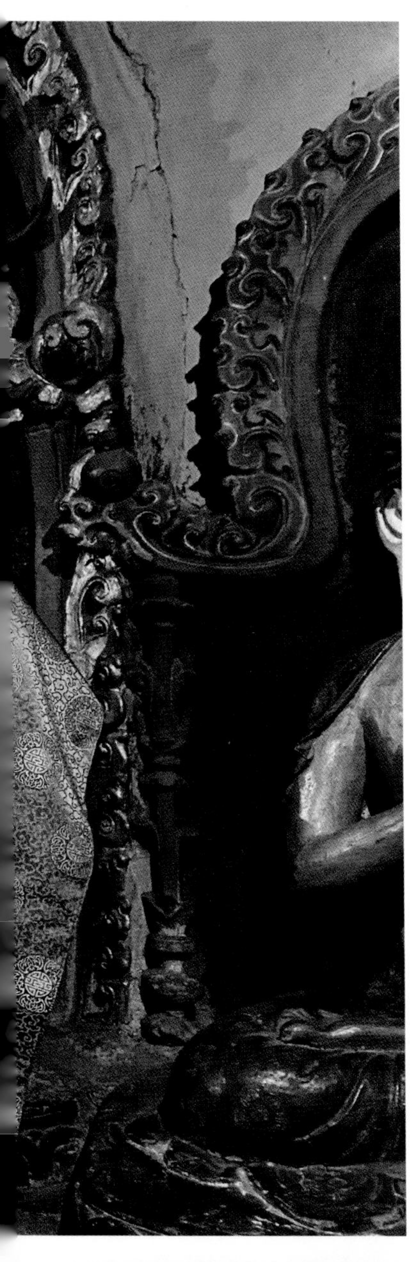

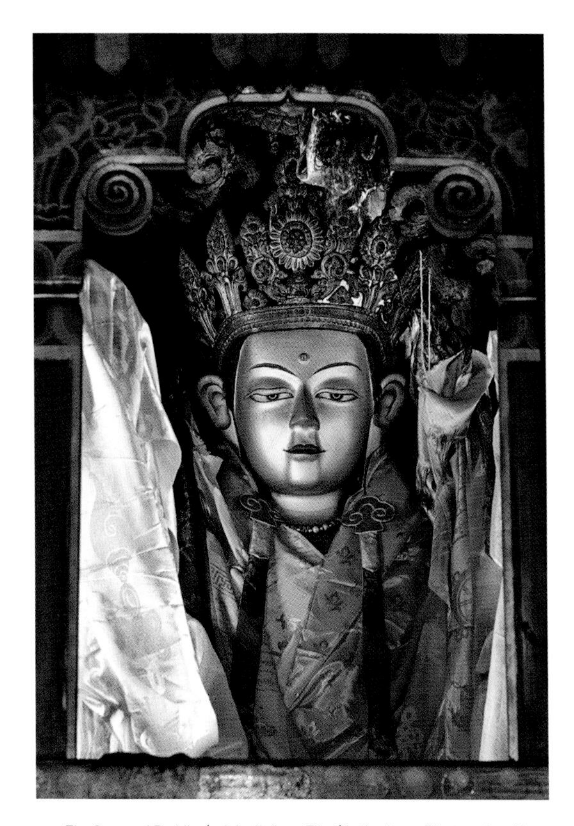

The Crowned Buddha (originally from Tibet) in the Jansa Bhu temple at Paro. It is said that when this statue – which resembles the 'Jowo', Lhasa's famous crowned Buddha – was about to be moved to the *dzong* at Paro, it spoke, saying 'I shall stay here.' 2007.

Left:
Clay statue of Padmasambhava in Tamchin monastery, Bumthang province, 2007.

Overleaf:
The wax and clay statue of Dilgo Khyentse Rinpoche, in his home at Paro Kyichu, lit up by the early morning rays, mingled with clouds of incense. 2007.

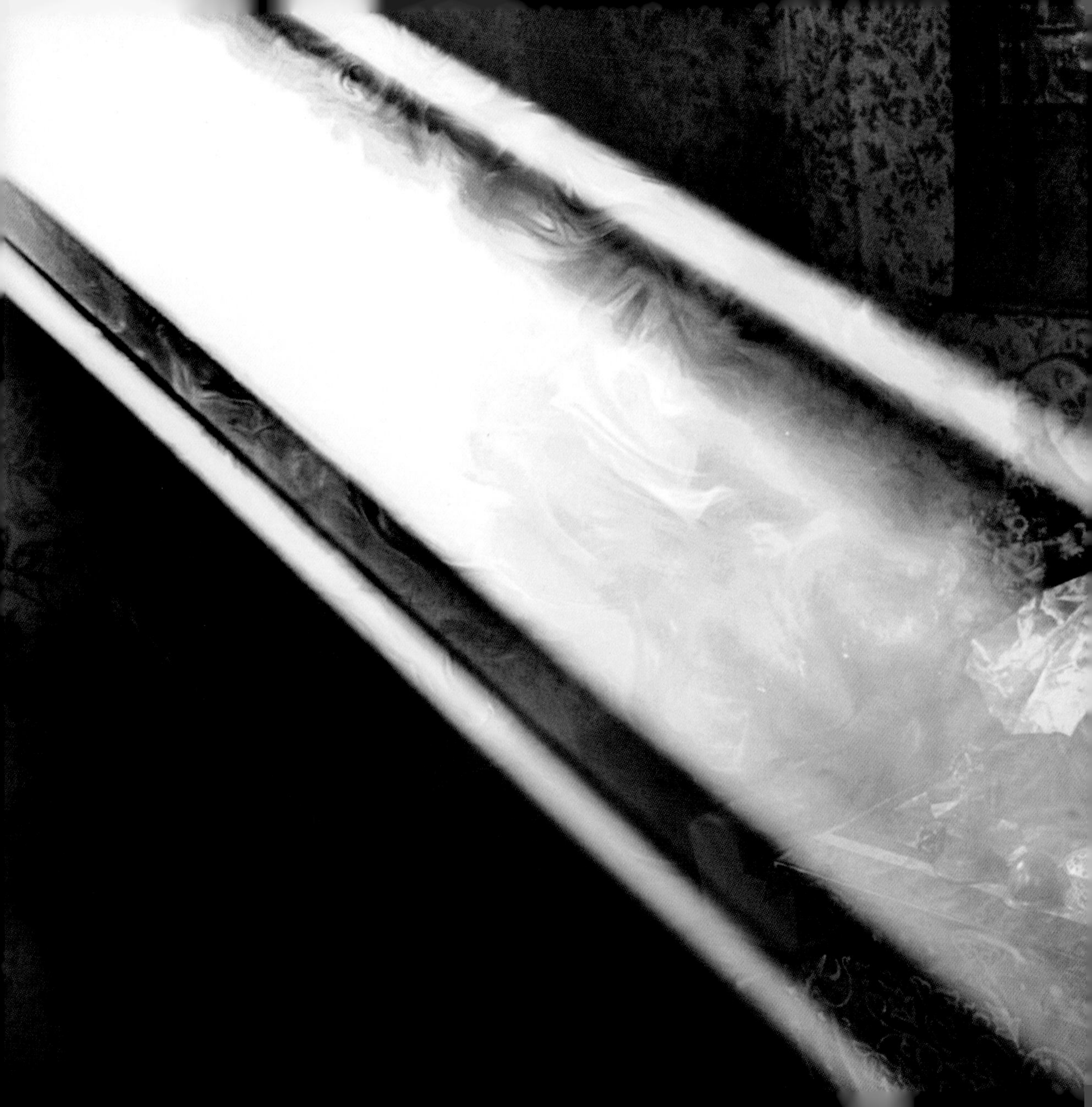

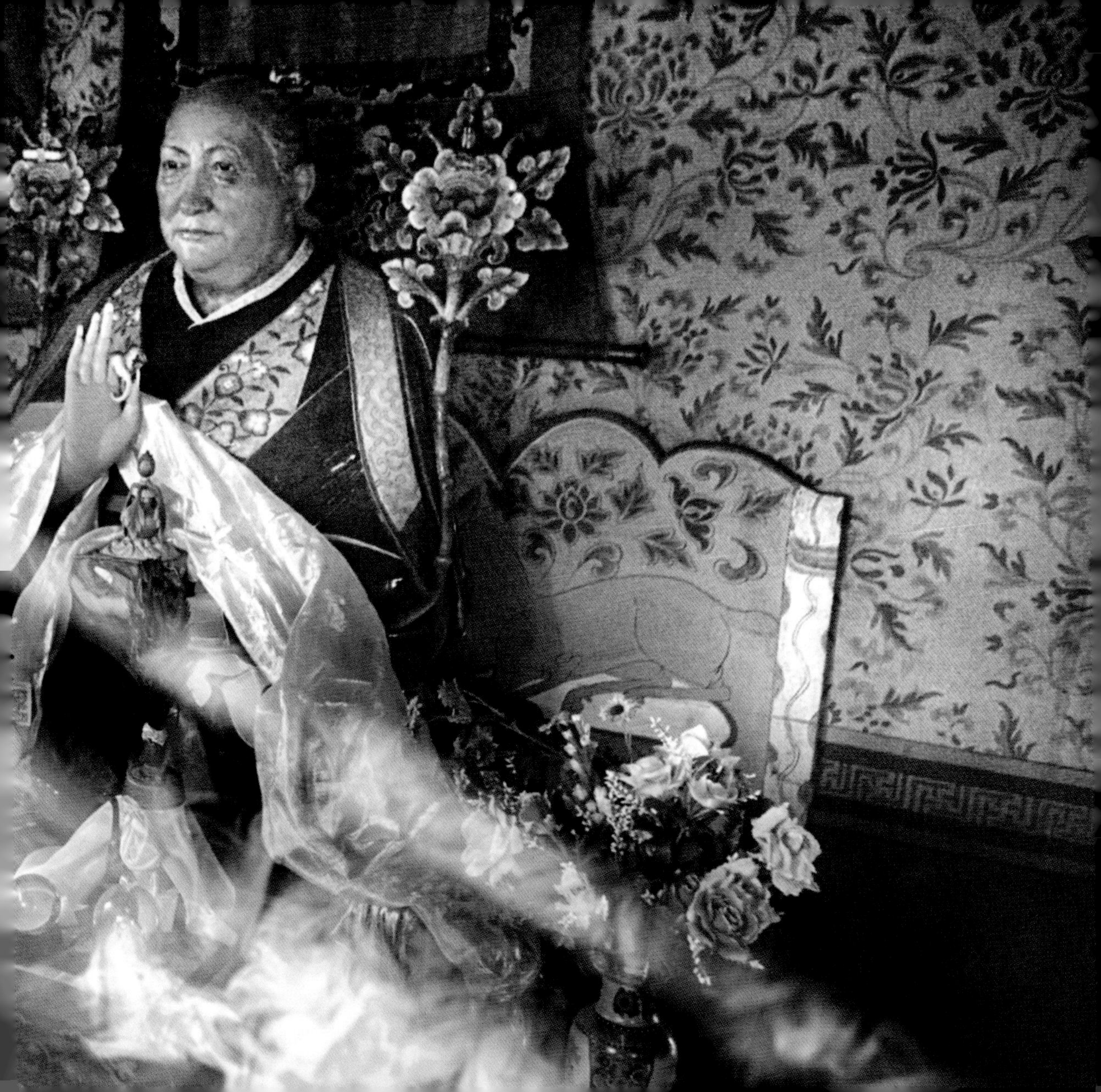

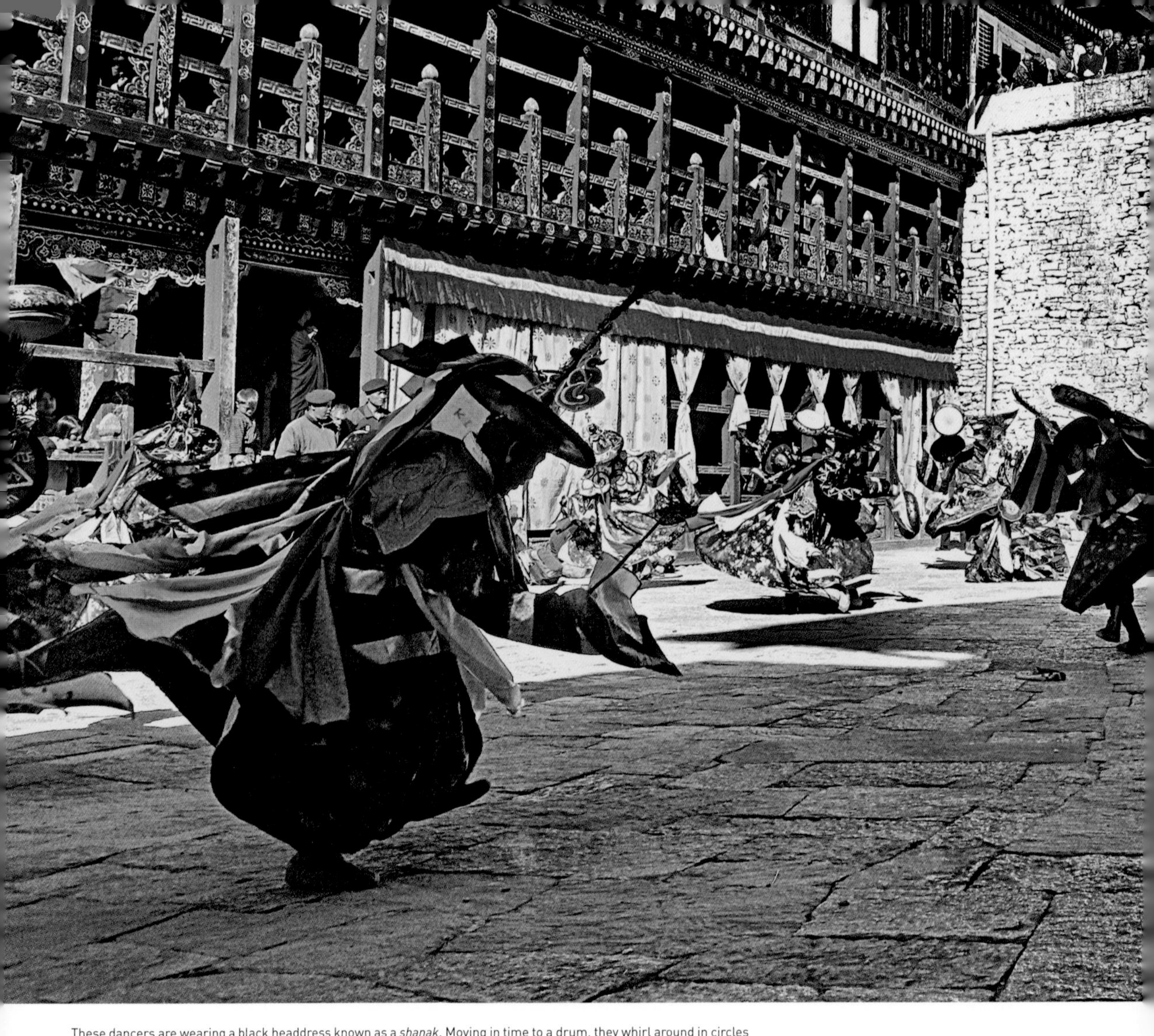

These dancers are wearing a black headdress known as a *shanak*. Moving in time to a drum, they whirl around in circles continuously for three quarters of an hour. Annual festival of sacred dance, Trongsar monastery, 2007.

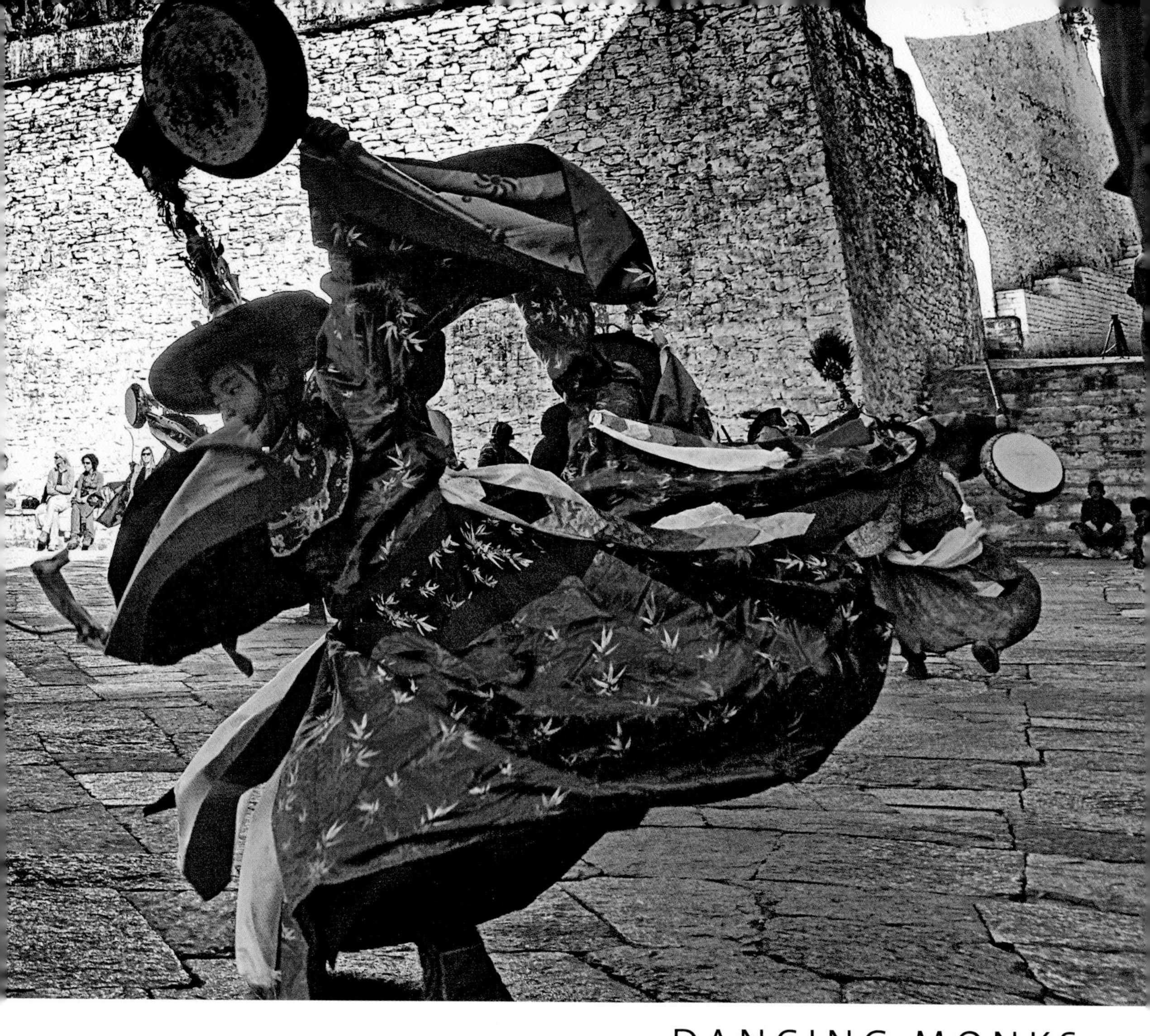

DANCING MONKS

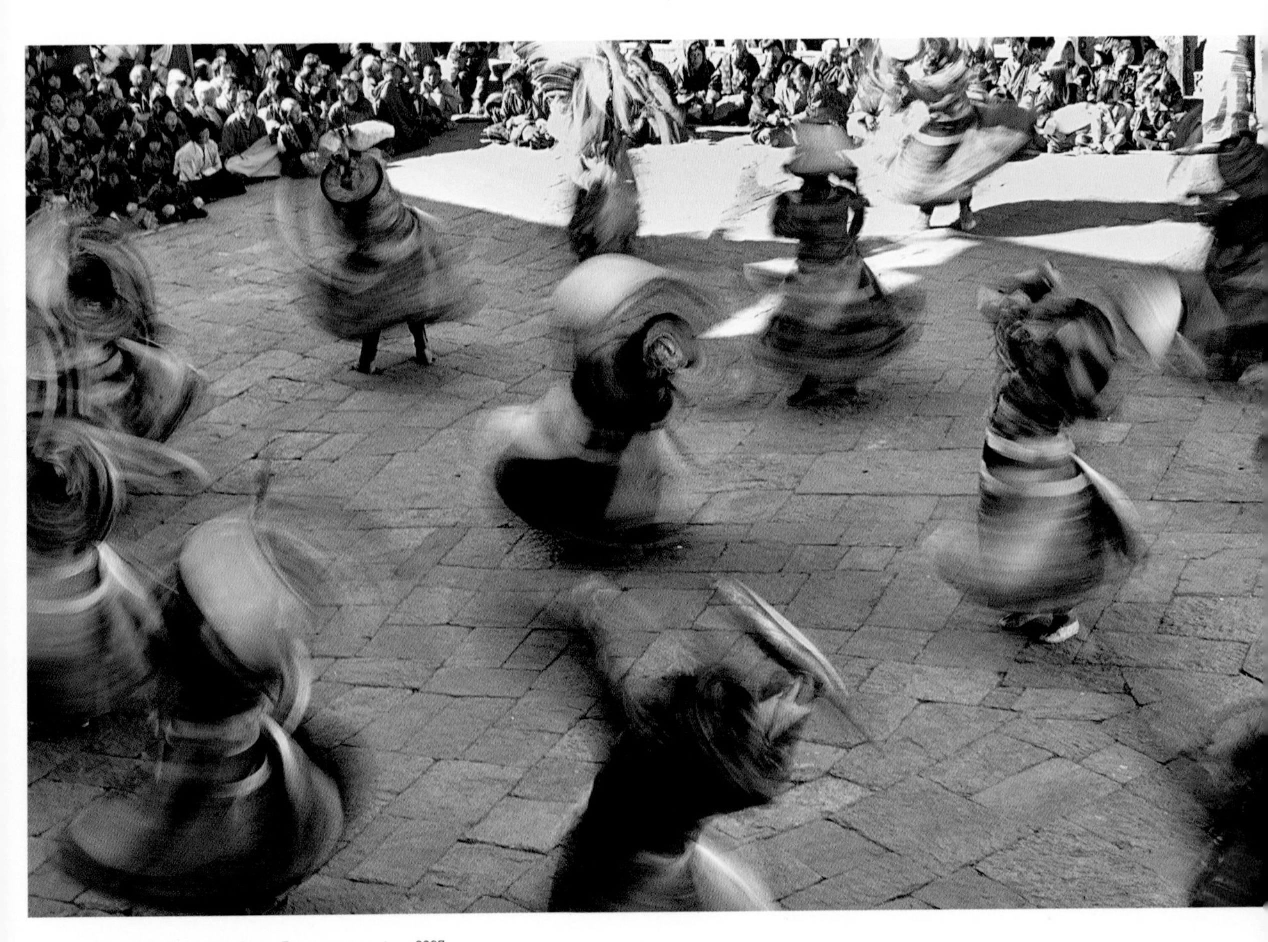

Annual festival of sacred dance, Trongsar monastery, 2007.

Dancing Monks

The very notion of monks dancing may seem incongruous. In the West, dancing is often an expression of sensual exuberance, sometimes with a connotation of seduction far removed from monastic contemplation. In fact, Buddhist monks are forbidden to indulge in secular music and dance. Sacred dances, or *tcham*, on the other hand, are a form of meditation and an opportunity to share a spiritual experience with the lay community, which lives in a relationship of close symbiosis with the monastery. What the monks share is an experience acquired in the course of long contemplative ceremonies, which is then offered up in symbolic gestures accompanied by sacred music. The sacred dances are said to 'liberate' by seeing, just as sacred music liberates through hearing, the blessing of a spiritual master liberates through touch, imbibing sacred substances liberates by taste, and meditation liberates by thought. 'Liberate' here means to liberate from the bondage of the five mental poisons which destroy our own and others' inner peace – hatred, covetousness, ignorance, pride and jealousy. It is in this context that sacred dances are understood in Bhutan, where their tradition has been faithfully preserved.

Every valley has its own festival of sacred dances, which is always one of the major events of the year and draws the crowds in their hundreds. The festival at Trongsar, the country's capital under its first king, Urgyen Wangchuck, is held in the *dzong*'s beautiful paved courtyard. No one, from the most important official down to the humblest peasant, would contemplate missing the five-day performance, which takes place during the eleventh lunar month of the Bhutanese calendar (generally corresponding to the month of December).

These events are a tough test of the monks' physical powers of endurance. The ceremonies that begin on the eve of the festival continue virtually throughout the night. Then, from seven in the morning, the monks perform their various dance sequences in the freezing cold courtyard still shaded from the sun. During the second half of the day, lay practitioners take over, performing dances for which they too have been rigorously trained, and some of them demonstrate extraordinary skill.

The sacred dances stem from the time that Buddhism was first brought to Tibet and Bhutan by Guru Padmasambhava in the 9th century. This early repertoire was enriched through visions, which continued to breathe new inspiration into the practice of sacred dancing. In the context of sacred art, innovations are not invented, but flow from the wealth of visionary experience which accompanies deep spiritual realization. The dance forms first appear in the mind of a spiritually advanced individual and are transmitted as accurately as possible by his disciples from generation to generation. Pema Lingpa (1450–1521), the great Bhutanese 'finder of spiritual treasures', had a dream in which Yeshe Tsogyal, Padmasambhava's principal follower and spiritual consort, said to him: 'This is how you dance the Rain of Blessings ritual', and she showed him the dance of the Five Dakinis (feminine deities, literally 'travellers in the sky of wisdom'). When Pema Lingpa woke up, the images of the dance were still crystal clear in his mind and he taught them to his followers.

Sacred dance is not limited to physical movements. The dancer recites mantras, and it is his task to visualize, clearly and without distractions, the deity he is embodying. The accessories used during the ceremonies and dances all have symbolic significance. Masks with a peaceful expression, for example, symbolize wisdom and loving kindness, while wrathful masks illustrate the elimination of the mental poisons that enslave us. The masks are usually made of several layers of glued fabric, though they can be carved from wood, which makes them heavier, or from sheets of beaten copper. Certain masks are regarded as precious relics imbued with blessings, such as the mask showing an aspect of Guru Padmasambhava made by Pema Lingpa.

THE EIGHT MANIFESTATIONS OF PADMASAMBHAVA

A festival comprises many dances, but the high point is the representation of Padmasambhava's 'Eight Manifestations' or more precisely 'Eight Names' (Guru Tsengye). While undertaking his various activities for the sake of all beings, Padmasambhava assumed a number of different forms – Buddha, king, yogi, scholar, and other, often wrathful, forms whose purpose was to remove the obstacles on the spiritual path. These Eight Manifestations symbolize different facets of Enlightenment: Tsokye Dorje, the 'Diamond Born-from-the-Lake'; Padmasambhava, the 'Lotus-Born'; Pema Gyalpo, the 'Lotus King'; Loden Choksey, 'Erudite Lover of Intelligence'; Sakya Senge, the 'Lion of the Sakyas'; Nyima Öser, the 'Sun's Rays'; Senge Dradrok, the 'Roaring Lion', and Dorje Drollö, the 'Loose Belly Diamond'.

Accompanied by a glorious procession, Padmasambhava leaves the temple and takes his place on a throne beneath a parasol of multicoloured silks. Then the crowd come to prostrate themselves before him and offer him white silk ceremonial scarves, while the Eight Manifestations dance, one by one, surrounded by other dancers. After Dorje Drollö has finished his leaping dance, overcoming the negative forces that stand in the way of world peace, Padmasambhava and his retinue return to the temple in a dynamic finale, amidst a great burst of music and an array of banners floating in the wind.

THE *ATSARA* CLOWNS

A large part of the spectacle relies on the clowns, or *atsaras*, who are present throughout, teasing and joking with the audience and indulging in all sorts of frequently bawdy antics. They are also responsible for controlling the crowd, who have a habit of invading the dance area, and for helping the dancers to tighten the fastenings on their masks or adjust an outfit that is coming undone. Nor are the dancers spared, for the clowns mimic and mock them too. All this adds a note of good humour and cheerful detachment to what is otherwise a profound meditation. There is a serene and happy atmosphere to the proceedings, reflecting the character of the Bhutanese people themselves. Beneath a frivolous exterior, the *atsaras* are the 'divine madmen' who, like the *mahasiddha*, the great Indian yogis, have understood the illusory nature of phenomena and abandoned all forms of conventional behaviour.

THE STORY OF THE HUNTER

Bhutan has preserved some dances that have disappeared from Tibet following the Chinese invasion. Among them are the didactic dances taught by the great visionary Karma Lingpa in the 14th century. They tell the story of two characters, a hunter who, at the moment of death, faces the consequences of his negative actions, and a good man who reaps the rewards for a well-spent life. The audience follows the thread of this edifying story illustrating the laws of karma with childlike amusement and a little frisson of anxiety.

The dance begins with the arrival, with great pomp and ceremony, of the Lord of Death, who takes his place on his throne. The wretched defendant then enters, wearing a black mask and a dark cape, and trembling with fear. The clowns shower him with abuse and keep making him jump up and down. A wild-haired demon lists the hunter's misdeeds, gesturing menacingly and stamping with impatience at the prospect of taking charge of the dying man and hauling him off to hell. It seems that the man has not merely spent a lifetime slaughtering animals but has also cultivated a talent for drunkenness, thieving and inveterate selfishness. The lawyer for the defence, a mild figure dressed in white and wearing a white mask, now takes his turn to speak, describing the hunter's few good deeds and arguing that if he acted badly it was out of ignorance rather than knowingly. The hunter himself makes a show of remorse. Judgment is swiftly passed and the messengers of the Lord of Death unroll a black carpet on which they drag the condemned man away to the lower realms of *samsara*.

A few moments later, another man appears before the Lord of Death. This man has led a virtuous and selfless life and the lawyer for the defence praises his good deeds – notably the fact that he saved six people from drowning in a flood. To the great displeasure of the public prosecutor, who keeps circling round him in a threatening fashion, the man is escorted towards a Pure Land by a procession of divinities that manifest themselves in the *bardo*, the intermediary state between death and rebirth.

These images may seem simplistic, but amid the lively and at times comic atmosphere of the dance, there is no sense of heavy moralizing or indoctrination. The lesson is clear: we are the architects of our own destiny. The last judgment is not given by an entity that exists outside ourselves: it is the result of the sum of our actions. It is always possible to compensate for a negative action with a positive one before our karma is expressed into suffering. But if we do nothing, we are the only ones to blame for our pain and misery. The dance reminds us too that the wisdom and compassion of the Buddha can guide us, but they cannot replace our actions. The Buddha cannot throw us towards Enlightenment like a pebble, nor prevent a negative action from bearing fruit. It is up to us to change the direction of our karma and to remedy our lack of discernment in the light of the teachings of the Buddha, who constantly reminds us: 'I have shown you the way: it is for you to take it.'

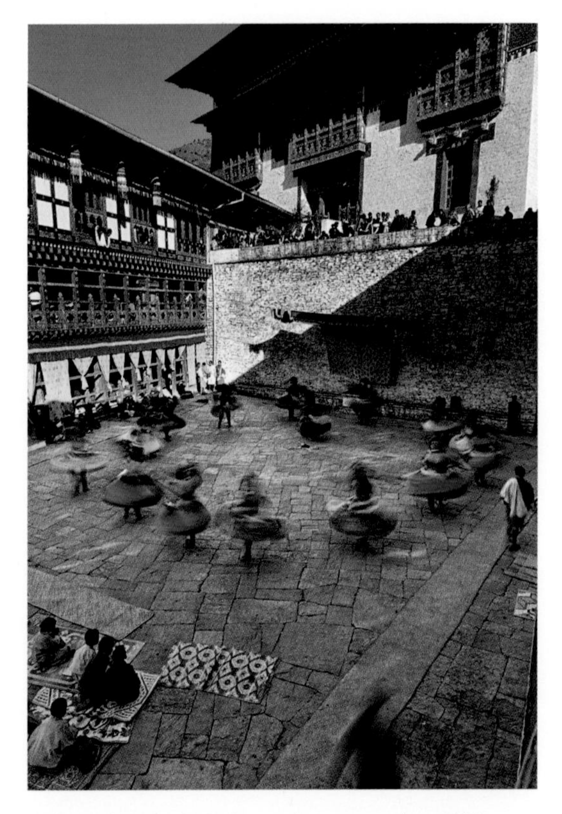

Whirling monks performing the *thun-nam* dance – representing wrathful deities – in Trongsar monastery's inner courtyard on a cold winter's morning. These deities symbolize a powerful aspect of compassion. Trongsar festival. December 2007.

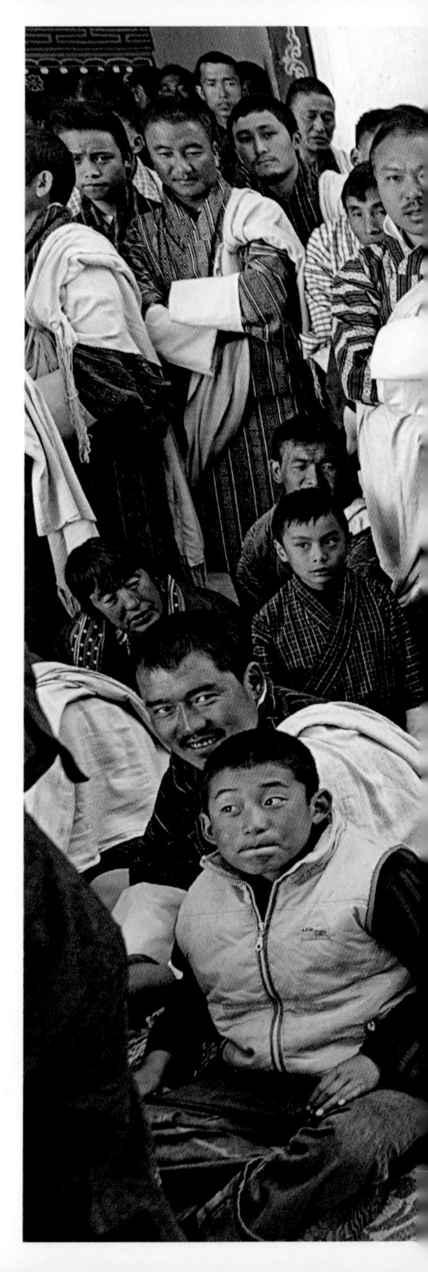

Clowns, or *atsaras*, mingle with the crowd, teasing people and playing the fool. 2007.

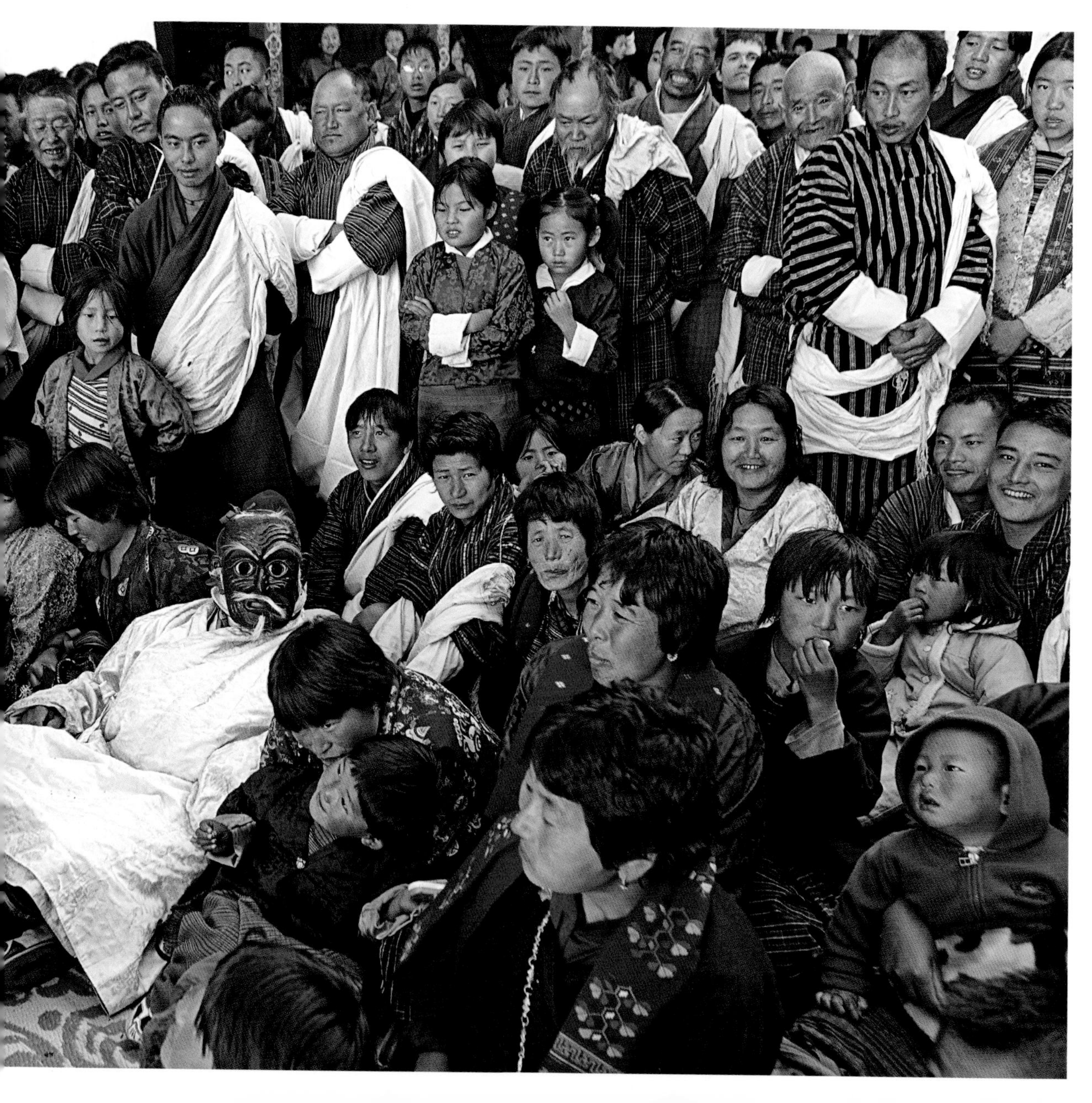

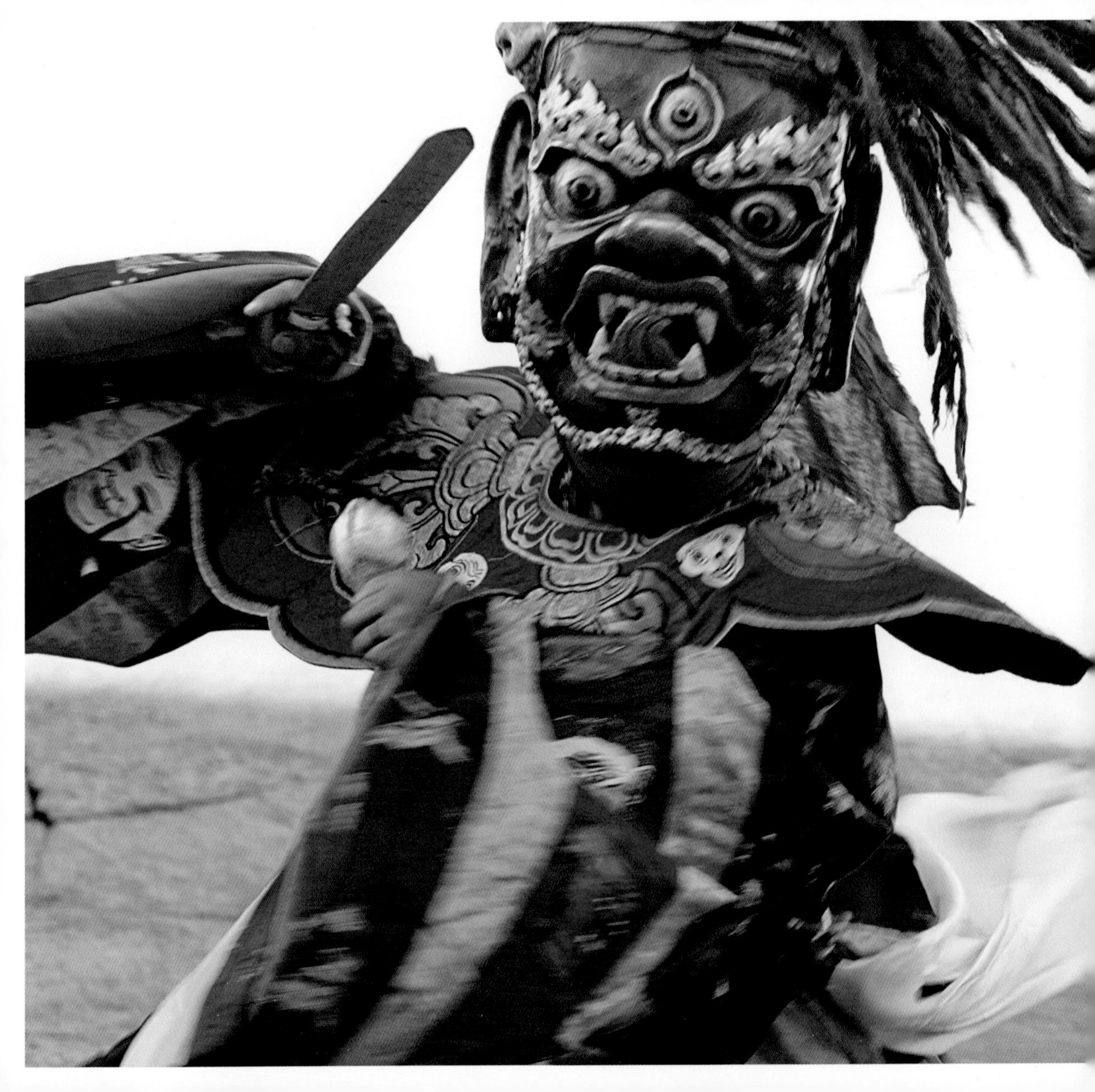

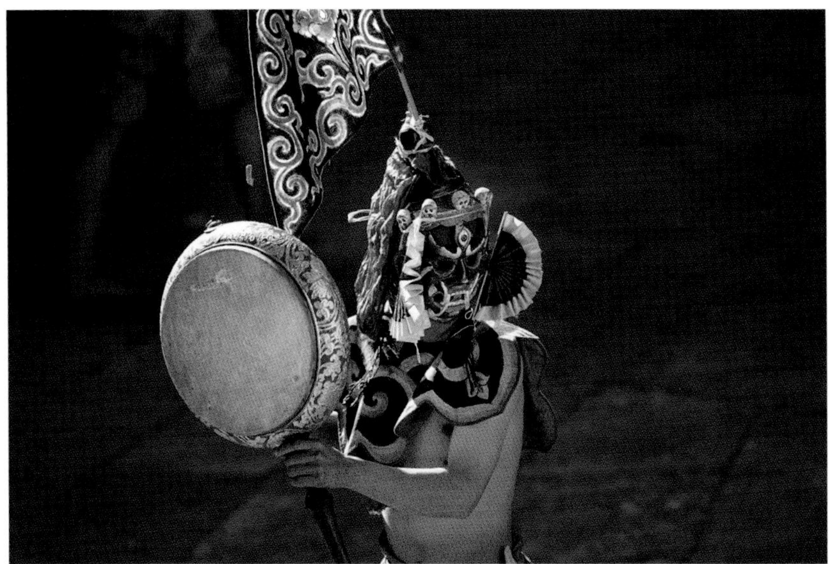

Above and pages 160–161:
The dance of the sixteen heroes (*gings*) has a particularly deep and complex symbolism concerning the spiritual energies linking the mind and the body. The sixteen 'heroes' (*gings*) represent the sixteen types of 'essence' (*bindu*) whose movements in the subtle channels (*nadi*) bring about transformations in the vital 'breath' (*prana*). The multicoloured fans on either side of their masks signify that they are surrounded by rainbow light. Their tiger-skin skirts symbolize the sublimation of ordinary passions. 2007.

This fierce masked deity is preparing to cleave the darkness of ignorance and cut through attachment to the ego, thereby removing the external and internal obstacles that lie on the path to Enlightenment. Trongsar festival, December 2007.

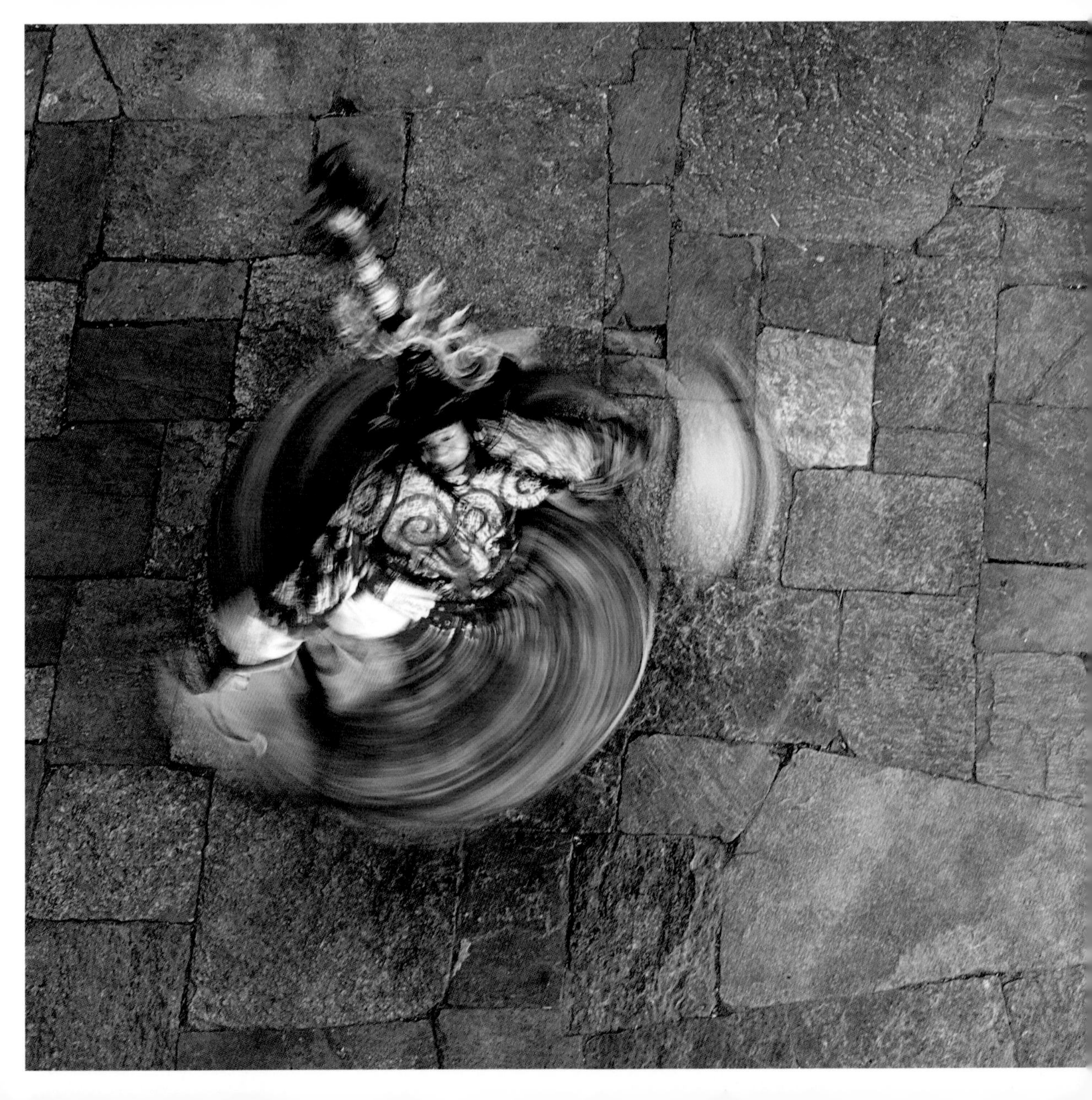

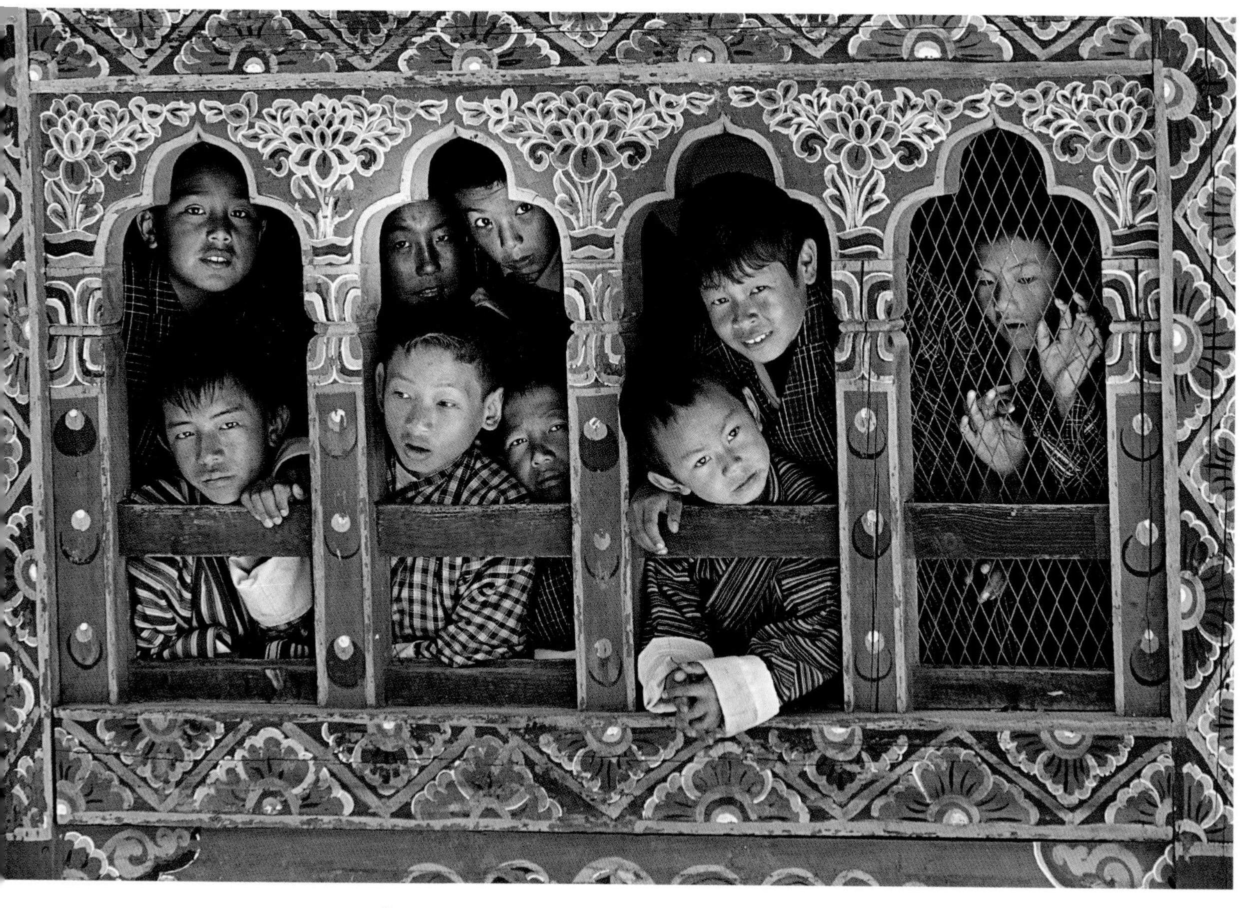

There are many eager young spectators of the sacred dances. Some of these boys stood for hours at the window overlooking the courtyard, drinking in every detail of the festival. Trongsar festival, 2007.

This dancer with his black hat spins for nearly an hour in the monastery courtyard. Trongsar, 2007.

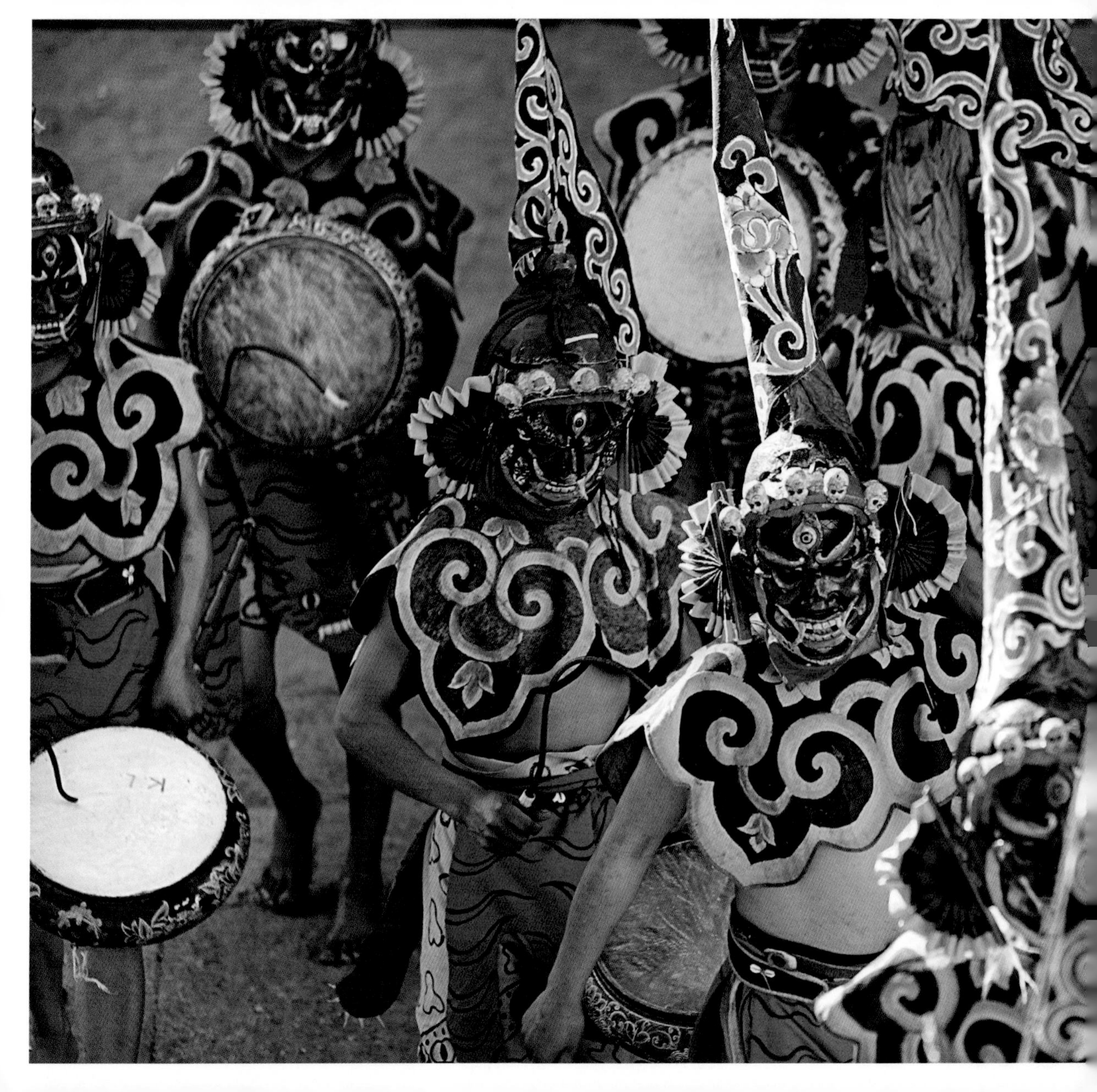

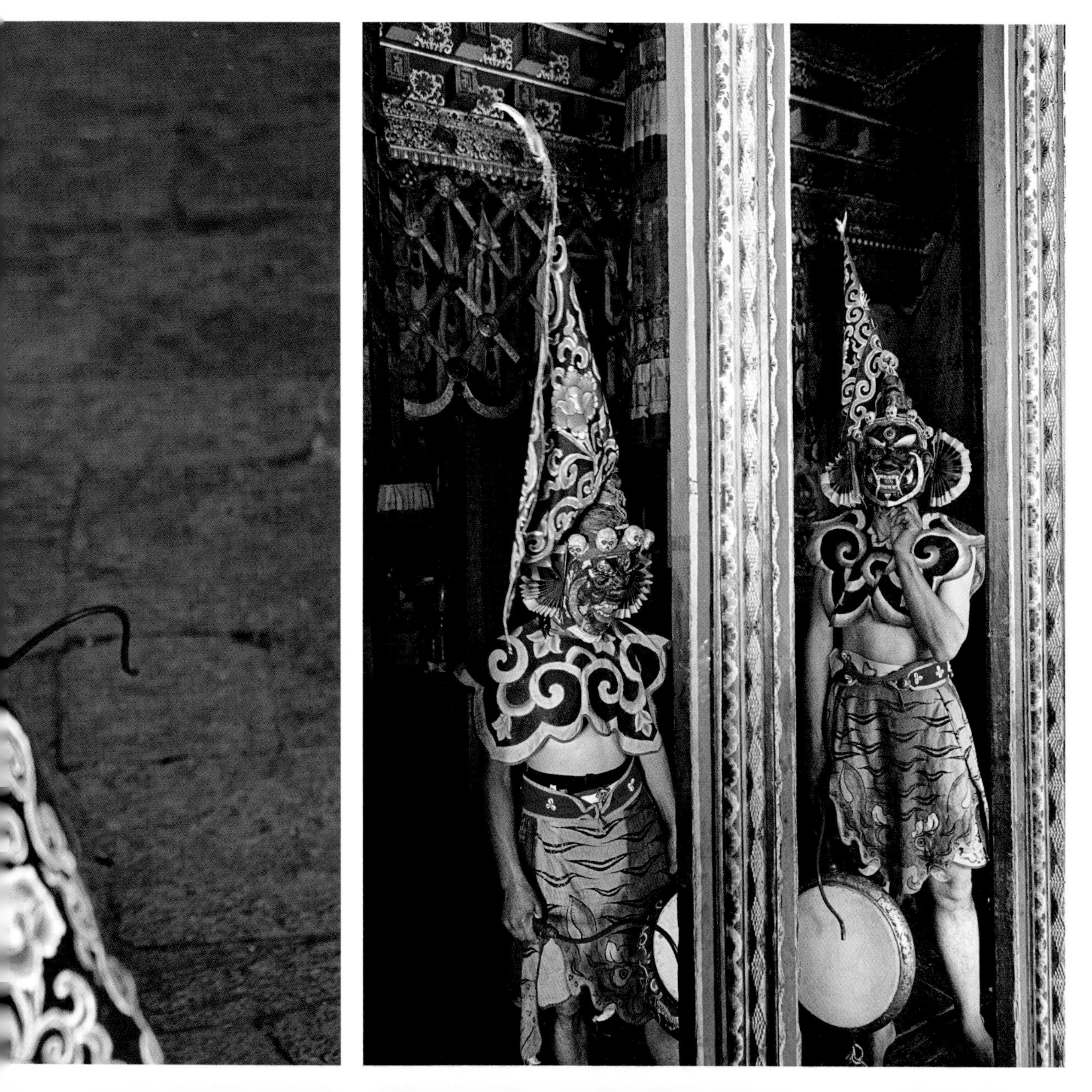

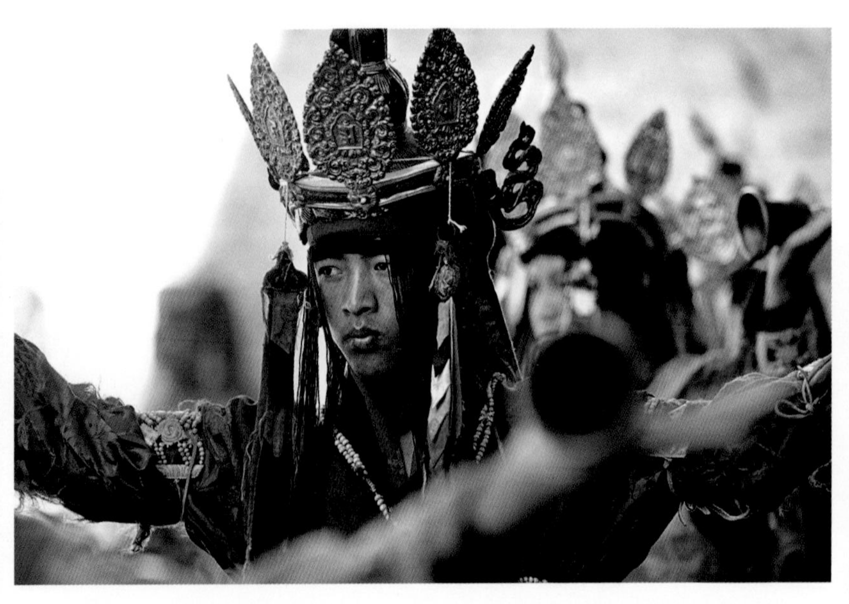

The beaten copper crown worn by these dancing monks symbolizes victory over the five mental poisons of hatred, desire, ignorance, pride and jealousy. 2007.

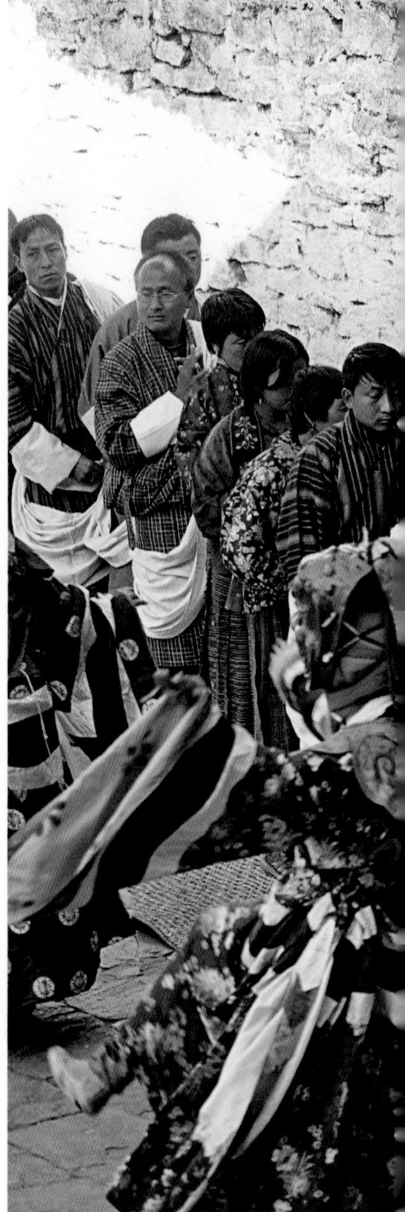

While the dance of the 'Eight Names' is being performed, the crowd files past the statue of Padmasambhava. They present their offerings – ceremonial scarves made of white silk – and receive the statue's blessing. 2007.

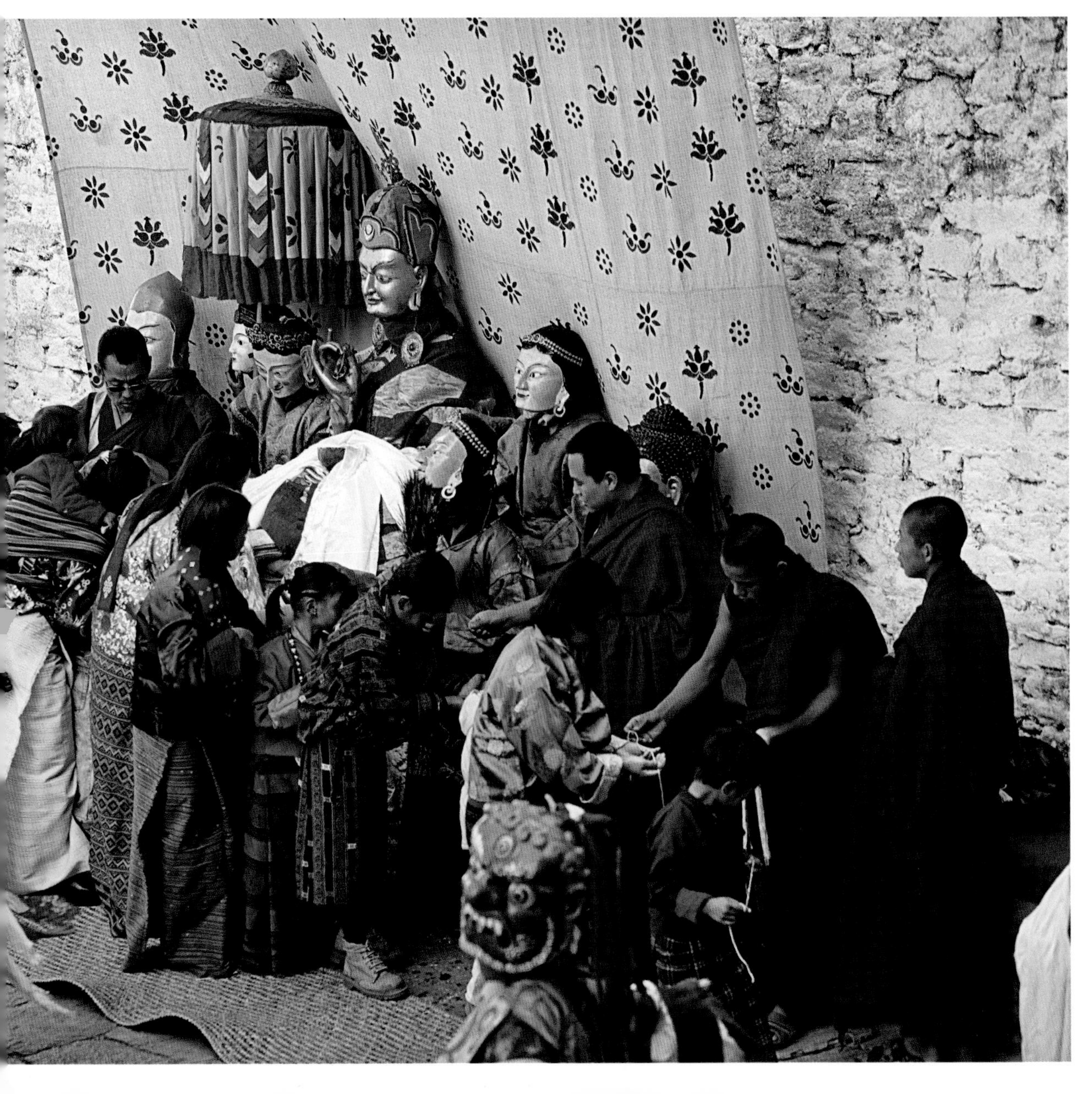

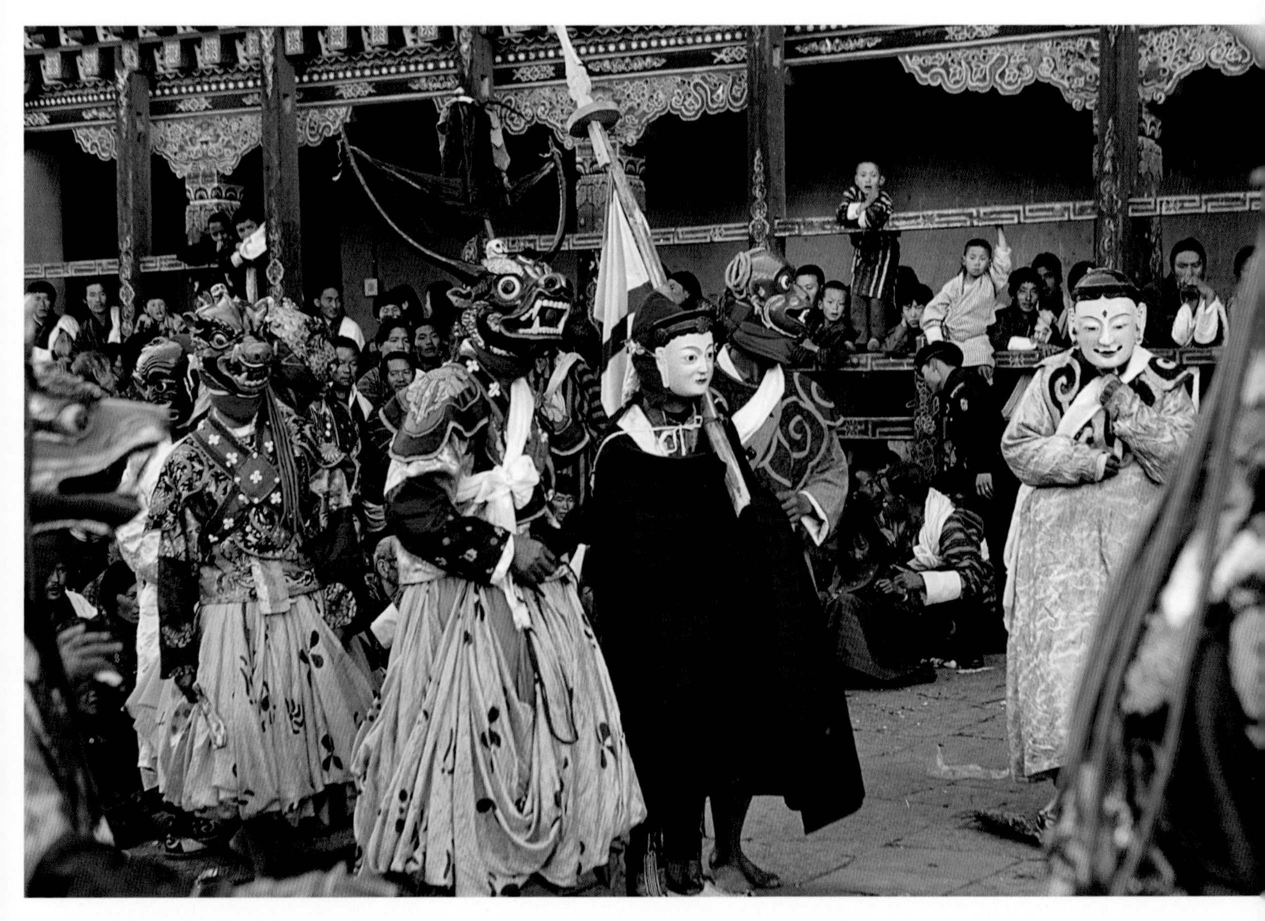

In a theatrical presentation of the laws of karma – performed as a dance – a man who has led a good life comes to face the 'last judgment'. The judgment is given by Yaramaraj, Lord of Death, who is not an external entity but represents the sum total of a person's actions, both good and bad. The man is led towards a 'pure land' by deities who appear in the *bardo*, the intermediary state between death and rebirth. Trongsar, 2007.

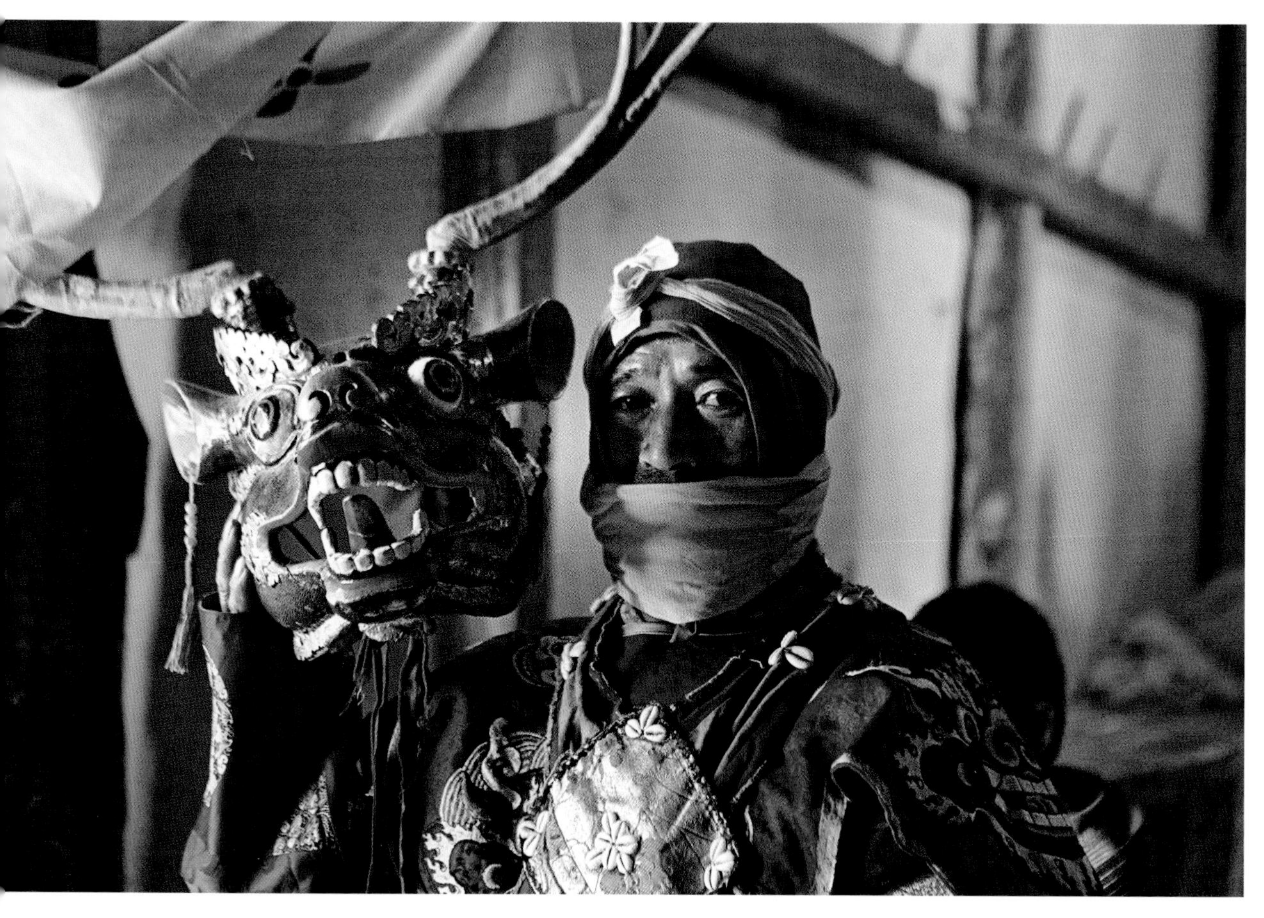

Above:
A lay dancer from a neighbouring village is getting ready to put on his deer mask. Trongsar, 2007.

Overleaf (from left to right):
The masks of a clown (*atsara*), an old village woman, Loden Choksey, 'Erudite Lover of Intelligence', and one of the wrathful deities of the *thun-nam* dance.

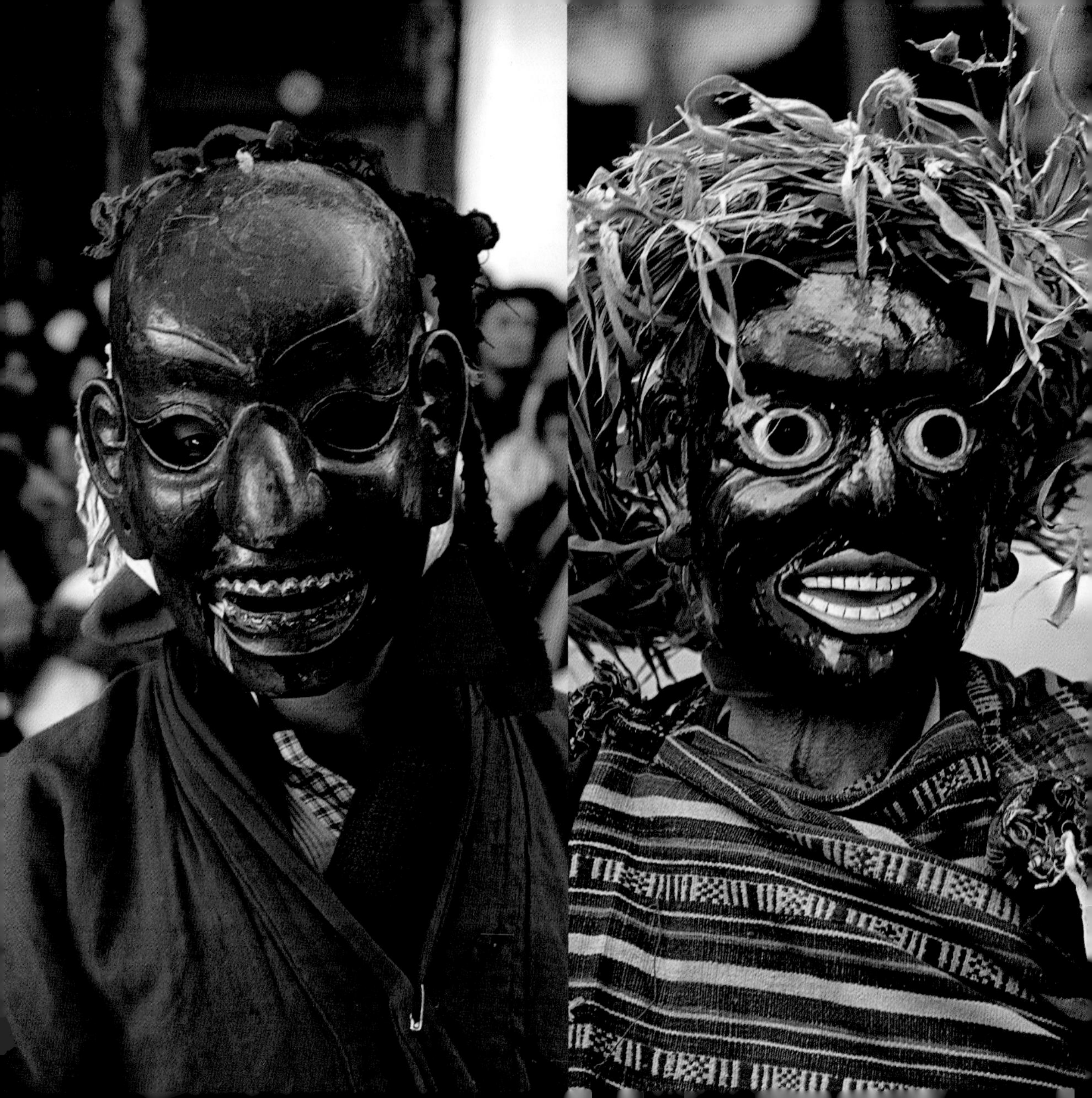

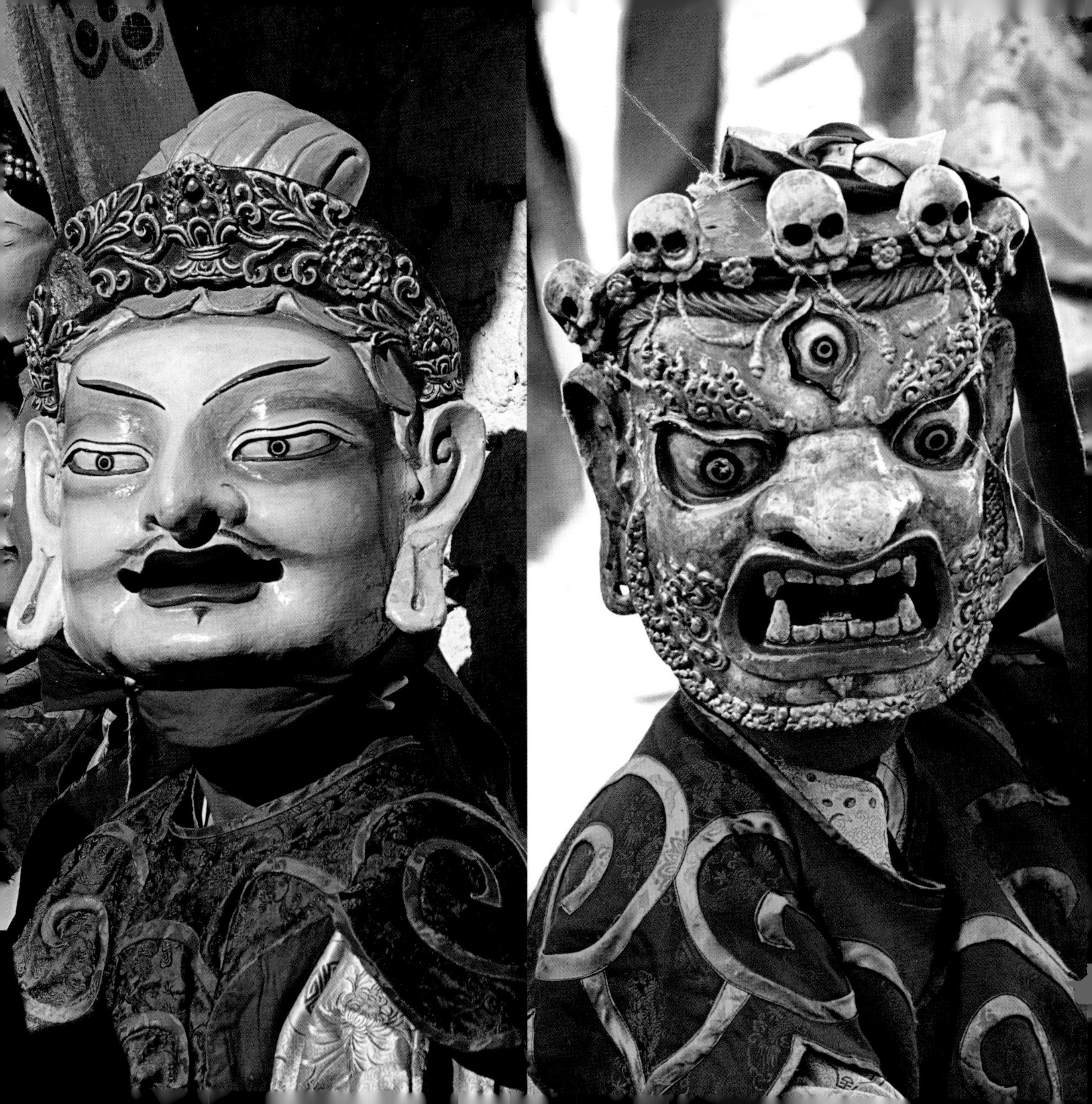

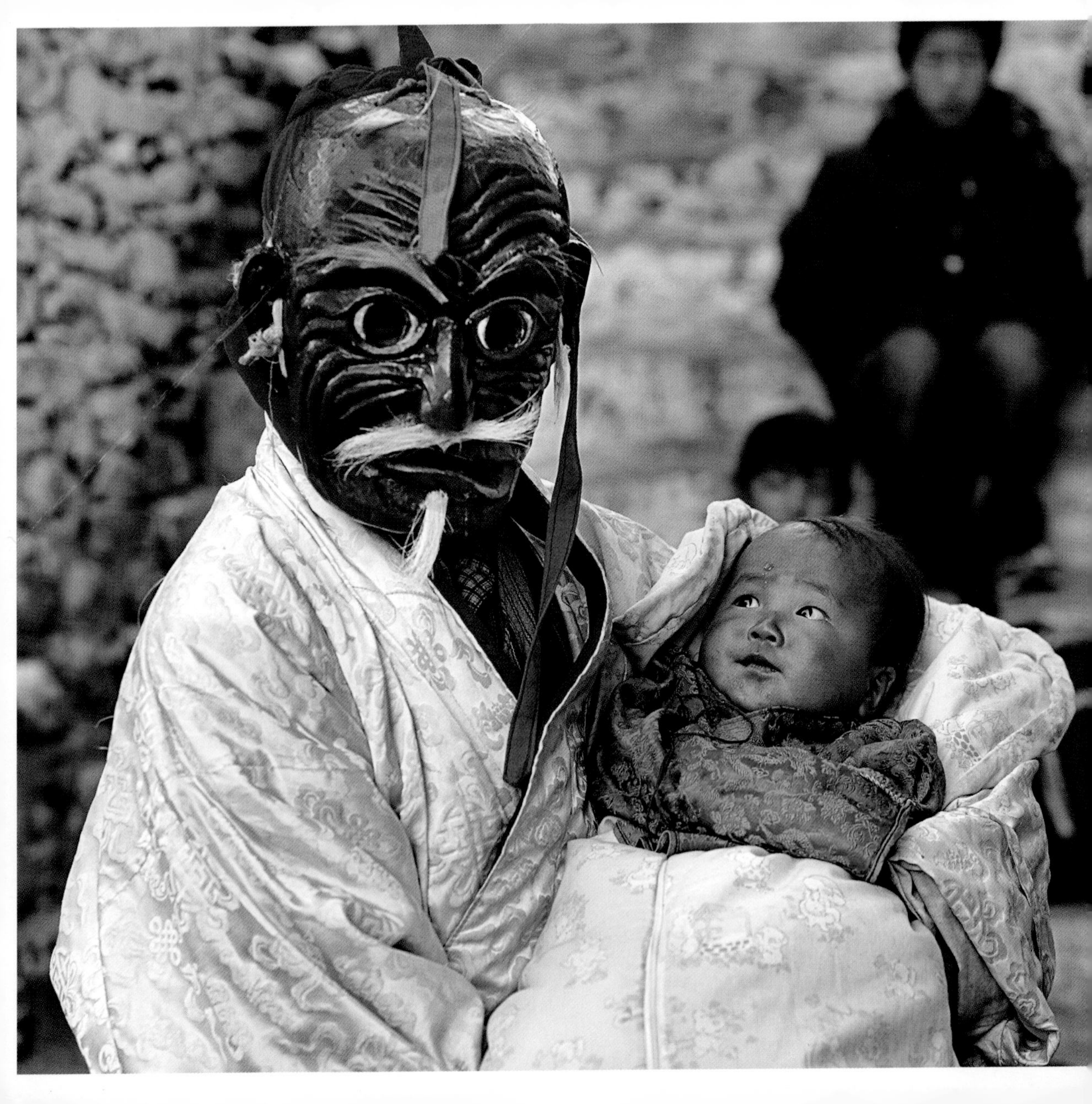

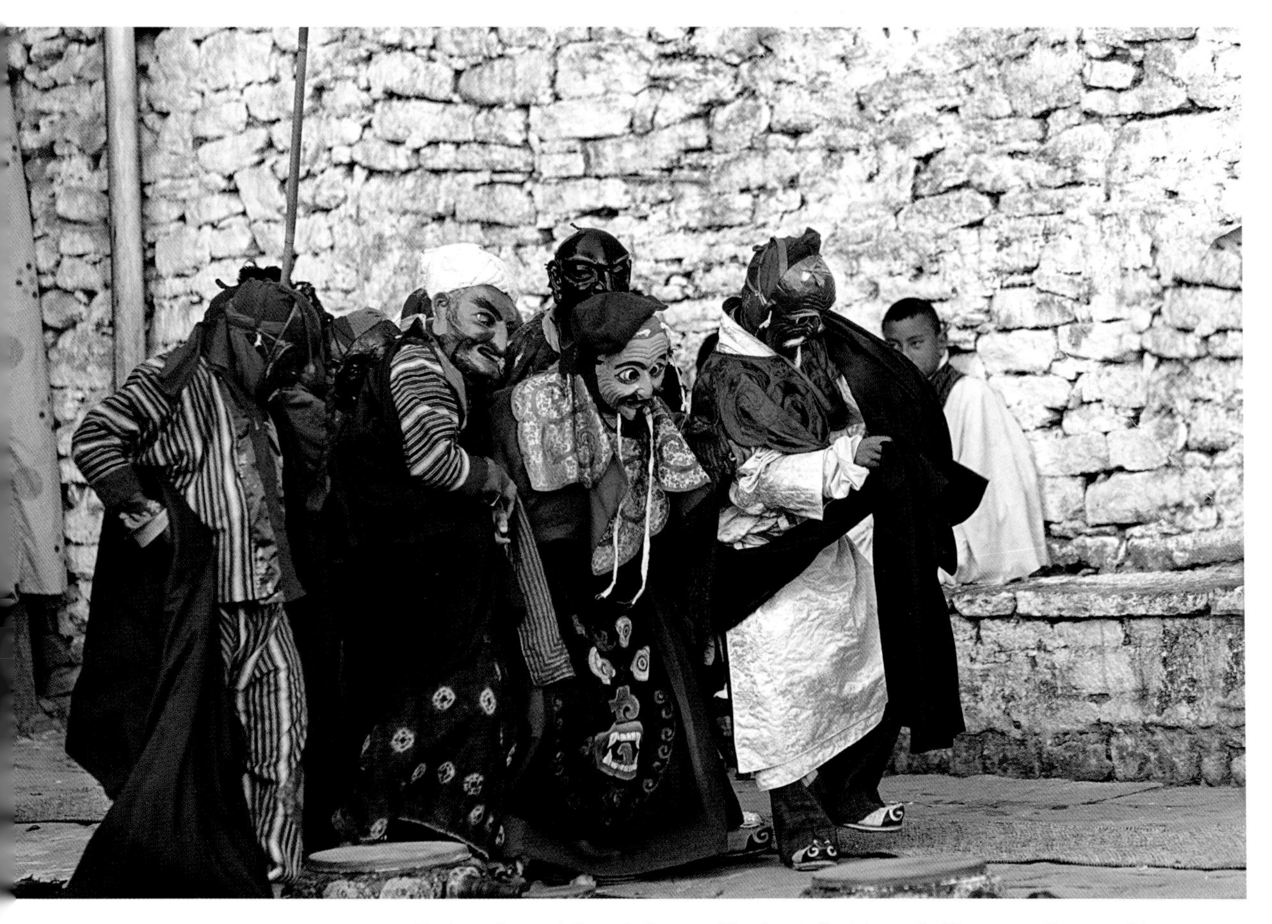

The clowns often parody the monks: here, one of them is pretending to be a senile old lama, escorted by a group of devotees. They are about to perform a spoof version of a ceremony, which will have the crowd hooting with laughter. Trongsar, 2007.

Opposite:
A mother has handed her surprised yet relatively unperturbed child to this clown, so that he can take it to receive a blessing from the statue of Padmasambhava, at the centre of the 'Eight Manifestations' dance.

Overleaf:
Dancer in a black headdress.

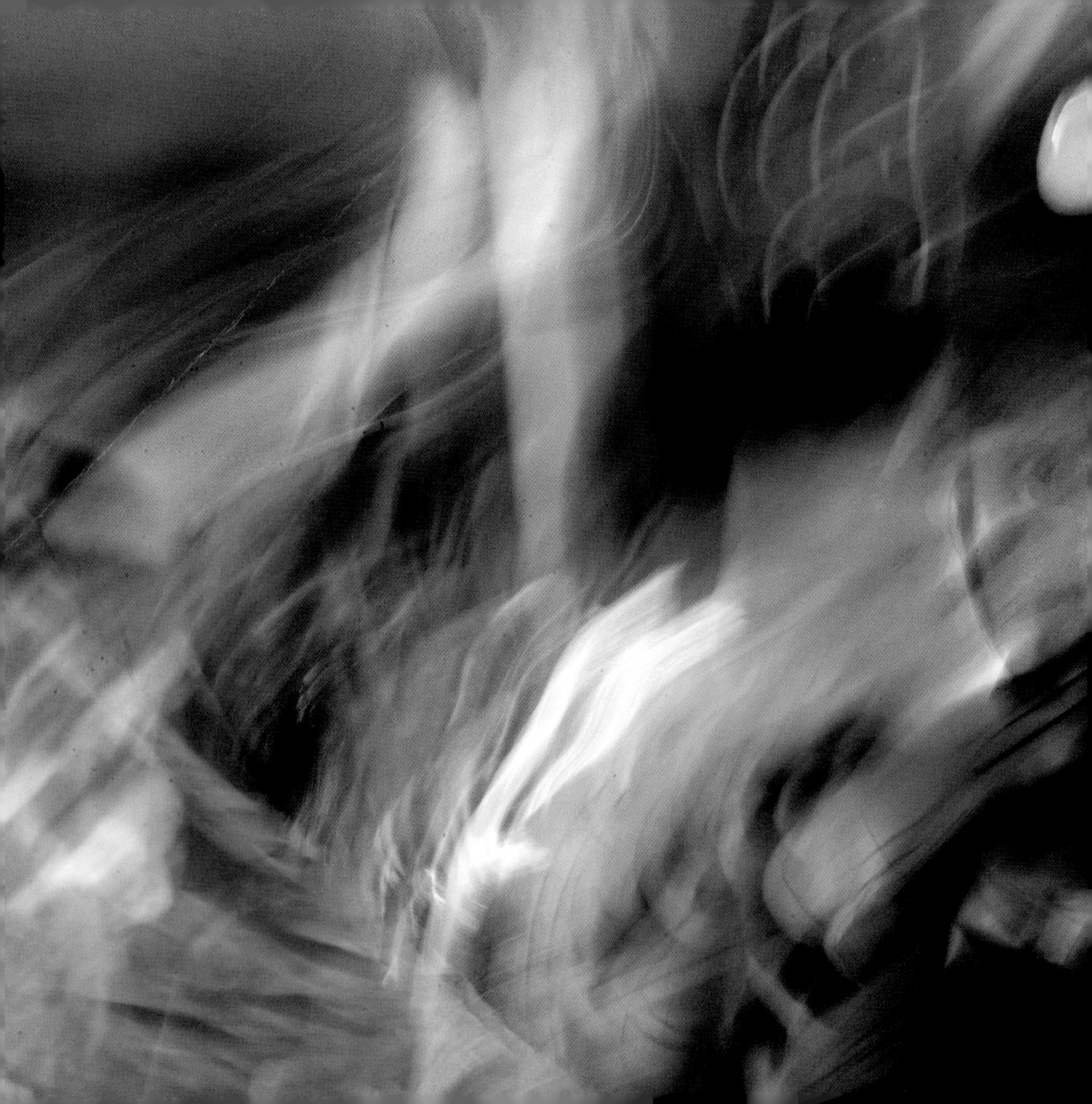

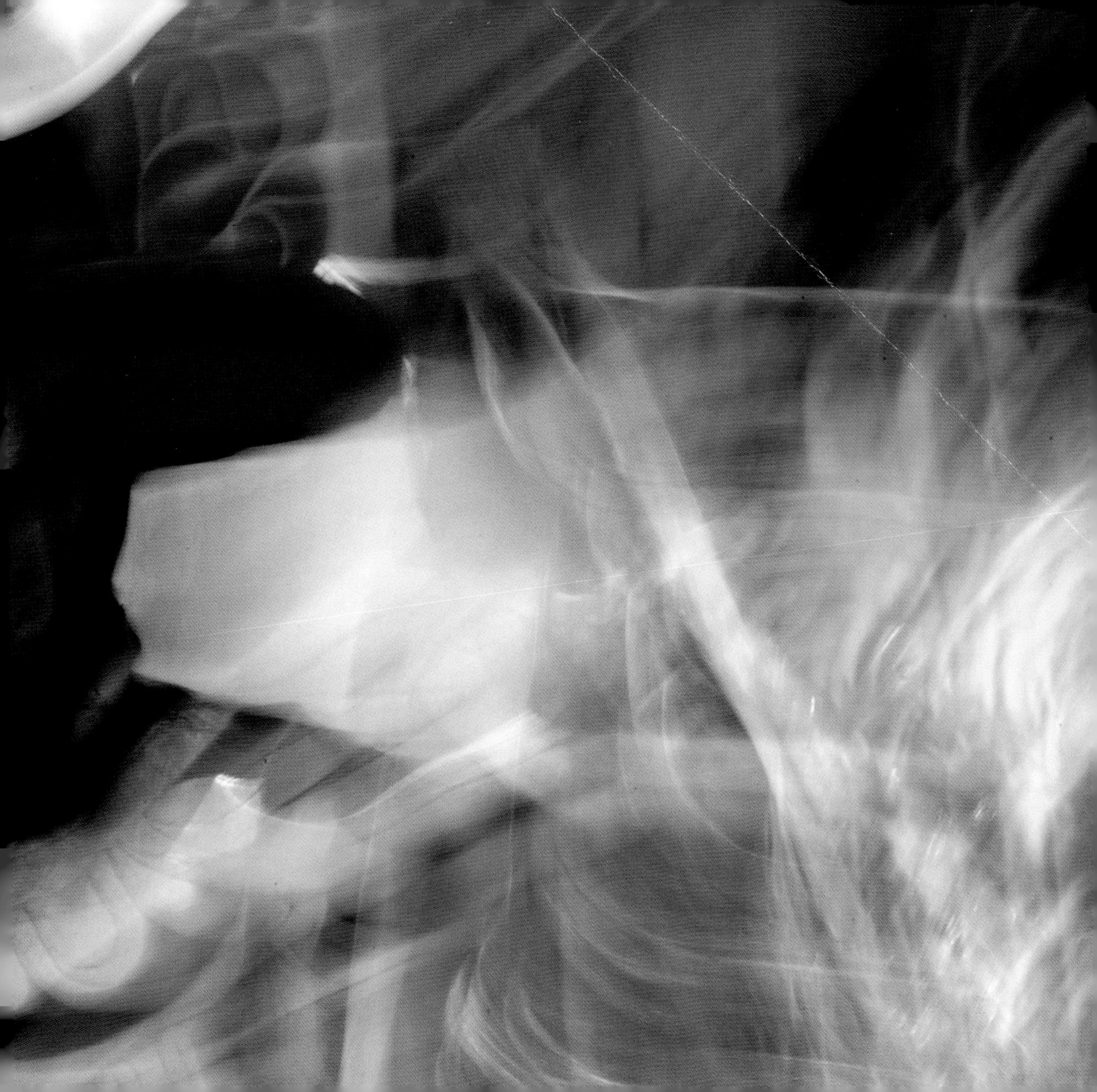

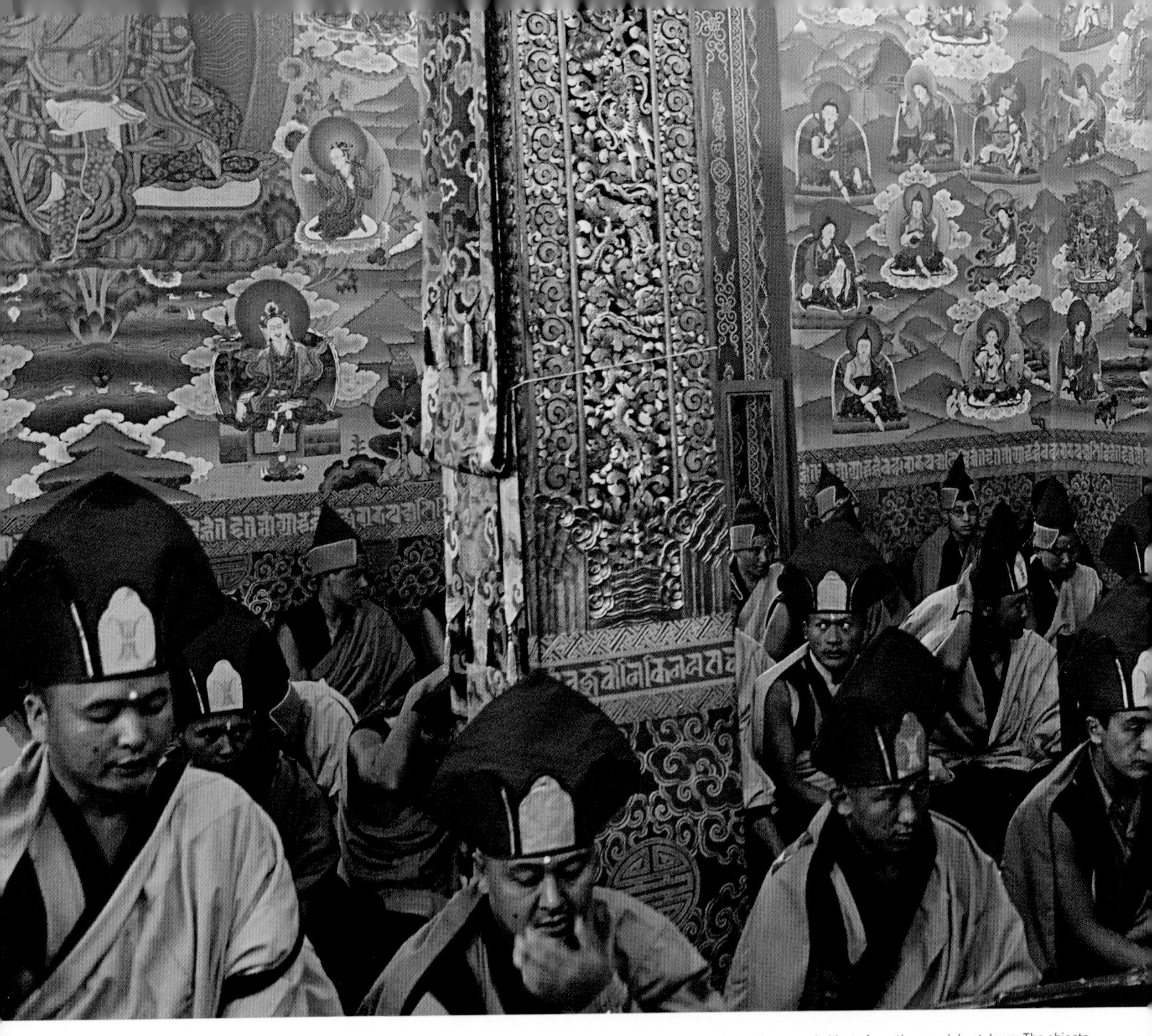

On the final day of the Great Accomplishment ceremony (*drupchen*), Rabjam Rinpoche and the principal officiants bring the sacred objects from the mandala at dawn. The objects have been placed in the mandala for the nine days and nine nights of the ritual, accumulating blessings through the participants' meditations, and these blessings are about to be bestowed on the assembled gathering. Paro, 2006.

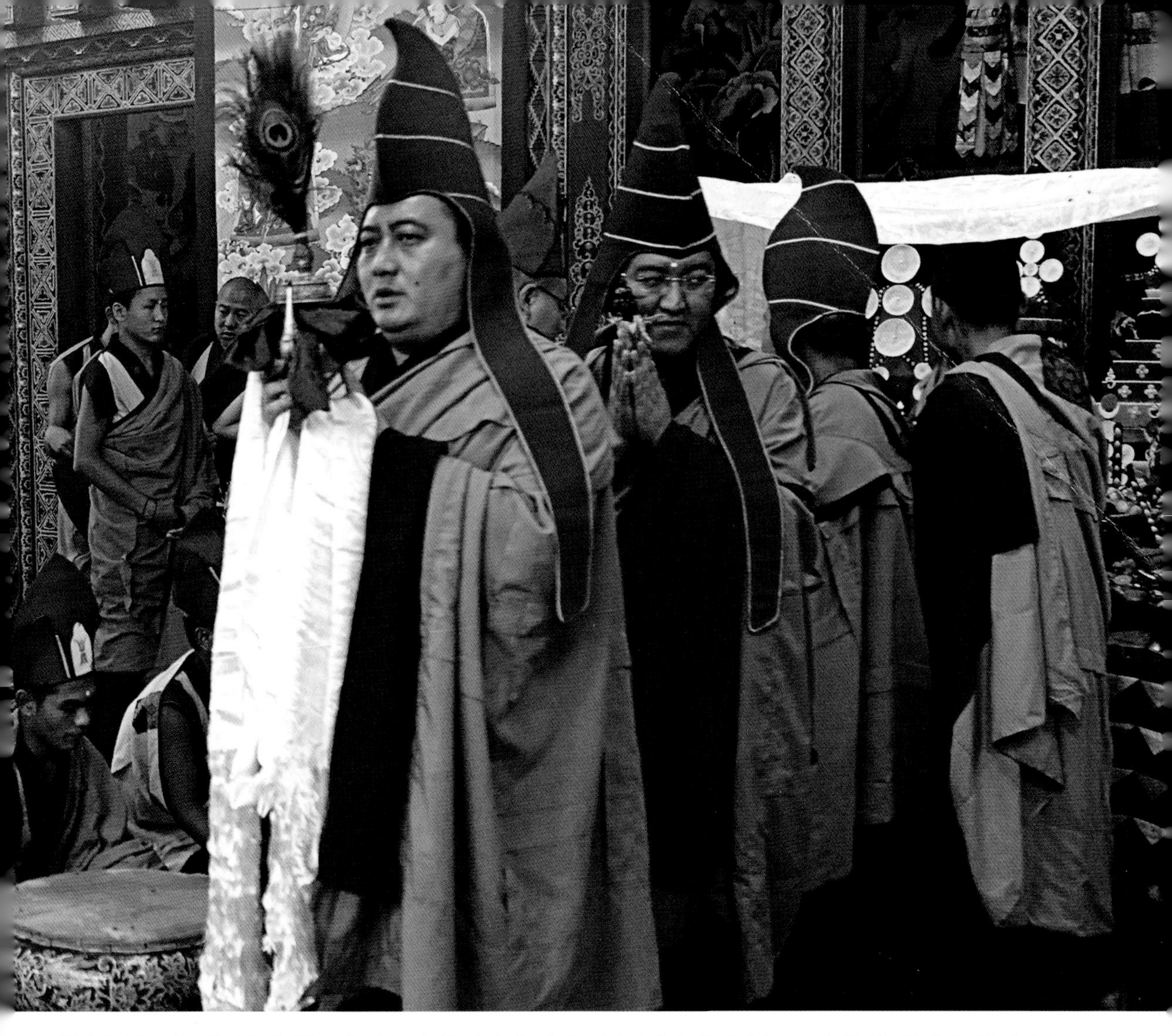

THE GREAT ACCOMPLISHMENT CEREMONY

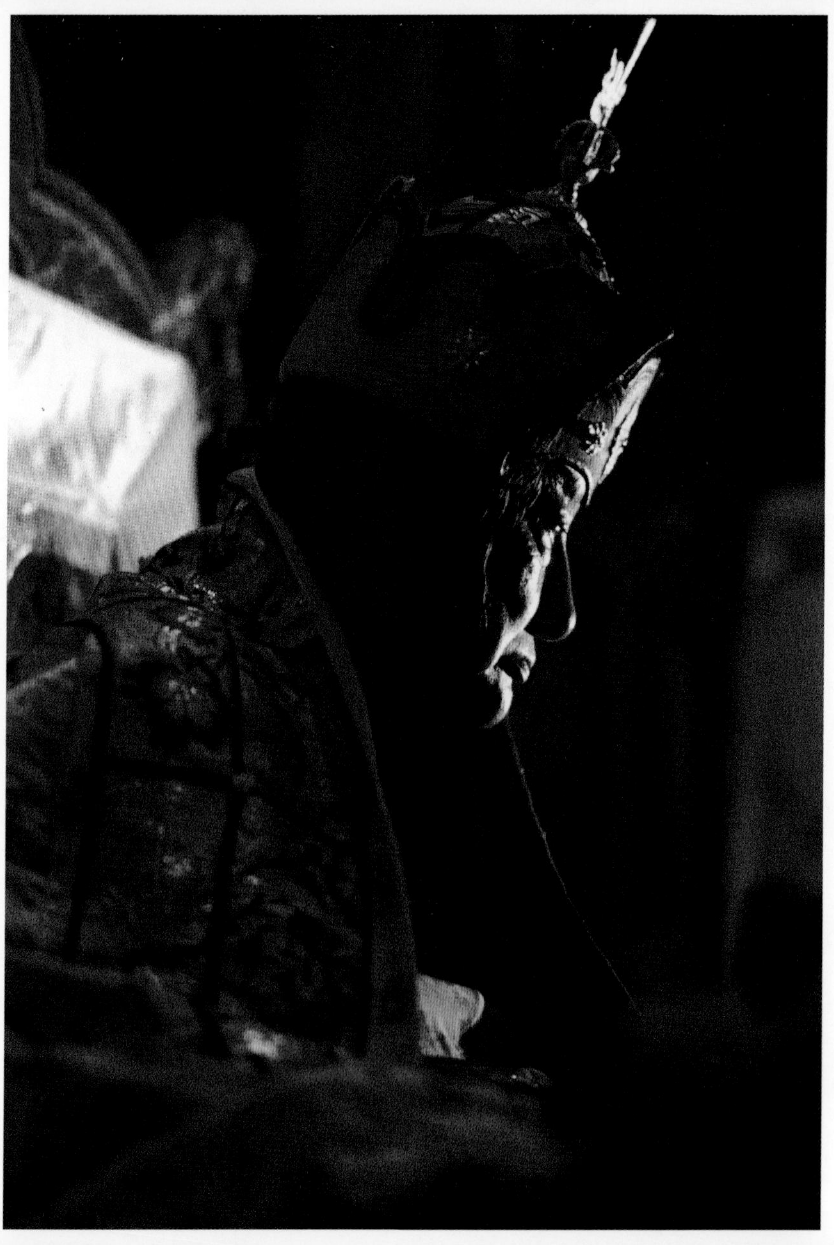

Dilgo Khyentse Rinpoche at a Great Accomplishment ceremony at Paro, in 1984.

The Great Accomplishment Ceremony

We are in the Paro valley, at Kyichu, in the temple courtyard, with its large grey paving slabs. We can already hear music, trumpet notes and oboes, cymbal clashes and the heavy thud of drums, which resound from within the temple. In Bhutan, religious ceremonies are magnificent events that usually go on for many hours. But this is no ordinary ceremony. The event that is unfolding here is a *drupchen*, a 'Great Accomplishment', and it will last for eight days and seven nights without interruption. *Drupchen* are in fact profound meditations using sacred texts as guides to the essential themes of Buddhist meditation, such as emptiness, love and compassion. For twenty-seven years Dilgo Khyentse Rinpoche used to preside over these special gatherings, inspiring the participants with his powerful and compassionate presence.

Founded in the 7th century by Songtsen Gampo, Tibet's first Buddhist king, Kyichu is one of Bhutan's great treasures, a place of profound spiritual importance. It has a small and very ancient chapel where a crowned Buddha sits enthroned amidst images of the eight *bodhisattvas*, the 'heroes of compassion'. Clearly visible in front of the altar, on the shiny dark floor, are a number of curious marks that look like toe prints embedded in the thick planks of hard wood. They have been made over the centuries by devotees prostrating themselves 100,000 times in front of the precious statue of the Buddha – a spiritual commitment that takes two months to accomplish, when carried on throughout the day. One practitioner after another has prostrated on the same spot and the light rubbing of so many feet has ended up hollowing the surface of the wood, as if it were as soft as clay – a tiny detail that provides a measure of the devotion and perseverance of those Buddhist practitioners.

Next to Kyichu's small ancient chapel is a more recent temple housing a majestic statue of Padmasambhava that was made in the 1960s. The statue was built by the Queen Mother of Bhutan following the advice of the great master Dilgo Khyentse Rinpoche at a time when the country was experiencing a troubled period in its history. On its northern border, Tibet had just been invaded by China, while its other great neighbour, India, regarded Bhutan as 'an autonomous kingdom enjoying a special relationship with India'. Internal turmoil was also threatening the peace and stability of the country. Dilgo Khyentse Rinpoche had a series of dreams and premonitory visions, on the strength of which he made two recommendations: that the great statue should be erected at Kyichu and a *drupchen* be held there every year in order to ensure a peaceful future for Bhutan. Khyentse Rinpoche consecrated the statue – made of painted clay, its face and hands covered in a fine layer of gold – on repeated occasions and the figure radiates a powerful blessing. The statue is not empty. It contains no fewer than 100,000 miniature statues of Padmasambhava and thousands of pieces of rolled-up paper on which prayers and mantras have been printed. The temple walls are decorated with magnificent frescoes, protected by yellow silk curtains, which are the work of a contemplative artist, a disciple of Khyentse Rinpoche, who lived in a hermitage a few hours' walk further up the mountain from the 'Tiger's Lair'.

During the *drupchen*, the deep-voiced chanting of the liturgy is interspersed with bursts of musical offerings, mingling the sounds of long trumpets, bells, drums, and cymbals. There are also long moments of silence, during which the participants quietly recite mantras, sacred formulas which have a subtle effect on the mind. The Sanskrit word mantra literally means 'that which protects the mind': a mantra protects the mind from confusion, distraction and the inner poisons of hatred, desire, pride and jealousy. Above all, repeating a mantra helps us to free ourselves from unhealthy grasping to the ego whose illusory nature is the source of so much unnecessary suffering.

The monks gather in the temple for the entire day, from seven in the morning until seven in the evening, and are joined by lay practitioners, who attend the ceremonies for a few hours at a stretch in order to absorb some of the blessings that flow from them. The Queen Mother, Ashe Kesang Choeden Wangchuck, the ceremony's benefactress since its inception, is regularly present. And while Dilgo Khyentse Rinpoche was alive, His Majesty the King sometimes came to visit during the proceedings, which would come to a halt momentarily so that he and Dilgo Khyentse Rinpoche could talk. Wearing the large yellow scarf made of raw silk which only he and the Je Khenpo (patriarch of the Bhutanese monasteries) are entitled to wear in Bhutan, the king prostrated himself three times in front of Khyentse Rinpoche before receiving his blessing. He often asked to be given a private initiation, thereby perpetuating the master-disciple relationship established many years earlier.

During the night, the masters of ceremonies and the monks take turns so that the prayers, meditation and repetition of mantras can continue uninterrupted. One group attends from seven to eleven in the evening; a second group takes over until three in the morning; then the last group ensures the continuity of the ritual from three to seven in the morning. A rota is set up so that the monks who attended the first session the previous evening take part in the second session the next night, and so on. Throughout the night, tea and rice flakes are served to the participants, and villagers come and walk round and round the mandala, chanting mantras.

As the days and nights pass, the intense commitment demanded by the *drupchen*, in terms of concentration and perseverance, gives rise to an increasing sense of inner peace and clarity.

Instrumental music, singing and sacred dances all play an important part in the ritual. Depending on circumstances, music can be an offering, an invocation, a call to prayer, a way of maintaining the rhythm, or a support for meditation.

When the offering prayers are sung in the morning, monks wearing brocade costumes, bone ornaments and gilded tiaras, and personifying the sixteen offering goddesses, circle slowly round the mandala, performing gestures known as *mudras*, which symbolize the flowers, incense, lamps, perfume and other offerings dedicated to the deities of the mandala. At regular intervals, tea is served, accompanied twice a day by red rice, which the monks receive in a square piece of cloth that rests on their crossed legs in lieu of a plate. And at the end of every afternoon, dances are performed inside the temple. In this confined space, the monks execute elaborate and sometimes highly acrobatic dances accompanied by prayers intended to remove any obstacles, both internal and external, that might lie on the path to Enlightenment.

The daytime sessions end with the masters of ceremonies and sometimes members of the royal family, walking three times slowly around the three-dimensional mandala in the middle of the temple. Amidst a great burst of music and chanting, they make swirling patterns in the air with long ceremonial coloured silk scarves, invoking a rain of blessings on the mandala, all the participants of the Great Accomplishment ceremony and all beings everywhere.

On the morning of the last day, an offering ceremony dedicated to the 'wisdom fire' takes place in the monastery courtyard, and at the end of the afternoon comes a moving ceremony involving an offering of light. Each participant holds a lighted butter lamp and a stick of incense which unite him with his neighbours, a union symbolized by the knotted white scarves that link all the participants of the assembled gathering. The master of ceremonies starts up a slow, melodious chant, pausing after each verse so that those present can repeat it as a chorus. By singing the words of this prayer, the participants express their wish to practise together throughout their future lives until they finally achieve Enlightenment. The week concludes with moving prayers dedicated to world peace, the elimination of the multiple forms of suffering that affect sentient beings, the perpetuation of the Buddha's teachings, and the long life of the spiritual teachers who transmit them. And then the participants finally disperse, deeply enriched by this powerful experience.

It is not uncommon for a second *drupchen* to begin a few days after the first has finished. The great Tibetan master Dilgo Khyentse Rinpoche used to lead seven or eight Great Accomplishment ceremonies a year. I was fortunate enough to take part in many *drupchen* in his presence, and these most precious moments are forever engraved in my memory.

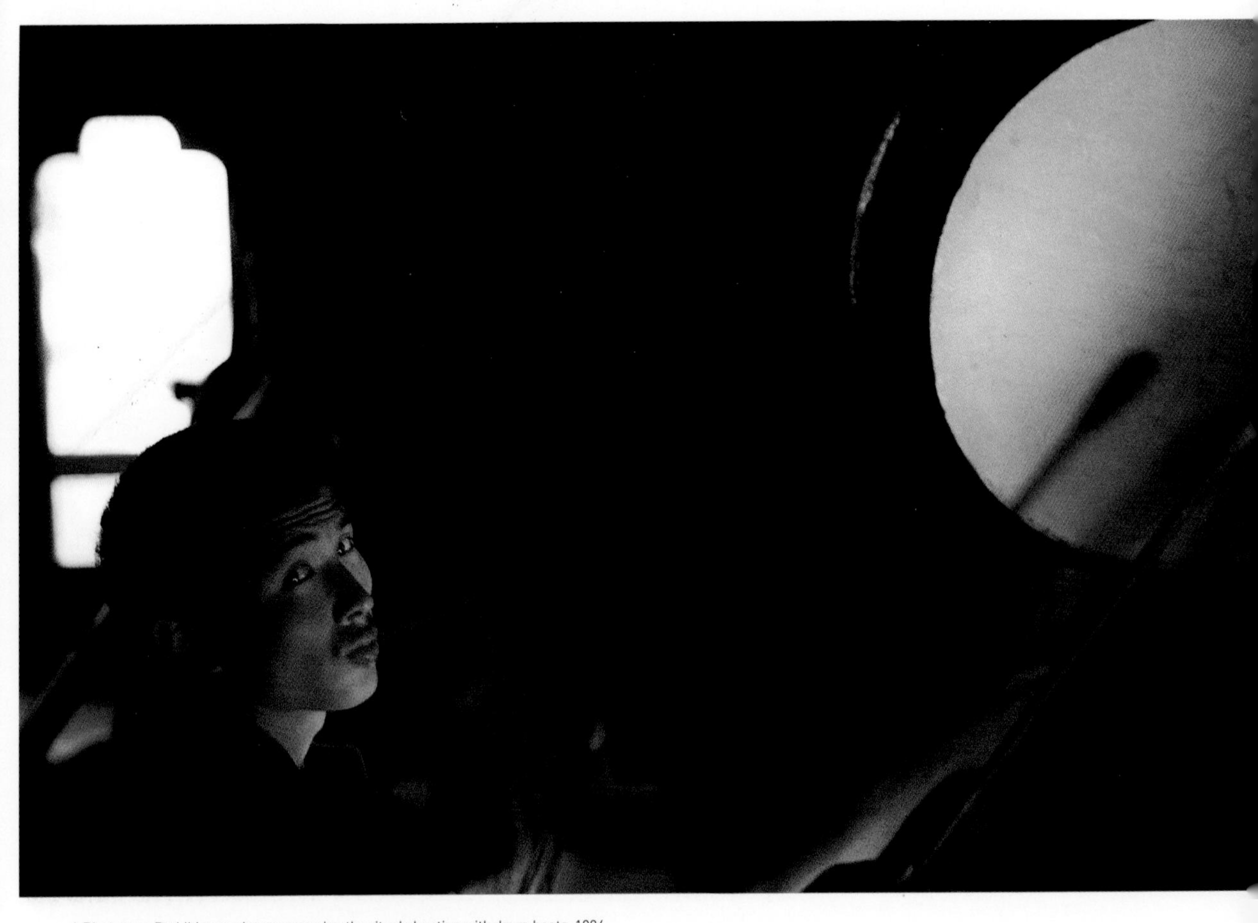

A Bhutanese Buddhist monk accompanying the ritual chanting with drum beats. 1984.

Dilgo Khyentse Rinpoche conducting a ritual by light from the butter lamps at dawn on the final day of the Great Accomplishment ceremony. Punakha, 1985.

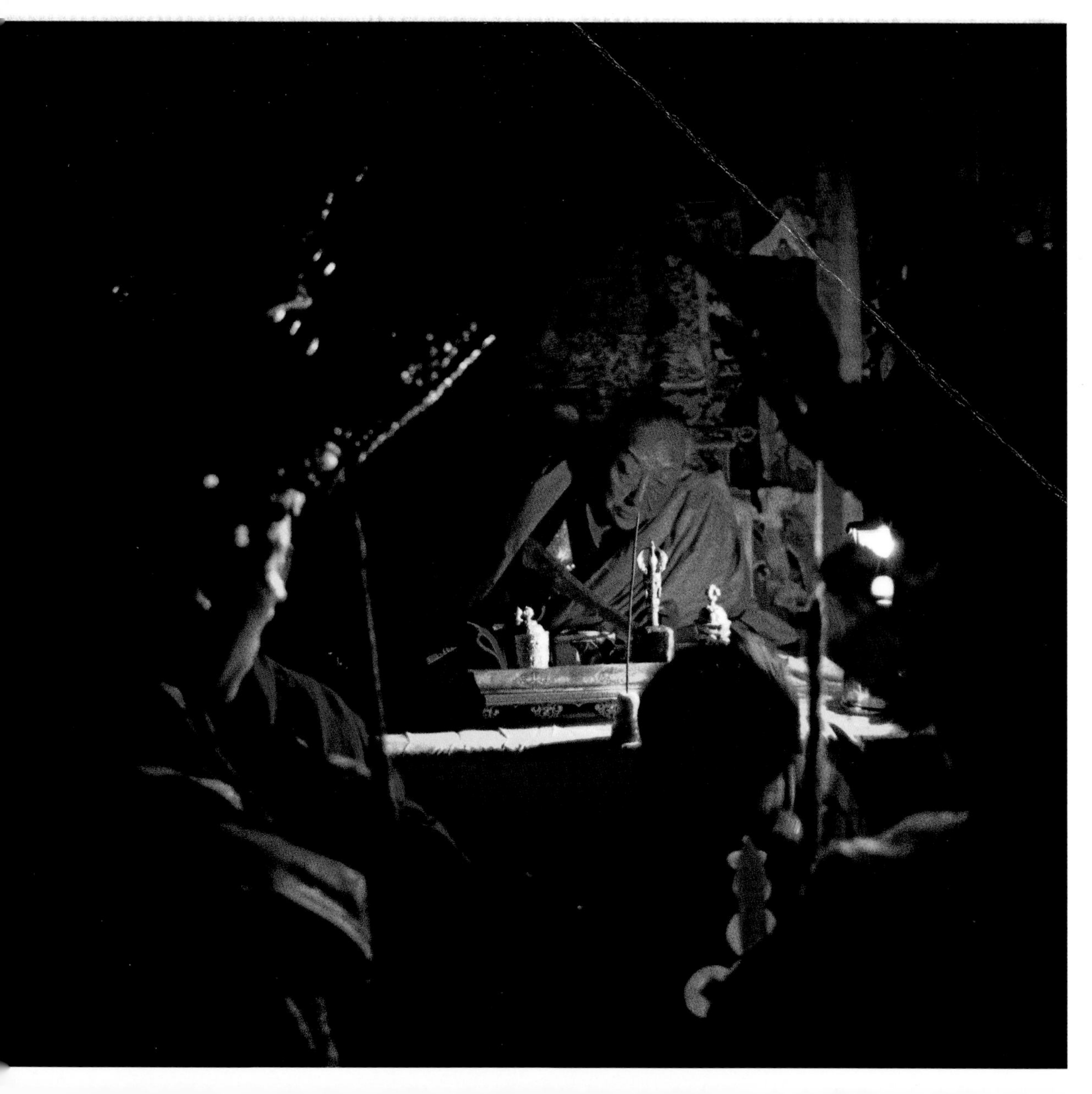

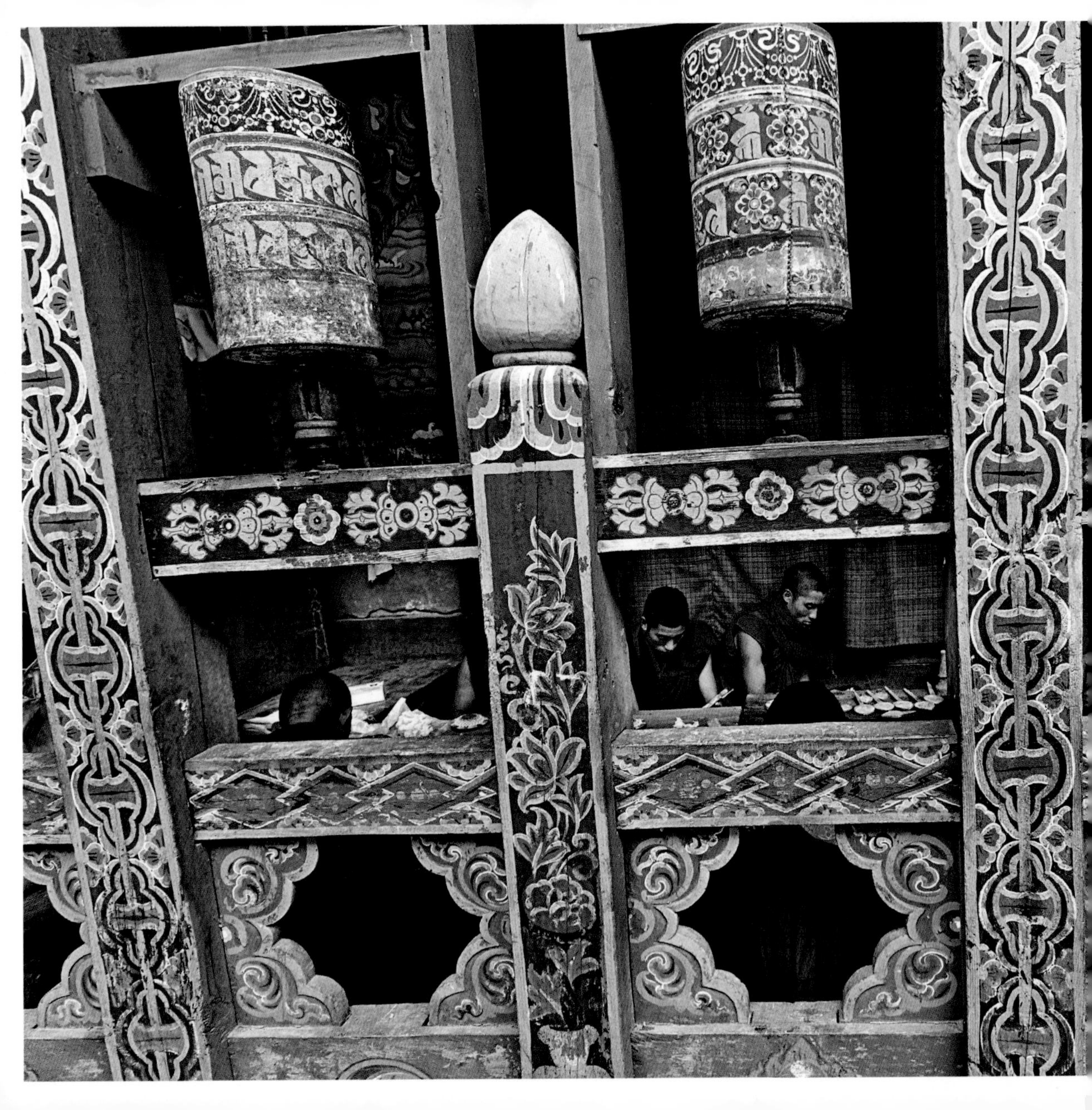

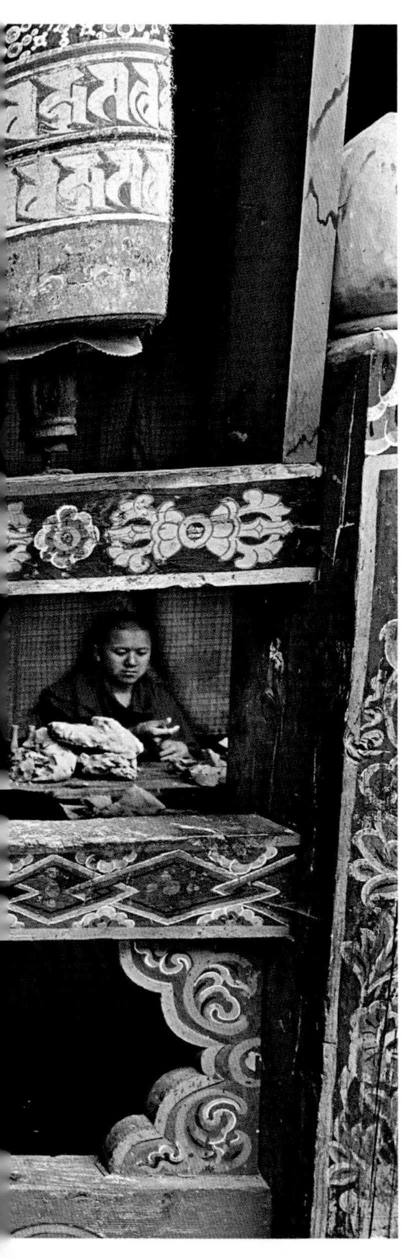

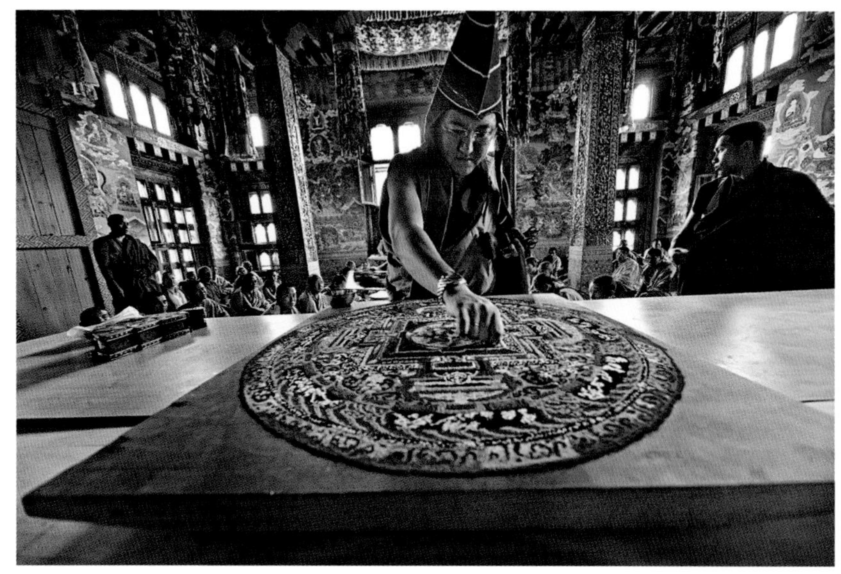

One of the masters of ceremony preparing to disperse the mandala, made from coloured powder, at the end of the annual Great Accomplishment ceremony. Temple of Satsam Chörten, Paro valley, 2007.

Left:
Behind the richly painted guard rail of a veranda, surmounted by prayer wheels, monks from Trongsar monastery are making offerings from flour and butter (*torma*) to place in front of the mandala. 2007.

Overleaf, left:
Monks from the Vajrakilaya temple (Phurba Lhakang) at Satsam Chörten in the Paro valley perform a ritual at the beginning of the Great Accomplishment ceremony to establish the sacred boundaries within which the ceremony will take place. This annual ceremony continues for nine days and nine nights. 2007.

Overleaf, right:
Led by their abbot, Shechen Rabjam Rinpoche, the monks walk in single file around the temple courtyard at the end of the Great Accomplishment ceremony. They are forming a 'circle of joy' (*gakyil*) after scattering the mandala powder in the river. Satsam Chörten, Paro, 2006.

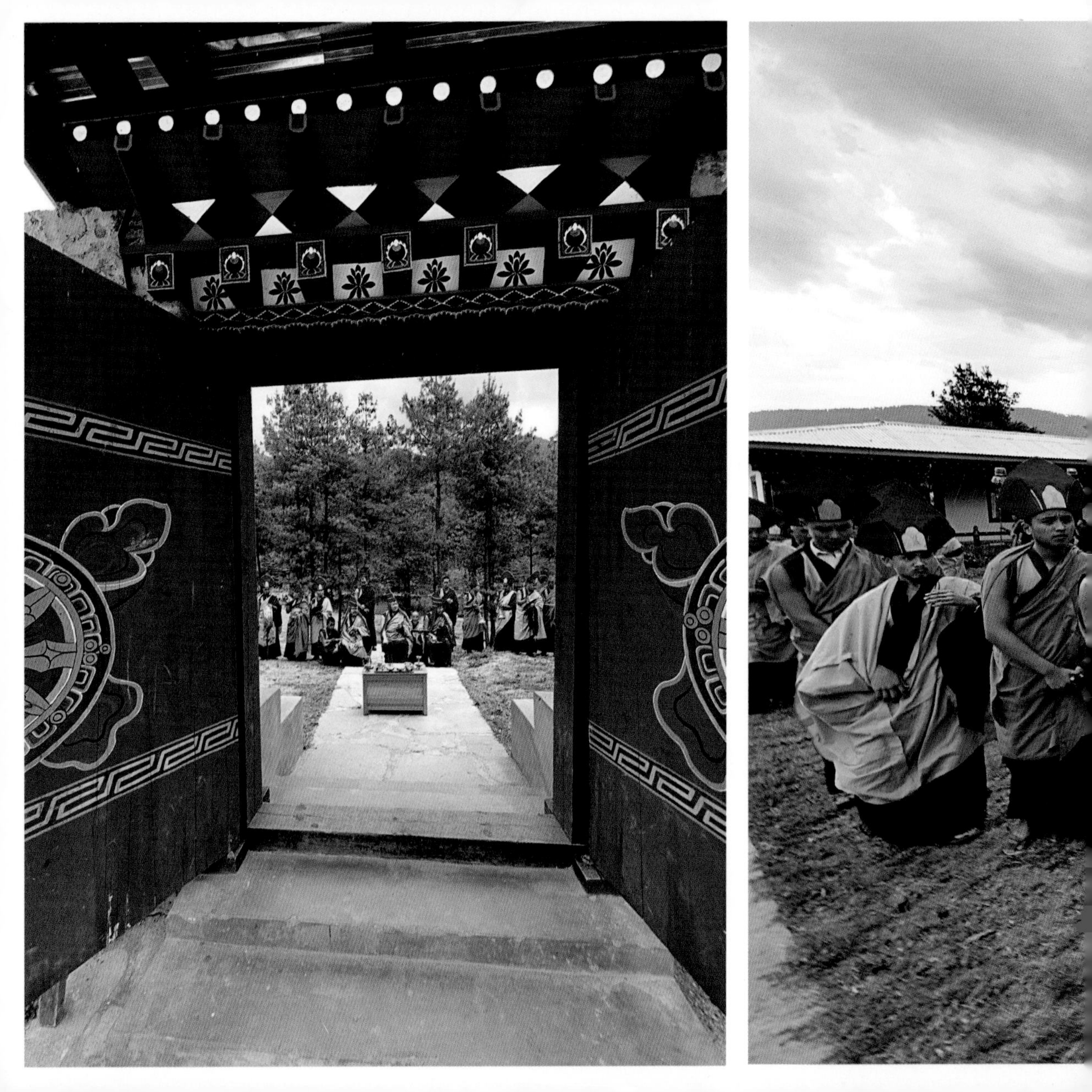

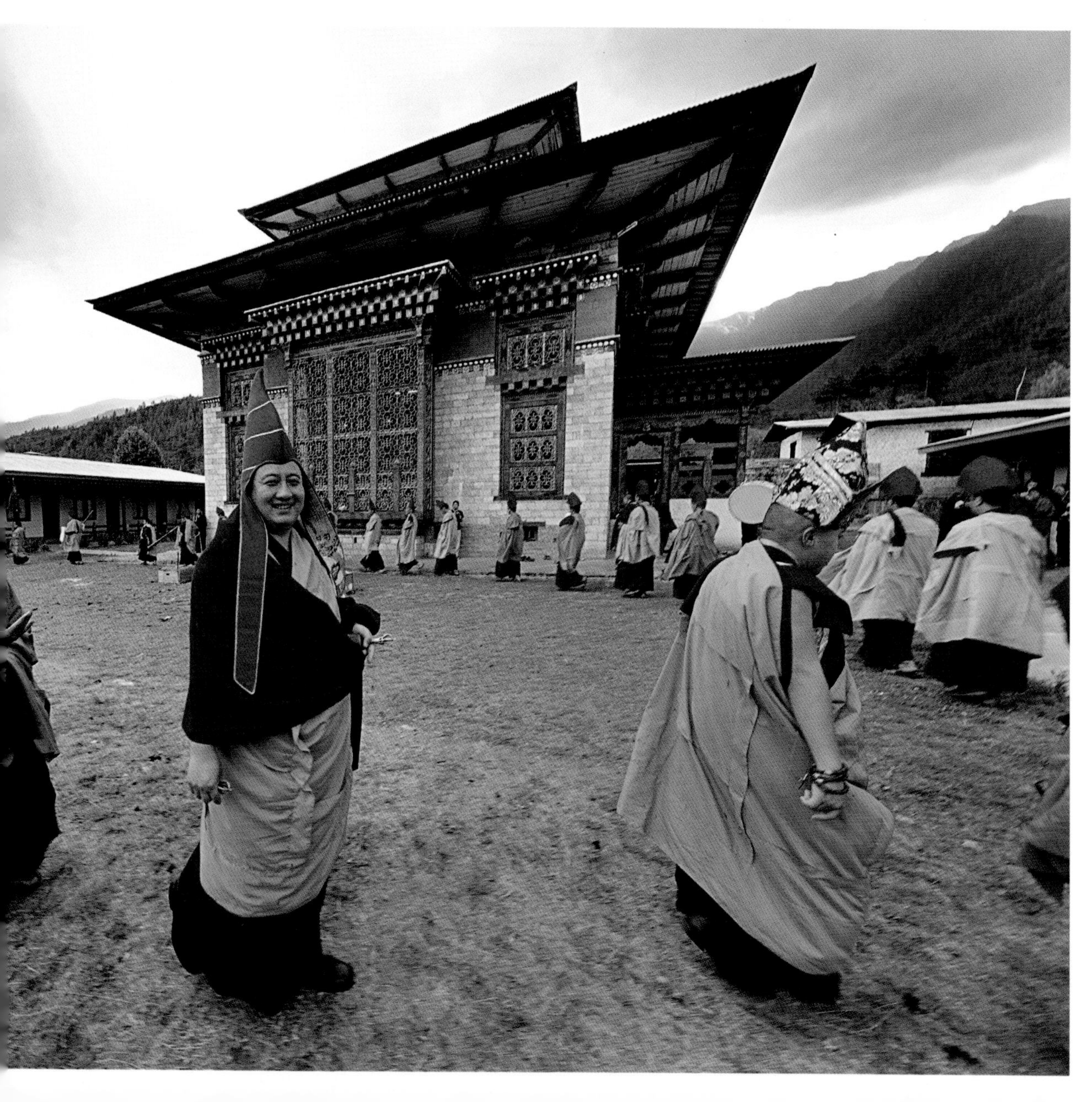

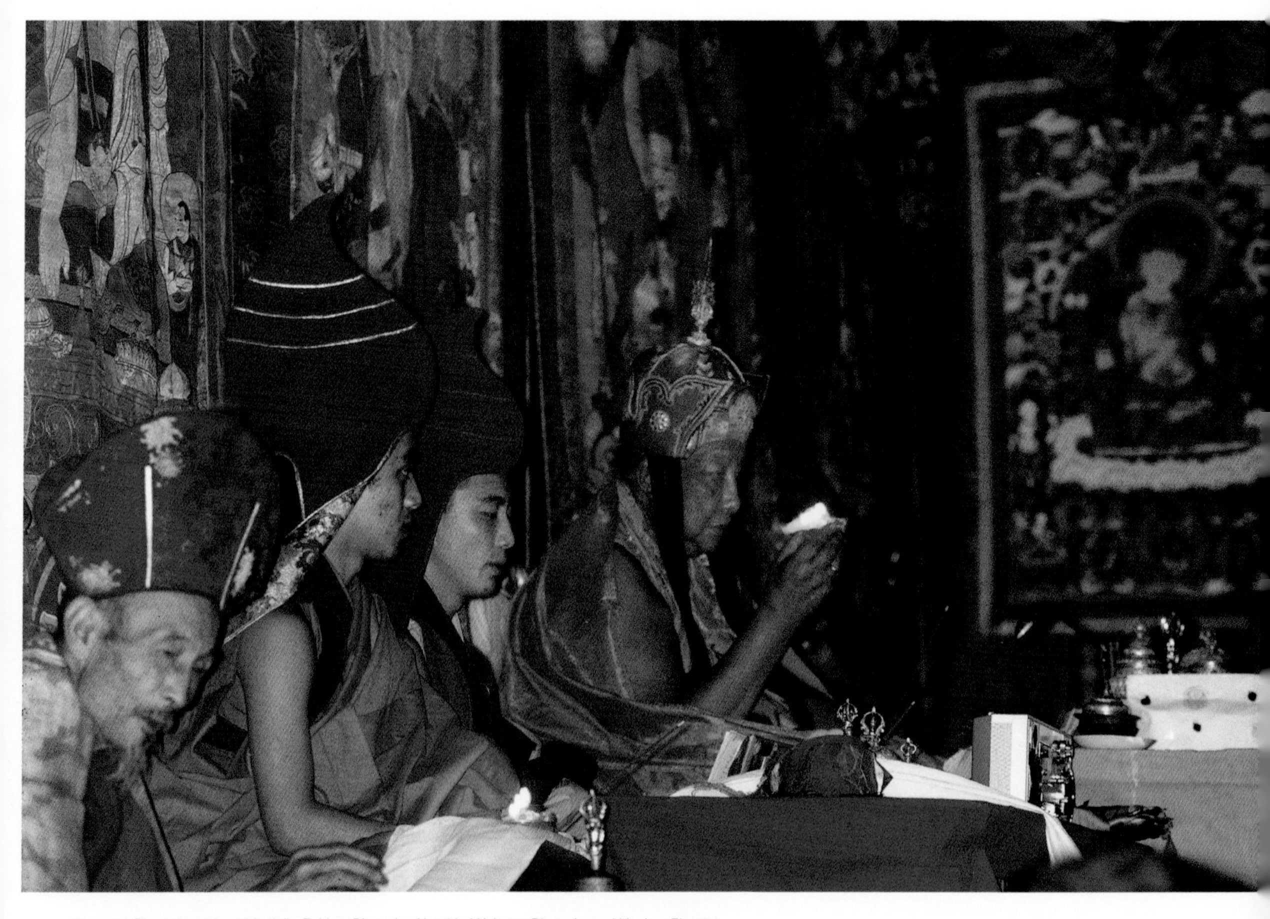

Khyentse Rinpoche with, on his right, Rabjam Rinpoche, Namkhai Nyingpo Rinpoche and Machen Zimpön, concluding the Great Accomplishment ceremony with an offering of light. Punakha monastery, 1982.

The statue of Guru Padmasambhava in the temple of Paro Kyichu. The statue contains 100,000 miniature statuettes as well as many sacred texts and the relics of spiritual teachers. It was built by the Queen Mother of Bhutan, following the recommendations of Dilgo Khyentse Rinpoche. 1989.

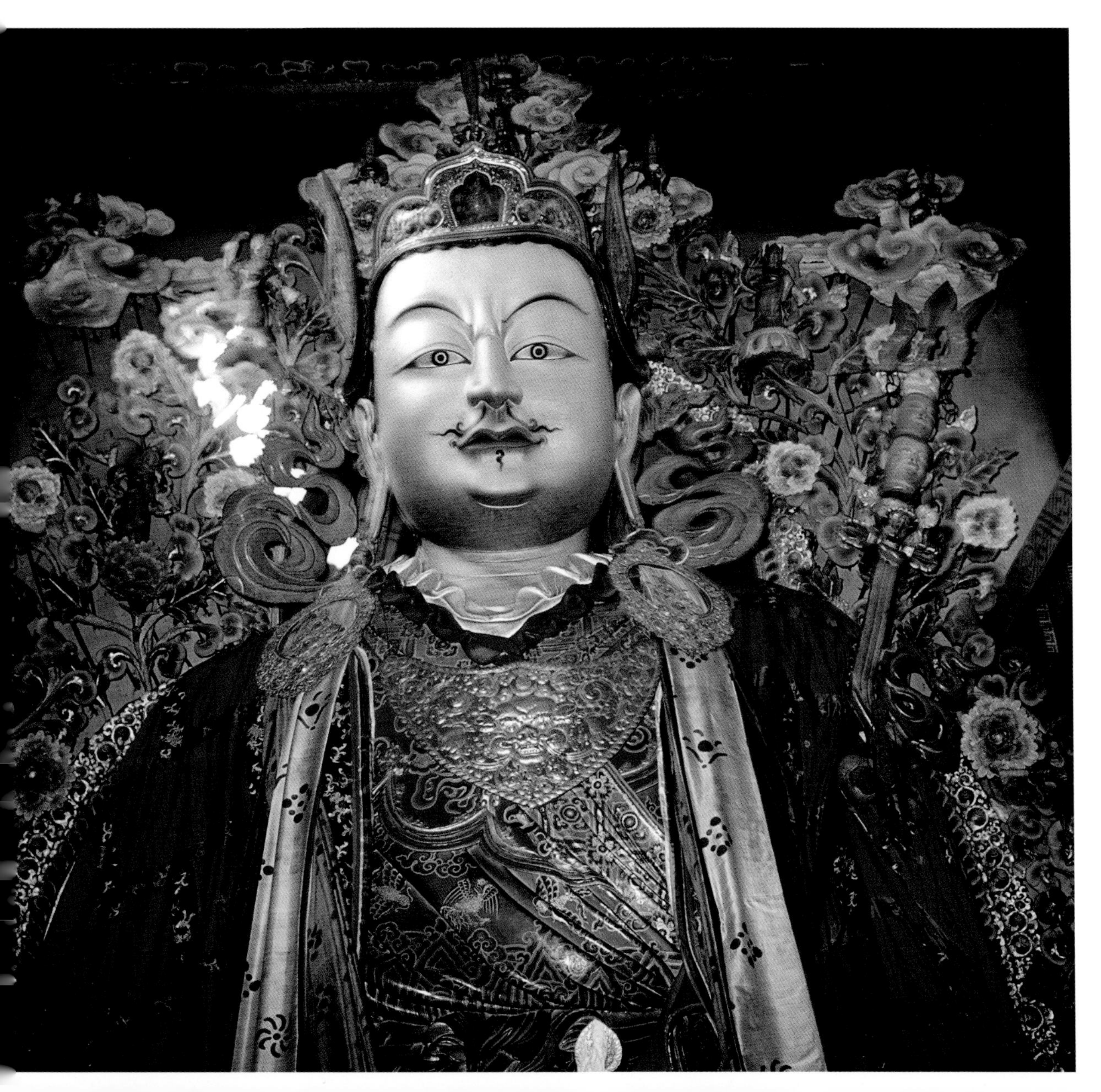

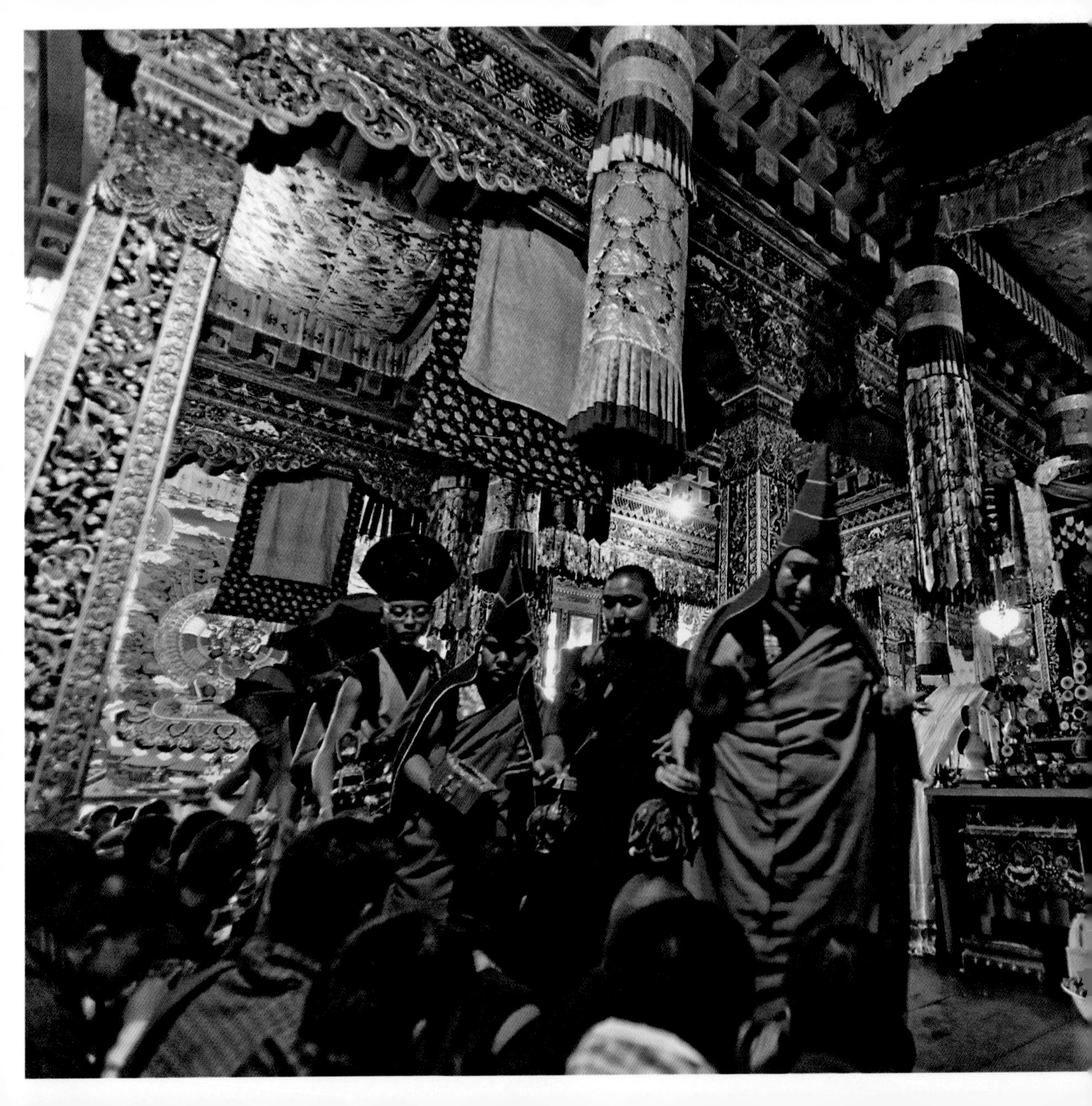

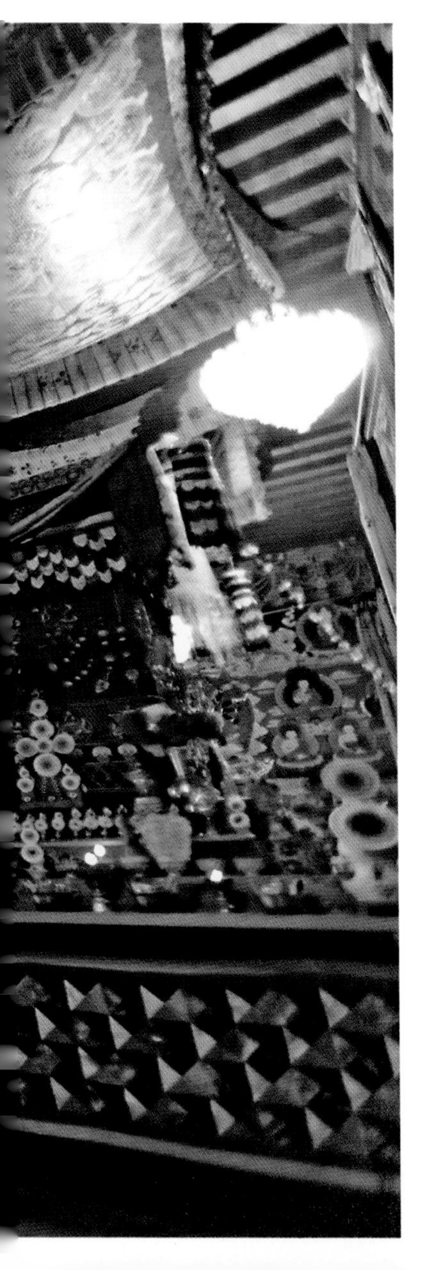

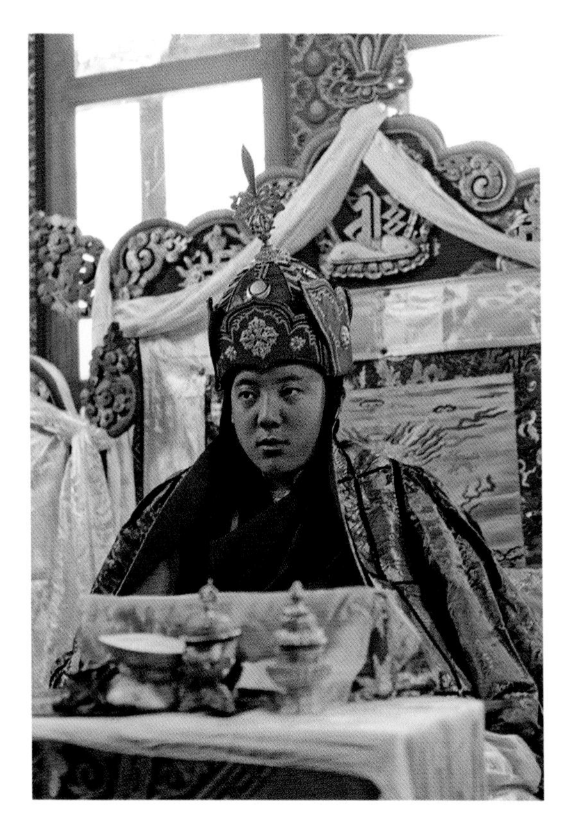

Dilgo Khyentse Rinpoche Yangsi at the age of thirteen. Kuje monastery, Bumthang province, June 2005.

Rabjam Rinpoche, abbot of Shechen monastery, accompanied by other lamas, blessing participants with sacred objects at the end of the *drupchen* ceremony. The objects have been placed inside the mandala during the nine days and nine nights of the ceremony. Kuje monastery, 2006.

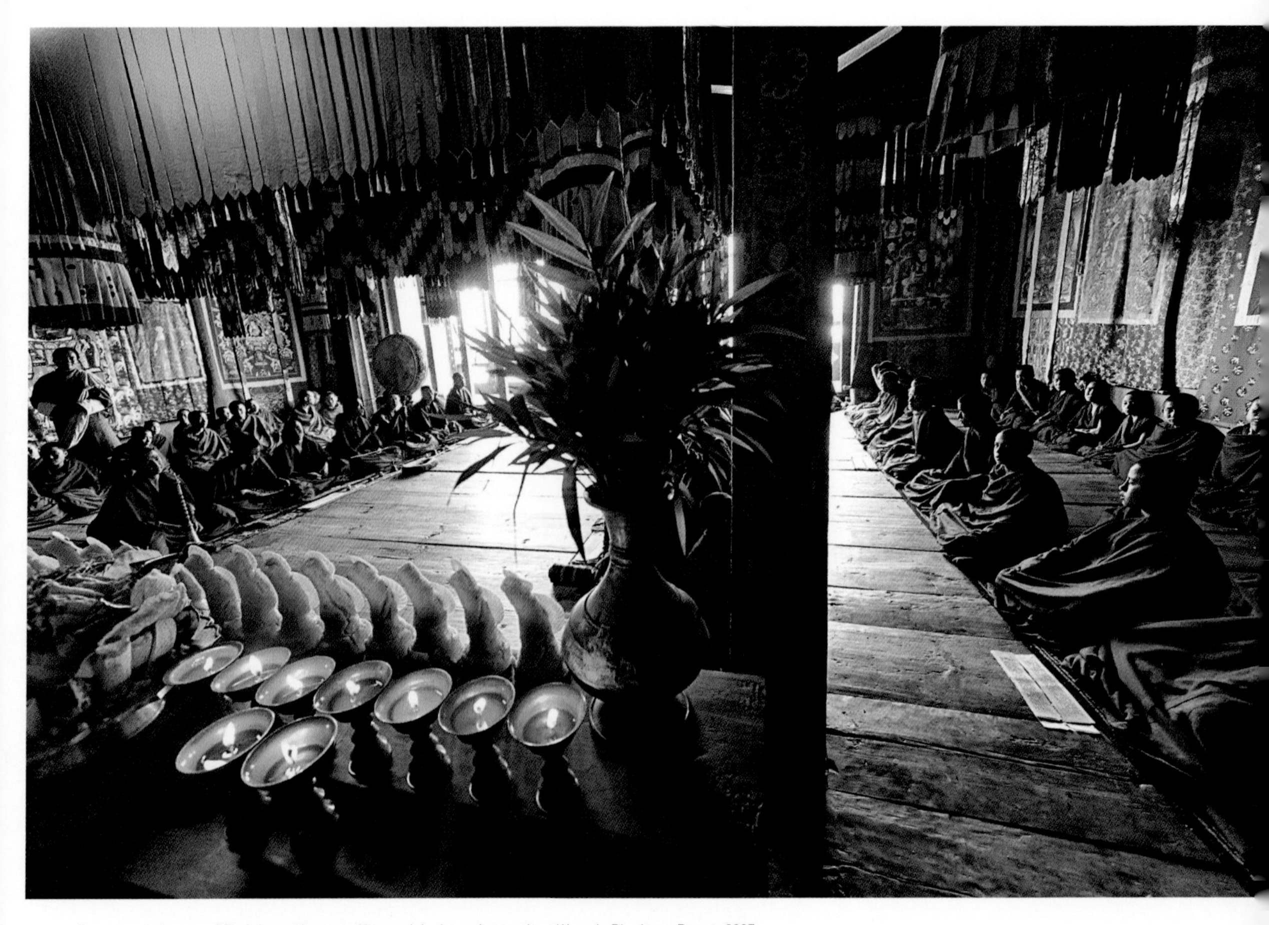

Ceremony in honour of Shabdrung Ngawang Namgyal, in the main temple at Wangdu Phodrang Dzong, 2007.

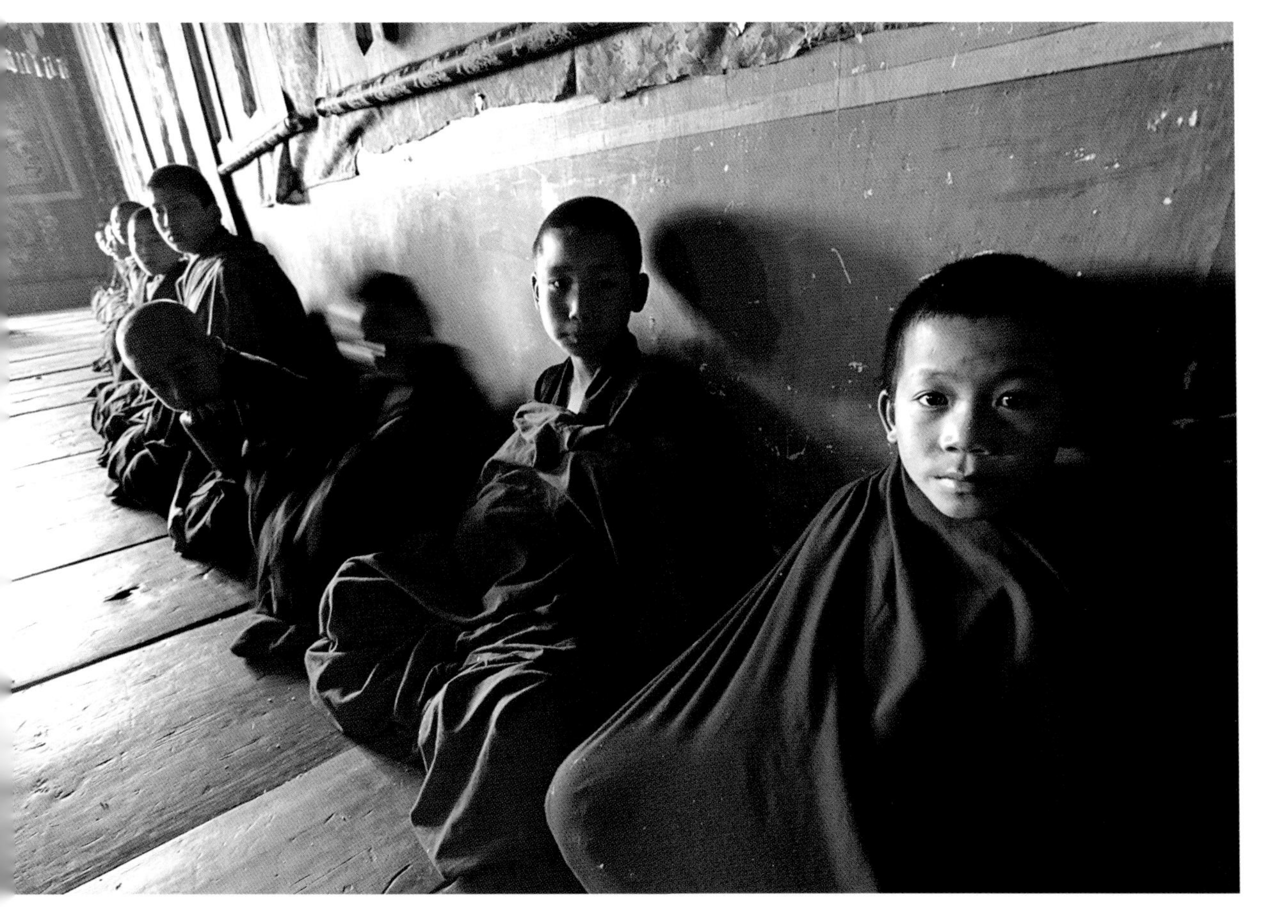

Young novices in the main temple at Wangdu Phodrang Dzong, 2007.

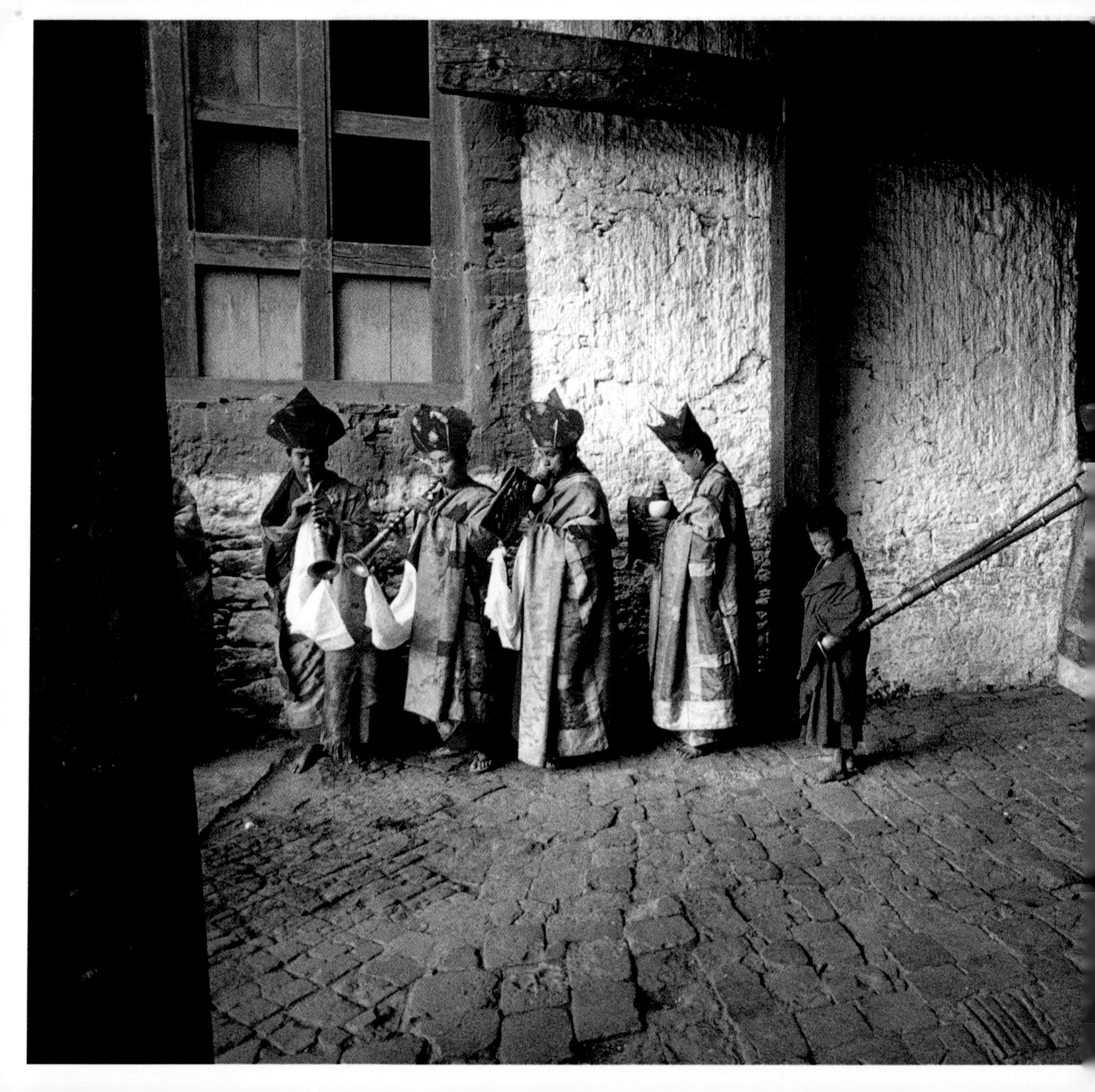

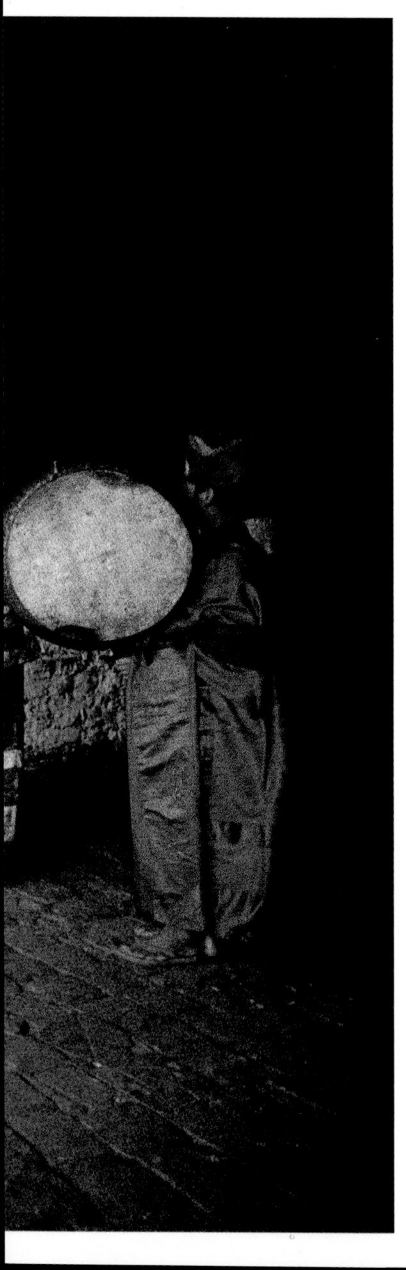

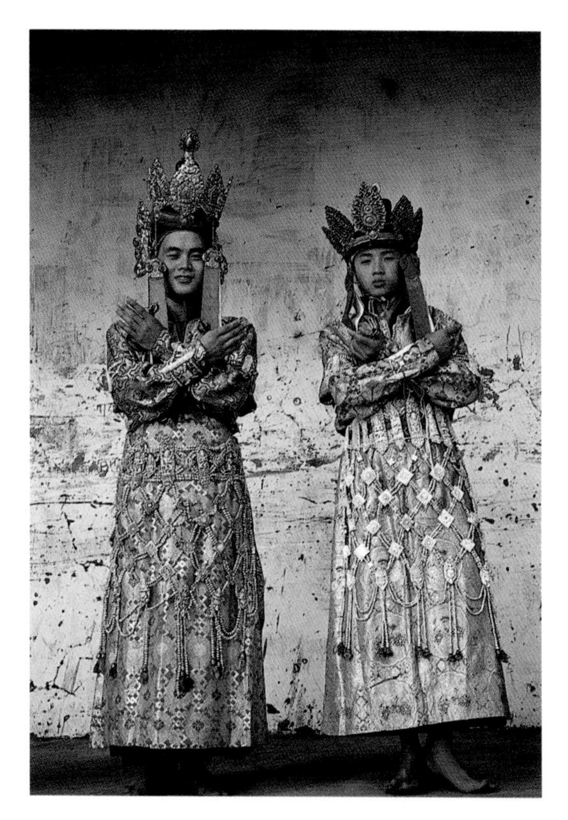

Bhutanese Buddhist monks dressed as offering goddesses and wearing golden tiaras and bone ornaments. Sixteen goddesses circle slowly round the mandala and perform gestures (*mudra*) symbolizing the offering of flowers, incense, lamps and perfume each morning while prayers are sung. Punakha, 1982.

Left:
A procession of monks, Punakha monastery, 1987.

Overleaf, left and right:
Rabjam Rinpoche, Khyentse Rinpoche's grandson, officiating late into the night during the conclusion of a week-long ceremony designed to remove the obstacles to world peace. Paro Kyichu, 1982.

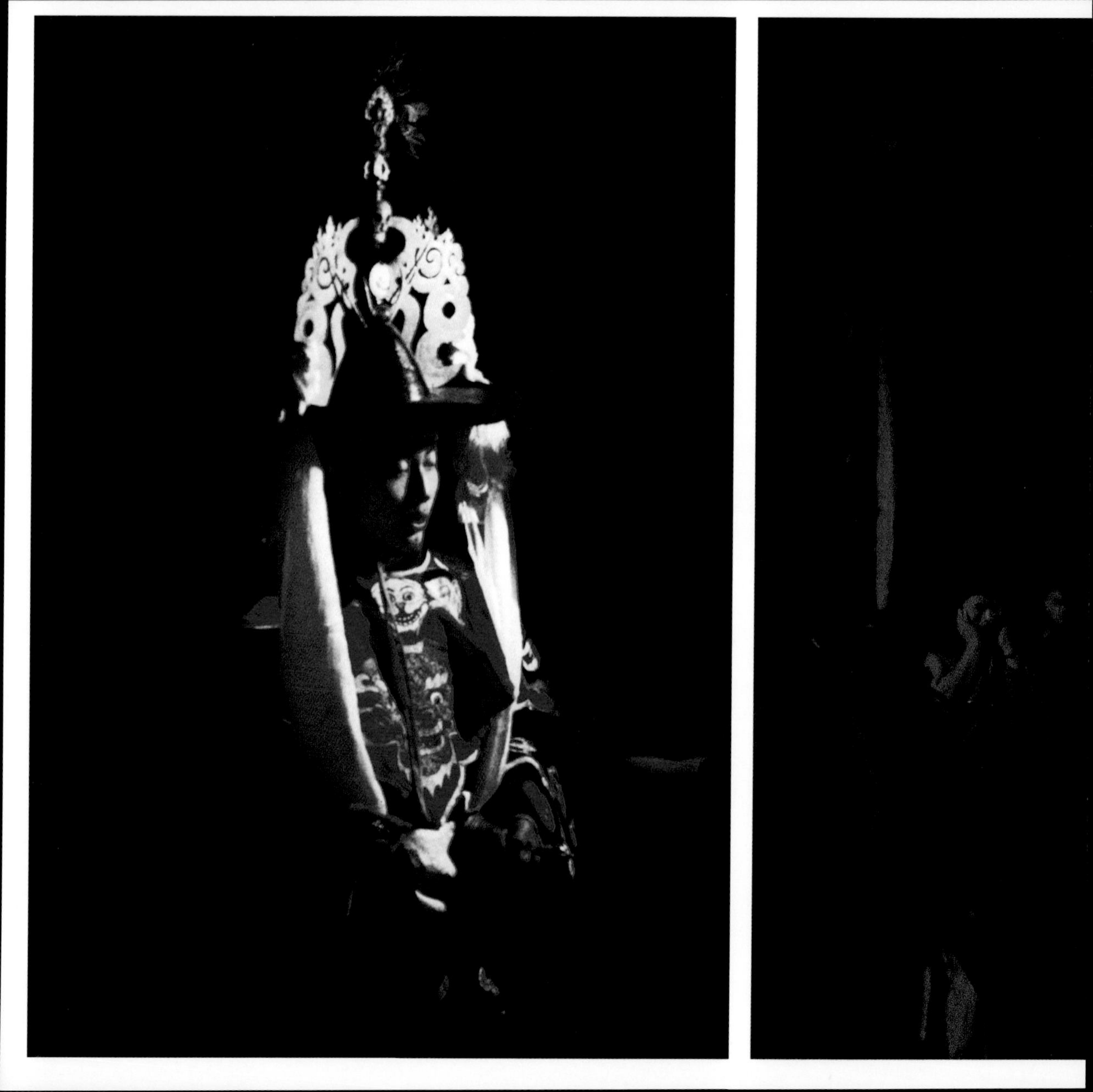

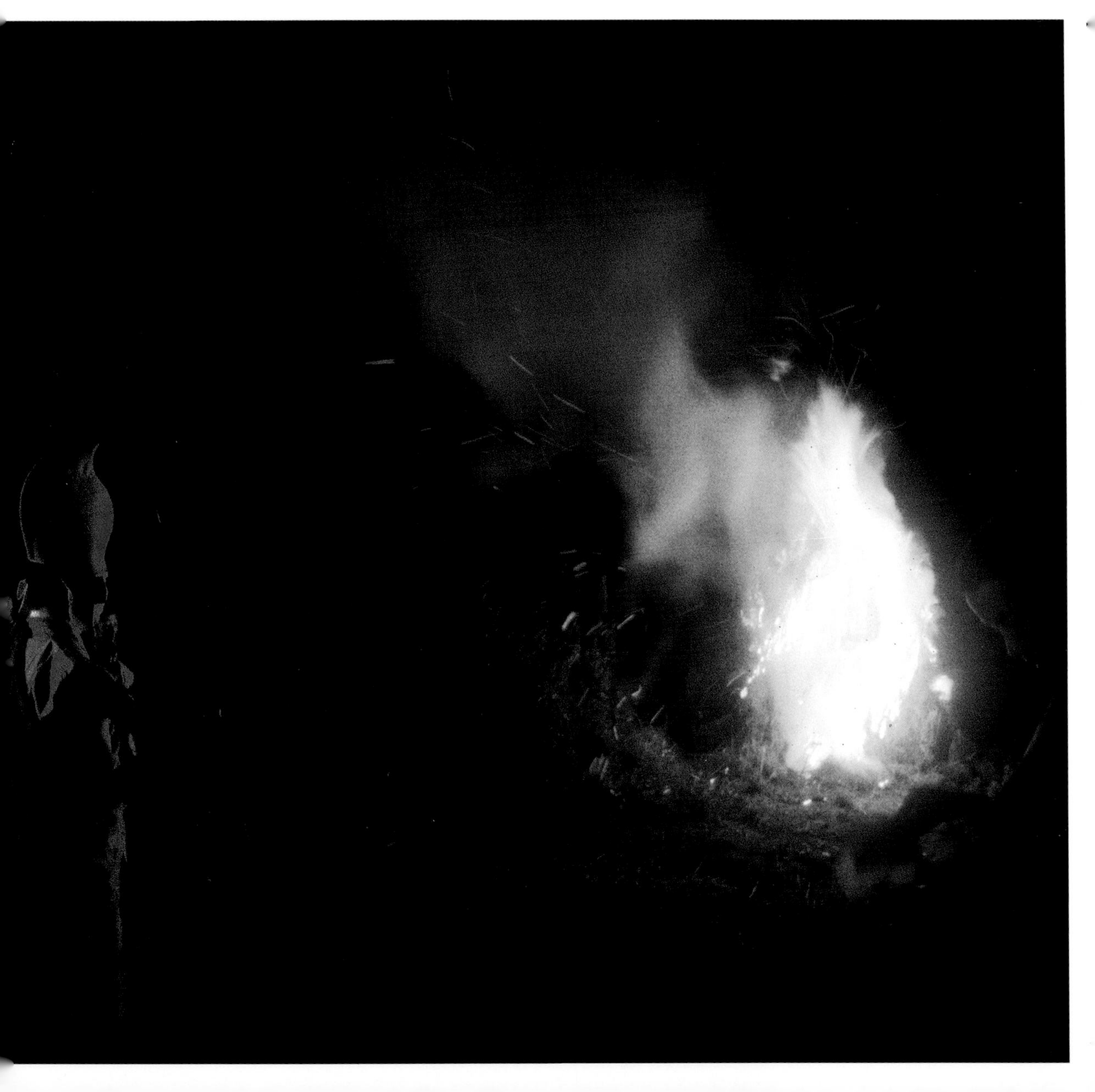

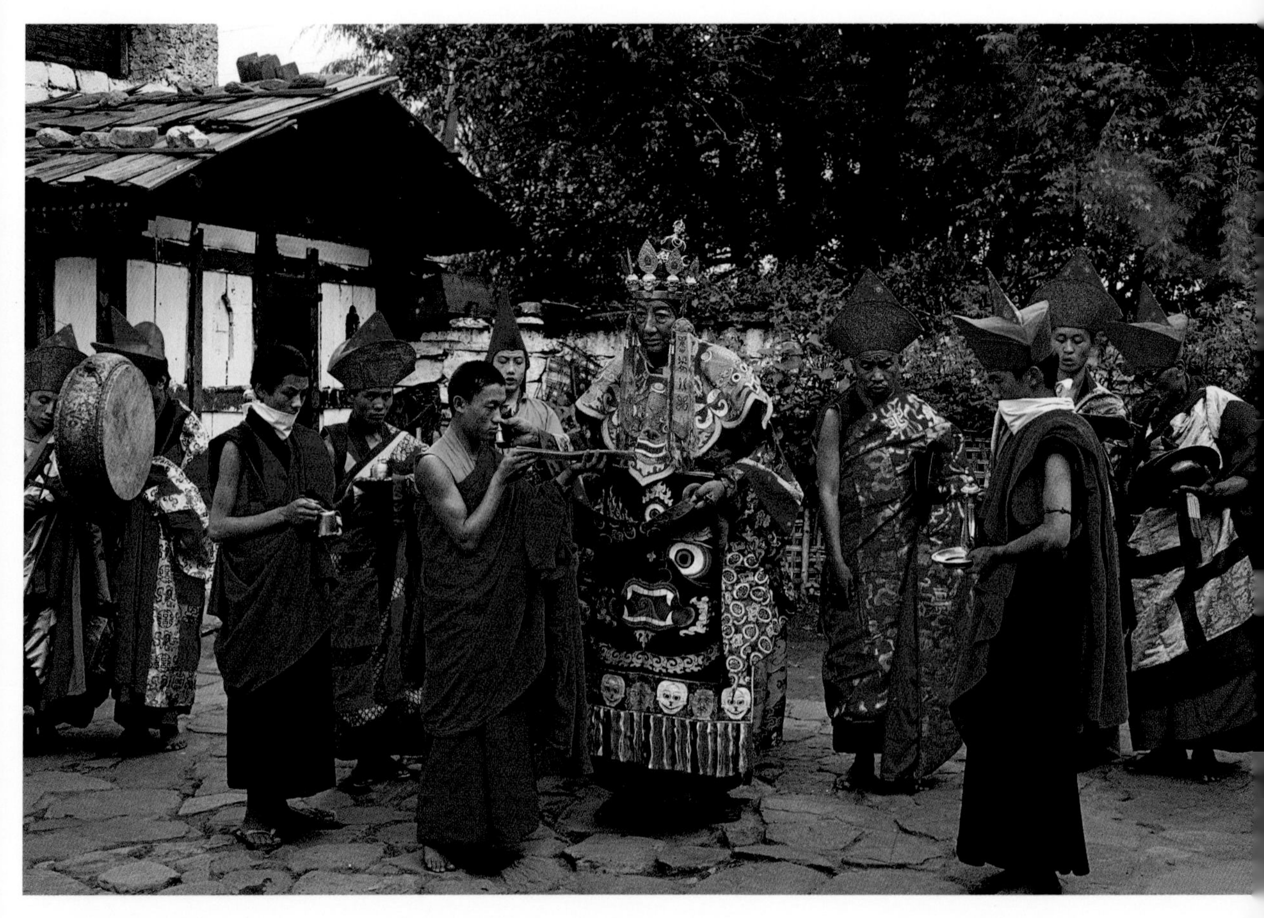

Above and opposite:
Khyentse Rinpoche at Paro Kyichu during a preliminary part of the *drupchen* ceremony, 1983.

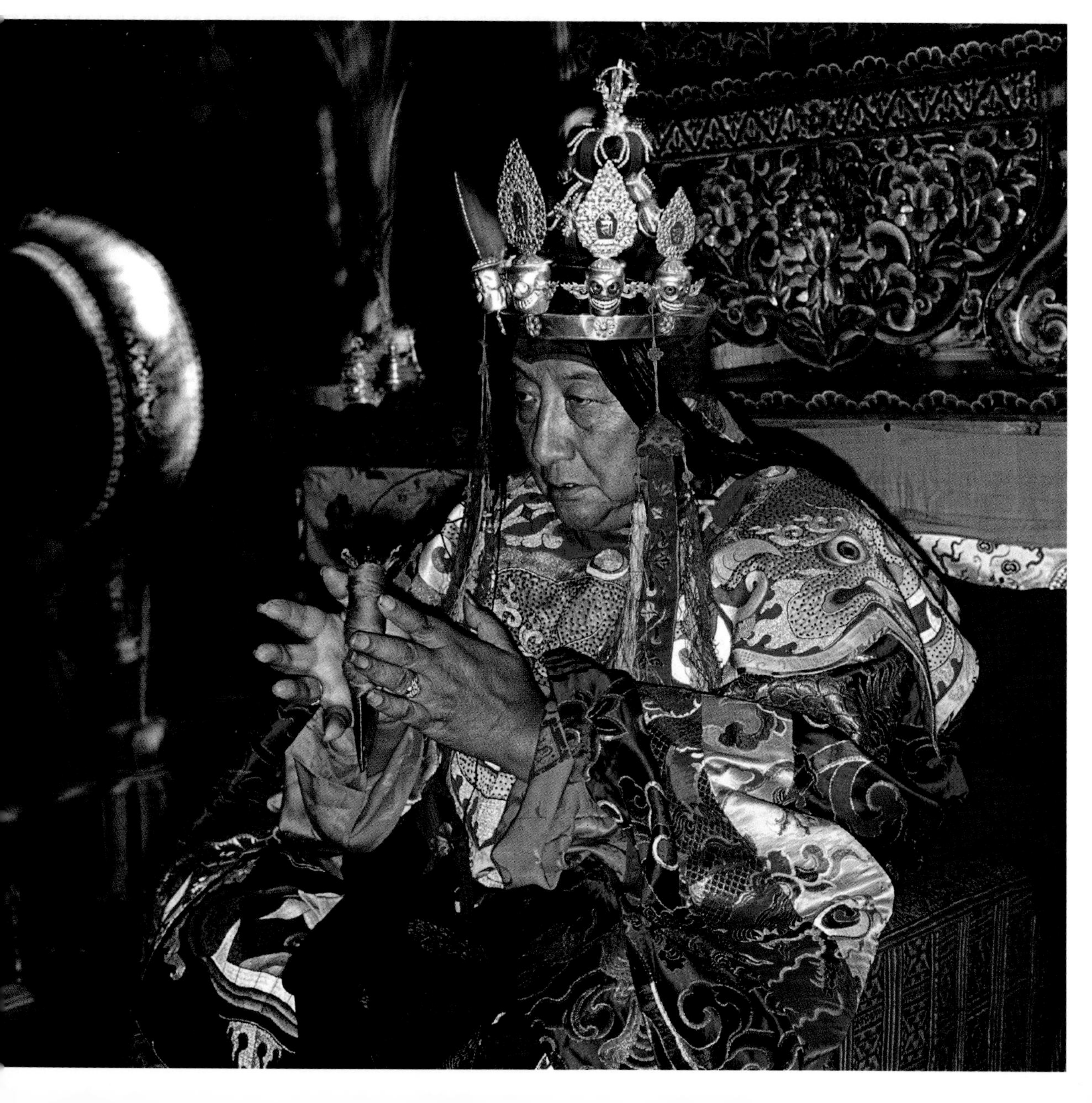

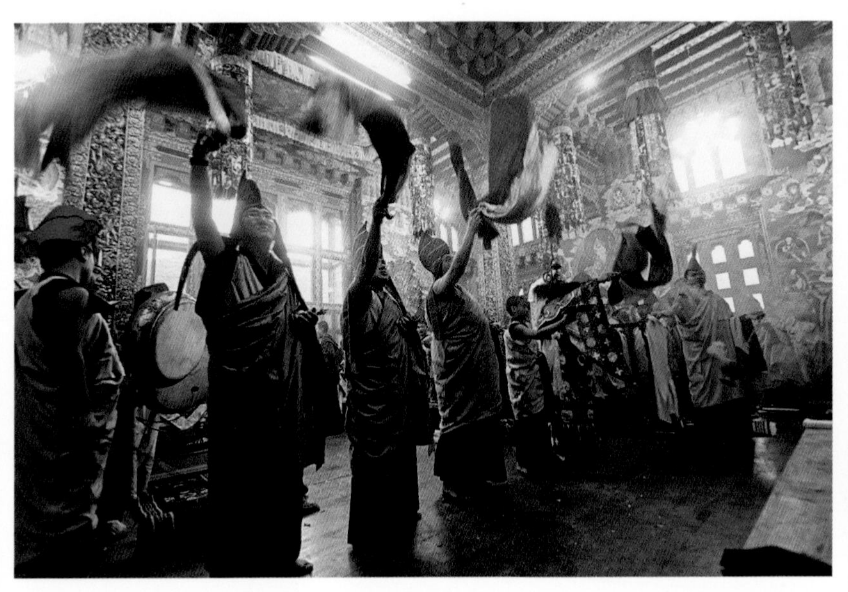

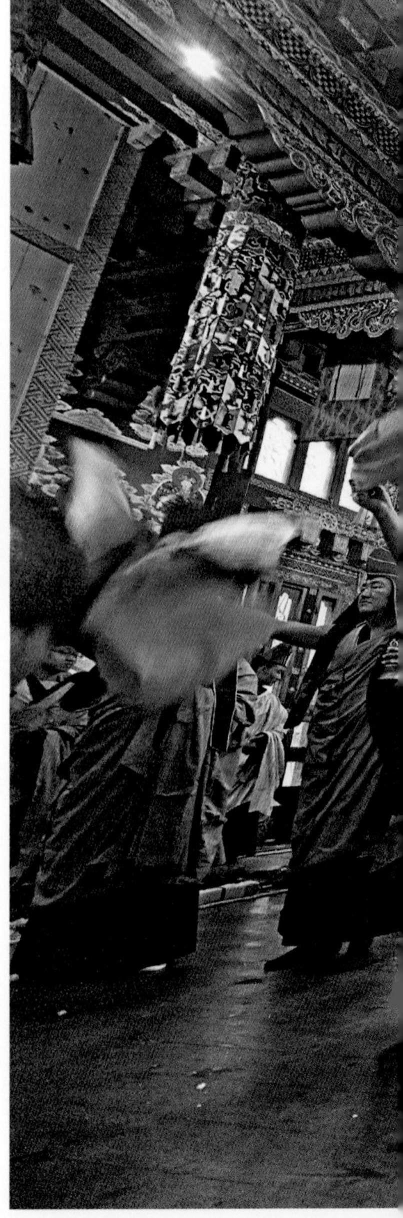

Above and right:
The principal lamas gathering round the mandala at the end of the afternoon in order to invoke a 'rain of blessings' on the mandala and all the participants of the *drupchen*. Phurba Lhakhang, Paro, 2006.

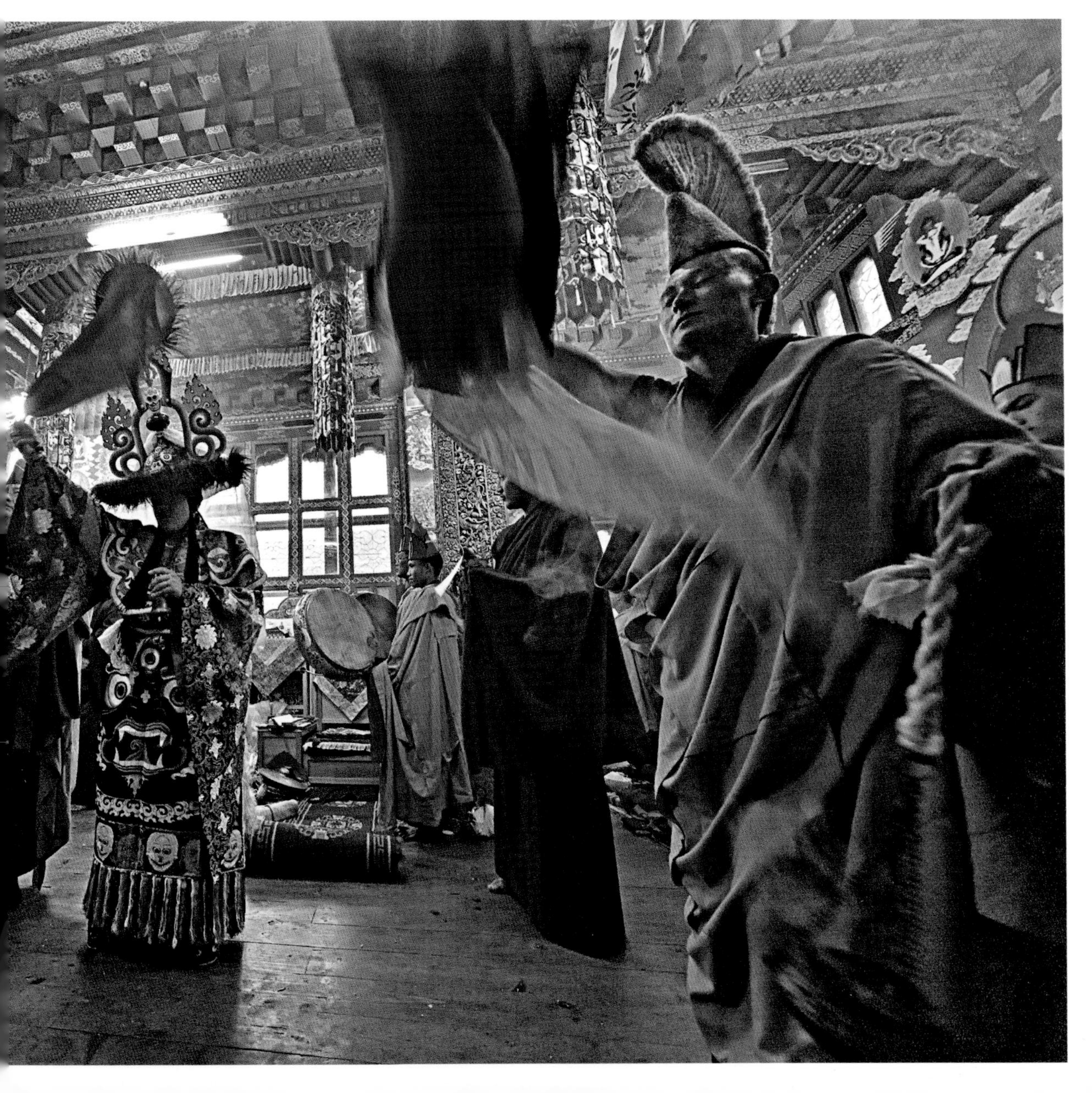

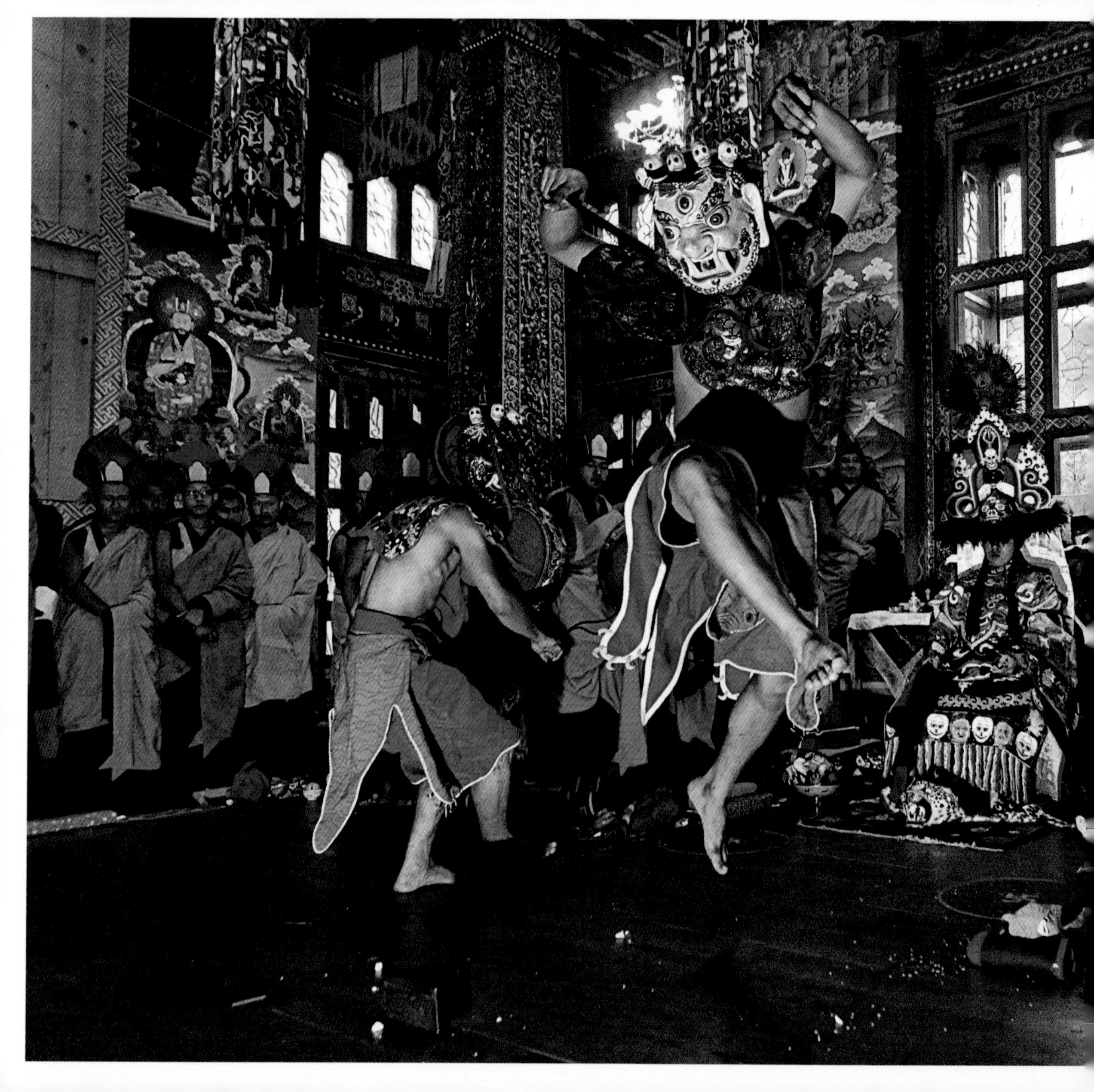

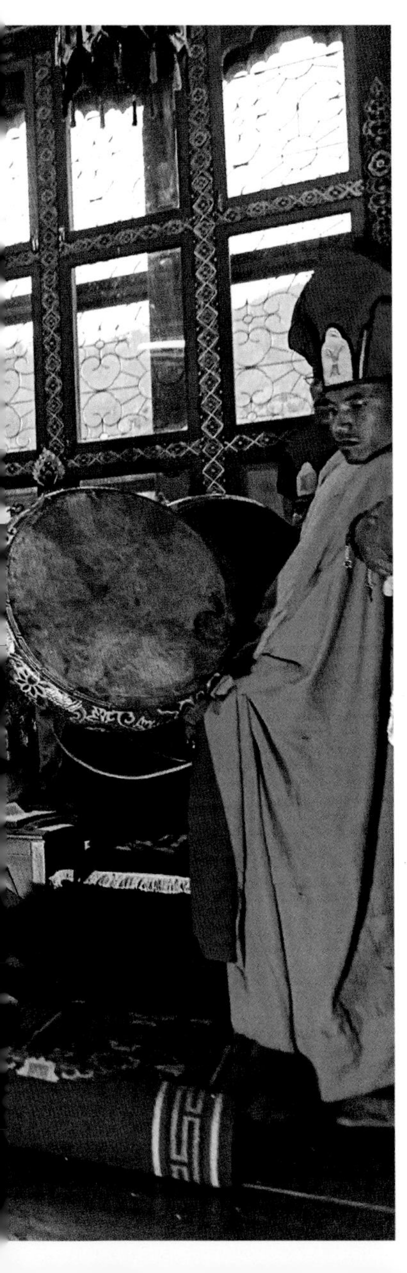

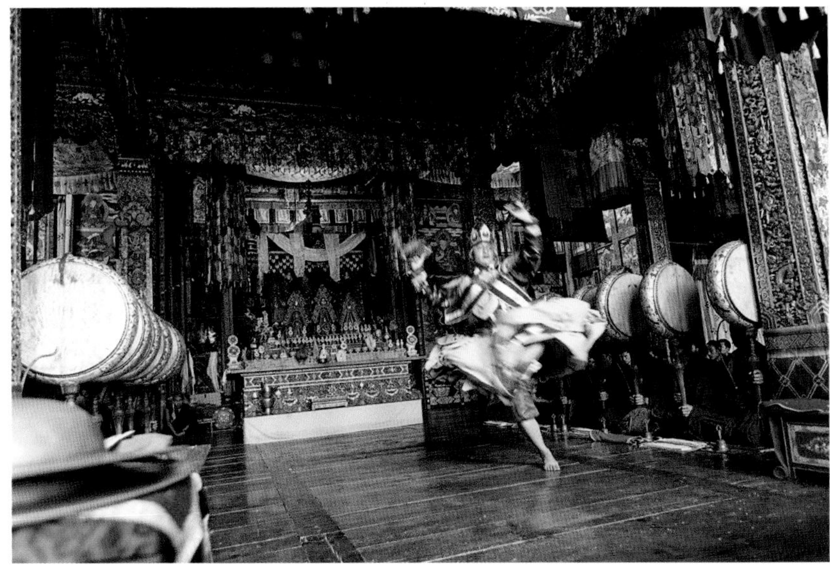

Above and overleaf:
This acrobatic whirling dance accompanies the 'prayer in seven chapters' (*leu dun-ma*), which describes the life and qualities of Padmasambhava. It is performed by two monks in a tiny area inside the temple. Kuje temple, 2006.

Dances being performed at the end of the afternoon at Satsam Chörten as part of the ritual designed to eliminate any obstacles that might interrupt the nine-day ceremony prior to its conclusion. 2007.

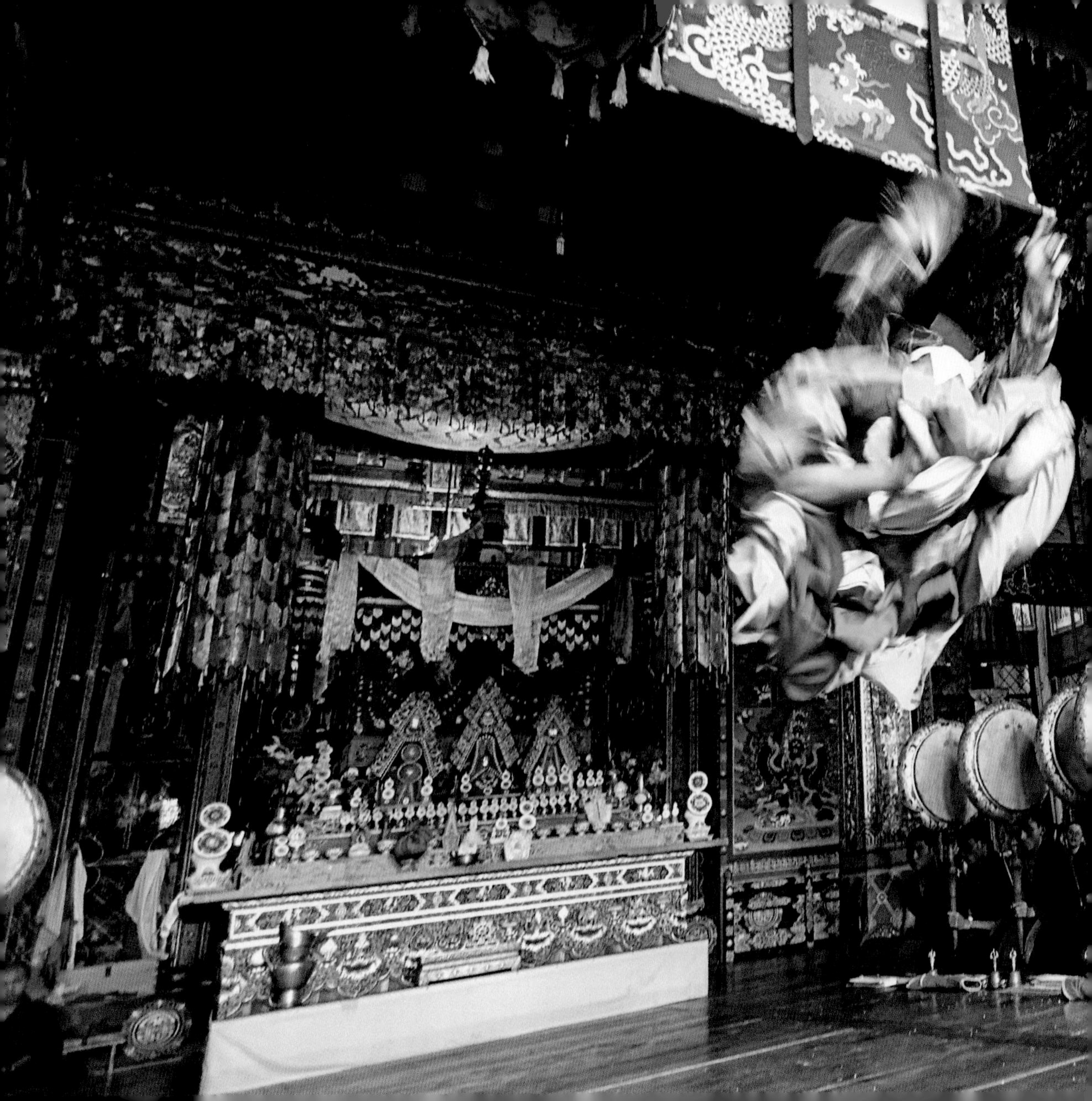

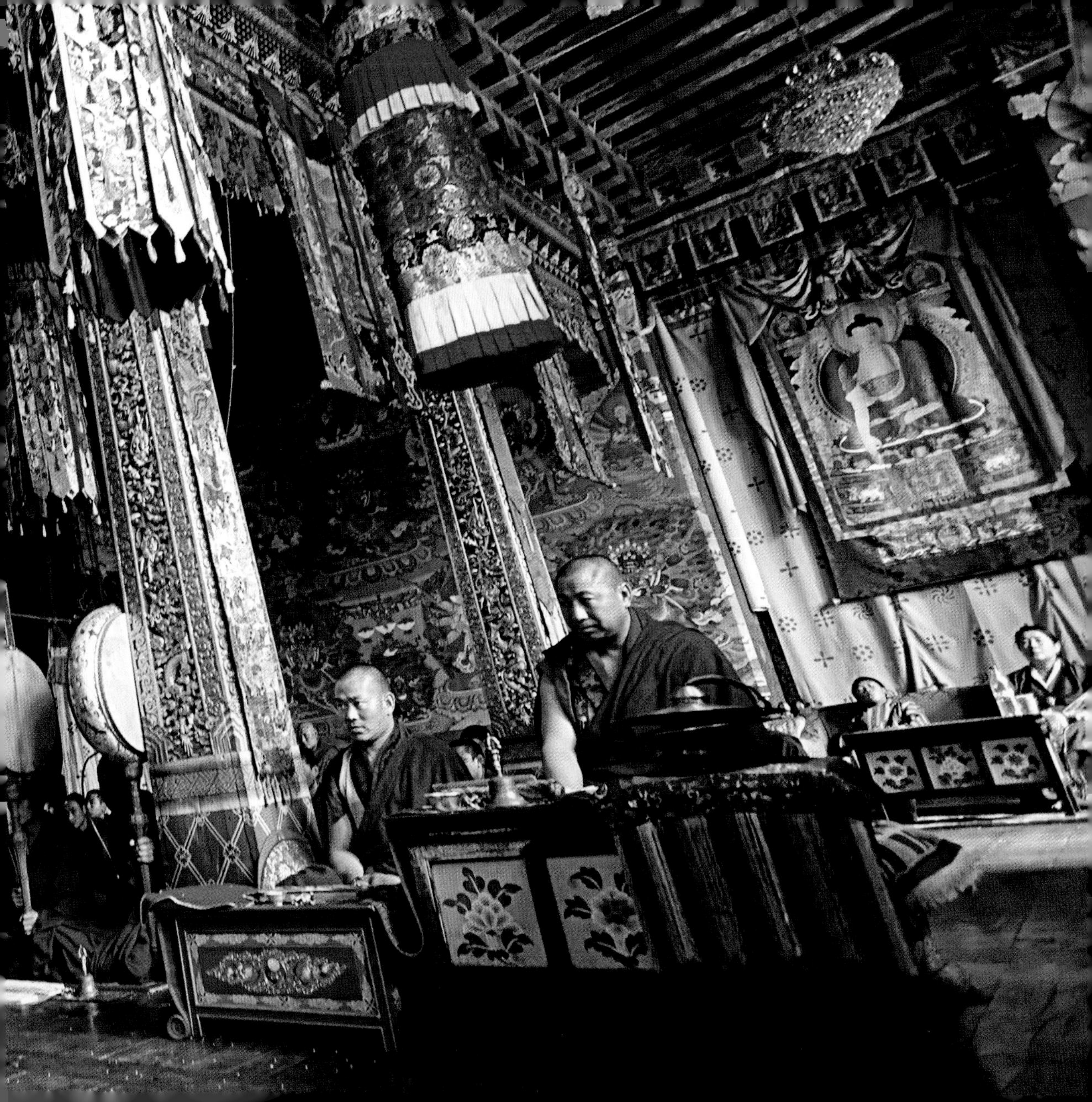

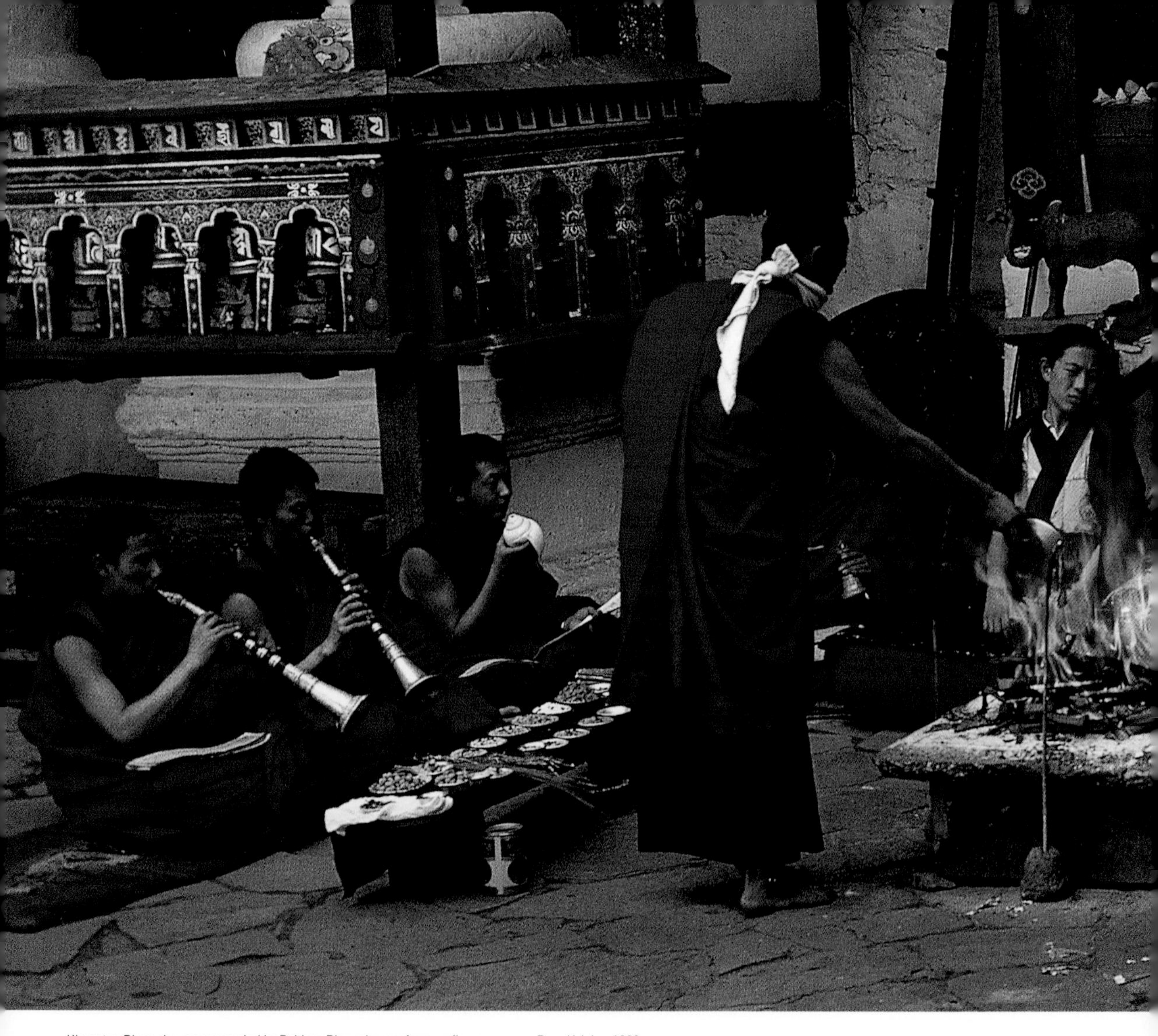

Khyentse Rinpoche, accompanied by Rabjam Rinpoche, performs a fire ceremony. Paro Kyichu, 1983.

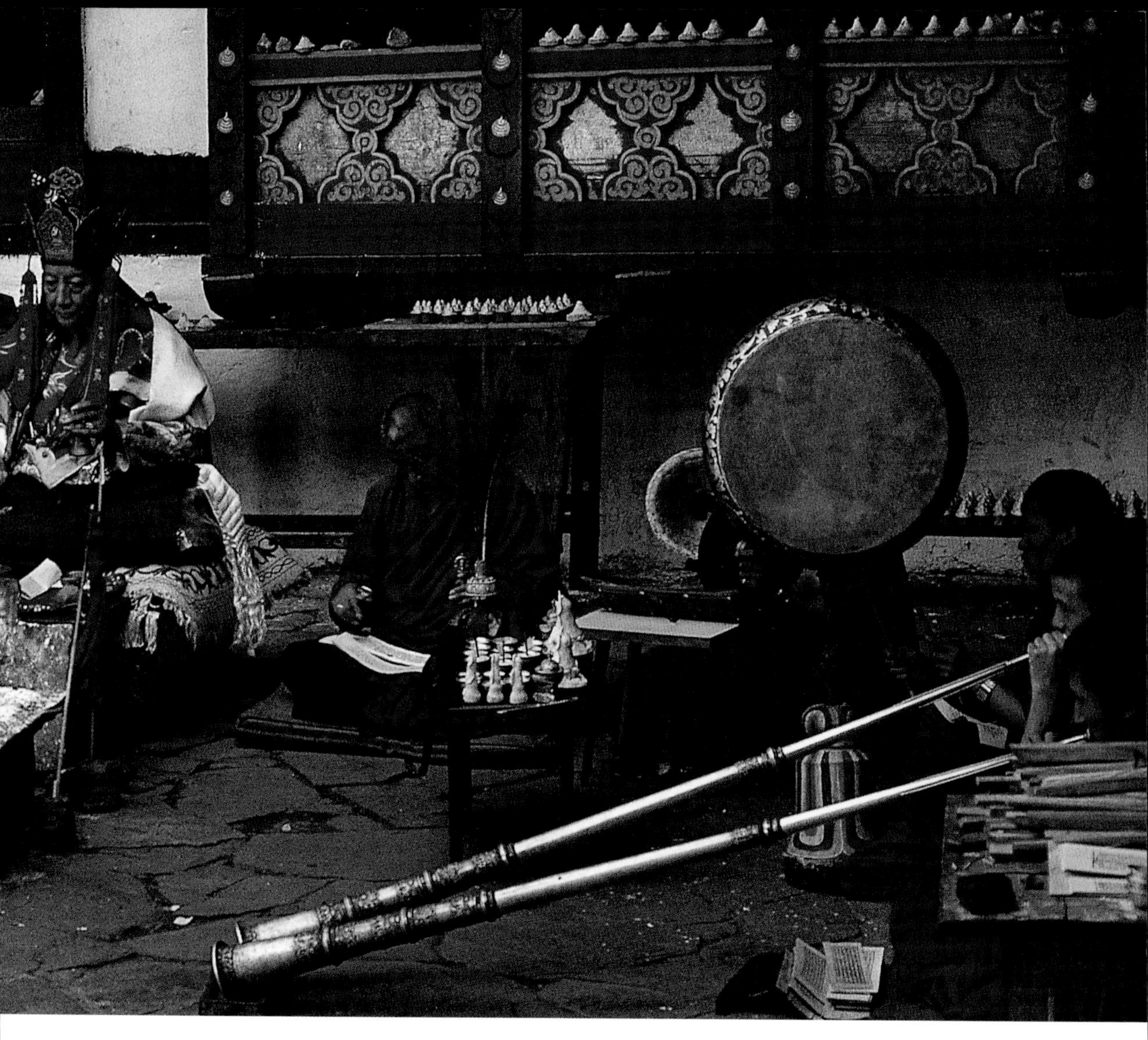

OFFERINGS OF FIRE AND LIGHT

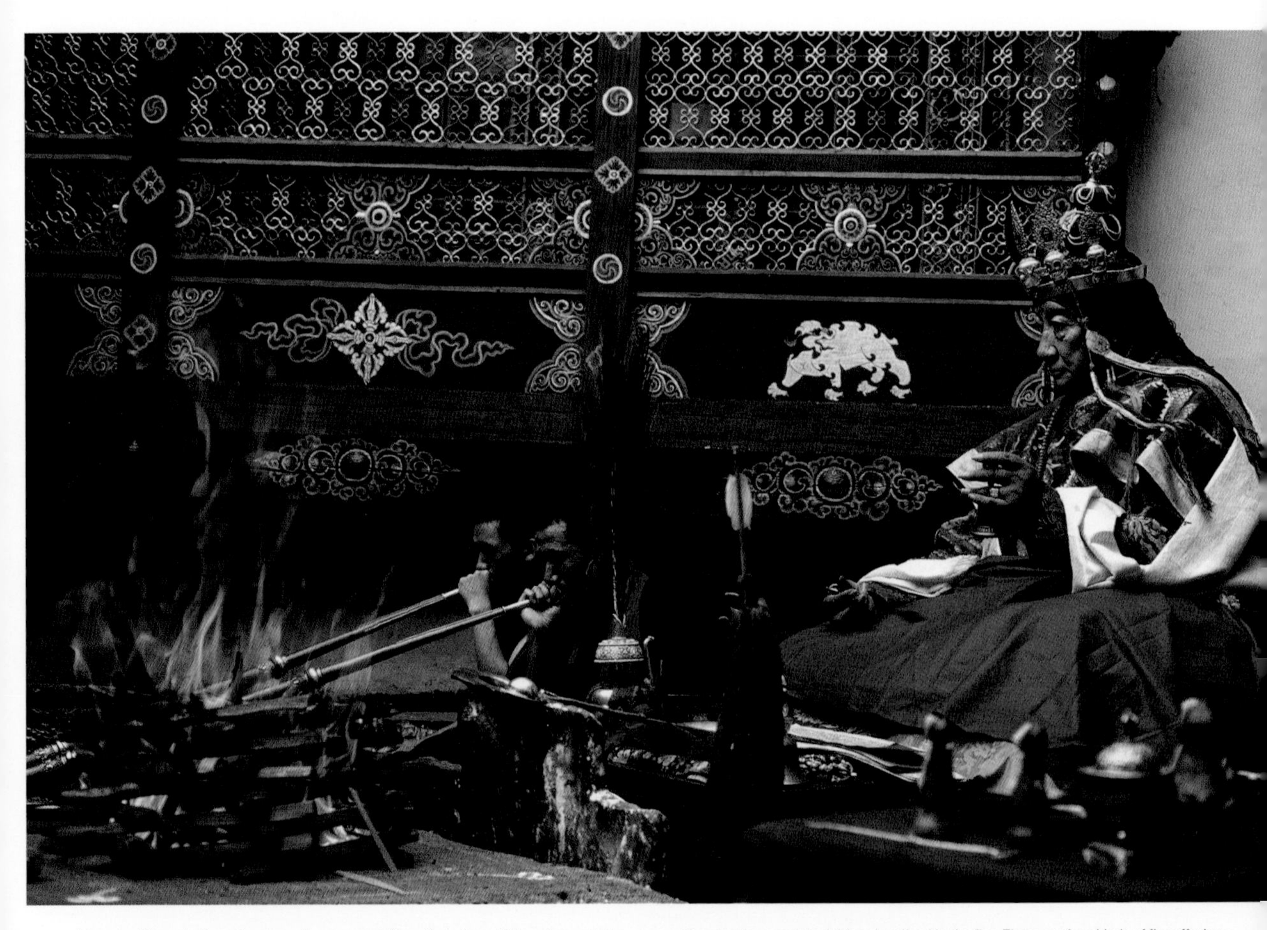

Khyentse Rinpoche is performing a fire ceremony (*jinsek*), during which various substances are offered to the mandala deities visualized in the fire. There are four kinds of fire offerings, corresponding to four types of enlightened activities. In each case, the instruments, substances, costumes and firewood used have a different colour. Here, the purpose of the ceremony is to *attract* favourable circumstances, and the colour is red. In other situations, the aim may be to *pacify* illnesses, wars and negative emotions, in which case white is used; to *develop* merit, longevity and meditative experiences, using yellow; or to *subjugate* internal and external obstacles and negative forces, using dark blue. 1983.

Offerings of Fire and Light

It is dawn on the last day of the great *drupchen* ceremony and the head lamas are slowly dismantling the mandala. First, they fetch the sacred objects and the sacred substances from the mandala and place them on the heads of the participants. The entire monastic community is blessed in this way, and likewise the crowd of lay practitioners who have come to share this solemn moment. While the lamas pass along the rows gathered inside and outside the temple, two monks play the *gyaling*, a reed instrument similar to an oboe. The musicians use a special technique called *uk-khor*, or circular breathing, which enables them to emit a continuous sound lasting several minutes. They fill their cheeks with air, then blow into the instrument using only the cheek muscles, while continuing to inhale through the nose.

During the course of the morning, there is an offering ceremony, which is meant to burn the veils of ignorance in the 'fire of wisdom'. In its elaborate form, this ritual consists in offering various consecrated substances to the mandala deities visualized within the fire. There are four fire offerings, corresponding to four types of enlightened activity: pacification, development, attraction and subjugation. In each case, the instruments, substances, costumes and firewood used have a different colour. When the aim is to *pacify* illnesses, wars and negative emotions, the dominant colour is white; when it is to *develop* merit, longevity and meditative experiences, the colour is yellow; if the ritual is designed to *attract* favourable circumstances, the colour is red; if the ritual serves principally to *subjugate* internal and external obstacles and negative forces, the colour is dark blue. Sometimes all four ceremonies are performed at once, outside the temple and facing in the four cardinal directions. Khyentse Rinpoche used to perform these offerings several times a year and frequently wore the corresponding costumes. And twenty-five years later his reincarnation, Khyentse Yangsi Rinpoche (*yangsi* signifying 'he who has returned to existence'), is performing the same rituals in the same places.

At the start of the *drupchen*, the monks create an elaborate mandala – representing the 'pure land' of the ceremony's central divinity – using coloured powders, and on the last afternoon of the ceremony the mandala is destroyed, to symbolize the impermanence of all things. One of the masters of ceremony sweeps through the delicate design with a ritual object, making the shape of a Greek cross. The powder is then brushed into a little pile and collected in a silver urn, the various colours mixing together to produce a dark, uniform grey. The urn is carried in procession to the nearby river and, following a short ritual, the powder is scattered in the water, while the monks invoke blessings for all those who drink the water and all the animals that live in it.

The procession returns to the monastery courtyard, where the monks, walking in single file, form a 'circle of joy' (*gakyil*), a complex, slowly evolving figure, resembling the Chinese symbol of yin-yang, whose purpose is to ensure an auspicious conjunction of future events. Finally, the monks return to the temple.

The meditation is an intense experience lasting nine days and nine nights and it concludes with a final offering of light, symbol of the knowledge that dispels the darkness of ignorance and mental confusion. The temple is transformed into a luminous ocean of butter lamps, punctuated by the glow from a myriad of incense sticks, and weaving through it the great bond of compassion symbolized by the ceremonial scarves held by monks, nuns and lay practitioners. The master of ceremonies begins a melodious, slow chant, which is taken up by the whole assembly in unison. These are the words that they chant:

By entering the supreme mandala of the unsurpassable secret,
I have taken the path of Enlightenment as very essence;
May I not fall into the great abyss of samsara,
Nor be born in the stony gorges of desire and hatred,
Nor be hurled into the copper cauldron of false views,
Nor hear the ferocious roar of the beasts of ill-will,
Nor be struck by the poisonous lance of emotions;
But from my excellent spiritual friend,
From my spiritual brothers and sisters linked to me by sacred links, from the strength of life, (...)
In this and all my future lives
May I never be separated, and through the profound concentration of those links,
May we together successfully ascend the ten levels.
At the moment of death, when the time comes to change my body,
I might fall again into the deep abyss of samsara;
But, opening the door of illumination by the pure light of these lamps,
Following in the footsteps of the Holders of Awakening,
Purifying my mind at the level of all-pervading luminosity,
May I spontaneously attain the level of the unsurpassable Enlightenment.

Note: Extract adapted from the 'Prayer of the Lamps',
translated from the Tibetan by the Padmakara Translation Group.

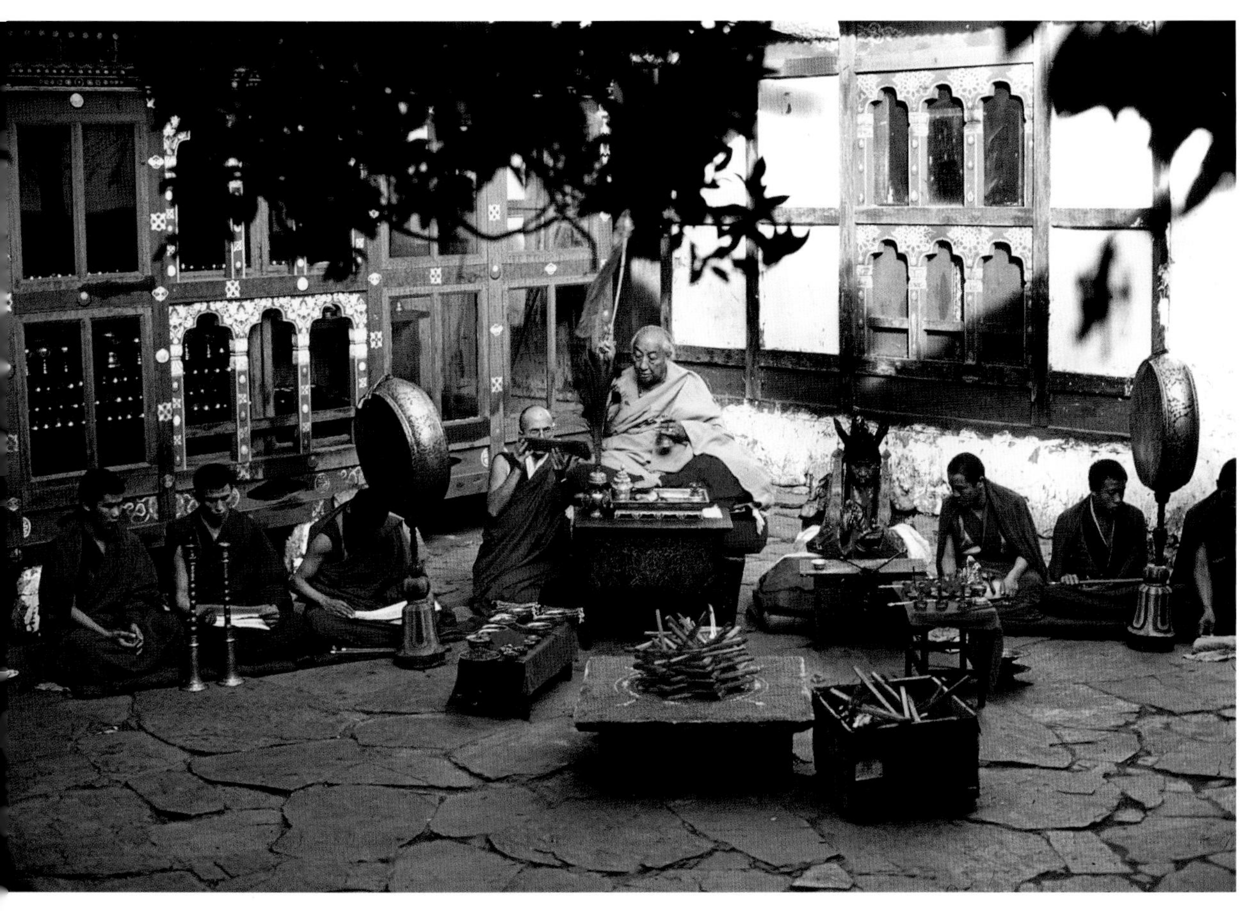

At Paro Kyichu, 1987.

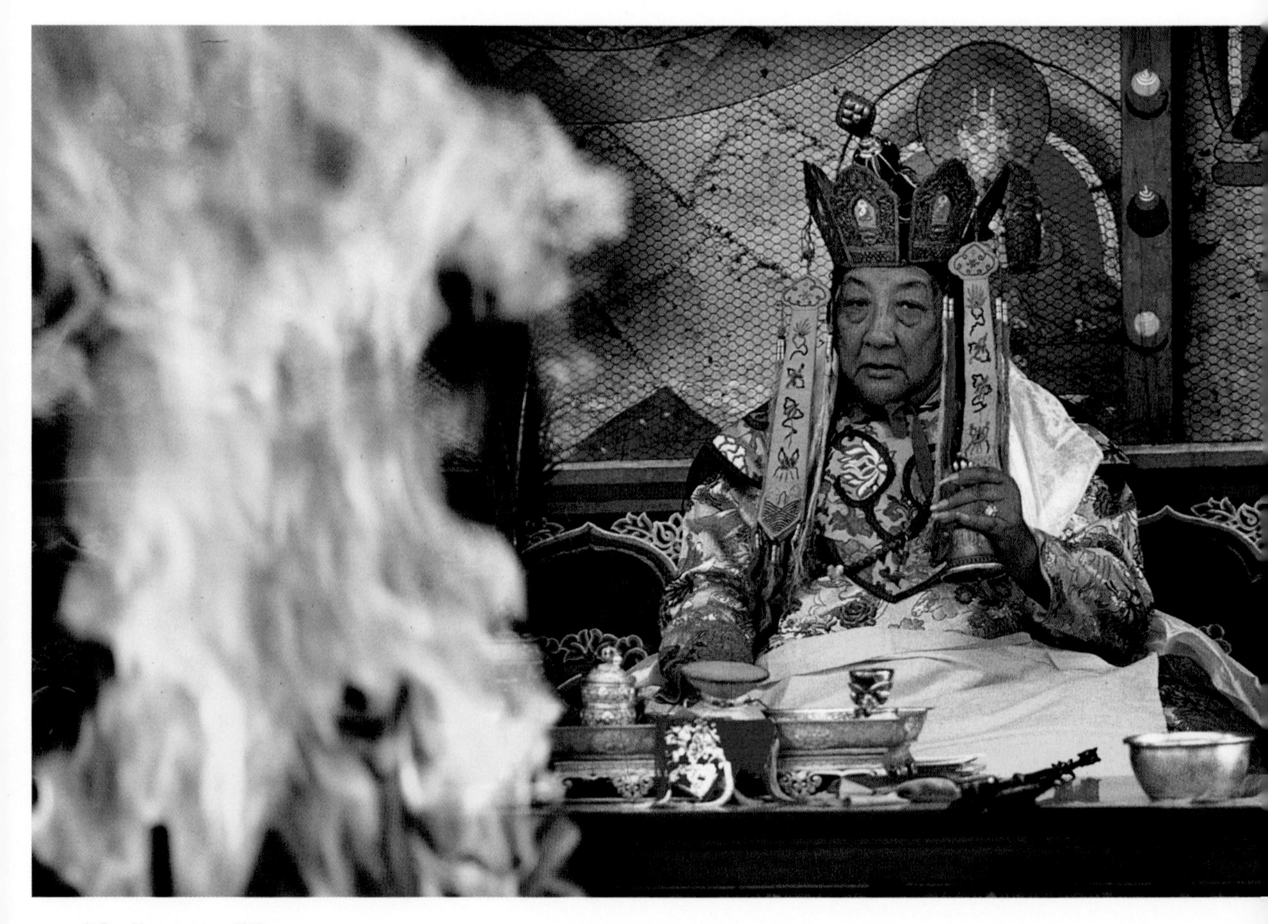

At Punakha monastery, 1982.

At Paro Kyichu, 1987.

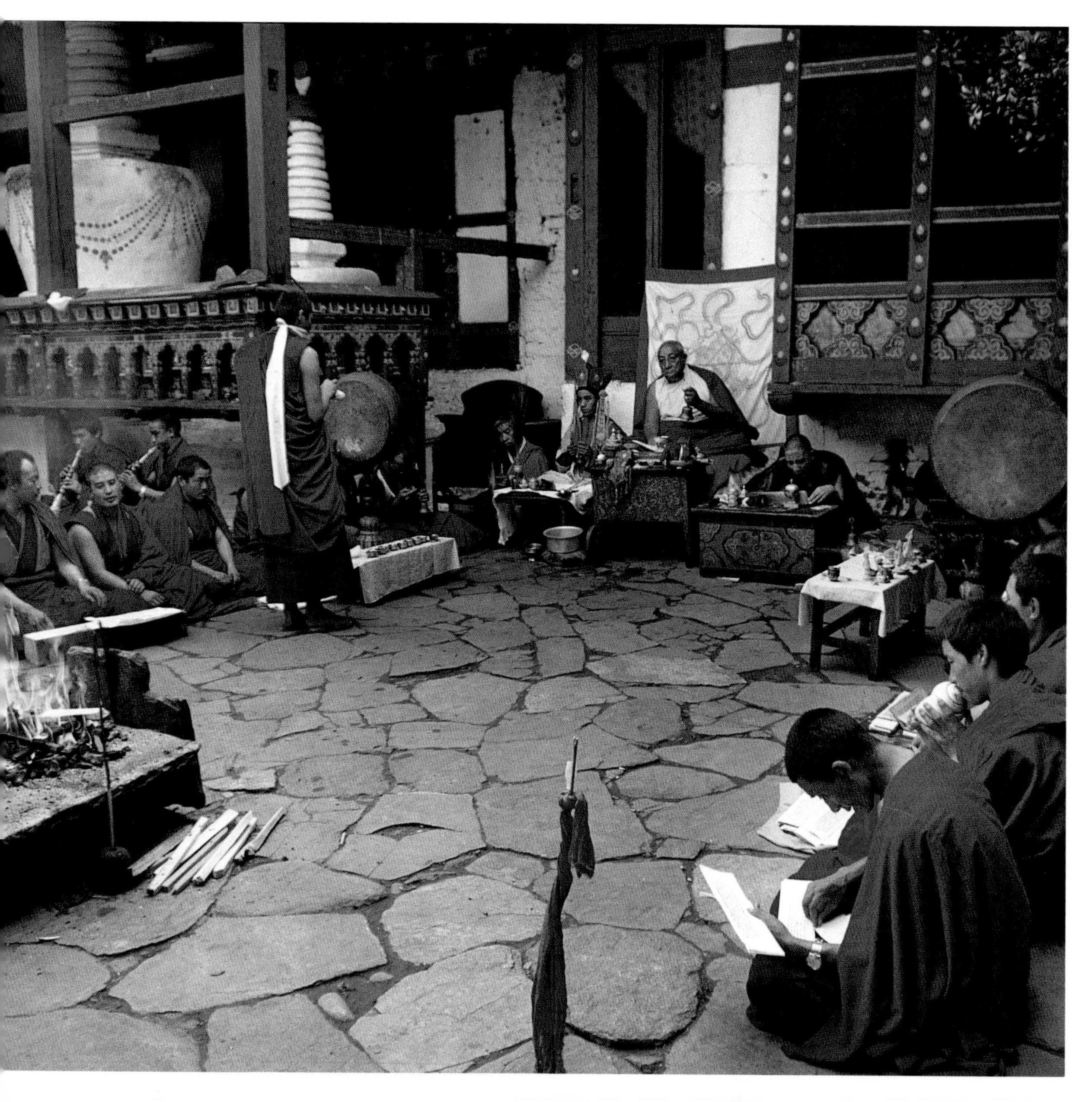

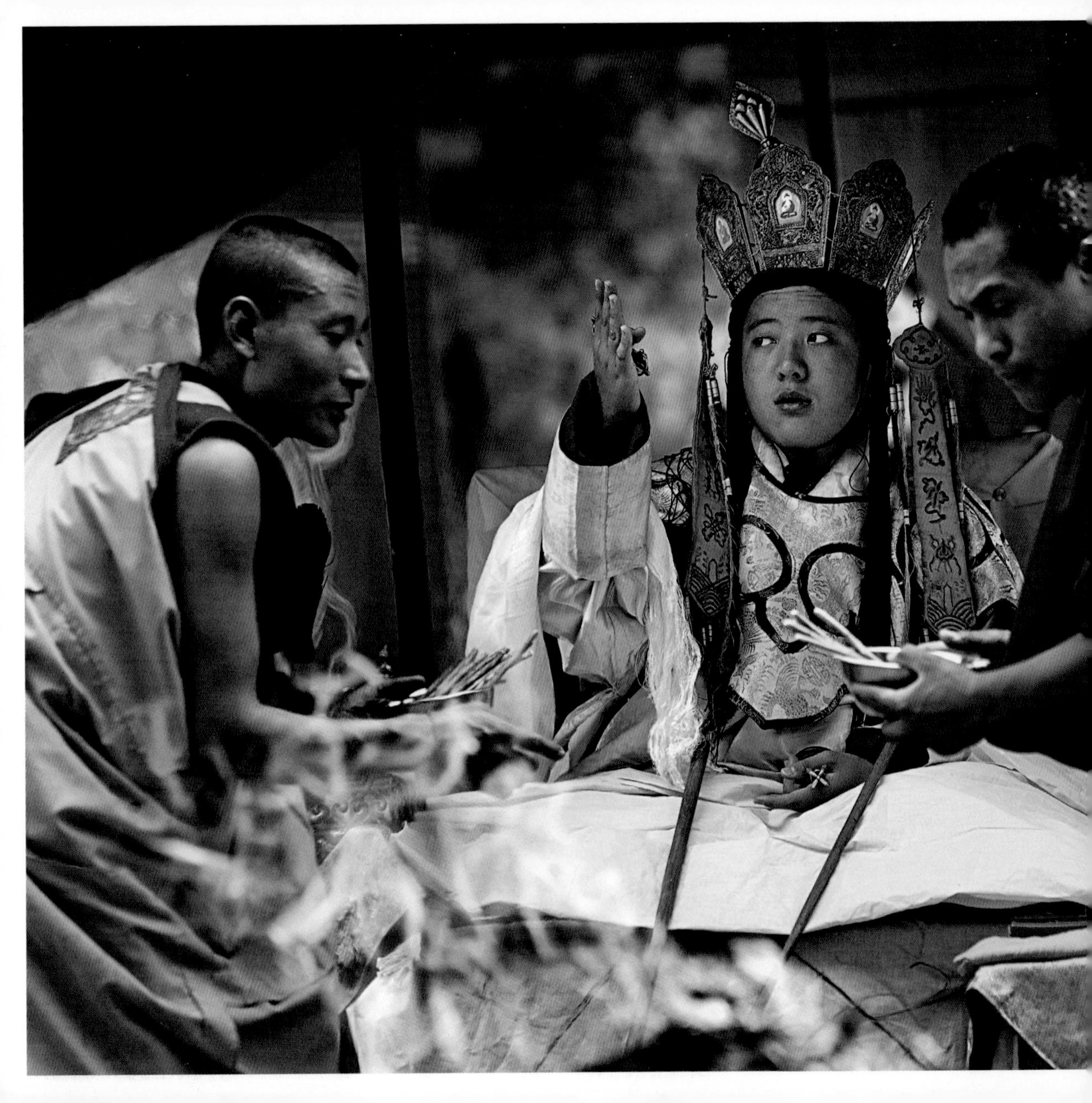

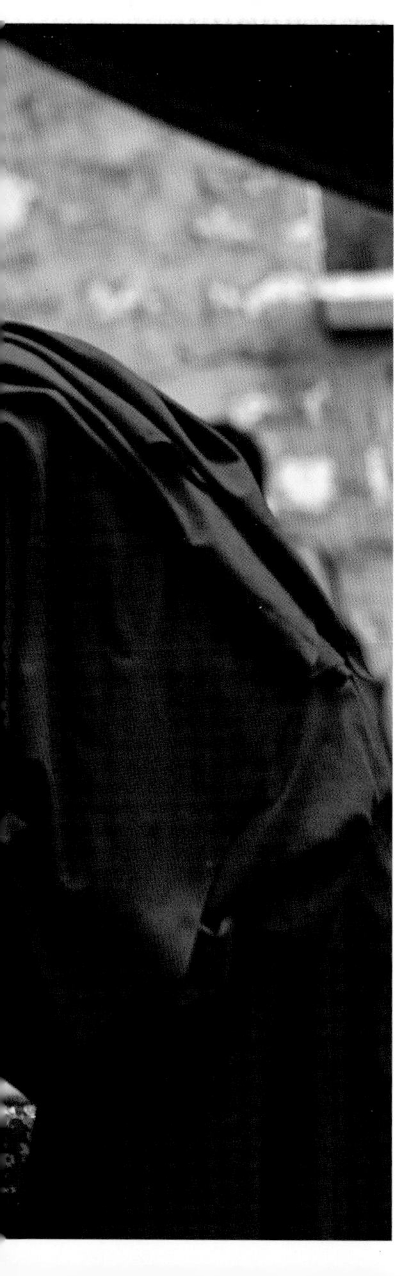

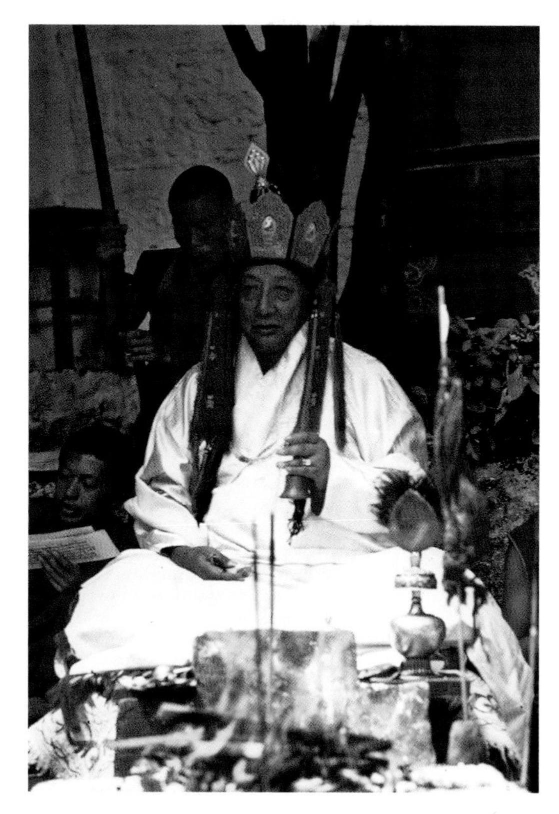

Khyentse Rinpoche wears white brocade robes for a ritual designed to dispel illnesses, wars, ignorance and negative emotions. Paro, 1980.

Left:
The thirteen-year-old Urgyen Jigme Tendzin Lhundrup – recognized as the incarnation of Dilgo Khyentse Rinpoche – performing the same ceremony in the same place, twenty-five years later. Paro, 2006.

Overleaf:
On the left, Urgyen Jigme Tendzin Lhundrup performing a ceremony of offering at the temple of Kuje, in 2006.
On the right: his predecessor performing the same ceremony at Punakha a quarter of a century earlier, in 1982.

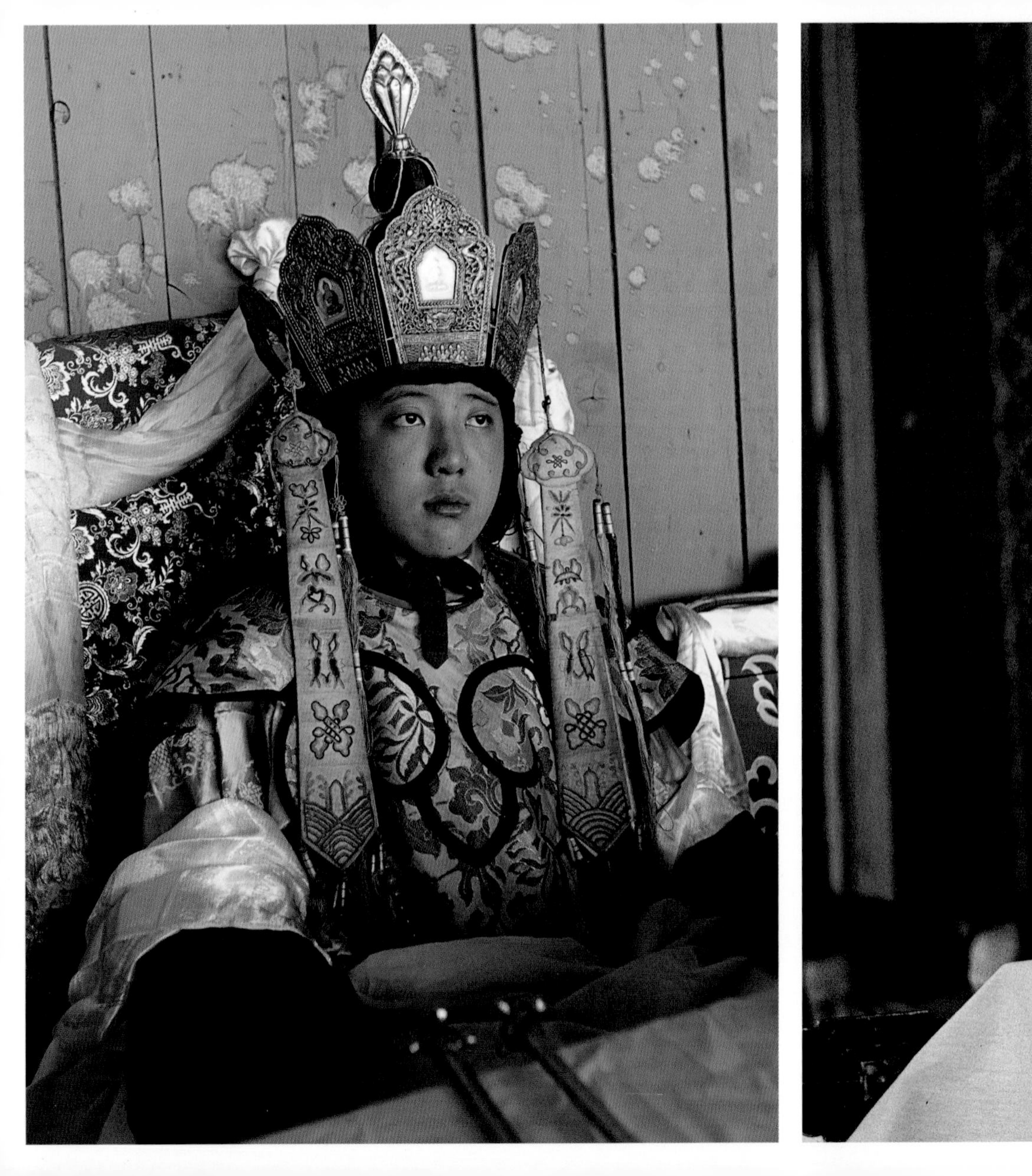

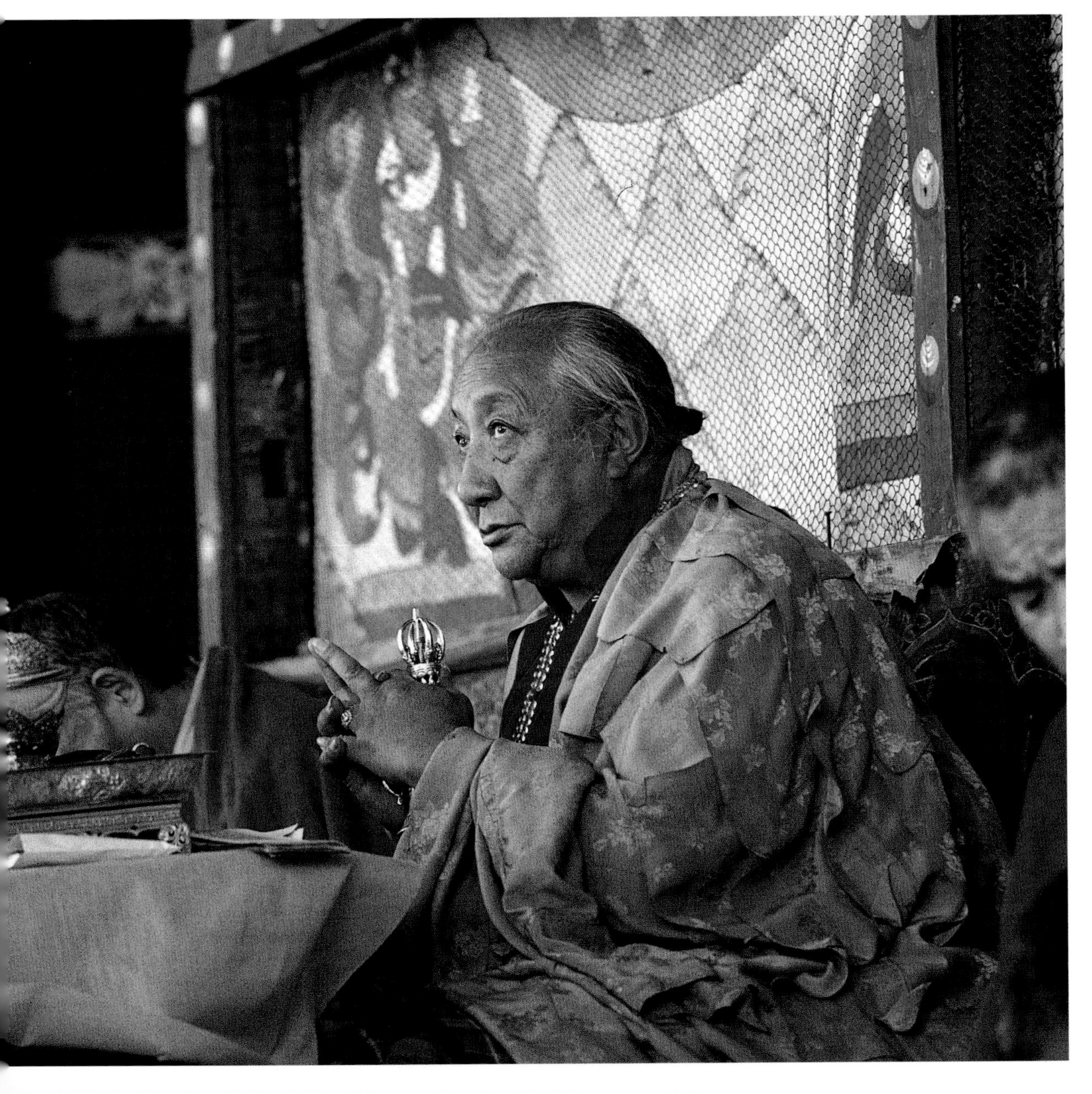

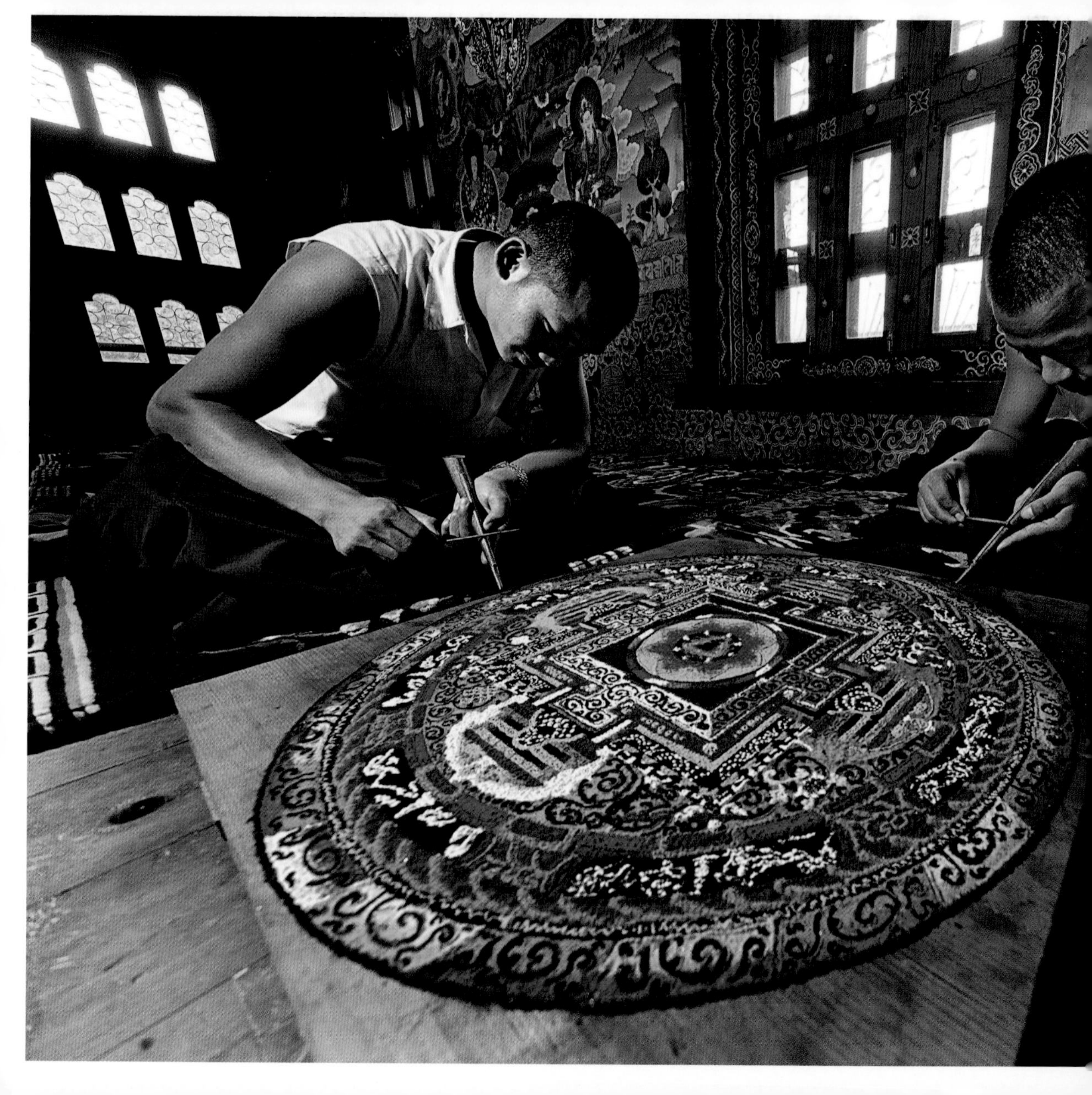

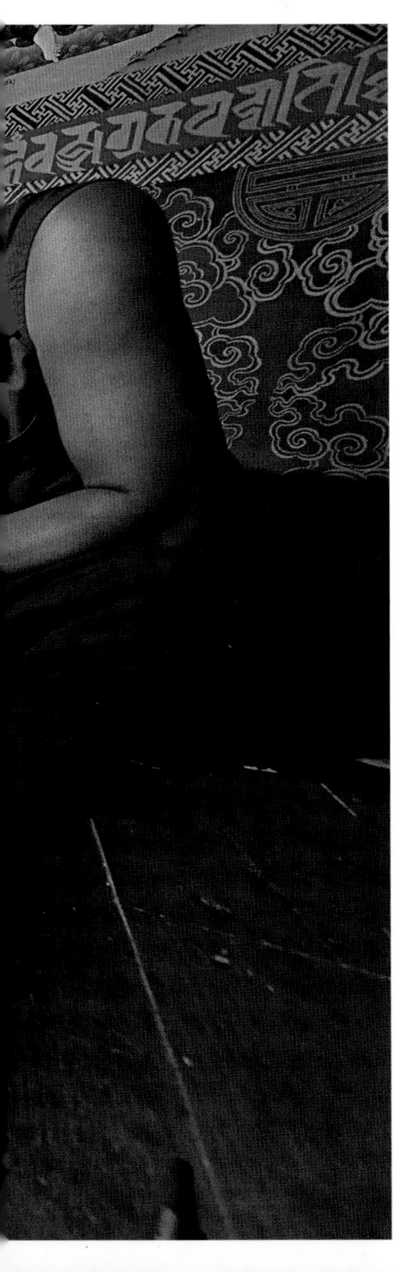

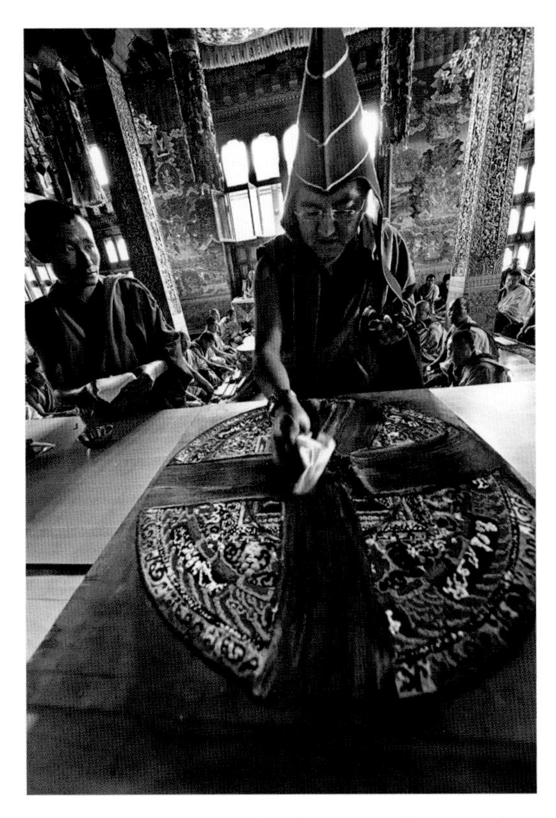

At the end of the lengthy *drupchen*, the delicate patterns of the mandala – drawn with different coloured sands – are destroyed and the sand is placed in an urn and carried in procession to the river, where it is dispersed. The destruction of the mandala symbolizes the ephemeral nature of all things. 2007.

Monks creating the Vajrakilaya mandala, in preparation for the annual Great Accomplishment ceremony at the temple of Phurba Lhakhang, Satsam Chörten, in the Paro valley. This mandala forms the centre of the ritual and takes two days to make, using coloured powders. 2007.

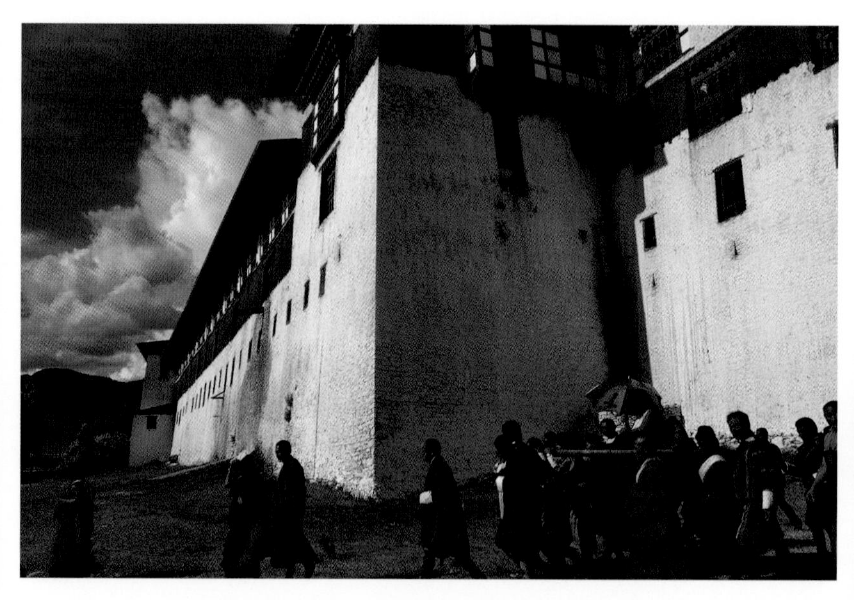

Dilgo Khyentse Rinpoche is carried on a litter from Punakha monastery to the nearby river. 1983.

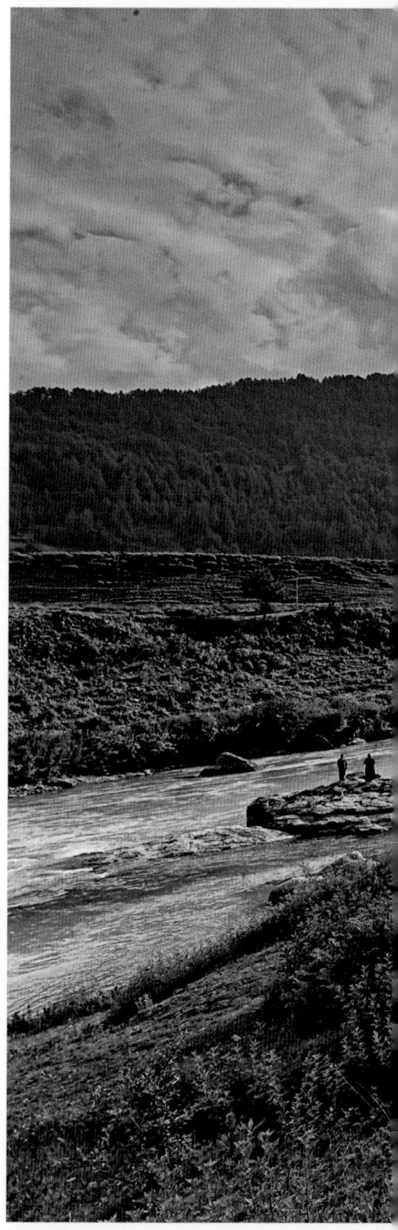

A procession of monks heading for the river, at an altitude of 2,800 metres, in Bumthang province.
They are going to scatter the coloured powders of the mandala into the water. 2006.

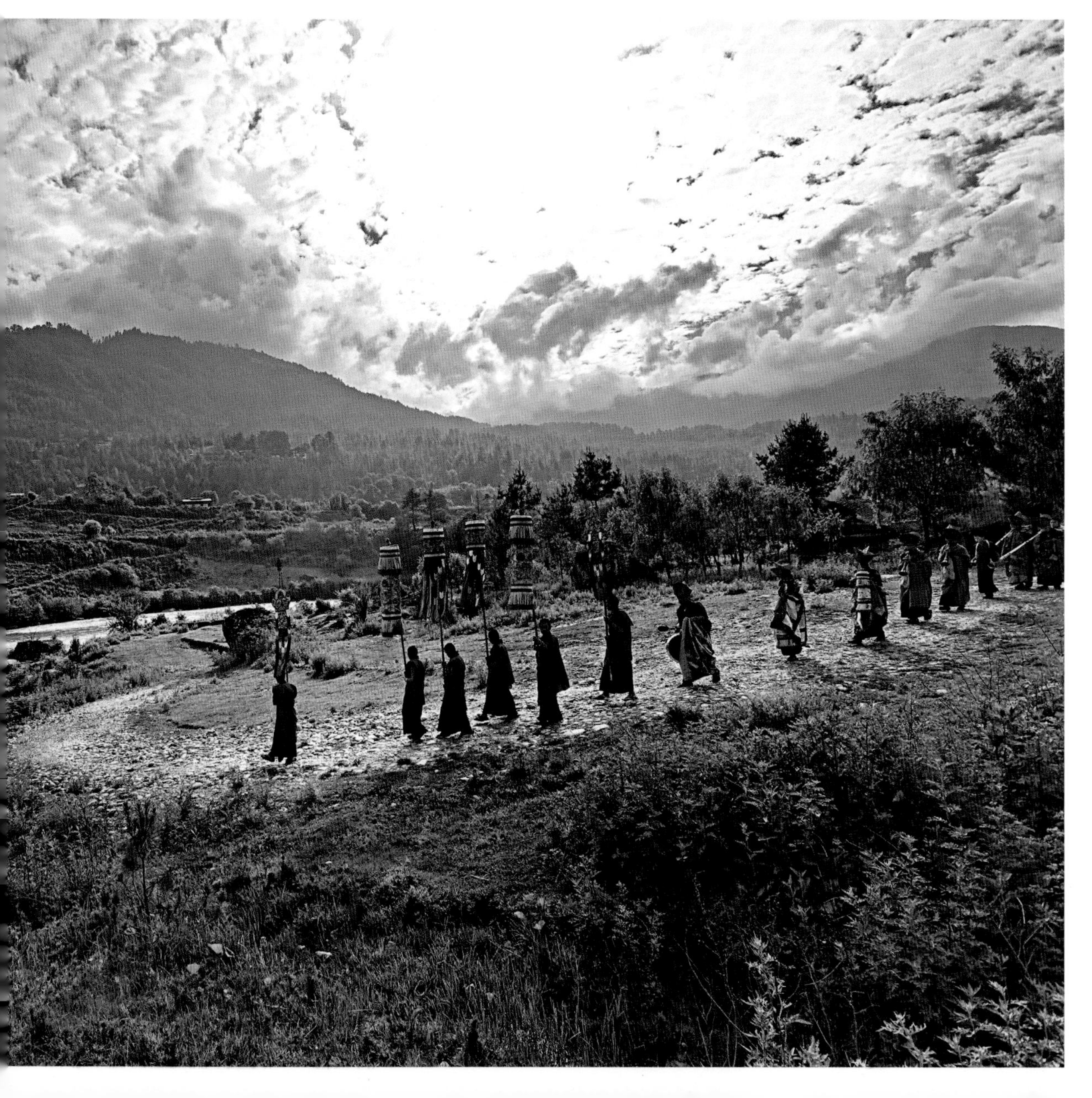

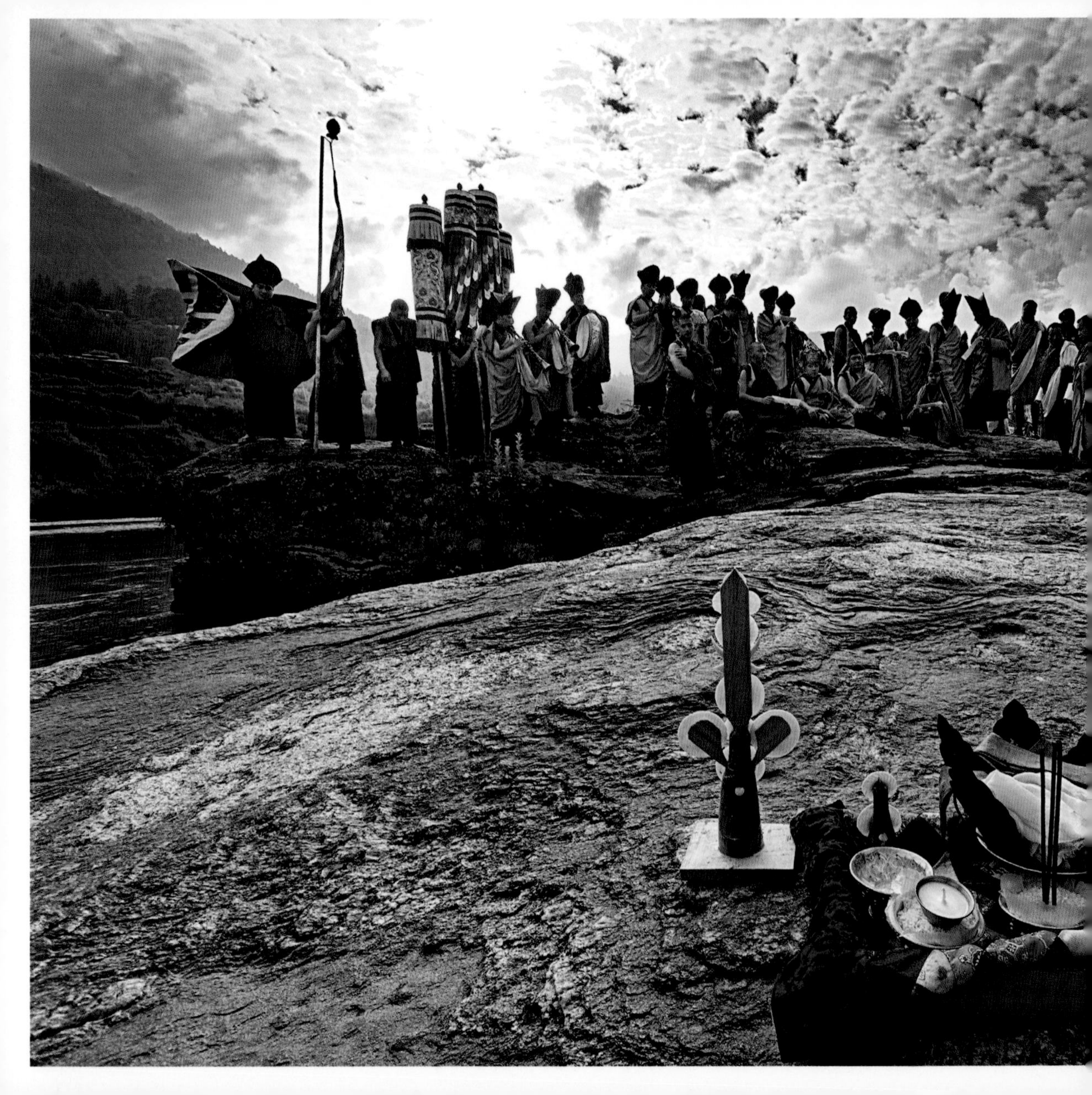

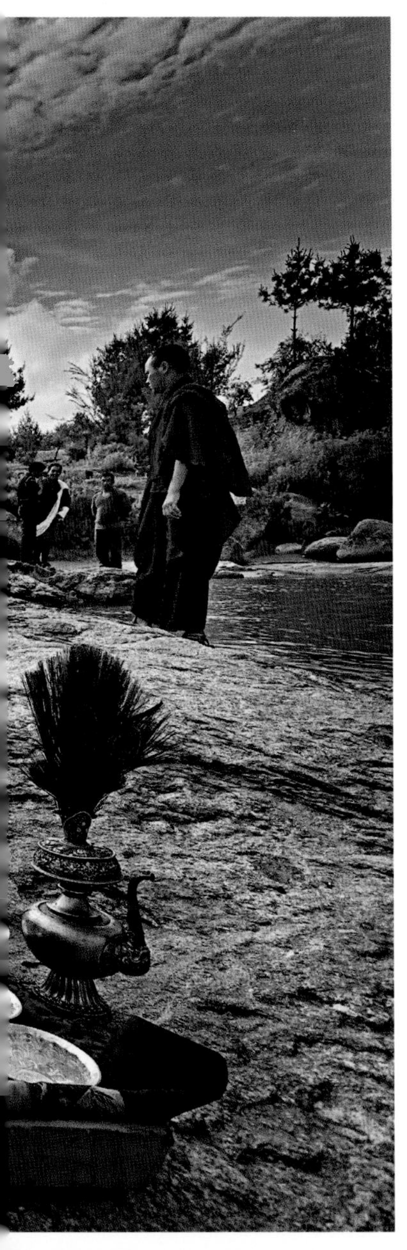

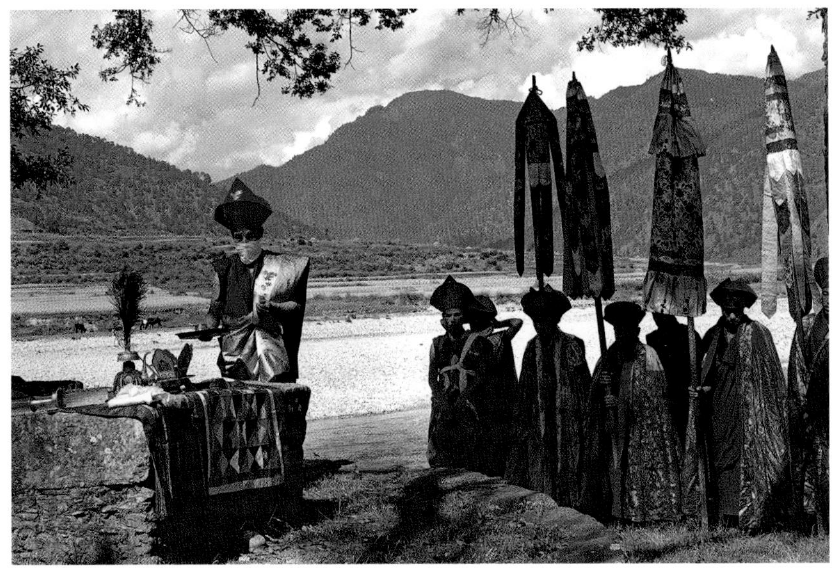

Left and above:
Monks preparing for the ritual scattering of the mandala powders, in 1981 at Punakha (above) and in 2006 at Kuje (left).

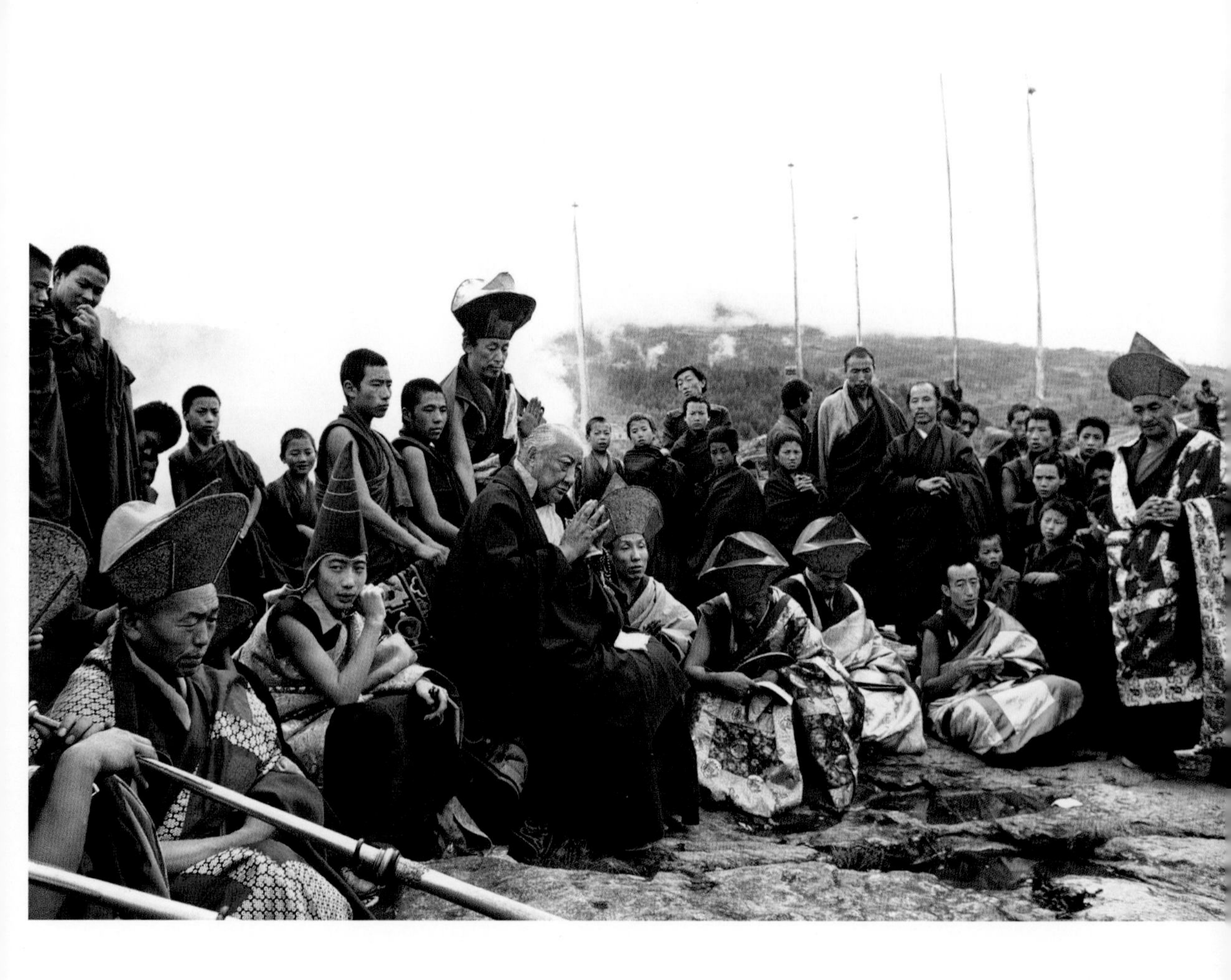

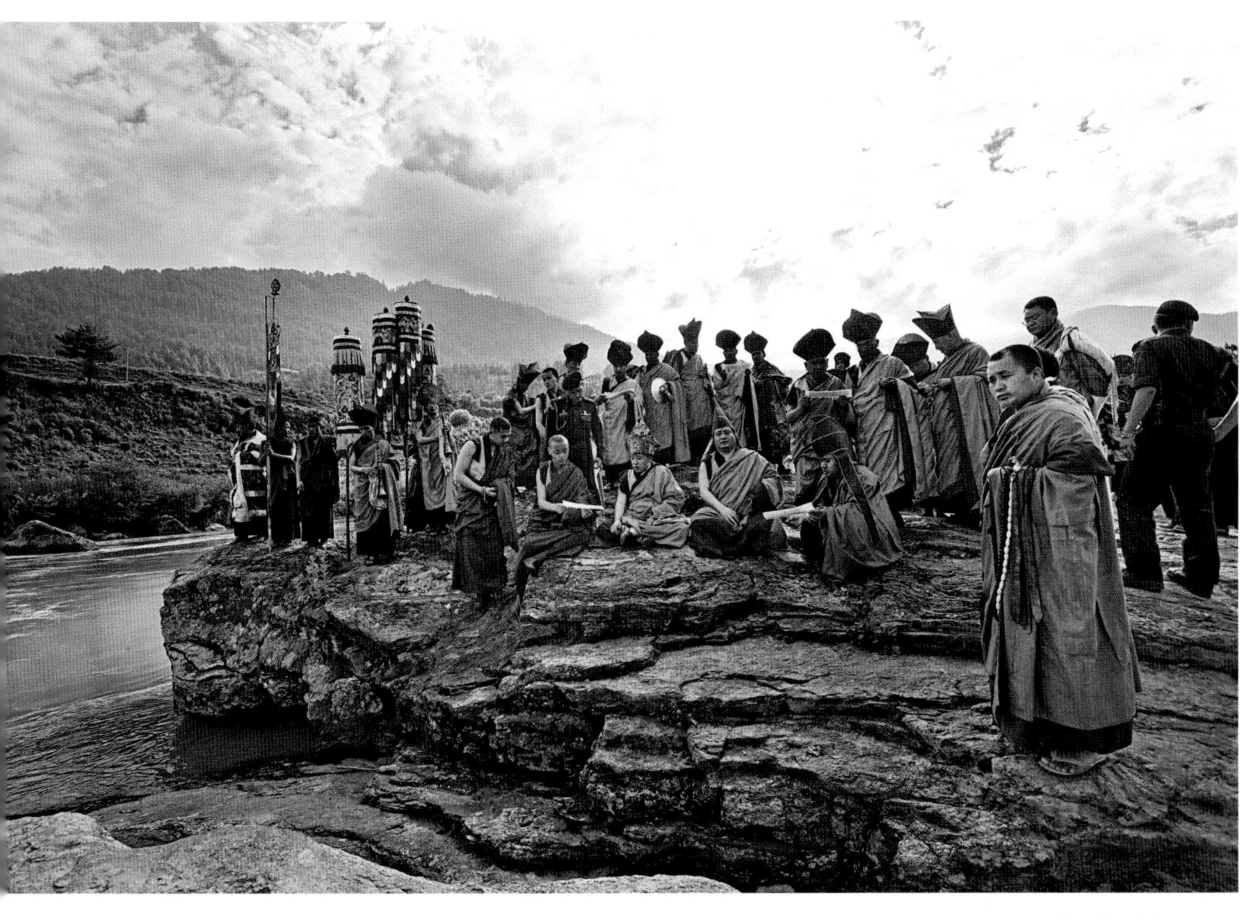

Opposite and above:
Dilgo Khyentse Rinpoche (opposite), in 1981, and his young reincarnation (above), in 2006, perform the same ceremony to disperse the powder of the mandala, on the same rock, overlooking the same river – but twenty-five years apart. They are in the Bumthang valley, at an altitude of 2,800 metres.

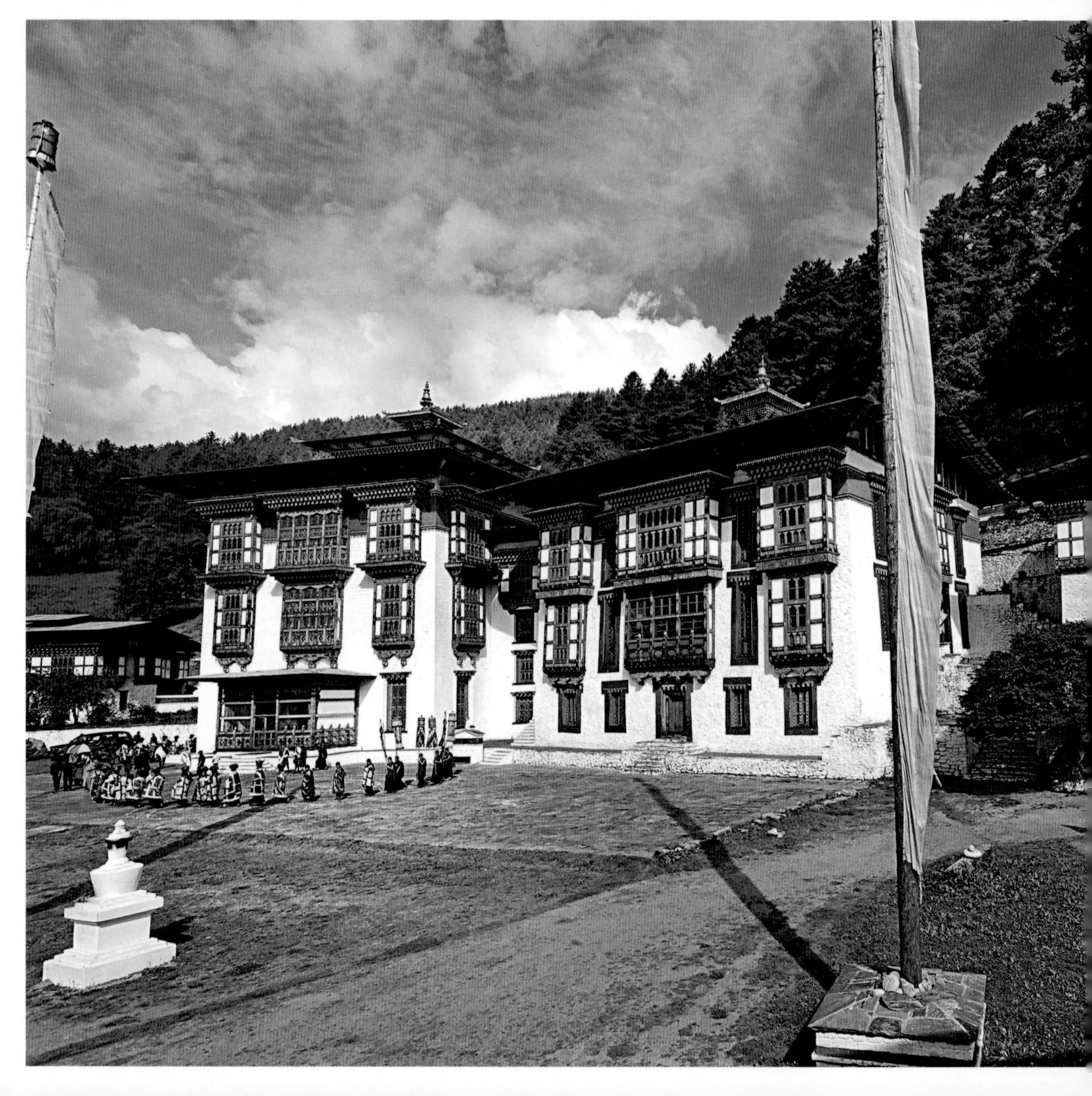

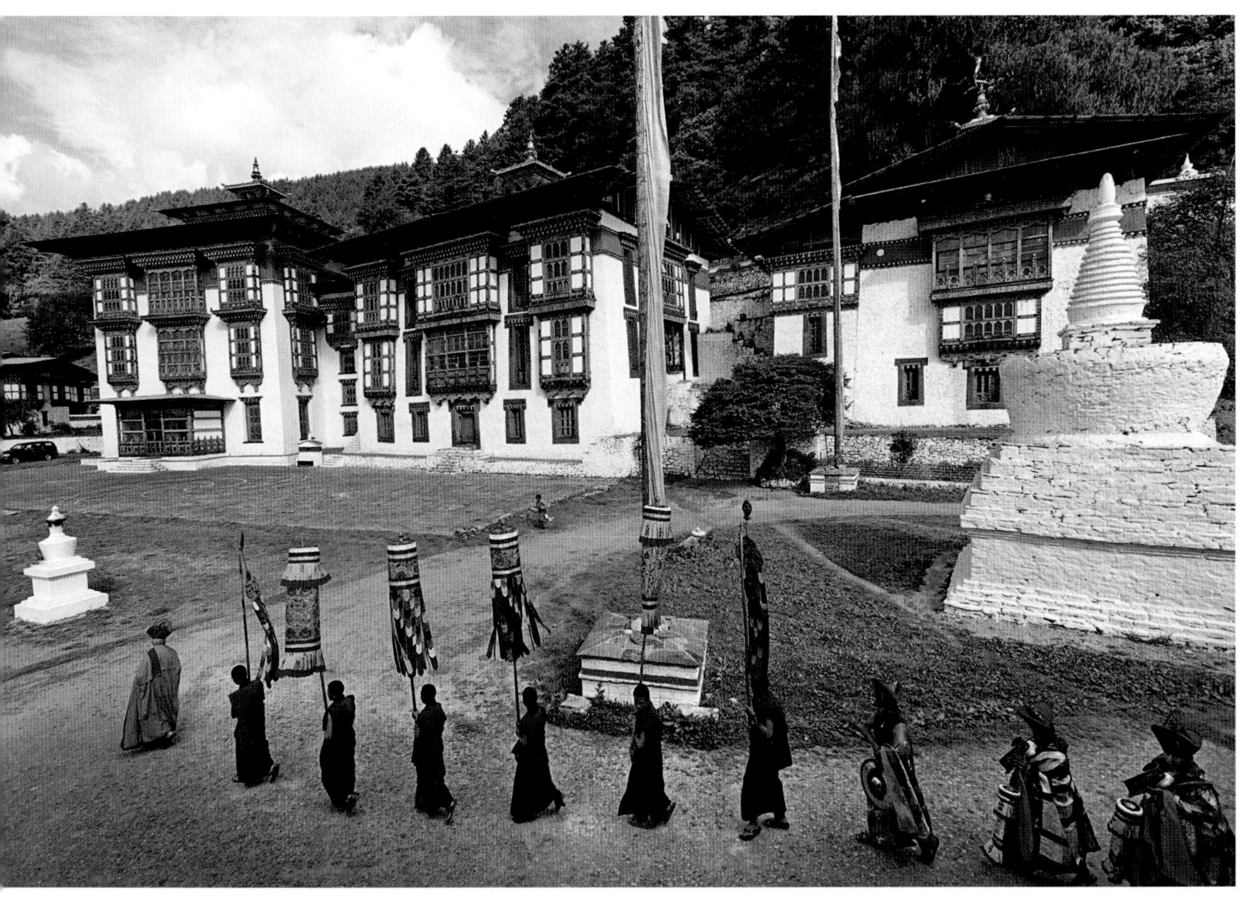

Above and left:
Back in the paved courtyard, the monks walk in single file and form a 'circle of joy' (*gakyil*), resembling the Chinese yin-yang symbol. They then return to the temple for the conclusion of the Great Accomplishment ceremony. Kuje, June 2006.

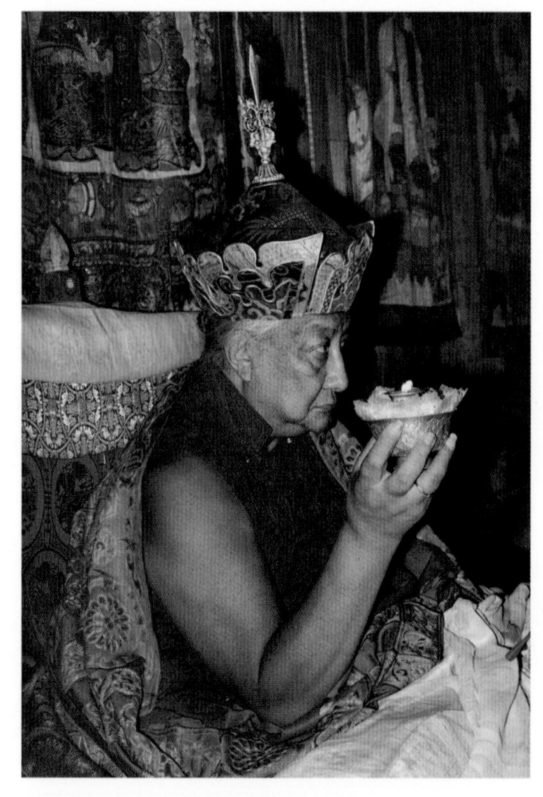

Khyentse Rinpoche during the offering of light ceremony at Punakha. He is wearing the lotus hat and holding a lighted butter lamp, symbolizing the light of knowledge. 1986.

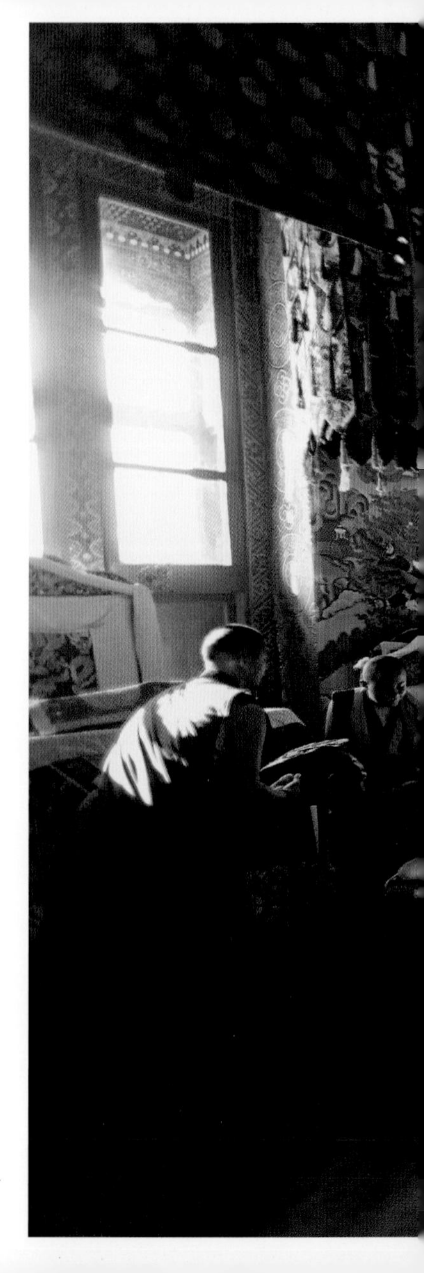

Monks at Kuje temple preparing to form a procession, 2006.

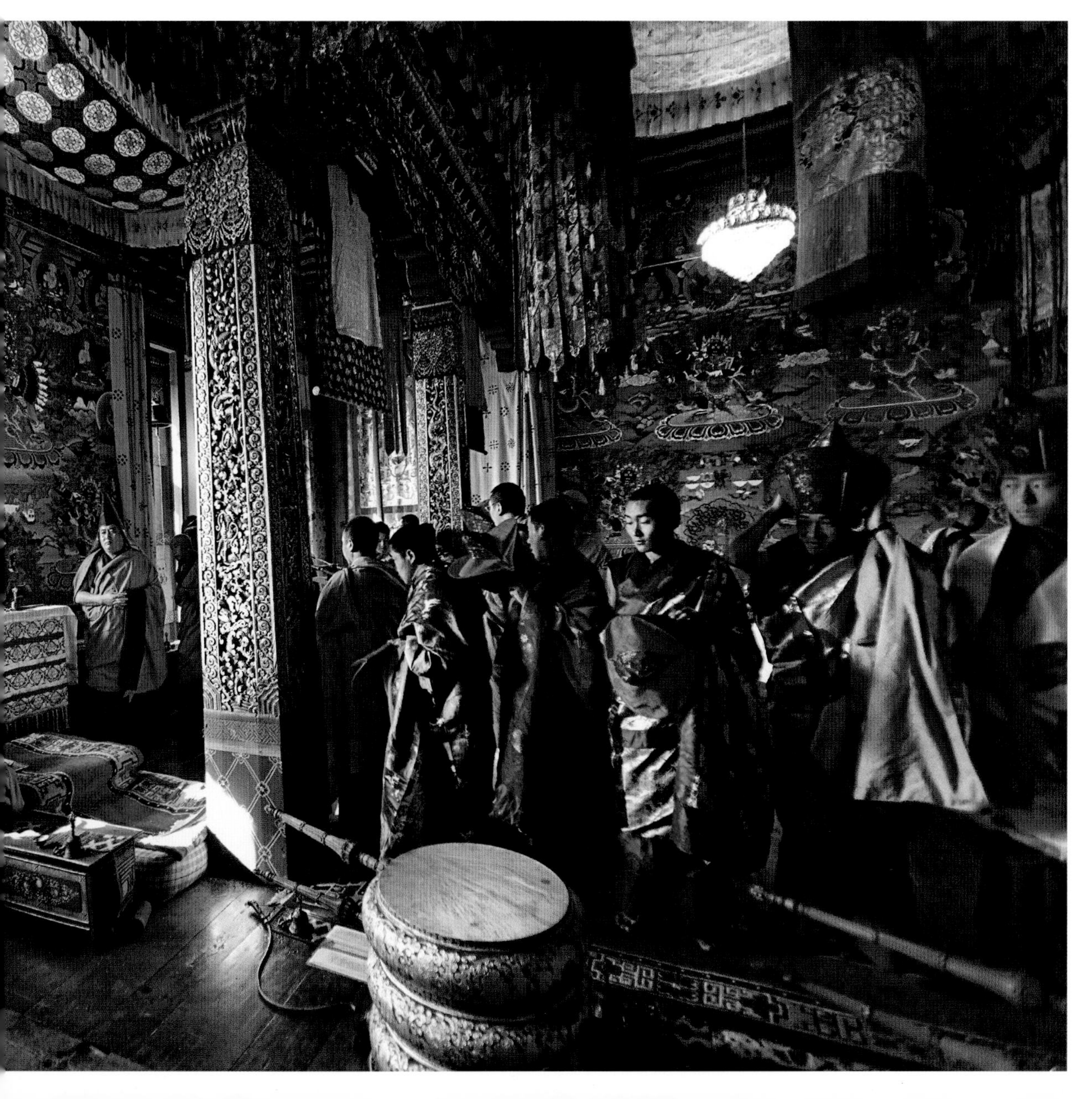

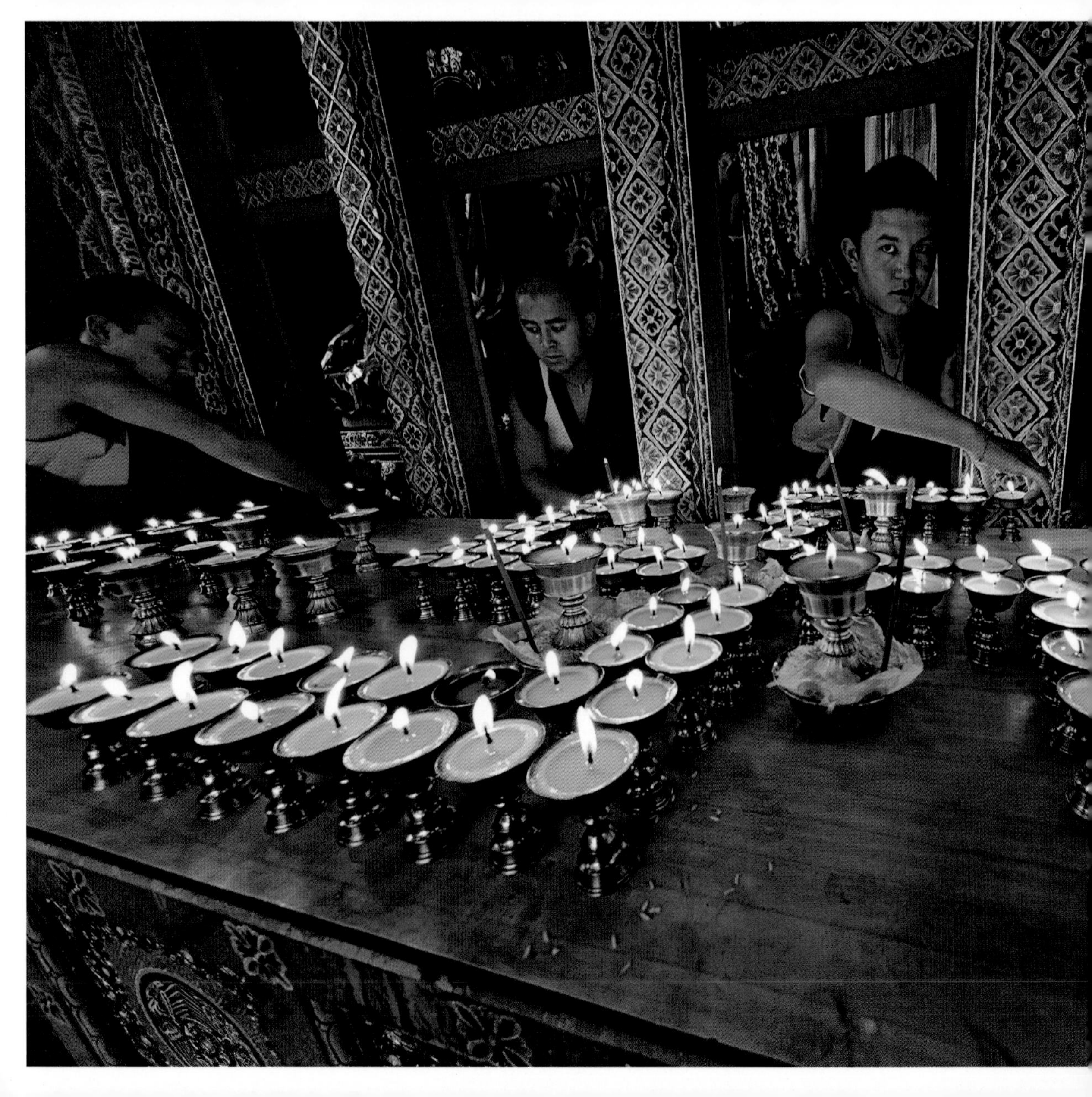

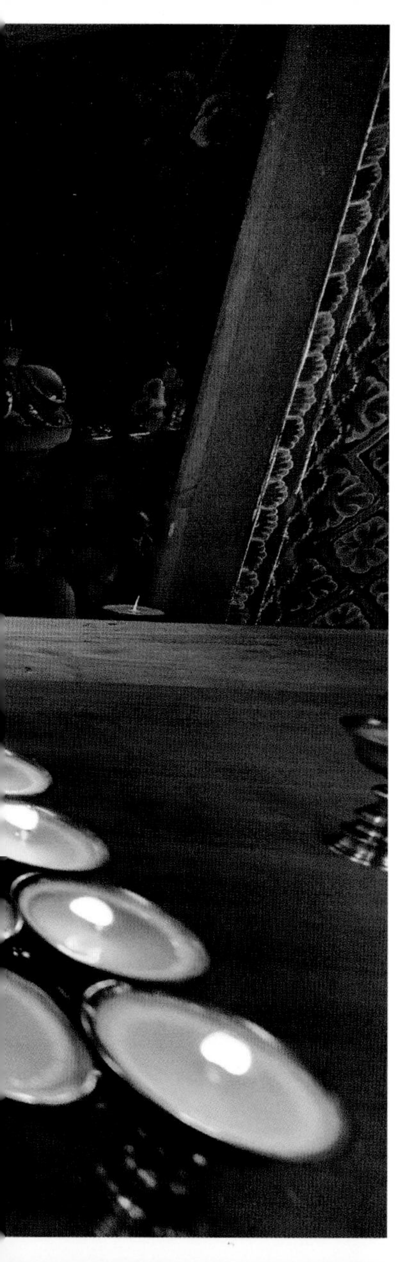

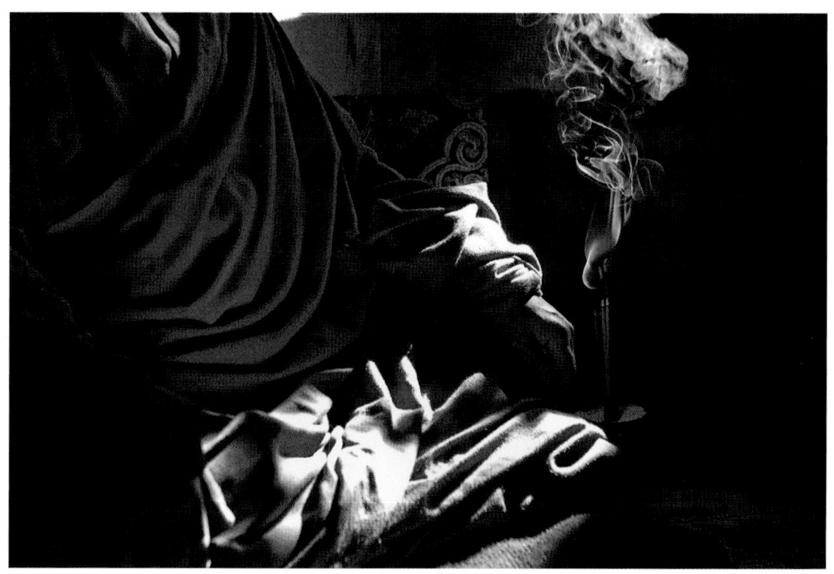

A monk holding a stick of incense during the offering of light ceremony.

Left:
When the offering of light ceremony is over, the lamps held by the faithful are arranged on the altar in the shape of a swastika, an ancient Asian symbol of immutability. 2007.

Overleaf:
Lamas making an offering of lamps as the long ceremony draws to a close. Each holds a lighted lamp and is connected with the rest of the assembly by a knotted rope of white scarves. In a slow, melodious chant, the practitioners pray that they may continue practising together through all their future lives until they attain Enlightenment. 2004.

Pages 230–231:
Jomolhari, Bhutan's highest mountain (7,326 metres), seen from the Dochula pass, lit by the last rays of the setting sun. December 2007.

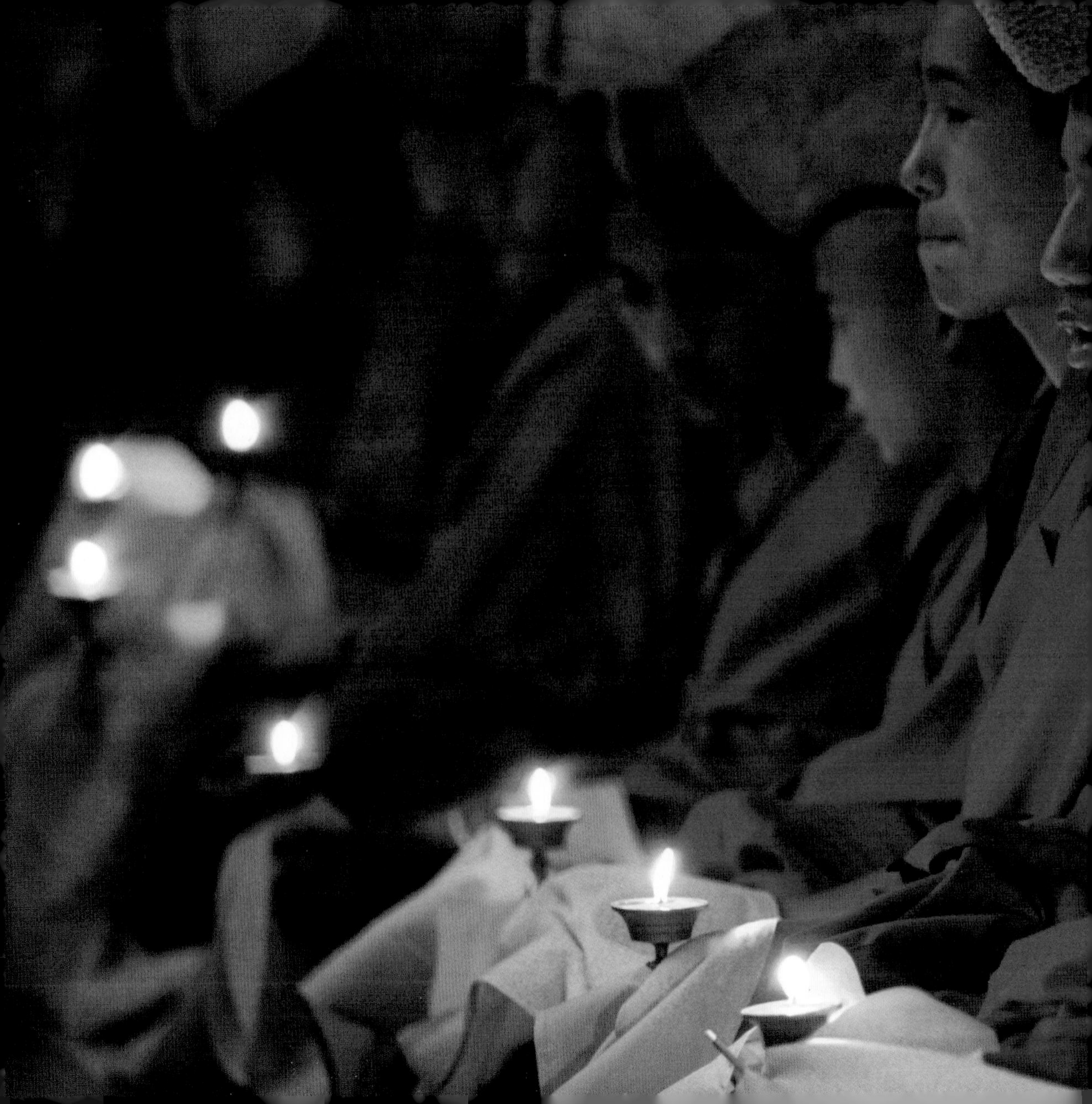

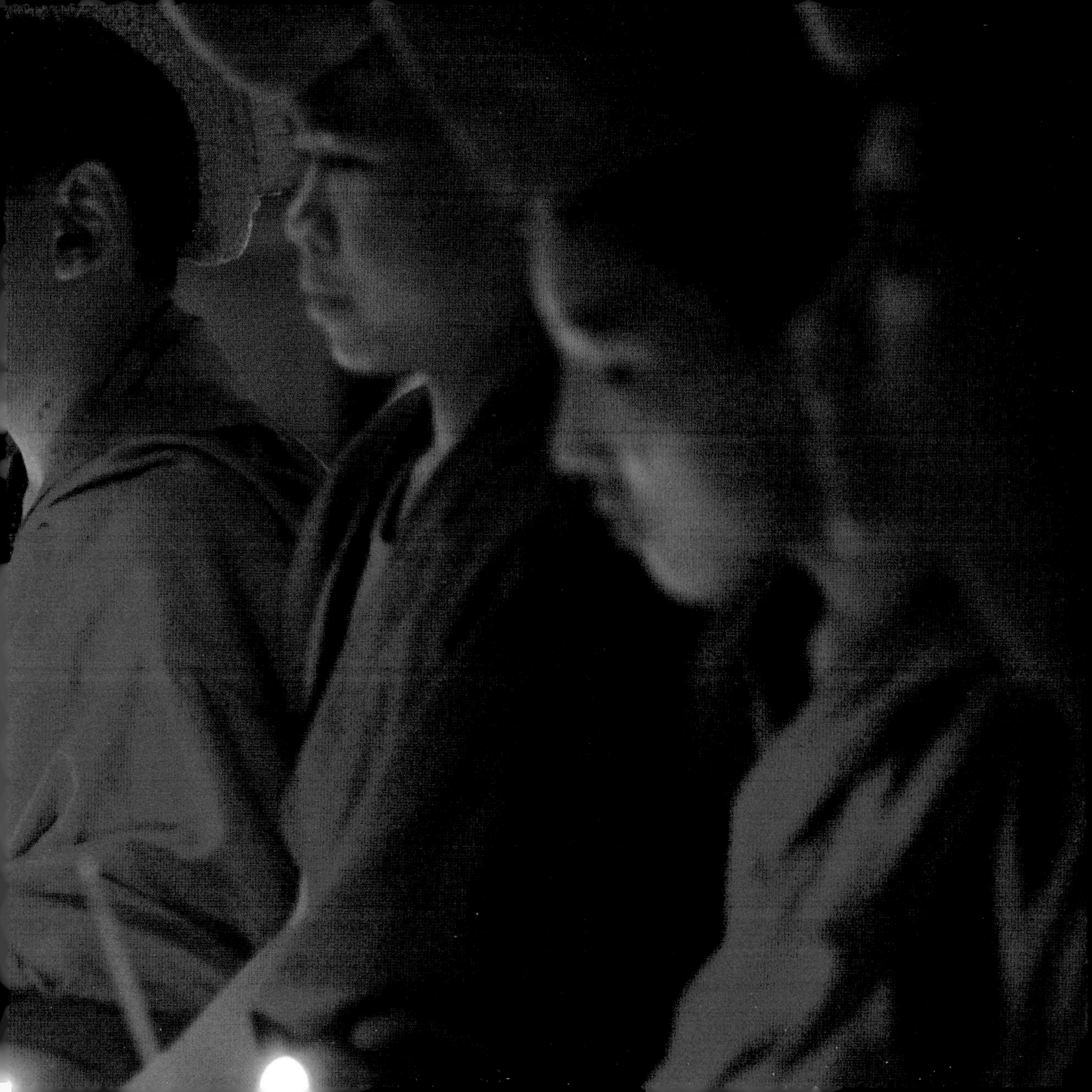

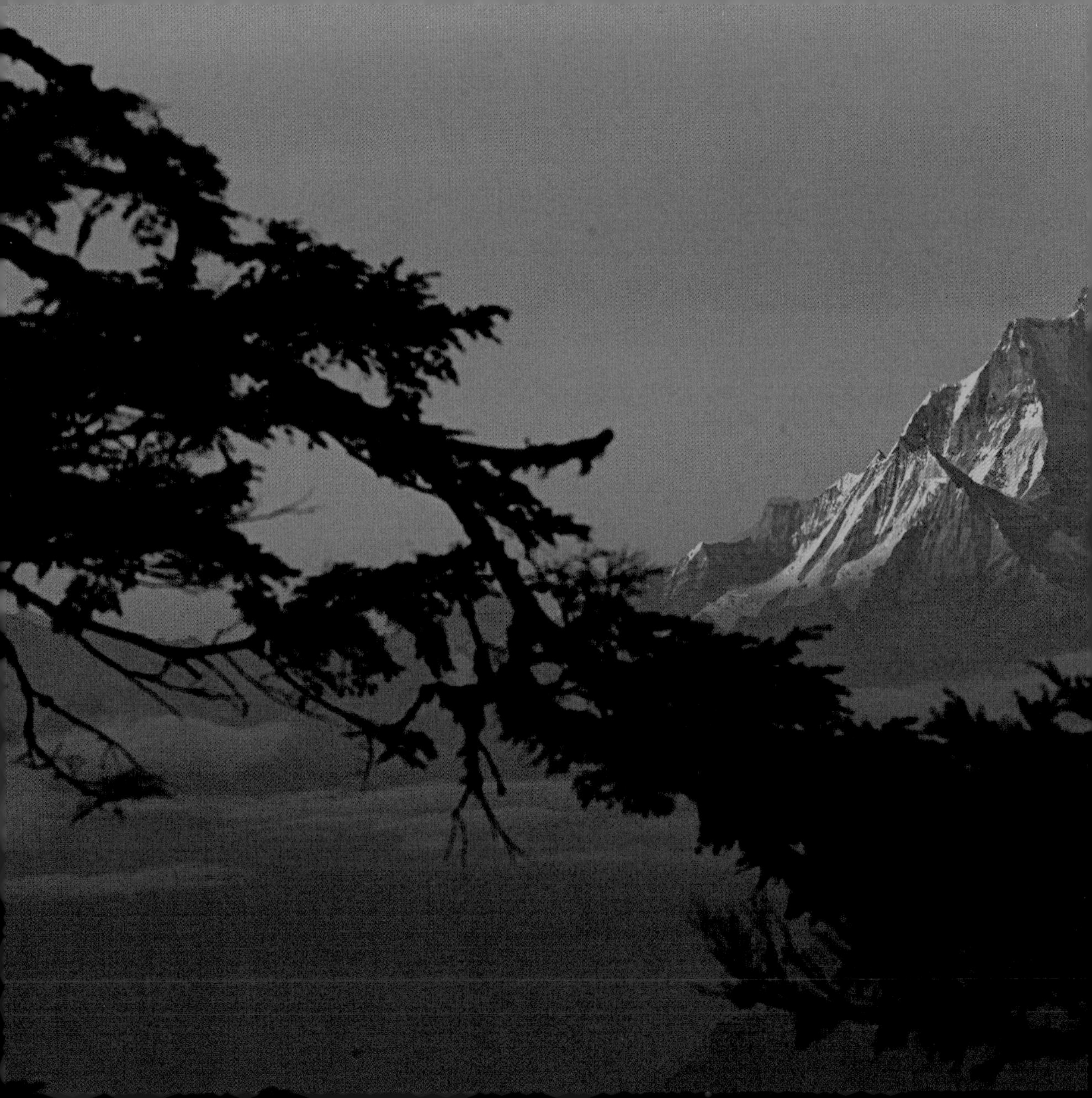

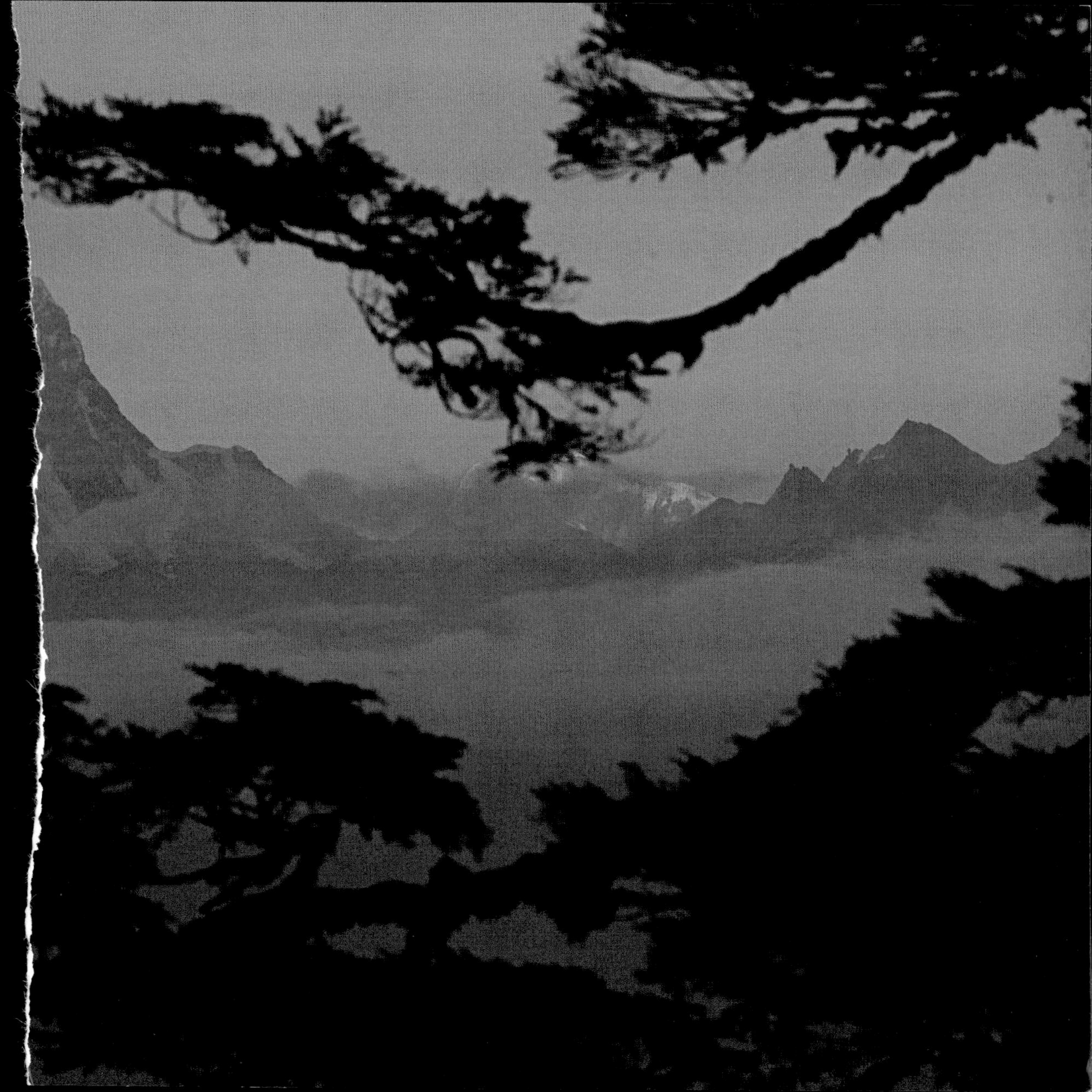

ACKNOWLEDGMENTS

I offer my boundless gratitude to Kyabje Dilgo Khyentse Rinpoche (1910–91), who inspires my entire existence and with whom I lived for twelve years, ten of them in Bhutan.

My deepest thanks to Rabjam Rinpoche, abbot of Shechen Monastery in Nepal, where I live, who encouraged me to produce this book and who inspired it.

I owe a great debt of gratitude to Her Majesty the Queen Mother of Bhutan, Ashe Kesang Choeden Wangchuck, to whom this book is dedicated, who allowed me to spend many years in Bhutan with Khyentse Rinpoche and granted me permission to take many of these photographs.

I am very grateful to our friends and benefactors, the Shelley and Donald Rubin Foundation and Klaus Hebben, for their support in the form of photographic equipment, in addition to their most generous support to our humanitarian projects.

Special thanks are also due to Vivian Kurz, Carisse and Gérard Busquet for their constant support and editorial assistance.

I would also like to thank my publishers and friends Hervé de La Martinière and Thomas Neurath, who were enthusiastic about this project, as well as Emmanuelle Halkin and Sandrine Bailly, who supervised the editing, Audrey Hette and Noémie Levain, who were responsible for the design, and all our friends at Éditions de La Martinière and Thames & Hudson.

My thanks also go to Captain Dondrup Gyaltsen and Captain Sonam Chödrak, pilots with Druk Air, who allowed me to take some beautiful shots from the cockpit, and also to Sonam Dorje and Tsering Thenphel, who assisted me during my travels in the Land of the Thunder Dragon.

The author's share of the proceeds from this book has been entirely donated to various humanitarian projects in Tibet, Nepal, India and Bhutan. To find out more about this work, please contact:

Karuna-Shechen
511 Avenue of the Americas
P.O. Box 339
New York, NY 10011
USA
shechen@sprynet.com and www.karuna-shechen.org

The photographs in this book are available as signed prints.
For more details please go to: www.matthieuricard.org and www.photoby.fr

Translated from the French *Bhoutan, terre de sérénité* by Ruth Sharman

First published in the United Kingdom in 2008 by Thames & Hudson Ltd, 181A High Holborn, London WC1V 7QX

www.thamesandhudson.com

First published in 2009 in hardcover in the United States of America by Thames & Hudson Inc., 500 Fifth Avenue, New York, New York 10110

thamesandhudsonusa.com

This paperback edition first published in 2012

Reprinted in 2016

British Library Cataloguing-in-Publication Data
A catalogue record for this book is available from the British Library

Library of Congress Catalog Card Number 2008932341

ISBN: 978-0-500-29044-6

Printed and bound in China